ROUTING THE OPPOSITION

Social Movements, Protest, and Contention

Series Editor: Bert Klandermans, Free University, Amsterdam

Associate Editors: Ron R. Aminzade, University of Minnesota
David S. Meyer, University of California, Irvine
Verta A. Taylor, University of California, Santa Barbara

For more books in the series, see page 310.

ROUTING THE OPPOSITION

Social Movements, Public Policy, and Democracy

David S. Meyer, Valerie Jenness, and Helen Ingram, Editors

Social Movements, Protest, and Contention
Volume 23

University of Minnesota Press
Minneapolis • London

Published by the University of Minnesota Press
111 Third Avenue South, Suite 290
Minneapolis, MN 55401-2520
http://www.upress.umn.edu

Library of Congress Cataloging-in-Publication Data

Routing the opposition : social movements, public policy, and democracy /
    David S. Meyer, Valerie Jenness, and Helen Ingram, editors.
        p. cm. — (Social movements, protest, and contention ; v. 23)
    Includes bibliographical references and index.
    ISBN 0-8166-4479-9 (hc : alk. paper) — ISBN 0-8166-4480-2 (pb :
alk. paper)
        1. Social movements—United States.   2. Political activists—
United States.   3. Social problems—Government policy—United
States.   4. Democracy—United States.   5. United States—Politics and
government—20th century.   I. Meyer, David S.   II. Jenness, Valerie,
1963–   III. Ingram, Helen M., 1937–   IV. Series.
    HN65.R68 2005
    322.4'4'0973—dc22
                                                            2005000434

Printed in the United States of America on acid-free paper

The University of Minnesota is an equal-opportunity educator and employer.

12 11 10 09 08 07 06 05   10 9 8 7 6 5 4 3 2 1

Contents

Acknowledgments

We are grateful to all of the participants at the conference "Social Movements, Public Policy, and Democracy" held in Laguna Beach, California, in January 2002. In addition to those who are represented in this volume, all of the papers benefited immensely from insightful comments by other conference participants, including Paul Burstein, Doug Imig, Cecelia Lynch, Calvin Morrill, Lina Newton, Belinda Robnett, David Snow, and Sidney Tarrow. The conference from which this book derives, as well as the book itself, would not have been possible without the support of the Center for the Study of Democracy, the School of Social Sciences, and the School of Social Ecology, all at the University of California, Irvine. We are grateful for the confidence and support of Dean William Schoenfeld, Dean C. Ronald Huff, and the director of the Center for the Study of Democracy, Russell Dalton. Finally, we deeply appreciate the heroic administrative work provided by Dianne Christianson, Judy Omiya, and Thomas Wicke, and the editorial expertise of Carrie Mullen, Nancy Sauro, and Jason Weidemann. Each in their own way made this volume come into being.

Introduction

Social Movements and Public Policy: Eggs, Chicken, and Theory

David S. Meyer

There were all kinds of good reasons to oppose U.S. participation in the Vietnam War in 1965, and as the war escalated, opponents found increasingly good reasons to take to the streets to make their claims. In July 1965, Lyndon Johnson announced that he would intensify the U.S. commitment to South Vietnam, increasing its military presence by nearly fifty thousand troops, necessitating more aggressive use of the military draft. The draft turned a distant issue,[1] the war in Vietnam, into a proximate one, and stoked the fledgling antiwar movement. The draft provided a focus for the antiwar movement as well as a sense of urgency on college campuses to do something to stop the war. The Johnson administration, probably not intentionally, aided activists who wanted to focus on the draft when, in October 1965, Attorney General Nicholas Katzenbach promised to investigate the antidraft movement even as local Selective Service officials revoked the student exemptions of protesters against the war when they were arrested (De Benedetti 1990, 120–30).

The salience of the draft invigorated what had formerly been small pacifist and leftist organizations mobilizing and coordinating the initial opposition to the war, flooding local chapters and national events with larger numbers of new activists than any of the organizations were prepared to handle (Gitlin 1980; Miller 1987). The draft allowed pacifists who normally reached small audiences to speak to much larger crowds, and groups that expressed a broad commitment to comprehensive democratic change in the United States, like Students for a Democratic Society (SDS), spread quickly to less elite college campuses (Heineman 1993). Resistance to the draft, often by the ritualized (and criminal) action of destroying a draft card, was a readily available tactic of expressing opposition to the war, physically accessible to millions of young men, a possibility that had to be confronted.

The rapid growth of the antiwar movement also created difficulties for those who would organize it. New recruits to organizations working against the war didn't necessarily share commitments to pacifism or "participatory democracy." The newly swollen antiwar organizations provided a larger venue, as well as the prospects of higher payoffs, for internecine fights about ideology and tactics, effectively encouraging bitter sectarian disputes and an internal social control problem for organizations concerned with managing their public face by constraining their expressed tactics and claims. Many organizations didn't survive.

If rapid growth created problems for the antiwar movement, these were certainly no less than the problems it created for political authorities. The larger, more volatile, more public, and more diverse antiwar movement made life more difficult for a government seeking, minimally, domestic peace. In his memoirs, Richard Nixon (1978, 396–404) admits that the antiwar protesters constrained his options in Vietnam, preempting the use—or the effective threat of using—nuclear weapons in Vietnam. One response to the antiwar movement was extending the franchise to eighteen-year-olds; another was instituting a draft lottery, before ultimately ending the draft.[2]

The end of the draft in 1972, following on the heels of the ratification of the Twenty-sixth Amendment in the previous year, altered the political terrain dramatically for the antiwar movement. As electoral possibilities opened, organizers lost some portion of the zealous new converts, terrified about their own lives even as they opposed the war. James Fallows (1981, 136) observes, "The history of Vietnam demonstrated the difference between abstract and self-interested actions. Resistance to the war went up in proportion as the effects of the war (primarily, the draft) touched the children of influential families." Although the antiwar movement may well have won (see Small 1988), as U.S. involvement in Vietnam ultimately ended, the pacifists lost their connections with movement politics; and broader claims about invigorated and genuine democracy, as expressed by SDS, mostly disappeared from American political life or were reformulated in much more moderate terms as procedural reforms.

The example of the draft points up a range of connections among protest, policy, and democracy; I mean to provide a framework for understanding those broader connections. I begin with a focused review of the literatures on public policy and on social movements, identifying notable omissions and areas of commonality. Scholars of public policy, for example, often assign social movements a role in the agenda-setting process, although the mechanisms by which this occurs are rarely specified: something out-side institutional politics affects the agenda within. Social movement schol-ars make analogous omissions. Although policy is almost routinely treated as one social movement outcome, the interaction of both substantive and symbolic changes in policy with the development of a challenging move-ment is undertheorized and understudied. Fundamentally, social move-ment scholars treat the policy process as a black box within the state, which movements may occasionally shake and upset into action, whereas policy scholars treat movements as undifferentiated and unitary actors who re-spond (or not) by disruption. But in their areas of central concern, scholars offer a much more nuanced recognition of complexity and contingency.

Of course, these questions are fundamental to the functioning of democ-racy in America. On one level, the emergence, indeed, the proliferation, of social movements suggests that established political institutions in the United States are widely perceived as inadequate to represent and manage citizen concerns. When government responds to social movements representing less than a majority, this also constitutes a challenge to the functioning of democ-racy. Here I will consider social movements as an addition to mainstream in-stitutional politics rather than as an alternative to them—as most activists do. To be sure, a movement without allies working in mainstream politics will be hard-pressed to make inroads in the policy process. The more provocative question to consider is whether participation in social movements has become necessary—although certainly not sufficient—to effect policy change for most groups. We will return to these issues in the conclusion, but we can start by thinking about the policy process and social movements.

From the literature, I suggest that as analysts we would do well to focus on the connections at this point in order to develop a broader understand-ing of the process, and stakes, of an increasingly common form of politics in democratic polities (see Meyer and Tarrow 1998). I briefly outline the particular set of constraints and opportunities that make the American context unique and then offer an integrated model that specifies multi-dimensional connections between social movements and public policy in the United States by recognizing the iterative development of both move-ments and policy. I conclude with a call for more focused research on the protest/policy connection.

Policy/Protest: A First Look

The initial example of U.S. policy on conscription puts in high relief a large number of connections between protest and policy, expressed over a period of only about seven years. The policy, increasing the yield of young men for the military by conscription, at once creates not only a grievance but also a constituency that feels that grievance most intensely: draft-eligible young men and their families. The policy of conscription became a provisional target for the antiwar movement ("Stop the Draft, End the War"), and its administration provided a series of sites or targets at which to launch protests (draft boards), as well as a set of tactics (burning draft cards, defacing files). The nature of American draft policy gave antiwar organizations a vehicle for servicing their constituents: draft counseling. It also forced young men to confront the policy concretely as well as abstractly, making personal decisions—with varying degrees of anxiety and information—about their own draft status and strategies (e.g., whether to pursue conscientious objector status, whether to flee to sanctuary in Canada). Both opposition to the draft in general and concern about one's individual fate pushed young men—and those who cared about them—into the full range of American political institutions, including the Selective Service bureaucracy, local draft boards, the courts, and electoral campaigns. The high stakes of the draft for young men gave the antiwar movement an urgency and a capacity for growth that is difficult to imagine for a foreign war fought without reluctant—to say the least—American conscripts. And the policy gave government a ready, albeit illegal, means for trying to control opposition to the war and enforce social discipline.[3]

What's more, opposition to the draft, in conjunction with the broader movement against the American part in the Vietnam War, has affected all sorts of policies since. Although draft registration of young men was restored in 1980, the U.S. has relied on a volunteer military force since Vietnam, at least partly because of the antiwar movement (Fallows 1981). More generally, the political fallout of the antiwar movement has served to constrain U.S. foreign policy since that time. The so-called Vietnam syndrome led to a reluctance to commit ground troops abroad unless the United States deployed overwhelming force and could reasonably expect to win and exit within a fairly short time period (Weinberger 1990).[4]

Ending the draft also changed a range of personnel practices within the military, which now had to manage employees who had the option of quitting. Absent a draft, policy makers and administrators must focus on the quality of life for military personnel, including devoting far more attention to recruiting, as well as issues of compensation, housing, child care, and career advancement for service people. Some period of service in the military, formerly a nearly universal part of the lives of young American men, is now an experience confined to a relatively small portion of the populace. Work in the military became a job (or career) chosen by service people rather than an obligation borne by all young men. Perceived adverse consequences of this change in the polity and in the military led a group of neoliberals (most of whom had not performed military service) to make a case for reinstituting some form of the draft (e.g., Fallows 1981). The effect of the antiwar movement's efforts against the draft, however, led cautious politicians to reframe new policy options as a broader "national service" program, including all sorts of non-military activities, to make sure that such a program was not compulsory, and then to scale it back and underfund it (see Waldman 1996).

I want to emphasize the range of mutual influences of policy and protest. To understand these relationships we need to take a broad interpretation of connections that allows for complex and iterative interactions, rather than discrete outcomes or origins, and to consider a longer period of time in seeking patterns of influence.

Extant Theory: Mutual Recognition and Neglect

Scholars concerned with public policy *or* with social movements often recognize the importance of other phenomena in their subject of interest, but don't generally go beyond that recognition. There is some irony in these reciprocal omissions, as some of the central work on movements in the 1960s and 1970s was focused on the policy payoff of social protest mobilization. Michael Lipsky's (1970) work vindicated protest as a political strategy for people who were poorly positioned to represent their interests by conventional means. His central point was that protest sometimes worked. Similarly, Frances Fox Piven and Richard Cloward's work has addressed very directly the connection between government policy toward poor people and their response. In *Regulating the Poor* (1971), they argued that welfare spending was essentially an effort by government to maintain social peace, policy directed to prevent protest.

In *Poor People's Movements* (1977), they examined the relationship from the other side, using extended treatments of four historical cases to show that disruptive protest was the best means available to poor people to influence government policy on their behalf—because, as they had pointed out earlier, welfare spending was a way to buy quiescence. They claimed that in times of electoral uncertainty, politicians could respond to disruption through policy concessions to groups represented in some fashion by the protesters. They framed their analysis as a prescription to organizers in clear and sharp terms, chastising organizers who failed to learn from the past that organization building "blunted or curbed the disruptive force which lower-class people were sometimes able to mobilize" (xxii). Although Piven and Cloward's work spurred a great deal of debate, primarily about the accuracy of their claims about poor people and welfare, there was much less in the way of careful examination of their premises of how protest worked to influence policy, or the extent to which their claims about poor peoples' movements were applicable to the social protest efforts of the nonpoor, who have been responsible for mobilizing most of the major social movements in the advanced industrialized world over the past three decades (Meyer and Tarrow 1998).

The other critical work on movements and policies, also from this period, William Gamson's *The Strategy of Social Protest* (1975), focused on the organizational attributes that correlated with success. Gamson identified fifty-three representative "challenging groups" that attempted to exercise influence in the United States between 1800 and 1945, then assessed their political fate. He was particularly concerned with whether each group had received formal recognition as a legitimate actor in American politics ("acceptance") and whether it had won some portion of its claims on policy ("new advantages"), using a sampling frame of fifteen years after the peak of its challenge. Predictably, Gamson's methodology raised a number of critical questions about how to define and measure success—and to his credit, Gamson reprinted some of the ensuing debates in the second edition of his book (1990). More to the point for our purposes, the work treated policy as an outcome and output but didn't examine the process by which protest translated (or didn't translate) into influence, focusing instead on the sorts of organizational resources, structures, claims, and tactics that were likely to be associated with success.

Although these critical works in the 1970s opened up an important area for research, few of the critical questions identified were pursued systematically in the ensuing decades. Scholars of social movements addressed the context and outcomes of political mobilization, but public policy was treated as a relatively minor part of the structure of political opportunities that might spur social movements. From the social movement side, policy is often treated as an outcome of mobilization, and changes in policy are traced back to find the influence of movements. In either case, the policy process appears as a black box, described without nuance and contingency. Indeed, in his important recent book on the influence of social movements, Thomas Rochon (1998) contends that a focus on policy explores only one arena of social movement influence (the other is cultural change), one that is generally less permeable to movement influence.

Students of public policy have recognized a place for social movements in the policy process, but it is a relatively small place. There is a generic pattern in which social movements are recognized as exogenous political factors that can affect some part of the policy process, most notably agenda setting (Baumgartner and Jones 1993; Kingdon 1984) or the construction of social problems, "target constituencies," and policy alternatives (e.g., Schneider and Ingram 1997). Rarely, however, does the analysis go beyond this or address the mechanisms by which movements affect the policy process. Nonetheless, drawing from the literatures on policy and movements, we can establish a framework for understanding relationships between policy and movements.

Movements and Policy: First Premises

We can establish first premises by starting with what we know about public policy and about movements. First, the policy process does not rigidly follow any of the linear frameworks offered in textbooks, and innovation and change can come from a wide variety of sources. Rational actor models, although useful heuristics, don't describe the way the policy-making process actually takes place, which is as a battle among various actors seeking to please distinct constituencies. Policy disputes include not only struggles about the relative influence of the range of interested parties, but also the definition of particular conditions as problematic and amenable to purposive intervention by government, the range of tools legitimately used by government, and the ultimate objectives of any policy intervention (Stone 1997).

Second, the modal pattern of policy in any particular area is one of stasis, although not one of satisfaction. Policies are maintained by policy monopolies, that is, a network of groups and individuals operating inside and outside of government, linked by their mutual recognition as legitimate actors concerned with a particular set of policies.[5] Members of this monopoly include elected officials, administrators in the bureaucracy, and activists in established interest organizations. Conflict among these actors plays out, generally, in a stalemate that allows only incremental reforms in the policy area. Efforts at reform launched from outside these networks are usually easily ignored. Scores of policy monopolies operate with autonomy from one another, often invisible to the larger body politic (Baumgartner and Jones 1993).

Third, opportunities for policy reform, or "open windows" in Kingdon's (1984) terms, occur on schedules that only sometimes line up with the development of a social problem. Changes in politics, policy, or problems, as Kingdon notes, can create an open window, but the key element to focus on is the possible reconfiguration of a policy monopoly (Baumgartner and Jones 1993). Policy reforms come from a change in the balance of political power within that monopoly, and those reforms can further alter the political balance, precipitating or frustrating subsequent reforms.

But sometimes open windows pass—or are passed—without anyone doing anything that promotes change effectively. Such unexploited windows, or "missed opportunities" (Sawyers and Meyer 1999), are significant even when largely unexploited, for subsequent chances for reform might not readily appear. Failure to effect some kind of reform can fortify the stasis within a policy monopoly. Witness, for example, Bill Clinton's initial attempt to reform American health insurance. The political price Clinton paid for his failure, particularly the Democratic party's loss of Congress in 1994, dissuaded Clinton—and probably his successors—from comprehensive efforts at reform.

Fourth, policies reflect, and then shape, dominant social constructions not only of problems but of persons associated with those problems (Ingram and Smith 1993; Schneider and Ingram 1997). By delineating certain actors as worthy, government legitimates political and social action on their behalf; more important, it enables those actors to mobilize on their own behalf. Of course, the reverse is also true: by identifying certain people as authors of their own misfortunes, government not only justifies official inaction (or punitive or paternalistic action), it also creates social, political, and psychological obstacles for their own mobilization.

The literature on social movements establishes a few key points. First, it helps to understand the distinct properties of a social movement. Sidney Tarrow offers a concise and useful definition of movements as "collective challenges based on common purposes, in sustained interaction with elites, opponents and authorities" (1998, 4). Key points of this definition are worth emphasizing: (a) the broad frame allows the inclusion of both institutionally oriented and extra-institutional activity; (b) a social movement is larger than any particular event, representing a challenge extended in time; and (c) a movement operates in some kind of dynamic interaction with mainstream politics (see also Meyer 1990, 8).

Second, it helps to remember that movements are not unitary actors. Although it is a grammatical convenience to speak of "the" movement or "a" movement, social movements are composed of coalitions of actors, acting on some element of shared goals, and competing for prominence in defining claims and tactics. To understand the influence of a social movement, we need to track a range of actors operating in a variety of venues over some period of time (Meyer and Rochon 1997).

Third, because the process of staging a large challenging movement entails building networks and coalitions among groups and individuals who do not always act in concert, it is important to consider the circumstances in which diverse actors are likely to work together. In the last few decades, scholars of social movements have increasingly focused on the circumstances under which movements emerge or fade. The focus on context, or "political opportunity structure," highlights the relationships among mainstream politics, public policy, and protest politics (see, e.g., McAdam 1982; Meyer 2004; Tarrow 1998; Tilly 1978).

Fourth, openings from government can provoke or preempt protest, depending on the positioning of a particular constituency. The premise on which such analysis is based is that the prominence of particular issues, coalitions, and tactics in a social movement is largely influenced by the prospects for those issues and constituencies within mainstream politics. The initial framing of political opportunity theory postulated that the relationship between systemic openings and extra-institutional protest was curvilinear (e.g., Eisinger 1973; Tilly 1978). Groups that can achieve their goals without protest politics will do so; groups that have little prospect for influence regardless of their tactics are unlikely to mobilize. Thus, government action to bring some constituencies into the polity and respond to their claims can spur protest, while the same pattern can dampen the prospects for protest for other constituencies.[6]

Fifth, social movement organizations work not only to achieve policy reforms, but also to support themselves (McCarthy and Zald 1977; Piven and Cloward 1977; Wilson 1995). Organizers prospect for issues and tactics mindful of two distinct audiences: authorities and supporters. One is a target for influence, another a source of resources. The audiences place conflicting pressures on groups. To the extent that groups can cooperate on goals and tactics, they maximize their influence with policy makers; to the extent that they can differentiate themselves from other groups, each can carve out an advantaged niche for cultivating support (Zald and McCarthy 1987).

Sixth, cooperation and differentiation among groups within a movement coalition change over time, at least partly as a function of resources. When public attention to an issue is growing, and resources are relatively readily available, groups are more likely to cooperate, and groups without a primary interest in an issue area are likely to develop one.[7] In looking at the nuclear freeze movement, for example, groups, ranging from community associations to churches to service organizations, expressed a newly found interest in nuclear weapons and foreign policy issues. When public interest wanes, however, groups are more likely to differentiate, pursuing different elements of connected issues or abandoning movement issues altogether. Coalition dynamics thus accelerate and accentuate the dynamics of a cycle of protest (Meyer and Imig 1993; Tarrow 1998).

Seventh, particularly in liberal polities, social movement activists can build institutions for pursuing their claims over a long period of time. Organizations forged during the peak of social mobilization generally survive, even if at the expense of the movements that gave rise to them (Piven and Cloward 1977; Wilson 1995). At the same time, those organizations provide an infrastructure for subsequent mobilization (Meyer and Whittier 1994; Minkoff 1995).

Activists can also find or build safe spaces within mainstream institutions, including political institutions. Mary Katzenstein (1998) describes such safe spaces as habitats, noting that women following on the second wave of the feminist movement in the 1970s established habitats in particularly unlikely places, including the Roman Catholic Church and the U.S. military. In addition to being safe places for particular ideas or constituencies, such habitats can also serve as venues to promote particular policies (e.g., Clemens 1997; Hansen 1991). One effect of the civil rights movement, for example, was the establishment of the Equal Employment Opportunity Commission, which served as a habitat not only for African-Americans but subsequently for other ethnic minorities and for women (Burstein 1985; Minkoff 1995). The establishment of the Arms Control and Disarmament Agency in 1963, partly as a response to the peace movement (Meyer 1993), and the Environmental Protection Agency in 1970, partly as a response to the growing environmental movement (Switzer 2001), has also sometimes provided habitats for individuals concerned with moderation in the arms race or in environmental despoliation. The degree to which these institutions have legitimately represented the interests and ideas of the movements that gave rise to them has been a cause of debate and merits more systematic research.

Eighth, the time during which a social movement can capture the political imagination of a large number of mainstream actors, including elected officials and the mass media, is limited, and it is useful to think about the process of decline in terms of coalitions. During a movement's peak, many actors identify with a particular identity or set of claims. This link stretches to unite actors in mainstream politics with those engaged in extra-institutional politics. As this peak passes, a large number of members of this broad coalition drop out in different ways; the largest number leave the issue for another more urgent or promising or take a break from political activity altogether. Some groups and individuals abandon the compromises necessary for coalition work or interchange with mainstream politics in favor of articulating their own claims more sharply and strongly. Others leave the broader goals and extra-institutional tactics of social movements to focus instead on incremental gains within mainstream political institutions (Sawyers and Meyer 1999). Taken together, this process of decline composes political institutionalization (Meyer and Tarrow 1998) as the polity and members of a social movement implicitly negotiate a more routinized and less disruptive relationship, one that can be maintained over a long period of time.

What we know about movements and policy suggests that this process of political institutionalization is an appropriate focus for research on their interconnections. Both substantively and processurally, institutionalization describes the ways in which changes in policy can be managed without provoking movement response, and the ways in which movement actors are either included in the policy process as legitimate actors or effectively dismissed from mainstream political relevance. The processes attending political institutionalization and policy outputs are determined, to a large degree, by the set of opportunities and constraints inherent in the structure of government. The American polity offers a peculiar mix of these opportunities and constraints. By understanding the basic structure of American institutions and the policy process, we can begin to develop a broader understanding of the movement-policy relationship.

Social Movements and Democracy in America

In writing on behalf of the American Constitution he had helped craft, James Madison described a government that he promised would allow—even encourage—people to organize and mobilize on behalf of their interests and yet would make it very difficult for them to influence government to act on their interests. Limiting liberty, Madison argued, would stifle democracy and ultimately produce another revolution, but both government and Americans had to be protected from organized groups—including minorities and majorities—who would try to get government to act for them. He and his colleagues established a system that essentially encourages the development of social movements and virtually ensures their frustration.

The Constitution laid out a blueprint for a government that was premised on distrust of Americans—trusting only that individuals and groups would look out for themselves at the expense of others. Its basic design divided power to make it hard for any interested group, or "faction" in Madison's terms, to use the power of the government without broad and sustained support from a range of other actors. By dividing power, the Constitution guarded against the abuse of power. Even if a faction gained control of a portion of the government, it would be unable to do much with it. At one level, this was an explicit attempt to avoid the tyrannies of monarchs and mobs. At another level, however, it was a recipe for a government that would be able to do less. This tension and reality, a slow and unresponsive government wrapped in rhetoric about democracy and participation, confronts all Americans to this day.

We see more when we look more directly at the constitutional design. The United States divides power and policy-making responsibilities between the federal government and state and local governments, and activists always face the dilemma about the appropriate level of government at which to target their efforts. In general, local governments are more receptive to their concerns but more constrained in responding to them. The political structure presents activists with multiple targets and provides authorities with reliable means for passing the buck.

Power is further divided within the federal government, between the legislative, executive, and judiciary branches. The legislature, clearly meant to be the most powerful branch of government, is further divided into the Senate and the House of Representatives, each serving different constituencies and elected on somewhat different timetables. Activists have multiple targets to confront, and multiple venues in which to press their efforts at the federal government level. But each branch of government, ultimately, depends on the others to effect—or at least to allow—policy change. As I write, for example, local elected officials, state legislatures, and state judges are sparring about their respective powers in allowing—or prohibiting—gay marriage. Members of Congress and the president have weighed in with their views and threatened action, and it is clear that the federal judiciary will be forced to address the issue in some way. It is not immediately clear to anyone exactly who is in the best position to change—or to prevent change—in policy.

Democratic influence on who holds these positions is also a matter of uncertainty for social movement activists. Because elections for the legislature and the executive office are relatively frequent, activists must always consider the possibilities of an electoral strategy. At the same time, electoral politics are expensive and time-consuming, and placing even a strong ally in a powerful position doesn't guarantee policy responsiveness. The nature of elected positions in the government, coming from large single-member districts, funnels conflict into the middle of the political spectrum. It also encouraged the development of a two-party system, both to contest elections and to form legislative majorities. Of course, given the breadth of interests in any district, much less the nation as a whole, parties in the United States quickly became broad coalitions themselves. This ensures that once in office, no matter how committed and partisan, elected officials have to compromise and coalition-build further, compromising, if not co-opting, the concerns of their supporters.

In essence, the Madisonian design was all about *institutionalizing dissent,* bringing political conflict into the government, in order to confine the boundaries of claims that activists might make and to invite partisans to struggle using conventional political means rather than taking up arms or opting out of the system. The theory was that conflict inside government was preferable to conflict between the government as a whole and dissenters. This choice, however, results in a nonresponsive and inactive federal government.

The ratified Constitution included a Bill of Rights, which formally protected the liberties of those who would seek to influence government. For our purposes, most relevant are the sections in the First Amendment guaranteeing the rights of assembly, press, and speech. To be sure, although the Bill of Rights is remarkably clear on basic premises, government has often violated its protections. Presidents since John Adams and up to George W. Bush have tried, with some success, to limit the access of their political opponents to meaningful audiences through the press. The American government has sometimes prosecuted people for their political beliefs and threatened others because of their religious commitments. It is important not to ignore such drastic departures from the principles of civil liberties. At the same time, throughout American history citizens have been generally afforded some amount of political freedom to try to recruit others to their causes. The principle of free speech is the belief that even the most heinous ideas are less threatening and more manageable when out in the open. In the United States, the largest share of social movement politics has taken place in public, with all of the constraints and opportunities offered there. Similarly, although there have been serious limitations on the freedom of the press historically, the principle of a free press means that activists can try to use mainstream media to glean information about issues of their concern and to convey their concerns and efforts to others. Again, the idea is to bring dissent into the open, without letting it build into a potentially revolutionary movement. But inviting dissent is not the same thing as responding to it, as we will see.

Having considered the American context and the central points of established, distinct literatures on policy and movements, we can now move to build a fuller synthetic approach to understanding the connections between movements and policy in the United States. Indeed, this connection provides a sort of diagnostic of the process of democracy in advanced liberal states. I now turn to the sorts of influences that movements and policies can affect on each other.

Policy and Movements: A Taxonomy of Effects

Policies, the actions of government, can do a large number of things to influence the development of social movements. First, policies can directly affect the permeability of the political arena, for example, by making voting easier or harder or by mandating citizen participation in hearings (or not). By including a range of actors as legitimate in the polity, government actions create openings or closings that affect the attractiveness of protest and social mobilization as a strategy. Peter Eisinger's (1973) insight on the curvilinear nature of political opportunities emphasized that people are unlikely to protest when they believe they have more direct, and less risky or costly, means to exercise influence on policy (see also Tilly 1978; Meyer 1993). Opening institutional venues for broad participation can diminish the attractiveness, and likelihood, of protest as a political strategy. At the other end of the curve, repression can raise the costs and risks of protest to the extent that few people are willing to broker them in pursuit of political influence that appears unlikely. Of course, some individuals, less concerned with the political effects of their acts than with witness or actualizing some vision of justice, may take extraordinary actions regardless of the risks to themselves or to particular constituencies. Only occasionally, however, do such dramatic actions spread to a broader public and create what we think of as a social movement. Openings are frequently not equally available to all constituencies, and states can enable or exclude particular constituencies, creating categories of actors such that opportunity is raced, classed, and gendered by public policy (e.g., McAdam 1982; Costain 1992; McCammon et al. 2001; Banaszak 1996). Policy thus creates constituencies and the terrain on which strategies are made.

Along the same lines, government action can advantage certain strategies of political organization. McCarthy, Britt, and Wolfson (1991), for example, show that American tax law encourages activist citizens to form nonprofit groups, and government policy mandates certain elements of the organizational structure and allowable tactics that those groups will employ (also see Minkoff 1995). Changes in the laws regulating the funding of American elections in the 1970s, for example, encouraged groups to adapt certain forms of organization and to embrace particular tactics, including direct mail fund-raising and campaign contributions (Berry 1989). By surveillance, repression, and harsh criminal penalties, government can also foreclose particular tactics. Federal and state enforcement of civil and criminal penalties on anti-abortion demonstrators who blocked clinics mostly shut down peaceful clinic protests during the early 1990s, even as some anti-abortion activists adapted more violent and disruptive tactics (Meyer and Staggenborg 1996). In effect, public policies about participation can channel advocates to adapt particular tactics, organizational forms, and even claims.

Policy also creates causes or grievances. Social movements express concerns about something that government is doing—or not doing. We can think of some kind of regular stasis, a time at which most people are content to express their concerns about policy through institutional politics or not at all. Changes in policy, or changes in exogenous conditions that seem to mandate a change in policy, provide the concerns that drive people into mobilization (Meyer 2002). The concerns can take root because of articulated policy reforms or because of changes in policy implementation that suddenly make some policies more salient. The example of the draft makes this point clearly, but we can also think about policies on a range of other areas as well, ranging from zoning hazardous waste disposal to conducting a military action abroad.

The framing of policies creates constituencies, which can be organized along a variety of lines. Constituencies can be united by belief or ideology, supporting some kinds of programs and not others. Any policy area offers the potential mobilization of constituencies on any side of a proposed reform, depending on the salience of the issue. Nuclear power development in the United States, for example, has moved dramatically on the public agenda, depending on a variety of factors, including the price of gas and reporting on the last nuclear power accident. Constituencies can also be united more directly by a policy that identifies certain persons as included or stigmatized. Social Security, for example, which pays benefits to older Americans, unites a large number of people as recipients with a common interest. If not for the program, such people might be more commonly mobilized (or not) on the basis of other affiliations. And people can be demobilized and disempowered by the construction of policy as well (Banaszak 1996; Mettler 1998).

If the policy process is often the source of social protest mobilization, it can also be the outcome. Social protest mobilization, in interaction with institutional politics, can produce immediate increased expenditures or regulations in an established policy area, such as welfare spending or environmental regulation (e.g., Piven and Cloward 1971). Protest movements can create new categories of policies, instituting payments or other benefits to a newly recognized political constituency (e.g., Amenta 1998; Amenta, Dunleavy, and Bernstein 1994) or regulation of a previously unregulated area (e.g., Switzer 2001).

Mobilization can affect policies that enable new actors to be present in the implementation and subsequent renegotiation of policies. Weed (1995), for example, shows how crime victims, by mobilizing for themselves, not only changed criminal justice policy but ensured their own presence in negotiations for subsequent reforms in criminal justice policy. In other words, they won a place as established actors within the policy domain. Monitoring the implementation of policy affects the success and evaluation of that policy and the subsequent mobilization by affected persons (Andrews 2001). The absence of mobilization from a recognized constituency can also have an effect on policy (Imig 1996; Sawyers and Meyer 1999). By altering the balance of power within a policy domain, organized interests can change outcomes—or not.

Seeing policy outputs as the outcomes of social movements is important, but movement effects are not limited to direct policy influence. Indeed, there is some dispute in the literature about how movements affect influence on the policy process. For Piven and Cloward (1977), the threat of social and political disruption, in the context of electoral uncertainty, leads policy makers to adopt reforms directed to reestablishing public order, and those reforms may include concessions to protesters. For Amenta (1998), movements' demands are mediated by political institutions; social unrest provides sympathetic legislators with an opportunity to enact their preferred programs. Burstein (1999) focuses on the specific mechanism of public opinion, arguing that elected officials in a democracy must, in some fashion, respond to public opinion, and social movements can influence policy by changing public opinion or by heightening the salience of a particular issue.

These observations all focus on fairly short-term effects on policy. Others note that policy outcomes are only one dimension of social movement influences and that movements can influence culture, values (Rochon 1998), organizations, subsequent social movements, and individual participants (Meyer and Whittier 1994). Even failing short-term influence on policy, by altering deeply held values or practices in the larger society, movements alter the composition of the political environment in which policy will be made.

Toward a Broader Model

The listing and categorization of mutual effects in the previous section underscores the importance of studying the web of interactions between challengers and the policies they challenge. It does not, however, constitute a theory that can guide subsequent research. In this section, I take steps in that direction, again building on theory developed by scholars of social movements and scholars of public policy.

For heuristic purposes, it makes sense to start with policies as the precursor to protest, even as we must acknowledge that there is a bit of a chicken and egg question about whether policy precedes protest or vice versa. Clearly there is a reciprocal effect, and analysis can be productive by starting with either source. At the same time, the existence of the modern state is a necessary precondition for the emergence of social movements (Tilly 1978; Tarrow 1998), and states necessarily are defined by the capacity to make and implement at least a minimal set of policies, particularly running a military to defend national borders and taxing to support itself.

Most of the time, policy is supported by stalemate, rather than satisfaction, with key figures in the policy monopoly committed to working within institutional politics to achieve marginal reforms in the direction of their preferred ultimate policy. Advocates of progressive taxation, for example, work to include some elements of progressivity, while their opponents work to flatten the tax code in steps. Most of these debates and discussions are invisible to a larger audience, and routine participation in politics supports the range of advocates on both sides of the issue in their efforts to manage conflict. Elected officials and bureaucrats are linked, via formal and informal networks, to each other and to a small set of engaged actors outside of government, including leaders of established interest groups, party activists, and independent experts, often in the academy. The broader general public is sufficiently satisfied, disinterested, or disaffected so as not to be a relevant factor in the day-to-day management of the policy area.

Mainly invisible, activists commit to some alternative vision of policy work, largely below government's radar and mostly insulated from the political debate or public attention. Some of these groups are unsuccessful in repeated attempts to reach a broader audience by mounting series of campaigns that are still fairly marginal. Others, when their leaders judge circumstances unfavorable for mobilization, focus on preserving the organization and its values, worrying less about mobilization (e.g., Taylor 1989). In either case, they are disconnected from influence in mainstream politics, culture, or the policy process.

Threats to the stability of a policy monopoly, which might arise from politics, policy, or other critical events (e.g., a foreign war, a nuclear reactor accident), create opportunities for mobilization that can reach a broader audience and for the potential renegotiation of the boundaries of the policy monopoly. Under such circumstances, political mobilization becomes more attractive to citizens because the pattern of institutional politics has changed. It may suddenly appear permeable to new claims (for example, civil rights for African-Americans) because of explicit articulated changes in policy or the presence of new actors in the policy monopoly, and this can spur mobilization that seems like it might be effective. Alternatively, the reconfiguration of a policy network is often signaled when the institutional losers go public for support (e.g., Meyer 1990) because institutional politics appears inadequate and citizen efforts appear necessary to generate a response to new circumstances.

In either case, the key change is in the composition of the relevant policy monopoly. Either by including new actors with extra-institutional ties or by excluding established actors who then seek movement ties, a change in the policy monopoly effectively changes the prospects for extra-institutional mobilization. During peak periods of mobilization, connections between the margins and the mainstream define social movement politics. The positions and criticisms of those on the margins no longer appear irrelevant and can reach a larger audience, and government policies, unusually visible and salient to a broad public, appear malleable.

Volatile social movement mobilization alters the calculations of institutionally oriented actors. The presence of an active movement can make previous patterns of managing policy untenable and make long-simmering ideas suddenly appear viable. At the same time, institutional actors need to address, more frequently and with more detail, a broader audience than is normally the case. Thus, during the period of anti-apartheid protests in Washington, DC, President Reagan was forced to explain and rearticulate his own policies toward South Africa far more than any of his predecessors, all of whom had managed essentially the same policy. Enhanced external scrutiny of policy and of the policy-making process can make more substantial reforms possible.

Social movements can then influence policy by altering the composition of the relevant policy monopoly by replacement, conversion, re-creation, or reconfiguration. *Replacement* is the mechanism perhaps most fundamental to conventional democratic politics: throwing a rascal out and empowering an ally instead. The direct influence of movements in electoral campaigns is generally on the margins, but margins can matter.

The threat of that marginal influence is one factor that can lead to *conversion*. Exposing a recalcitrant legislator or administrator to the power of a movement's ideas—or alternatively to the power of the idea's promoter—means altering the composition of a policy monopoly without replacement. It is not important, for the purpose of this analysis, to determine whether conversions, such as George Bush's decision to oppose abortion rights in 1980 or Jesse Jackson's decision to adopt a pro-choice position in 1983, come from opportunistic calculation or reflective soul-searching. In either case, the policy process and product are altered. Indeed, the calculator may be more likely to display the zeal of the newly converted and perhaps to operate more effectively and strategically within institutional politics.

Creating a new policy monopoly by opening a new policy area is a third way to reconfigure, often radically, the balance of power on an issue. In this regard, the creation of institutional habitats mentioned above, such as the Arms Control and Disarmament Agency, the Environmental Protection Agency, or the Department of Agriculture, means the permanent institutional presence of concerns that would previously be represented idiosyncratically, dependent on the concerns and skills of elected officials. Political mobilization can encourage established policy makers to create these habitats, perhaps to institutionalize, perhaps to confine, but once established, they develop lives, constituencies, and concerns of their own. Jenness and Grattet (2001) show how the establishment of a new category of crime enabled new political actors to make other sorts of claims, quite apart from criminal justice.

Finally, political mobilization can *reconfigure* existing policy monopolies by establishing new actors within it. Weed's (1995) tale of the victim's rights movement shows how the newly institutionalized presence of actors who were formerly only spectators changes what happens not only in the courtroom but also in the legislatures. Similarly, Matthews's (1994) analysis of the feminist antirape movement shows how political mobilization by feminists against rape altered the content and implementation of policy as well as establishing new institutions, rape crisis centers, that ultimately negotiated an alliance with local law enforcement agencies (also see Gornick and Meyer 1998). Essentially, activists in both cases expanded the scope of a political conflict to alter the bias in the arena.

But changes in policy alter the conditions under which activists mobilize. As policy makers respond to social movements, the environment in which the movement makes claims—the "structure of political opportunities" in particular—changes, advantaging and foreclosing particular claimants and strategies of influence. A government may respond to a movement not only by narrowly defined policy outputs, but also by rhetorical appropriation, official recognition of movement groups or individuals within a policy domain, and the placement of movement actors within elected or bureaucratic positions. Thus, the feminist campaign against rape as the most threatening and egregious element of patriarchy was turned into a public safety effort. From eliminating oppression of women, activists and government established a working relationship, in Matthews's (1994) terms, with the goal of "managing" the problem of rape. At the same time, government's appropriation of the campaign against rape, using its resources to control the image of the issue and to enlist and employ activists as service workers, made it more difficult for activists to mobilize.

The institutionalization of movement concerns can mean changed policies, if not what activists ask for; it also makes it harder for activists to mobilize on the same terms. Generally, organizers see their most visible policy demand, be it banning the pesticide DDT, passing a voting rights act or an equal rights amendment, or freezing the nuclear arms race, as the leading edge in a broad movement to remake the world substantially. Institutionalization of concerns means, to varying degrees, settling for something less than that. Thus, appointees to the Arms Control and Disarmament Agency learn to speak only of the first objective in the agency's name, and opponents of pollution learn to negotiate acceptable levels of contaminants. And feminists learn to rely on legislators who make it easier to convict and punish rapists, even if ignoring larger oppressions in society.

Social movement coalitions often respond to these changes by redefining themselves, their claims, and their allies. Policy reforms split movement coalitions and fracture and demobilize movements. Because participating groups enter social movements with a range of goals, it isn't surprising that they would view acceptable outcomes differently. Coalition dynamics are inherently unstable, as participants are constantly aware of the changing viability and value of particular alliances. In the United States and, for that matter, in liberal polities where political institutions are relatively permeable, coalitions are particularly fluid.

A recent example illustrates this point. Laboratory research on the human genome rarely gets much public attention or understanding, but periodic decision windows offer an invitation for concerned groups to speak. The decision about whether to fund research on human stem cell lines revisits, and reconfigures, old coalitions from the abortion debate. Research scientists, absent en bloc from the abortion debate, weighed in heavily on the question of stem cell research, mobilizing victims of a range of diseases that might be treated with new scientific discoveries. Some portion of the anti-abortion movement, seeing research on discarded embryonic cells (or embryonic cell lines created to be research material) as disrespectful for life, threatened to mobilize if such research were legitimated.

Each side offered the threat of more substantial mobilization, something imaginable only if the policy outcome were sufficiently egregious. President George W. Bush sought to craft a decision that, above all else, preempted this kind of mobilization. By responding to the concerns of all constituencies, the administration crafted a response intended to create an equilibrium point that made extra-institutional mobilization and continued vigorous opposition unattractive to each opposing side. It is not clear at this point if this effort was successful for the short term, but we have seen activists on each side decrying the decision even while announcing that it is acceptable—for the moment. The opting-in of some portion of each coalition is good news for the administration that wants to manage and institutionalize the issue. For the longer term, however, it is clear that the stability of this policy point is temporary. Supporters of embryonic stem cell research shifted the venue of the struggle, successfully mobilizing in California to get the state to fund basic research. State-level innovations and scientific advances—or setbacks—will test the viability of the Bush compromise and reinvigorate—or fracture—movement coalitions on each side.

Conclusion: Thinking Dialogically

I started this introduction with the intent of synthesizing the findings of scholars of policy and scholars of social movements in order to focus closely on the interchange between movement coalitions and the American polity. The permeability of American political institutions to social movement actors and ideas makes participation in such movements a recurrent feature of democratic life. But while the role of social movements in contemporary democracy is well established, the viability of particular movement coalitions cannot be.

Changes in policy, particularly in the composition of a policy monopoly, mean that the terrain on which social movements mobilize can shift—abruptly or gradually. Opportunities for inclusion always threaten to undermine the urgency of particular claims or the perceived necessity of extra-institutional mobilization to make them. Government does not have to satisfy even the largest part of a movement coalition to make subsequent social mobilization much more difficult.

For elected officials, understanding this reality means a constant search for equilibrium points to stabilize policy monopolies and to palliate political constituencies, giving enough to quell disturbances but not so much as to generate disruption from the other side. For activists, understanding this interaction means making hard calculations about the costs, as well as the benefits, of concessions on matters of policy and political inclusion. Realizing that the prospects for continued mobilization are limited, in no small part due to the dynamics of coalition politics, should help in considering the trade-offs inherent in cultivating institutionally oriented allies, recognizing better deals, and negotiating them.

And for analysts, the recognition of the ongoing interaction between social movements and policy makers means adopting an analytic focus that accepts a long time frame for mutual influence and an iterative approach to the process of political institutionalization.

Notes

This chapter benefited from the helpful comments of participants in the "Social Movements, Public Policy, and Democracy" workshop held at the University of California, Irvine, January 11–13, 2002, and from participants in the Social Movement/Social Justice Workgroup at the University of California, Irvine. I'm also grateful for helpful comments from Helen Ingram, Val Jenness, and Annulla Linders; and I thank Deana Rohlinger for both comments and research assistance on this project.

1. The term "distant issue" is from Dieter Rucht (2000), who uses it to refer to political issues that don't directly affect those who mobilize for them.

2. De Benedetti (1990, 308) emphasizes that efforts to reform, then end, the draft were accelerated by implementation problems and inequities in the United States and military discipline problems in the field, including an increased incidence of "fragging" of officers by conscripts ("fragging" refers to efforts to kill unpopular officers by such means as shooting them in combat or rolling a grenade under their tents).

3. Of course, there are all kinds of additional "spillover" effects (Meyer and Whittier 1994). By allowing student deferments, the draft encouraged thousands of young men to stay in college or even graduate school, and others to marry and have children. Pressures on faculty to save the lives of their students may be the root of the much-maligned grade inflation on American college campuses.

4. It is this syndrome, as well as Saddam Hussein, that President Bush confronted directly in his plan to invade Iraq in 2002.

5. Burstein (1991) refers to basically the same network as a "policy domain," a term adopted by Jenness and Grattet (2001) and Sawyers and Meyer (1999). Heclo (1978) uses the term "policy network."

6. Middle-class constituencies, who mobilize on issues such as environmental protection or peace, appear most likely to mobilize in response to bad news in policy and exclusion from political decision making, whereas constituencies that mobilize on the basis of some ascribed identity, such as race or gender, appear most likely to mobilize in response to inclusion (Meyer 2002).

7. Of course, the expansion of a movement coalition breeds the conditions for subsequent dissension within it, even about basic terms and goals (e.g., Benford 1993).

References

Amenta, Edwin. 1998. *Bold Relief: Institutional Politics and the Origins of Modern American Social Policy.* Princeton, NJ: Princeton University Press.

Amenta, Edwin, Kathleen Dunleavy, and Mary Bernstein. 1994. "Stolen Thunder?

Huey Long's 'Share our Wealth,' Political Mediation, and the Second New Deal." *American Sociological Review* 59: 678–702.

Andrews, Kenneth T. 2001. "Social Movements and Policy Implementation: The Mississippi Civil Rights Movement and the War on Poverty, 1965–1971." *American Sociological Review* 66: 21–48.

Banaszak, Lee Ann. 1996. *Why Movements Succeed or Fail: Opportunity, Culture, and the Struggle for Woman Suffrage.* Princeton, NJ: Princeton University Press.

Baumgartner, Frank R., and Bryan D. Jones. 1993. *Agendas and Instability in American Politics.* Chicago: University of Chicago Press.

Benford, Robert D. 1993. "Frame Disputes within the Nuclear Disarmament Movement." *Social Forces* 71: 677–701.

Berry, Jeffrey M. 1989. *The Interest Group Society.* 2nd ed. New York: Harper Collins.

Burstein, Paul. 1985. *Discrimination, Jobs, and Politics.* Chicago: University of Chicago Press.

———. 1991. "Policy Domains: Organization, Culture, and Policy Outcomes." *Annual Review of Sociology* 17: 327–50.

———. 1999. "Social Movements and Public Policy." In *How Social Movements Matter,* ed. Marco Giugni, Doug McAdam, and Charles Tilly, 3–21. Minneapolis: University of Minnesota Press.

Clemens, Elisabeth S. 1997. *The People's Lobby: Organizational Innovation and the Rise of Interest Group Politics in the United States, 1890–1925.* Chicago: University of Chicago Press.

Costain, Ann N. 1992. *Inviting Women's Rebellion.* Baltimore: Johns Hopkins University Press.

De Benedetti, Charles. 1990. *An American Ordeal: The Antiwar Movement of the Vietnam Era.* With Charles Chatfield. Syracuse, NY: Syracuse University Press.

Eisinger, Peter. 1973. "The Conditions of Protest Behavior in American Cities." *American Political Science Review* 81: 11–28.

Fallows, James. 1981. *National Defense.* New York: Random House.

Gamson, William A. [1975] 1990. *The Strategy of Social Protest.* 2nd ed. Belmont, CA: Wadsworth.

Gitlin, Todd. 1980. *The Whole World Is Watching.* Berkeley: University of California Press.

Gornick, Janet C., and David S. Meyer. 1998. "Changing Political Opportunity: The Anti-Rape Movement and Public Policy." *Journal of Policy History* 10: 367–98.

Hansen, John Mark. 1991. *Gaining Access: Congress and the Farm Lobby, 1919–1981.* Chicago: University of Chicago.

Heclo, Hugh. 1978. "Issue Networks and the Executive Establishment." In *The*

New American Political System, ed. Anthony King, 87–124. Washington, DC: American Enterprise Institute.

Heineman, Kenneth J. 1993. *Campus Wars: The Peace Movement at American State Universities in the Vietnam Era.* New York: New York University Press.

Imig, Douglas R. 1996. *Poverty and Power: The Political Representation of Poor Americans.* Lincoln: University of Nebraska Press.

Ingram, Helen, and Steven Rathgeb Smith, eds. 1993. *Public Policy for Democracy.* Washington, DC: Brookings Institution.

Jenness, Valerie, and Ryken Grattet. 2001. *Making Hate a Crime: From Social Movement to Law Enforcement.* New York: Russell Sage.

Katzenstein, Mary F. 1998. *Faithful and Fearless: Moving Feminist Protest inside the Church and Military.* Princeton, NJ: Princeton University Press.

Kingdon, John W. 1984. *Agendas, Alternatives, and Public Policies.* Boston: Little, Brown.

Lipsky, Michael. 1970. *Protest in City Politics.* Chicago: Rand-McNally.

Matthews, Nancy. 1994. *Confronting Rape: The Feminist Anti-Rape Movement and the State.* New York: Routledge.

McAdam, Doug. 1982. *Political Process and the Origins of Black Insurgency.* Chicago: University of Chicago Press.

McCammon, Holly, Karen Campbell, Ellen Granberg, and Christine Mowery. 2001. "How Movements Win: Gendered Opportunity Structures and U.S. Women's Suffrage Movements, 1866 to 1919." *American Sociological Review* 66, no. 1: 47–70.

McCarthy, John D., David Britt, and Mark Wolfson. 1991. "The Institutional Channeling of Social Movements by the State in the United States." *Research in Social Movements* 13: 45–76.

McCarthy, John D., and Mayer N. Zald. 1977. "Resource Mobilization and Social Movements: A Partial Theory." *American Sociological Review* 82: 1212–41.

Mettler, Suzanne. 1998. *Dividing Citizens: Gender and Federalism in the New Deal.* Ithaca, NY: Cornell University Press.

Meyer, David S. 1990. *A Winter of Discontent: The Nuclear Freeze and American Politics.* New York: Praeger.

———. 1993. "Political Process and Protest Movement Cycles." *Political Research Quarterly* 46 (September): 451–79.

———. 1995. "Framing National Security: Elite Public Discourse on Nuclear Weapons during the Cold War." *Political Communication* 12: 173–92.

———. 2002. "Opportunities and Identities: Bridge-building in the Study of Social Movements." In *Social Movements: Identity, Culture, and the State,* ed. Nancy Whittier Meyer and Belinda Robnett, 3–21. New York: Oxford University Press.

———. 2004. "Protest and Political Opportunity." *Annual Review of Sociology* 30: 125–45.

Meyer, David S., and Douglas R. Imig. 1993. "Political Opportunity and the Rise and Decline of Interest Group Sectors." *Social Science Journal* 30: 253–70.

Meyer, David S., and Thomas R. Rochon. 1997. "Toward a Coalitional Theory of Social and Political Movements." In *Coalitions and Political Movements: The Lessons of the Nuclear Freeze,* ed. Rochon and Meyer, 237–52. Boulder, CO: Lynne Rienner.

Meyer, David S., and Suzanne Staggenborg. 1996. "Movements, Counter-movements, and the Structure of Political Opportunity." *American Journal of Sociology* 101: 1628–60.

Meyer, David S., and Sidney Tarrow, eds. 1998. *The Social Movement Society: Contentious Politics for a New Century.* Lanham, MD: Rowman & Littlefield.

Meyer, David S., and Nancy Whittier. 1994. "Social Movement Spillover." *Social Problems* 41: 277–98.

Miller, James. 1987. *Democracy Is in the Streets.* New York: Simon and Schuster.

Minkoff, Debra C. 1995. *Organizing for Equality: The Evolution of Women's and Racial-Ethnic Organizations in America, 1955–1985.* New Brunswick, NJ: Rutgers University Press.

Nixon, Richard M. 1978. *RN: The Memoirs of Richard Nixon.* New York: Grosset & Dunlap.

Piven, Frances Fox, and Richard A. Cloward. 1971. *Regulating the Poor.* New York: Vintage.

———. 1977. *Poor People's Movements.* New York: Vintage.

Polsby, Nelson. 1984. *Political Innovation in the United States.* New Haven, CT: Yale University Press.

Rochon, Thomas R. 1998. *Culture Moves: Ideas, Activism, and Changing Values.* Princeton, NJ: Princeton University Press.

Rucht, Dieter. 2000. "Distant Issue Movements in Germany: Empirical Description and Theoretical Reflections." In *Globalizations and Social Movements: Culture, Power, and the Transnational Public Sphere,* ed. John A. Guidry, Michael D. Kennedy, and Mayer N. Zald, 76–105. Ann Arbor: University of Michigan Press.

Sawyers, Traci M., and David S. Meyer. 1999. "Missed Opportunities: Social Movement Abeyance and Public Policy." *Social Problems* 46: 187–206.

Schneider, Anne Larason, and Helen Ingram. 1997. *Policy Design for Democracy.* Lawrence: University of Kansas.

Small, Melvin. 1988. *Johnson, Nixon, and the Doves.* New Brunswick, NJ: Rutgers University Press.

Stone, Deborah. 1997. *Policy Paradox: The Art of Political Decision Making.* New York: Norton.

Switzer, Jacqueline Vaughn. 2001. *Environmental Politics: Domestic and Global Dimensions.* 3rd ed. Boston and New York: Bedford/St. Martin's.

Tarrow, Sidney. 1998. *Power in Movement: Social Movements and Contentious Politics.* 2nd ed. Cambridge: Cambridge University Press.

Taylor, Verta. 1989. "Social Movement Continuity: The Women's Movement in Abeyance." *American Sociological Review* 54: 761–74.

Tilly, Charles. 1978. *From Mobilization to Revolution.* Reading, MA: Addison-Wesley.

Waldman, Steven. 1996. *The Bill: How Legislation Really Becomes Law; A Case Study of the National Service Bill.* Rev. ed. New York: Penguin Books.

Weed, Frank. 1995. *Certainty of Justice: Reform in the Crime Victim Movement.* New York: Aldine de Gruyter.

Weinberger, Caspar W. 1990. *Fighting for Peace: Seven Critical Years in the Pentagon.* New York: Warner Books.

Wilson, James Q. 1995. *Political Organizations.* 2nd ed. Princeton, NJ: Princeton University Press.

Zald, Mayer N., and John D. McCarthy. 1987. *Social Movements in an Organizational Society.* New Brunswick, NJ: Transaction.

I

Context Matters and Patterns of Influence: Agendas and Alliances

David S. Meyer

Following the logic of the introduction, this part focuses on the explicit connections between the state and challenging social movements. These chapters start with explicit consideration of the rules, routines, and structure of American political institutions. Taken together, they also suggest a sequence of political development over the fifty or so years covered here. The major point unifying all of them is that the notion that social movements are completely separate from the state doesn't really describe reality. Rather, movement actors are deeply intertwined with policy makers inside the state—or at least portions of government. Policy makers incorporate *some* of the ideas, personnel, and concerns of social movements into the governmental process. At the same time, challenging social movements look to government not only for policy response, but also assets in waging a political struggle.

In chapter 1, Edwin Amenta examines the politics of old-age security in the 1930s. He starts with a brief overview of the American political system, paying particular attention to the challenge of federalism. Large-scale economic dislocation in the 1930s created an opportunity for policy reform and unleashed a spate of social movements addressing economic insecurity. The influence of social movements on public policy, in this case, the Townsend Plan's influence on old-age policy, Amenta argues, can only be seen by focusing on the matching of movement tactics to political contexts—or political opportunities. He describes a situation in which much social movement action generated nothing in the way of response at the local level because sympathetic policy makers were not in position to make the most of Townsend pressures. In short, he argues that social movement actors need to be cognizant of the circumstances around them in order to choose strategies and tactics most likely to work.

The New Deal of the 1930s expanded the scope of government activity to an unprecedented extent, but government expansion didn't stop with Franklin Roosevelt. The basic social policy safety net of the New Deal continued, and the growth of the United States as a world actor during and after World War II led to further expansion of government on military and foreign policy issues. Using a unique database of government activity, Frank Baumgartner and Christine Mahoney track the composition of congressional agendas over time. Although some policy areas have diminished, the basic agenda has grown larger and more diverse, with many—but not all—areas a response to social movements. The establishment of ongoing policy debates about social movement areas, for example, the status of women or protecting the environment, has supported the growth of a relatively permanent sector of Washington-based social movement organizations that monitor government, represent interests, and make claims. The very crowded government agenda may make it more difficult for new issues and new movements.

In the final chapter of this part, John McCarthy examines a new form of organization, the community advocacy coalition, by looking at antidrug efforts. He finds no strict boundaries between government and the advocacy coalition and, in fact, that much citizen mobilization is the direct result of government policy and the efforts of elected officials. The advocacy coalition is defined by very loose membership rules, extraordinary breadth of actors and interests, and extensive elite support. Tracing citizen activism to elite sponsorship and government action, McCarthy offers a nuanced portrait of civil society and political advocacy.

Taken together, these chapters establish government as, simultaneously, a target, a venue, and an initiator of citizen action.

1

Political Contexts, Challenger Strategies, and Mobilization: Explaining the Impact of the Townsend Plan

Edwin Amenta

Social movements typically mobilize resources and engage in collective action in order to make an impact. Recently scholars have attempted to go beyond understanding mobilization to explain these impacts, often focusing on state-oriented consequences, especially those regarding public policy, yet little progress has been made in theorizing and studying these consequences (Giugni 1998). Given the number of actors involved and the complexity of political contexts, establishing the causal influence of any challenger has proved difficult, and it is even more difficult to appraise theoretical arguments about the consequences of challengers.

In this chapter I confront these theoretical and methodological issues. In the broadest sense I am arguing that the collective action of state-oriented challengers is politically mediated. To make an impact challengers must influence the thinking and actions of institutional political actors. More specifically I am arguing that political circumstances will influence the effectiveness of different sorts of collective action of well-mobilized challengers. I build on arguments about resource mobilization (McCarthy and Zald 2001), collective action strategies (Gamson 1990; Cress and Snow 2000), and "political opportunities" (Kitschelt 1986; McAdam 1996), but go beyond them, too. My claim is that mobilizing resources and deploying them in collective action does not necessarily lead to any predictable rate of return, as often expected by rational models of collective action (Chong 1992) or bargaining models (Burstein, Einwohner, and Hollander 1995). I am arguing also that gaining an impact is not merely a matter of choosing the one best strategy (Piven and Cloward 1977) or choosing appropriate organizational forms or goals (Gamson 1990). What is more, having an impact is not merely a matter of being mobilized at the right time (Goldstone 1980) or in the right place (Kitschelt 1986). Instead, gaining results for political challengers depends on a coincidence of strategy and political context.

I specify these arguments and give them a preliminary appraisal by examining the U.S. Depression-era group called the Townsend Plan, named after Dr. Francis E. Townsend, a California physician. The Townsend Plan, initially known as Old Age Revolving Pensions, Ltd. (OARP), provided the name for both the organization and its program, which called for a national, generous old-age pension for any citizen aged sixty or older who agreed to be retired and to spend the money quickly.[1] It was designed to end both poverty in old age and the Depression. Although no version of Townsend's plan ever became law, its influence over old-age policy has often been considered great among scholars (Schlesinger 1960, 43; Holtzman 1963, 207–10; Piven and Cloward 1993, ch. 3), who have argued that the Townsend Plan advanced both the timing of the Social Security Act and the content of its old-age programs (cf. Achenbaum 1983; Berkowitz 1991; Orloff 1993, ch. 9).

My analyses center on public social-spending policy making for the aged—the main collective benefit pursued by the Townsend Plan and one of central importance for aged Americans, as well as Americans of all ages. Programs for the aged today, including Social Security, Medicare, and Supplemental Security Income, account for the vast majority of U.S. social spending, which in turn accounts for the majority of U.S. government spending. It is no major exaggeration to say that the U.S. state has become a welfare state for the elderly. Just as important for my purposes, the Townsend Plan is useful for assessing theoretical claims about the impacts of challengers: its support waxed and waned and was greater in some polities than in others; it engaged in different strategies of collective action in varied political circumstances over more than a decade. I examine the impact of the Townsend Plan across a number of episodes of old-age policy making and collective action campaigns at the national level. I also address briefly old-age policy making in the states in order to take analytical advantage of their variability in political conditions and the strategies employed by the Townsend Plan. The Townsend Plan's efforts provide some puzzles, for it did not have its greatest influence when it was best mobilized, when it pursued its most aggressive collective action, or when political conditions were most favorable for social spending policies. I hope to solve these puzzles with my arguments.

A Political Mediation Model

In a democratic political system, mobilizing relatively large numbers of committed people is probably necessary to win new collective benefits for state-oriented challengers. However well mobilized, challengers are most likely to win results when institutional political actors see some benefit in aiding the group the challenger represents. Only rarely by their own actions can challengers effect the adoption of new state policies or regulations or enforce them, so challengers need to engage in collective action that alters the calculations of relevant institutional political actors, such as elected officials and state bureaucrats. These actors need to see a challenger as potentially facilitating or disrupting their own goals—which might include improving electoral prospects by augmenting or cementing new electoral coalitions or gaining in public opinion, acting on political beliefs, and increasing the support for the missions of governmental bureaus, among others. To secure new benefits, challengers will typically need help or complementary action from like-minded institutional actors or other movement organizations. I see states and political institutions as influencing challengers and the latter influencing states in a recursive process (see also Amenta et al. 2002). In discussing causal influences, it is best to start with political institutions, for all movements come into existence in particular political circumstances, and states and other organized political groups, such as parties, tend to dwarf movements and are usually impervious to rapid change.

Discouraging U.S. Political Institutions

My view is that U.S. political institutions and processes have been unfavorable to the collective action of challengers—which stands in opposition to the conventional wisdom that sees the U.S. polity as more susceptible to the influence of movements because of its federal structure and relatively under-bureaucratized executive bureaucracy (Kriesi 1994). The political institutional hindrances of the U.S. political and party systems usually reduce the effectiveness of the collective action of political challengers (Amenta et al. 2002; see also Meyer, introduction to this volume).

U.S. political institutions have been unfavorable to challengers in three main ways. One key aspect of the polity for social movements is the way and the degree to which it is democratized (Tilly 2000)—a polity characteristic that is systemic and slow to change. Like Switzerland and Australia, the United States was an early democratizing state for white men, but was largely a democratic laggard in the twentieth century, especially in the South (Kousser 1974; Piven and Cloward 1989). In the twenty-first century, the

United States retains restrictions on voting greater than those in other rich democracies (Lijphart 1997). The extreme horizontal dispersion of authority in the United States is a second key barrier. The fact that the executive office, legislature, and courts all share legislative powers provides members of the polity with great veto power over new legislation and discourages challengers' activity by undermining their ability to make new claims stick (Huber and Stephens 2001; Pierson 1994). The two legislative bodies are also divided into committees and have rules that hinder majorities (Brady 1988). The third key barrier is that the U.S. electoral system is tilted against challengers. Winner-take-all voting systems, such as those in America, Australia, Canada, New Zealand, and the United Kingdom, discourage challengers from forming political parties (Lipset and Marks 2000). American presidential electoral rules raise the bar even further by applying a winner-take-all formula to the electoral votes of each state and making a separate process of securing ballot lines for candidates in each state. The decentralization of national American political authority aggravates the situation. It is far easier for a new party to win a few seats in Congress than to win a presidential contest, but these seats buy much less influence than seats in a parliamentary system like Canada's.

The U.S. political party system has been systemically discouraging to the claims of state-oriented challengers. One main reason is that U.S. parties have often been patronage-oriented: hierarchical organizations that extend their presence through contesting and winning elections and then providing individualized benefits to supporters by the spoils of office (Mayhew 1986, 19–20; Katznelson 1981). Patronage-oriented political parties tend to deflect claims for the automatically provided collective benefits sought especially by social-spending challengers. What is more, U.S. parties are of the catchall variety, competing for the votes of different groups but with no organic connections to them. In many states where parties are not patronage-oriented, U.S. parties have been more open to the influence of challengers, but they are also open to capture by the challengers' better-funded opponents. The major parties have no outside impulses toward discipline, with party caucuses mattering less and less over the twentieth century, and factions of parties and individual legislators increasingly act on their own, especially since the 1980s, as the cost of political campaigns has skyrocketed. By the middle of the twentieth century, the Republican party had been transformed into a relatively unified right-wing party backed by most business interests, whereas the Democrats became an odd centrist party, with its northern wing fairly left in orientation, but its under-democratized southern wing far to the right on many issues (Hicks 1999). As southern Democrats drifted into the

Republican party in the wake of the democratization of the South in the last quarter of the twentieth century, the parties have become more polarized over issues of social spending and taxation, but the Democratic party has remained centrist largely because of the enormous influence of money on U.S. political campaigns.

The progress of the democratization of the polity and the nature of the political party system has varied greatly across the country as well as over time. In the first half of the twentieth century the former Confederacy was beset by under-democratized polities, and the most dominant patronage-oriented parties were located in various states in the Northeast and Midwest. These parties have become weaker in the second half of the twentieth century, and their patronage orientation has declined. Figure 1.1 shows the variability in U.S. polities at the middle of the twentieth century. The U.S. polity provided a hostile climate for challengers, but it varied greatly across the country. Most of the West was both democratized and lacking patronage parties.

Political system

	Extensive political rights	Restricted political rights
Party system / Program-oriented	**Open polity** 11 Western states (Arizona, California, Colorado, Idaho, Montana, New Mexico, Utah, Washington, Wyoming, Nebraska, Nevada); 7 Midwestern states (Iowa, Kansas, Michigan, Minnesota, Wisconsin, North Dakota, South Dakota); 4 Eastern states (Maine, Massachusetts, New Hampshire, Vermont); 1 Southern state (Oklahoma)	**Under-democratized polity** 11 Southern states (Alabama, Arkansas, Florida, Georgia, Louisiana, Mississippi, North Carolina, South Carolina, Tennessee, Texas, Virginia)
Patronage-oriented	**Patronage-based polity** 7 Eastern states (Connecticut, Delaware, Maryland, New Jersey, New York, Pennsylvania, Rhode Island); 5 Midwestern states (Missouri, Ohio, Illinois, Indiana, Kentucky) 1 Southern state (West Virginia)	**Under-democratized, patronage-based polity** None

Figure 1.1. U.S. polities according to type of political and party systems.

Strategies and Contexts of Protest

There are two main lines of argument about what accounts for the impact of well-mobilized challengers. On the one hand, it is often argued that specific sorts of strategies and goals of collective action are productive or unproductive of collective benefits—regardless of the political circumstances in which the strategies are undertaken (Piven and Cloward 1977; Gamson 1990). On the other hand, it is sometimes argued that once a challenger is mobilized the main thing influencing its impact is the political context or "opportunity structure" (Goldstone 1980; Kitschelt 1986). I suggest instead that in order to get results the strategies of state-oriented challengers need to fit the political situation. Different sorts of strategies are likely to be necessary to win collective benefits in different political circumstances. The basic idea is that the more favorable these circumstances are, the less a mobilized challenger has to do to win collective benefits; the more difficult the political circumstances, the more assertive a challenger has to be. Less assertive strategies are likely to work only in the most favorable circumstances; more assertive strategies are likely to work in many circumstances. However, in favorable ones they may waste resources and good will and their efforts might backfire.

What constitutes favorable and unfavorable political situations, and what constitutes more and less assertive collective action strategies? For political situations, a central middle-range aspect of the political context is the orientation of the regime in power toward the goals of challengers. A favorable regime is expected to amplify the impact of a challenger's mobilization and collective action, while an unfavorable regime would dampen it. Often parties have long-standing commitments to ideological positions or groups whose interests and goals may conflict with those of challengers (Klandermans and Oegema 1987). For state-oriented challengers seeking collective benefits through sustained public spending, the position of the regime on higher taxation is key. Since the 1930s the U.S. Republican party and its representatives have tended to oppose automatic, programmatic spending claims because they imply higher taxation, whereas the national Democratic party and Democrats outside the South have tended to be "reform-oriented"—more open to taxation and to claims requiring taxation on relatively well-off people (Amenta 1998; Hicks 1999). Another important part of the political context comprises the missions, activities, and powers of state bureaus in charge of domestic programs related to the challenger. Programs related to a challenger's interests will be more easily generated when relevant state actors are present and have initiative, talent, and power (Skocpol 1985). Domestic bureaucrats may see the creation of collective benefits for a group as advancing the mission of their bureau and may intensify the impact of challengers by their own actions. Conversely, the absence of such proficient state actors may make the public believe that new programs will be mismanaged and waste money (Orloff 1993). Not all implementation capacities will work to the advantage of challengers, however. If important and powerful state bureaus have missions that oppose the claims of a challenger, I would expect them to diminish the impact of a challenger's collective action.

I expect different sorts of strategies to work best in different contexts. If the political regime is supportive and the domestic bureaucrats are professionalized and supportive, limited protest based mainly on the evidence of mobilization is likely to be sufficient to provide increased collective benefits (see Figure 1.2). The challenger needs merely to demonstrate that it has support. Organizing additional members might serve this purpose. This might be done by time-honored activities such as rallies, petitioning, letter writing, or public awareness and education campaigns. The sequences of thinking and action—the "mechanisms" of influence—would probably work something like this: Members of a reform-oriented regime are likely to use the evidence of mobilization and modest protest as a confirmation of the beneficiary group's relative importance in an electoral coalition. In a regime likely to promote social spending, the claims of the mobilized may receive special attention. Domestic bureaucrats are likely to portray the mobilization as

| | | **State bureaucrats** | |
		Strong and aligned with challenger's interests	Weak and/or opposed to challenger's interests
Elected officials	Aligned with challenger's constituency	Sheer mobilization, limited protest	Sanction or urge creation of state bureaus
	Opposed to challenger's constituency	Sanction or displace elected officials	Highly assertive strategies

Figure 1.2. Collective action strategies expected to produce collective benefits, given the configuration of political regimes and state bureaucrats, in democratic and program-oriented polities.

indicating the need for the augmentation, a more rapid implementation, or greater enforcement of its program. If the regime hopes to add to its coalition or if domestic bureaucrats have a mission that is not yet realized, those groups best mobilized are likely to win the greatest benefits in public policy for their constituencies.

By contrast, achieving collective benefits through public policy is likely to be more difficult in the absence of either a supportive regime or a supportive administrative authority. When the regime is opposed to the challenger or sees no benefit in adding its beneficiary group to its coalition, and when state bureaucracies in the area are hostile or absent, minimally assertive collective action is likely to have at best a minor effect. Some political actors may dust off old proposals or think about new ones—tactical maneuvers to delay action until the challenge dwindles. If the bureaucracy is hostile to the mission, it ignores the challenge or engages in similar tactical maneuvers. Given the circumstances, a challenger engaged in minimally assertive action is unlikely to influence either the legislative agenda, the content of legislation, its potential passage, or its implementation, and thus has a minimal impact on the provision of collective benefits.

Matching Strategies to Contexts

As political circumstances become more difficult, represented by movement from the upper left-hand corner to the bottom right-hand corner of Figure 1.2, more assertive or bolder collective action is required to produce collective benefits. By more assertive I mean the use of increasingly strong sanctions that influence things political actors value—such as their positions, their beliefs, or their functions or prerogatives. They work largely by mobilizing large numbers of people behind a line of action, often with electoral implications. This collective action may be designed to convince the general public or like-minded officials of the justice of the cause, but may also demonstrate to officials that a large segment of the electorate is willing to vote based on a single issue.

I refer specifically to assertiveness rather than making the usual distinction between "assimilative" and "disruptive" strategies (Kitschelt 1986) or "institutional" and "noninstitutional" strategies (McAdam 1982). The assimilative category is often stretched to include all collective action that engages institutional politics, despite the fact that this collective action can vary greatly in its sanctions, and noninstitutional action, such as protest, may be less assertive than institutional action. The following examples, though far from exhaustive, give a sense of possible variations in sanctions and assertiveness in political institutional action by challengers. Engaging

in education campaigns and promoting the acceptance of a specific proposal or aid for a group is minimally assertive, though possibly necessary
to have an impact. Similarly less assertive is merely mobilizing support
behind a program. Gaining commitments of time from participating members is more assertive than compiling mailing lists of like-minded donors.
Letter-writing campaigns are more assertive, but can vary depending on the
claims in them. Making public statements of endorsement for individual
legislators or proposals goes further than education campaigns, and more
assertive than that is engaging in protest campaigns targeting programs or
administrators. Public campaigns to replace administrators subject to election or to prevent the appointment of others is more assertive still—elected
officials in democracies fear recall efforts far more than protest campaigns.
Contesting elections is also on the more assertive side, as it applies a key
sanction to legislators, who seek to be reelected as well as support specific
ideologies or policy ideas. Although the assertiveness of an action and its
potential systemic effects are not the same, many extremely assertive lines of
institutional action have a systemic bent to them. In some polities, standard
institutional political actors can be bypassed with institutional action, such
as initiatives, which can be more assertive than contesting elections. With
initiatives, a challenger can potentially put its issue on the agenda, specify
the proposal, and lead the campaign to have it voted into law. A challenger-
led initiative may not only produce great collective benefits, but also greatly
alter the political context in favor of the challenger and promote the future
growth of the challenger. However, only in a few U.S. polities are direct
democratic devices available, and they can also be employed by opponents,
who are likely to be better funded. Equally assertive but more systemic is
for a challenger to elect its own leaders or adherents to these offices by way
of a new party, an option highly limited in the U.S. setting.

Challengers are likely to benefit by targeting their actions to fit administrative or legislative contexts. If the relevant state bureaucratic actors are
present and either supportive or neutral and if the political regime is not supportive of the challenger's group, collective action will be most productive
if it focuses on elected officials. Such action might induce those who would
otherwise be indifferent or hostile to legislation to support it or at least not
to challenge it. If the political regime is supportive or neutral and domestic bureaucrats are either absent or hostile to the challenger's constituency,
domestic bureaucratic capabilities must be created or existing bureaucratic
actors must be sanctioned. When both the political regime and the relevant
state bureaucracy are unfavorably disposed to the challenger's constituency,
only the most assertive strategies will be likely to win collective benefits.

The most direct way to overcome these circumstances is for challengers to take political power through democratic processes, such as through initiatives or creating new parties. Less assertive electoral strategies would work better than limited protest, which in turn would be better than minor education or information campaigns. Assertive strategies might produce results in relatively favorable political environments, but they might backfire and risk alienating potential allies within the polity as well as waste resources better used for other purposes. In some circumstances, when the regime is highly unfavorable to the challenger's issue or constituency, no collective action has hopes of being productive.

There are direct and indirect ways that assertive collective action might work in unfavorable political contexts. The direct ways are easiest to see and are most likely to produce the greatest benefits. The electoral support of sympathetic legislators can tilt political contexts more in favor of the challenger and may lead to new legislation in favor of the challenger's constituency if the legislature is otherwise closely aligned. Successful initiative and referendum drives can produce new laws and often new administrative authority. Collective action that brings the replacement of unfavorable administrators—through firings or electoral challenges—can improve the enforcement of laws in favor of the challenger's constituency. Productive effort in creating new parties may also bring new legislation in favor of the challenger. In the best-case scenario challengers would be able to control a government or political regime and, possibly, alter the political context in a more permanent way.

Assertive collective action that does not meet its ostensible goals, however, can still lead to benefits for a challenger's constituency in political circumstances that are largely unfavorable. A vigorous if failed bid to unseat a legislator may soften his or her views against the program or other programs, benefiting the constituency of a challenger, in order to avoid a later challenge. A well-supported initiative effort that fails is likely to show legislators that the issue is of great significance to an important segment of their constituents and may lead to pressure to provide concessions for the constituency. Protests against the actions of administrators may lead to their eventual replacement, to legislation to alter the practices of administrators, or to changes in the practices of administrators, in order to prevent their replacement. The indirect benefits of failed third-party bids work somewhat differently. Making a plausible threat shows a major party candidate, who is already favorable to the constituency or issue, that more attention needs to be given to it. The process works indirectly when the new party candidate demonstrates support and then gains concessions in exchange for withdrawing from the election. But fighting until the bitter end will often backfire and harm the constituency of a U.S. challenger.

The policy situation facing the challenger is an important part of the political context. It is worth dividing the process of creating new laws containing collective benefits into the agenda setting, legislative content, passage, and implementation of legislation (see Kingdon 1984; Burstein 1993). Placing a bill on the political agenda is not a process that social movements can typically negotiate by themselves, and often such processes depend on the political regime, the relevant bureaucracies, and the nature of current programs. That said, mobilized challengers will have to do far less work if their issue is slated for entry onto the political agenda or is already there. In instances when a bill is coming onto the agenda, through presidential proposals or congressional hearings, groups merely need to mobilize in order to keep the issue from leaving the agenda and to show its importance. This may aid in increasing benefits for the challenger's constituency. Afterward, challengers may aim to increase the benefits in the legislation at hand or attempt to influence representatives to join the coalition behind legislation. At this stage social movements can provide "alternatives," which, if sufficiently supported, might be used as wedges to alter the content of legislation in favor of a constituency. There may be opportunities for compromise that should not be foreclosed by action on the part of the challenger. It is easier for challengers to influence policy in its earliest legislative phases, before a program or policy becomes highly institutionalized. If movement actors are involved in the institutionalization of policy—that is to say, if they are installed in a bureaucracy implementing policy or influence the selection process for these positions—the chances for later bids to change policy in a favorable direction are improved. This is not usually the case, however. Somewhat less advantageous are situations in which domestic bureaucracies are well run by state authorities with firm missions, recruit experts committed to the mission, and have a strong esprit de corps. In such instances, the bureau will press for the mission, which will often run in the same direction as the interests of the constituency of a challenger, but not always. Worse for movements is when domestic bureaus are captured and their missions subverted by nonexpert political operatives. Patronage political parties will often fill bureaucratic positions with nonexpert party loyalists, and, worse, domestic bureaucracies can be captured by opposing interest groups—as when regulatory bureaucracies are filled by appointees from the industry that they are meant to regulate. These groups may also cultivate ties with key members of Congress and form iron triangles or policy monopolies (Baumgartner and Jones 1993) that become more difficult over time for challengers to influence.

I am making no major claims about why challengers choose the strategies they do. Different groups within similar movements often employ diverse
strategies (Dalton 1995; Tarrow 1996).[2] Even challengers with the greatest
strategic capacities (Ganz 2000; Andrews 2001) usually need to make decisions quickly and with limited information, making it doubtful that optimal
matches of strategy to situation will typically happen. Some challengers may
choose strategies as matters of moral commitment or taste (Jasper 1997) or
identity (Polletta 2002). Others may employ strategies that match the political situation of the time of their founding, but find themselves unable to
change with political circumstances (Valocchi 1990; Cohn 1993). National
or international challengers working in several polities may employ a standard
strategy across polities that is appropriate to only some of them.

Assessing the Impact of the Townsend Plan: A First Cut

Before I appraise my arguments, let me introduce the Townsend Plan.
Old Age Revolving Pensions, Ltd., was founded in January 1934 by Dr.
Francis E. Townsend, a laid-off, sixty-four-year-old Long Beach physician,
and Robert Earl Clements, a thirty-nine-year-old real estate broker (see
Amenta 2003, ch. 2). The purpose of the organization was to promote the
enactment of the Old Age Revolving Pension plan, which Townsend had
first outlined in some letters to the editor of the *Long Beach Press Telegram*
in September 1933. The plan, with its $200 monthly pensions to all non-
working citizens over sixty years of age, excluding criminals, was designed
to end the Depression and ensure prosperity through extensive and mandatory spending, as well as to end poverty in old age and elevate the status of
the aged. Clements sold the pension plan in the manner of real estate, attaching Townsend's name to it, and Townsend was OARP's corporate per-
sonification and spokesman, something like Colonel Sanders. To maintain
enthusiasm and ensure a stable flow of resources, Clements and Townsend
inaugurated Townsend clubs. These local affiliates had no formal decision-
making role—indeed, they were largely fan clubs—but congregated regularly to hear speakers, discuss events, and make donations.

Though largely forgotten today, the Townsend Plan was a major political phenomenon. In 1936, the Townsend Plan was the subject of more
than fifty front-page stories in the *New York Times,* and its coverage that
year made it the seventh most publicized challenger in twentieth-century
America. That year OARP had organized two million older Americans into
Townsend clubs, quickly becoming one of the only fifty-seven voluntary
membership associations to attract 1 percent or more of the U.S. adult
population—a level never reached by any organization in the feminist or

civil rights movements (Skocpol 1999). At the end of 1935, OARP was raising funds at a rate comparable to that of the Republican party and far more rapidly than the ruling Democratic party (Amenta 2003, introduction).

To determine why a movement had consequences means ascertaining first whether it had any at all and, if so, which ones—not an easy task (Giugni 1998; Tilly 1999; Earl 2000; Amenta and Caren 2004). I approach these issues from several directions. Through intensive historical study, I ascertain whether institutional political actors changed their thinking and actions in response to the Townsend Plan. I employ comparisons of the results of a series of Townsend Plan campaigns and old-age policy-making episodes, noting changes in political contexts and strategies along the way. In addition, I make comparisons across U.S. states, where structural and short-term political contexts varied dramatically. The Townsend Plan's approach to the states changed over time, paying little attention to them during the 1930s but contesting them in different ways in the 1940s.

I start by addressing some plausible alternative arguments. According to the view that social movements are rational efforts to gain influence, their collective action is expected to yield collective benefits (Jenkins 1983; Chong 1992). The mobilization of resources constitutes a key constraint on a challenger's ability to engage in collective action (Tilly 1978). Similarly, bargaining models (Burstein, Einwohner, and Hollander 1995) hold that a challenger's resources should aid it in achieving goals, other things being equal, and so the connection between resources and influence is worth exploring. After all, the Townsend Plan sought resources in order to wage its collective action campaigns.

However, the historical trajectory of the mobilization of people and money behind the Townsend Plan does not line up neatly with its influence. In the heyday of the Townsend Plan, at the beginning of 1936, its impact on old-age policy was minimal (see Figures 1.3 and 1.4). By contrast, the Townsend Plan helped to improve the proposals for the aged in the administration's Economic Security Act in 1934 even though it had only begun to mobilize. In 1935, the Townsend Plan was better mobilized, but Congress watered down old-age benefits in the administration's security legislation. Although it is sometimes claimed that the Townsend Plan spurred the Social Security Act, the Townsend Plan was largest *after* its passage. The organization lost most of its influence when the bulk of its membership left later in the 1940s, despite continuing impressive efforts in gaining financial resources. In short, the Townsend Plan had influence over public policy at wildly different levels of support, suggesting that a membership base was necessary for influence on old-age policy, but not the only requirement.

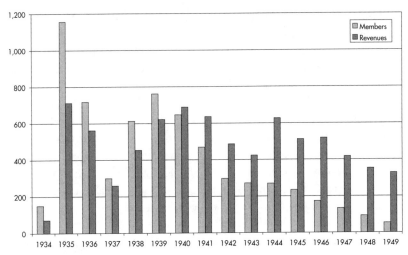

Figure 1.3. Townsend Plan paid membership and revenues, 1934–48 (membership in thousands, and revenues in thousands of dollars). (Data from Townsend National Weekly; *Holtzman 1963, 49, 80.)*

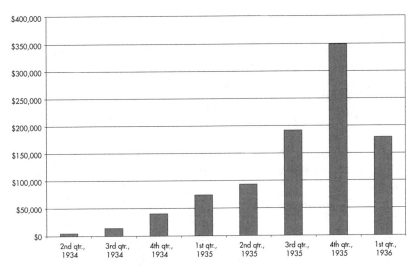

Figure 1.4. OARP revenues, by quarter. (Data from Modern Crusader; Townsend National Weekly.*)*

The lack of a close connection between mobilization and results was not a matter of political leaders acting according to misconceptions of support for the Townsend Plan. The Committee on Economic Security dispatched a staffer to follow the progress of the organization (Berkowitz 1995, 29–30), and OARP's publicist complained in 1935 that the administration was not fooled by exaggerations of support printed in news media. What is more, Clements ascertained that the backing in the House that year for an amendment based on Townsend's plan came only from congressmen in districts with many clubs, suggesting that they, too, had a good sense of OARP's support.

Nor did the Townsend Plan's influence relate directly to the degree to which it engaged in collective action. The Townsend Plan's collective action often proved a waste of time and resources, as during the debate over the Social Security Act in 1935, when it may have backfired. What is more, although it was mainly nationally focused in the 1930s, the Townsend Plan had some of its greatest effects on Old Age Assistance (OAA) programs at the state level. This happened despite the fact that the Townsend Plan sometimes fought improvements in OAA.

It is sometimes argued that the use of "constraints" in collective action is likely to lead to results for challengers (Gamson 1990). However, the Townsend Plan's strategy of aiding the organization's congressional friends and punishing its enemies did not automatically bring it influence in old-age policy making. As Figure 1.5 shows, this strategy had not even begun when the Townsend Plan had its initial influence on old-age policy in 1934. What is more, the endorsement strategy peaked in apparent productivity in the early 1940s, when there were more than one hundred members of the House endorsed by the Townsend Plan. Yet during the early 1940s the augmentation of old-age policy was removed from the political agenda.

What is more, the impact of the Townsend Plan had no close connection to shifts in the political context in favor of social policy, as arguments about the influence of political opportunity suggest (Goldstone 1980; Jenkins 1983). Figure 1.6 traces the political fortunes of northern Democrats and left-wing party representatives in Congress—which I am calling "prospective pro–social spenders."[3] The dominance of this group is often argued to be necessary to gains in social policy (Amenta 1998; Hicks 1999). I focus on this group as providing the main systemic fluctuations in the political context. Roosevelt, a northern Democrat, was president from 1933 to 1945, making his influence mainly constant. It seems unusual that the Townsend Plan had influence in 1934 in the proposal stage of the security bill, but not in 1935 or 1936, when the Congress was augmented with

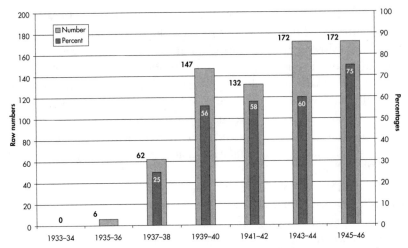

Figure 1.5. House members endorsed by the Townsend Plan, in raw numbers and percentages elected, 1933–46. During the 1934 elections for the 1935–36 House, OARP made no official endorsements. (Data from Townsend National Weekly; *Holtzman 1963, 127.)*

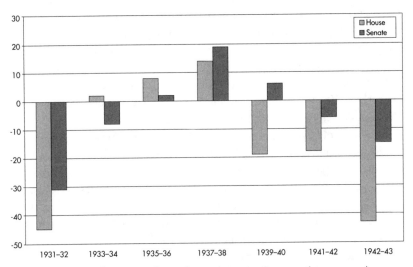

Figure 1.6. Size of pro–social spender margins in Congress (percentages), 1931–44. "Pro-spender" indicates likely supporters of generous, nationally controlled social programs. The margin is the difference between the pro-spenders and others. (Data from Congressional Quarterly.*)*

new northern Democratic members after the party's unusual midterm triumph. The Townsend Plan had little influence when the political alignment in Washington was even better suited to social spending gains, in 1937–38, but had better results in 1939 after an election in which pro-spenders in Congress took a beating and had their ranks greatly reduced. The figure does suggest, however, that once the systemic political context had turned greatly against social spending, as it did in 1943, there was little chance for the Townsend Plan or any challenger to do much to augment social policy.

Strategies, Contexts, and the Impact of the Townsend Plan, 1934–1939

The influence of the Townsend Plan is better explained by my arguments regarding strategy and context. These are summarized in Figure 1.7, which is similar to Figure 1.2 but includes a number of different episodes of Townsend collective action and old-age policy making—at both state and national

		State bureaucrats	
		Strong and aligned with challenger's interests	Weak and/or opposed to challenger's interests
Elected officials	Aligned with challenger's constituency	Sheer mobilization, limited protest *(National level, 1934)* **(National level, 1935)** *(Some states, late 1930s)*	Sanction or urge creation of state bureaus *(Anti-lien campaign, 1939)*
	Opposed to challenger's constituency	Sanction or displace elected officials *(States with initiative drives, 1940s)* **(States without initiatives, 1940s)**	Highly assertive strategies **(California before 1939)** *(National level, 1939)*

Figure 1.7. Collective action strategies expected to produce collective benefits, given specified political conditions, and Townsend Plan campaigns, 1934–46. Campaigns in italics are ones in which the Townsend Plan matched strategy and context; campaigns in bold are ones in which the Townsend Plan failed to match strategy and context, according to the model. In each instance, matching strategy and context led to gains by the Townsend Plan, and failing to match strategy and context resulted in no gains for the Townsend Plan.

levels. When the Townsend Plan matched appropriate strategies to political contexts it was influential, and when it did not it was not. In what follows I discuss a number of collective action campaigns and old-age policy making (Amenta 2003). I break up the episodes of contention and policy making into two time periods, from 1934 through 1939 when the Social Security Act was first proposed and passed, and from 1940 onward when the old-age issues left the national agenda and the Townsend Plan focused on the state level.

The Making of the Economic Security Act, 1934

The political strategy of the Townsend Plan in its first year was minimally assertive and the political context was largely favorable. OARP made no official congressional endorsements and did no work for candidates. For the most part OARP attempted to educate people about the pension plan, to build enthusiasm for it, and to organize clubs. Old-age and other social programs, notably unemployment insurance, were already on the political agenda before OARP really got going, with the Dill-Connery old-age pension bill and the Wagner-Lewis unemployment compensation bill receiving support in Congress prior to 1934. After these two bills were voted on in Congress in spring 1934, Roosevelt called for the creation of a Committee on Economic Security (CES) to write a comprehensive bill for social policy, including old-age policy. Both Houses of Congress had Democratic majorities, and the presidency was held by a reform-oriented New York Democrat. The congressional forces likely to be in favor of social spending—northern Democrats and left-wing party representatives—were not in a majority status in Congress, however, and thus were not quite sufficient in numbers to overcome opposition from Republicans and southern Democrats if they combined. At the bureaucratic level, the situation was also a good one for old-age policy. The Federal Emergency Relief Administration was running the most extensive social policy program in American history, and among its efforts was aiding the impoverished aged (Brown 1940, ch. 8–12; Brock 1988, 162–73). Old-age policy apparently moved far ahead on the administration's priorities that autumn in response to the Townsend Plan. The Committee on Economic Security recommended the adoption of Old Age Assistance and an old-age insurance program—which was to include a payroll tax that would finance it and the assistance program (U.S. CES 1935). The Dill-Connery bill had called for a program on the order of Old Age Assistance, but with lower matching payments and a lower appropriation. Also, Aid to Dependent Children, another proposal by the CES, was funded at a lower matching rate than Old Age Assistance was, and health insurance was placed completely on the back burner. There is no smoking gun, but there is every reason to believe that the upgrading of old-age policy came because of the mobilization of the aged by OARP behind its generous pension plan. After all, the committee had a staffer follow OARP and had letters from OARP supporters forwarded to it from the White House, and then the committee proposed more than it had initially planned for old age. The Townsend Plan's strategy of sheer mobilization, educational efforts, and minimal collective action helped to advance the content of a proposal already on a reform-oriented administration's legislative agenda.

From Economic Security Act to Social Security Act, 1935

By 1935, the political situation had improved sharply for proponents of old-age and other social spending programs. The 1934 congressional elections, which would have been expected to lead to the loss of about twenty-five House seats by the Democratic or presidential party, and thus lower the prospects for social spending innovations, instead brought enormous gains in seats by the Democrats in both House and Senate. The newspapers chalked up the election results not to the Townsend Plan or other extant social movement organizations, but to the popularity of Roosevelt's responses to the Depression, including his emergency relief programs. In the House, social spending programs could now pass without the backing of southern Democrats, though given their seniority and strategic position some of them could delay or reduce benefits in bills, and in any case the situation was not as favorable in the Senate (see Figure 1.6). The administration went forward with its economic security bill and demanded $5 billion for a work relief program—an unprecedented sum that would amount to about one-tenth of the national income and more than half of the budget.

OARP changed its strategy in 1935, hoping to take advantage of the fact that old-age policy was on the political agenda (see Amenta 2003, ch. 4). After the New Year, the Townsend Plan introduced a bill by Congressman John McGroarty, an older gentleman himself, who was just elected from Townsend and Clements's congressional district and who ran largely on the basis of his support of the Townsend pension plan. OARP took a much more direct and assertive approach to Congress than it had in the autumn, mobilizing Townsendites behind a letter-writing campaign to members of the House Ways and Means Committee and other influential congressmen, demanding that they support the McGroarty bill—or else. Townsend and other OARP witnesses also testified in favor of the bill. The Townsend Plan leadership took a fairly hard line and refused to compromise with anyone on old-age benefits. It attacked the administration's bill as providing "pauper's" benefits.

The results were unproductive. The McGroarty bill received harsh criticism, for its proposed taxes would generate only about a quarter of the revenue needed to pay for the pensions. This bill was replaced on April 1 by a second McGroarty bill, which would pay pensions, to all those eligible, of a lower amount, about $40 or $50 per month, that could be supported by the taxes. While the OARP worked on rewriting the McGroarty bill, the House Ways and Means Committee reduced benefits in the old-age portions of the security bill. Old Age Assistance was altered to allow more discretion for states to pay lower benefits and set higher eligibility restrictions, the liberal Federal Emergency Relief Administration was removed from authority over the program, and merit hiring practices in the states were dropped. Also, old-age insurance benefits removed additional agricultural workers and domestic servants from coverage. On the House floor, the Townsend Plan congressional contingent gained a standing vote on an amendment similar to the Townsend plan, which lost handily, 206–56. OARP did not throw its weight behind a better-supported amendment, which upped the federal matching ratio for OAA and would have provided larger benefits to many more recipients, and it failed, too. The security bill probably would have passed one way or another, given the Democrats' November triumph. OARP probably did not cause the cutbacks in old-age benefits, but its actions did little to help, and the resources and good will expended on them were largely wasted.

The Heyday of the Townsend Plan, 1935–1936, and the Aftermath

In the summer of 1935, OARP attempted to learn from its mistakes. Clements noticed that the Townsend amendment received support only from representatives in districts where Townsend clubs were well organized—mainly in California and a few pockets of the West. As a result he launched a national recruitment drive (Amenta 2003, ch. 5), relying on commission-earning state area organizers, who were to hire one subcontracting organizer for each congressional district in the country. OARP's cause was also aided by the passage of the Social Security Act—which was the opposite of the administration's intentions, for the act validated the claim of the aged to old-age benefits but did not immediately provide them. In October OARP organized a convention in Chicago, drawing six thousand Townsend club members. An off-year House election in Michigan saw the victory in a crowded Republican primary of an OARP-endorsed candidate. Both events brought favorable national publicity behind OARP and aided recruitment. As for its political strategy, the organization dropped its hectoring letter-writing campaign and instead began to ask House members, politely, to provide written confirmation that they would support the second McGroarty bill. As Congress prepared to reconvene in the New Year, the number of House members who had signed in support numbered in the sixties.

By 1939 the Townsend Plan was riding high (see Amenta 2003, ch. 6). The organization was featured in January in the *March of Time,* a series of documentary shorts that played in the nation's movie theaters. Also, OARP was drawing enormous revenues (see Figures 1.3 and 1.4). The $350,000 it raised in the last quarter of 1935 was similar to the sum raised by the Republican party on the eve of an election year and far outstripped the fundraising of the Democrats. By March there were more than seven thousand clubs with probably as many as two million members. Although OARP's club affiliates remained strongest in numbers in the West, as Table 1.1 shows, they were starting to break through in other parts of the country, such as Florida, Minnesota, Iowa, and Maine. What is more, the political context

Table 1.1. Townsend Clubs per congressional district, circa spring 1936: lowest and highest states.

Rank	State	Clubs per district
1.	Oregon	138
2.	Colorado	88
3.	North Dakota	88
4.	Washington	83
5.	Arizona	82
6.	Montana	75
7.	Idaho	70
8.	Nevada	61
9.	Wyoming	61
10.	Vermont	61
48.	South Carolina	1.8
47.	Virginia	2.2
46.	Louisiana	2.9
45.	Rhode Island	3.0
44.	North Carolina	3.1
43.	Mississippi	3.2
42.	Georgia	6.1
41.	Tennessee	6.2
40.	Alabama	6.2

Sources: Harry B. Presson, "Tells History of First Townsend Clubs," *Townsend National Weekly,* November 2, 1936, 10. Abraham Holtzman, *The Townsend Movement: A Political Study* (New York: Bookman, 1963), 50–51.

Note: Data for top ten are based on Presson's approximations for 1936; the data for the bottom nine include all clubs ever in existence from Holtzman (and thus likely overstate the number of clubs in 1936).

had changed little from 1935, which was the most favorable in American history for national social spending policy.

Despite its great resource mobilization and the favorable political context, the Townsend Plan did not greatly spur old-age policy in 1936. This surprising deficit of influence was most notable in Congress, where the Townsend Plan targeted its pressure (see Amenta 2003, ch. 6). It was not unexpected that the McGroarty bill did not go far. OARP was about one hundred votes short in the House of being able to discharge it from committee. But no other bill to improve old-age benefits came up for consideration. At the national level, the main story regarding old age had to do with the rapid growth of the Social Security Board, especially its Bureau of Public Assistance, which advised states on their Old Age Assistance programs and made recommendations for approval (McKinley and Frase 1970). It was promoting somewhat restrictive "family budgeting" needs assessments in state OAA programs (Coll 1995, 81–84), but OARP did not target this body or its actions. The greatest amount of old-age spending activity was happening at the state level. National incentives had placed the issue on the political agenda of all states. Here it seemed that the Townsend Plan mobilization had at least indirect effects, as state governments were passing and demanding national certification for new Old Age Assistance programs far more rapidly than for Aid to the Blind and Aid to Dependent Children programs. By New Year's Day, sixteen states had passed and requested approval of old-age programs compared to eleven for the blind and ten for dependent children. In many states, too, old-age programs were favored, treated more like pensions—relatively unfettered grants—than public assistance with its often great restrictions and annoying caseworkers. California, Washington, Massachusetts, Nevada, and Colorado quickly opted for such old-age "pension" systems. Three of these states harbored quite extensive networks of Townsend clubs (McKinley and Frase 1970, 23, 26; Coll 1995, 81–88; U.S. CES 1937; Cates 1983, 112–14).

The difference between the impressive influence of OARP at the state level and its low impact at the national level mainly has to do with differences in the status of old-age policy on political agendas. The new availability of national matching payments and the end of the Federal Emergency Relief Administration aid to the aged forced the old-age issue onto the political agenda of all states. Because of the strength of the Townsend organization, political regimes gave benefits for the elderly a higher priority among the new public assistance programs. In states where Townsend clubs were particularly prevalent, state officials were more likely to pay higher old-age benefits in a pension-like manner, despite no encouraging moves in this direction by OARP and the occasional attempt at prevention.

At the national level, the administration was not proposing any legislation, so there was no chance to alter any proposal before it was submitted to Congress as there was in 1934. Nor was there an opportunity to alter old-age legislation for the better in Congress, which had been a live possibility in 1935. OARP was far stronger and savvier in political matters, but did not have nearly enough support in Congress to force old-age policy onto the docket through the discharge-petition process. In this way OARP's situation compared unfavorably to that of the veterans' organizations, such as the American Legion, which successfully concluded a long campaign of gathering support in Congress for a World War I veterans' "bonus" bill. The development of OAA at the state level provides further evidence for my claims about the coincidence of strategy and context. In its first years the Townsend Plan engaged in no action to improve state Old Age Assistance programs, but Townsend clubs were differentially mobilized across the states, which provided vastly different political circumstances. Here I examine all states that were similar in that they were from a democratized polity not dominated by patronage parties (those states in the upper left-hand corner of Figure 1.1), and they had a prominent presence of Townsend clubs. In these seven states the Townsend Plan had a differential impact according to whether a favorable political regime was in power or not. In five states (Colorado, Idaho, Minnesota, Montana, and Wyoming), Democrats or left-wing parties controlled the government for most of the period after 1935, and in two others (California and New Hampshire) they did not. For the two states without favorable regimes in power during the 1935–38 period, the average old-age benefit prior to the Townsend Plan was 47.1 percent of the state's per capita income. By 1939, this figure had increased to only 52.6 percent—about a 5.5 percentage-point increase. By contrast, the five states with Democratic or third-party regimes in power saw their benefit levels jump from 27.4 percent of per capita income to 53.3 percent—a much more substantial increase. They caught up with and slightly surpassed states that had got off to far greater head starts.[4]

California, home of the Townsend Plan, provides an example of a lost opportunity to advance old-age policy. The Townsend Plan paid little attention to OAA there, as elsewhere, and instead pressed the legislature to pass measures "memorializing" Congress to adopt the Townsend plan. The Townsend Plan's high mobilization and "think nationally/act nationally" strategy was not enough to boost California old-age policy. The Republicans controlled the governor's mansion and the state House for most of the period, and the California Department of Social Welfare shared responsibility over old-age policy with the more restrictive county boards of supervisors (Pinner, Jacobs, and Selznick 1959, 16–17). OARP lent no support to bills sponsored by EPIC legislators to boost old-age benefits to $50 per month. California had been a leader in old-age politics before OARP existed, but after its emergence California's old-age program began to trail those of other states (U.S. CES 1937), especially in promoting eligibility. Only 18 percent of those sixty-five and older received old-age payments, dropping California to twenty-fourth on this basis (see also Amenta, Halfmann, and Young 1999).

In Colorado, by comparison, an organization similar to the Townsend Plan, indeed, one begun by leaders and clubs that broke with OARP, pressed for a state initiative to create generous old-age pensions where the political regime was similarly unfavorable. This group, the National Annuity League, not only succeeded in its drive to place its initiative on the ballot, creating immediate pressure on state officials to increase pensions, but the initiative was approved in the general election—despite some opposition from the Townsend Plan, which saw the effort as distracting attention from the national level (Cates 1983). As a result of the National Annuity League's advocacy, Colorado's version of old-age assistance shot to the top of the nation's programs in terms of both benefits and coverage. This episode suggests that had the Townsend organization attempted to influence state-level politics, it might have had a significant impact in similarly situated states in the middle 1930s.

Strategies, Contexts, and the Impact of the Townsend Plan, 1939–1946

The Townsend Plan faltered in 1936. Dr. Townsend was now in charge and found himself on a steep part of the learning curve. As a result of a congressional investigation and Townsend's own mistakes—including his purge of Clements, McGroarty, and other key leaders; his neglect of organizing; and his hopeless crusade against Roosevelt—the Townsend Plan shed supporters in 1936 and 1937. Under his new organization, the Townsend National Recovery Plan, Inc. (TNRP), however, Townsend was eventually able to rally his followers. By 1939 the TNRP counted 700,000 members. The comeback was sparked by a reemphasis on organizing, a sharp economic decline in 1937–38 that the administration's opponents called the "Roosevelt Depression," and a consensus among the administration and both parties in Congress that old-age policy needed to be revisited (Amenta 2003, ch. 7).

In 1938 and 1939, the political situation was different, as the Roosevelt administration returned old-age policy to the political agenda. The Social Security Board wanted to make changes and with the aid of an advisory council suggested a number of amendments, including the creation of survi-

POLITICAL CONTEXTS, STRATEGIES, MOBILIZATION

vors' insurance. In Congress, partisan forces on both sides of the aisle sought to make old-age insurance a "pay-as-you-go" program. Liberal Democrats were concerned that the old-age payroll tax was building up reserves at the expense of the economy and potential existing beneficiaries; old-age insurance was not scheduled to pay benefits until 1942. The Republicans and other conservatives were concerned with the high cost and produc- tivity of the tax; they feared that if the program was perceived as running a surplus Congress would be induced to provide much higher benefits. The previous year's congressional election, however, saw many losses for north- ern Democrats, diminishing the ranks of prospective "pro-spenders" (see Figure 1.6). Different, too, was the Townsend Plan's strategy of action. It refocused energy on House elections and ended up endorsing 147 winning members, including three on the important Ways and Means Committee.

It was not enough to bring the passage of a new Townsend Plan bill in Congress, but the TNRP influenced the 1939 amendments to the Social Security Act. Although the Townsend Plan congressional forces were un- able to pass a bill, they were able to sweeten an administration-backed bill, once one returned to the political agenda. Because of its congressional endorsement strategy, the influence of the Townsend organization on leg- islation was far greater than that evidenced in 1935, when the Townsend Plan was unable to prevent decreases in benefits for the aged in the Social Security Act (Amenta 2003, ch. 8).

In 1941, little had changed, except that the administration had again completed its agenda regarding old age. The political alignment remained moderately favorable to advances in social spending, Roosevelt being re- elected again with approximately the same level of congressional support, and the Townsend Plan returned a similar endorsed contingent to Congress (see Figures 1.3, 1.4, and 1.5). The old-age issue had some life in hearings led by California's Senator Sheridan Downey, a proponent of the Townsend plan who was elected in 1938. In response to the hearings and against its inclinations, the SSB drew up plans for a "double-decker" old-age program: each aged person would receive a pension of a flat amount, and a qualified subgroup would receive higher amounts according to previous earnings (Cates 1983, ch. 3). This was in case a Townsend plan bill would emerge from committee with a significant following. But the hearings were inter- rupted by the news from Pearl Harbor, removing social policy from the political agenda.

Worse, however, for the prospects of social policy, the 1942 elections decimated the ranks of northern Democrats, undermining the political align- ment for social policy reform (see Figure 1.6.) A coalition of Republicans and southern Democrats delayed previously enacted and scheduled increases in the old-age and survivors' insurance payroll tax. This happened despite the fact that there were more Townsend-endorsed members of Congress than ever. The evidence of the middle war period suggests that a moderate level of Townsend Plan strength in membership and high effectiveness in political endorsements was not enough even to prevent retrenchment in old-age spending policy. The congressional alignment was soundly anti–social spending and the president was preoccupied by foreign affairs.

As the war continued, the Townsend organization paid more attention to the states, though in most states the political circumstances had also turned against social policy reform (see Amenta 2003, ch. 9). The Townsend Plan's strategies varied. In some states, notably, the organization embarked on drives for "little Townsend plan" initiatives. These called for $60 per month for all citizens sixty years old and older, and by 1944 the TNRP had placed these initiatives before the voters in Arizona, Washington, and Oregon, as well as in California. The initiatives lost in each state; in California there were about two million opposed and one million in favor (Holtzman 1963, 193–98).

Yet the drives were not totally in vain, as some comparisons across states indicate. Again, I examine states that were similar in having an extensive Townsend club presence in political systems that were not under-democratized or patronage-oriented. But this time each of the states had an unfavorable regime in power, with the main difference being that some states had initiative drives for little Townsend plans, a highly assertive form of action, and others did not. The results of these campaigns can be seen by comparing what happened afterward in the three states (California, Oregon, and Washington) where the Townsend Plan sought "60 after 60" with the seven similar states (Colorado, Maine, Minnesota, Montana, New Hampshire, South Dakota, and Wyoming) in which it did not. Despite the fact that they failed, the little Townsend plan campaigns likely boosted the average OAA pension in the three states. Beforehand, the three states targeted for initiatives had slightly less generous benefits than the seven states that did not. The average OAA pension was 35.6 percent of per capita income in the seven states, but after five years the sum held steady, ending at 35.5 percent of per capita income by 1946 (Amenta 2003, ch. 9). In the three states targeted for initiative drives, the average pension stood at 31.7 percent of per capita income in 1940–41, but this figure shot up to 42.4 percent by 1946, an increase of more than ten percentage points and approximately seven percentage points higher than in the similar states without initiatives (see also Amenta, Halfmann, and Young 1999).

California again provides a case in point—this time a more positive one. Near the end of the 1930s, TNRP began to contest specific aspects of the California OAA law, especially the unfavorable administration of it, and in an increasingly assertive manner. In 1939 Townsendites marched on conservative county boards in both Los Angeles and San Francisco, protesting their enforcement of liens on old-age beneficiaries' estates. According to these rulings, old-age beneficiaries could not bequeath their possessions, preventing many of the aged from applying for benefits (California Department of Social Welfare 1943, 5–7). Townsend Plan protesters asserted that California should provide pensions as a right to citizens and drew attention to the boards' policy on liens. Although an initiative to end the lien policy did not make the ballot, the bid for change likely helped to place the issue on the political agenda. At the start of the 1940 legislative session, Governor Culbert Olson, a Democrat originally with EPIC, asked for the repeal of the lien provision, despite the fact that he had stated that he was hoping to avoid pension issues that session (Burke 1953). Two repeal propositions passed by more than a half million votes with the support of TNRP.

Although Democrats never ruled in California, the political situation there took a turn for the worse for them after the elections of 1940 and 1942, when a Republican was elected governor and Democratic representation in the legislature dropped. All the same, augmentations in old-age benefits occurred in the wake of the little Townsend plan initiative drives. In 1943, as the first drive began, California adopted legislation to raise the maximum grant from $40 to $50 in order to reduce the responsibility of relatives to support the aged, to increase the amount of personal property a recipient could own, and to provide that the state pay five-sixths of non-federal costs, up from one-half. California's average grant jumped more than $10 per month, putting it at the top of all states, and California's rank in terms of old-age coverage improved to seventeenth (Amenta, Halfmann, and Young 1999). In the wake of the little Townsend plan campaigns, California's old-age program was altered in the direction of the Townsend plan. This was the last hurrah for the Townsend Plan, however, which was done in by the end of the Depression, by attrition—Townsendites were literally dying off—and the competition of new pension challengers.

Conclusion

My main claim has been that the collective action of state-oriented challengers and their influence on public policy is politically mediated in specific ways. Under certain political institutional conditions, notably restrictions on democratic practices and the entrenchment of patronage-oriented political parties, both the presence and impact of state-oriented challengers is likely to be greatly dampened. The American polity at midcentury was comparatively less favorable to the action of social movements, especially because of distinctly unfavorable political institutional circumstances in some parts of the polity. Only about half of the state-level U.S. polities were structurally favorable to influence by challenger collective action. Even when polities are structurally and systemically favorable or mixed, however, I argue that in order to have an influence challengers need to match specific collective action strategies to specific short- and medium-term political conditions. Generally speaking, collective action is more likely to be productive when a reform-oriented regime is in control and when state bureaucrats in charge of social spending are favorable and powerful. In such situations, mobilization and mildly assertive strategies of action are likely to produce collective benefits for the group represented by the challenger. Under more difficult medium- and short-term circumstances, mobilization is necessary but not sufficient to achieve collective benefits. A focused and assertive collective action program is also necessary to win gains. In addition, the place of an issue on the political agenda has an important mediating effect on the productivity of challengers' collective action. If the issue is on the political agenda, which is related in part to the existence of a favorable regime, it greatly increases the probability of influence. But the place of the issue on the political agenda offers shifting opportunities for action that are usually short-lived and change in setting from political executives to legislators to administrators.

The history of the campaigns of the Townsend Plan and U.S. policy for old-age benefits provides support for these claims. Under favorable circumstances at the national level in 1934, when the Roosevelt administration had placed old-age policy on the political agenda, OARP's rapid mobilization was enough to increase collective benefits for the aged in proposed social legislation. In an even more favorable situation in 1935, OARP took too hard a line for the circumstances and did not advance old-age policy any further in Congress. In many states after 1935, the Townsend Plan had an influence over old-age policy, despite the fact that it engaged in almost no collective action to advance it—largely because the passage of national legislation placed the old-age issue on the political agendas of states. At the national level in 1936, after the old-age issue had been removed by the administration from the political agenda, a tremendous mobilization of the aged by OARP and a regime favorable to social spending was not enough to provide gains in old-age policy. A reorganized Townsend Plan was able to gain influence in 1938 and 1939 when the administration and Congress brought the old-age issue back to prominence, and the political alignment remained moderately favorable for social spending advances. The Townsend Plan made its first real efforts to elect members of Congress, providing leverage in that body that it did not have four years earlier. Townsend forces helped to induce Congress to increase the matching payments for Old Age Assistance. In the 1940s the TNRP began to pay more attention to politics in the states and engaged in assertive action, initiative drives, in political circumstances that were unfavorable in the short term. These failed campaigns nonetheless resulted in gains in average old-age benefits in California and two other states.

All of this suggests that scholars need to pay closer attention to challenger strategies and political contexts in democratic polities to understand the impact of challengers on states and their public policies. Political contexts vary dramatically in the short, medium, and long run, all with implications for the productivity of the collective action of challengers. Challenger strategies that are lumped together as "assimilative" or "institutional" can vary greatly in their assertiveness, sanctions, and direction, with implications for the productivity of action. Thinking through these possibilities matters because collective action differs in its effectiveness according to the contexts in which it is undertaken.

Notes

This is the fourth draft of a paper initially presented at the conference on "Social Movements, Public Policy, and Democracy," organized by Helen Ingram, Valerie Jenness, and David S. Meyer, University of California, Irvine, January 11–13, 2002. For comments on previous versions I thank Belinda Robnett, Bruce Hemmer, and the organizers and participants in the conference; Russ Dalton and the participants in Center for the Study of Democracy dinner, January 14, 2002; Mildred Schwartz, Julie Stewart, and the participants in the NYU Sociology of Politics, Power, and Protest workshop meeting of February 8, 2002; Kate Strully and the participants in NYU's Political Sociology class of spring 2002; and the conference organizers, especially David S. Meyer, for detailed comments. This research was supported in part by National Science Foundation grant SBR 9709618.

1. Although scholars mainly refer to the "Townsend movement," following the 1963 study by Abraham Holtzman, I am referring to this group as the "Townsend Plan." That is how most contemporaries, including the *New York Times,* referred to the organization and its followers, as well as the program. Also, from the perspective of social movement scholarship, OARP and the Townsend clubs and supporters were not a movement, but the major movement organization in an old-age pension movement. I use the uppercase when referring to the organization and the lowercase when referring to the pension proposal.

2. I am also making no claims about which forms of challengers are most likely to develop the appropriate and telling collective action strategies. Presumably the best case is to have many talented and committed activists ready and able to pursue different sorts of strategies and be open to tactical innovations as situations develop (Andrews 2001). It is not clear, though, what form of organization might best accomplish this matching. The literature suggests that centralization of authority is likely to lead to more coherent strategic action that can be carried out consistently in many places (Gamson 1990). Yet this might also lead to the pressing of idiosyncratic and inappropriate strategies for longer than might otherwise occur. Similarly, participatory democracy is often held to be at odds with strategy, providing extensive discussion when quick action is needed. Yet democratic processes in movements may also lead to the sort of experimentation that helps leaders test out strategies and avoid the calcification of strategic thinking (Polletta 2002).

3. By prospective pro–social spenders, I mean those elected to Congress who would be likely to support generous and nationally controlled social spending programs. The most favorable group includes radical third-party members and Democrats elected from democratized polities and from program-oriented political parties. Somewhat less enthusiastic, but overall favorable, are Democrats from democratized polities but patronage-oriented political parties. By contrast, Republicans are treated as being in opposition to social spending policy, as are Democrats from under-democratized polities (see Amenta 1998, ch. 1; Amenta and Halfmann 2000).

4. In these analyses, I include only states with functioning old-age pension programs in 1934, the first year of OARP and the year before the Social Security Act. For additional discussion and analyses, see Amenta, Halfmann, and Young 1999.

References

Achenbaum, W. Andrew. 1983. "The Formative Years of Social Security: A Test Case of the Piven and Cloward Thesis." In *Social Welfare or Social Control: Some Historical Reflections on Regulating the Poor,* ed. Walter I. Trattner, 67–89. Knoxville: University of Tennessee Press.

Amenta, Edwin. 1998. *Bold Relief: Institutional Politics and the Origins of Modern American Social Policy.* Princeton, NJ: Princeton University Press.

———. 2003. *When Movements Matter: The Impact of the Townsend Plan and U.S. Social Spending Challengers.* New York: Cambridge University Press.

Amenta, Edwin, and Neal Caren. 2004. "The Legislative, Beneficiary, and Organizational Consequences of State-Oriented Challengers." In *The Blackwell Companion to Social Movements,* ed. David A. Snow, Sarah A. Soule, and Hanspeter Kriesi. Malden, MA: Blackwell.

Amenta, Edwin, Neal Caren, Tina Fetner, and Michael P. Young. 2002. "Challengers and States: Toward a Political Sociology of Social Movements." *Research in Political Sociology* 10: 47–83.

Amenta, Edwin, and Drew Halfmann. 2000. "Wage Wars: Institutional Politics, the WPA, and the Struggle for U.S. Social Policy." *American Sociological Review* 64: 506–28.

Amenta, Edwin, Drew Halfmann, and Michael P. Young. 1999. "The Strategies and Contexts of Social Protest: Political Mediation and the Impact of the Townsend Movement in California." *Mobilization* 4: 1–24.

Andrews, Kenneth T. 2001. "Social Movements and Policy Implementation: The Mississippi Civil Rights Movement and the War on Poverty, 1965–1971." *American Sociological Review* 66: 21–48.

Banaszak, Lee Ann. 1996. *Why Movements Succeed or Fail: Opportunity, Culture, and the Struggle for Woman Suffrage.* Princeton, NJ: Princeton University Press.

Barkan, Steven E. 1984. "Legal Control of the Southern Civil Rights Movement." *American Sociological Review* 49: 552–65.

Baumgartner, Frank R. and Bryan D. Jones. 1993. *Agendas and Instability in American Politics.* Chicago: University of Chicago Press.

Berkowitz, Edward D. 1991. *America's Welfare State: From Roosevelt to Reagan.* Baltimore: Johns Hopkins University Press.

———. 1995. *Mr. Social Security: The Life of Wilbur J. Cohen.* Lawrence: University of Kansas Press.

Brady, David W. 1988. *Critical Elections and Congressional Policy Making.* Stanford, CA: Stanford University Press.

Brock, William R. 1988. *Welfare, Democracy, and the New Deal.* New York: Cambridge University Press.

Brown, Josephine Chapin. 1940. *Public Relief, 1929–1939.* New York: Holt and Co.

Burg, Stephen Bret. 1999. "The Gray Crusade: The Townsend Movement, Old Age Politics, and the Development of Social Security." PhD diss., University of Wisconsin, Madison.

Burke, Robert E. 1953. *Olson's New Deal for California.* Berkeley and Los Angeles: University of California Press.

Burnham, W. Dean. 1984. "Partisan Division of American State Governments, 1834–1985" [computer file]. Conducted by Massachusetts Institute of Technology, ed. ICPSR. Ann Arbor, MI: Inter-University Consortium for Political and Social Research [producer and distributor].

Burstein, Paul. 1993. "Explaining State Action and the Expansion of Civil Rights: The Civil Rights Act of 1964." *Research in Political Sociology* 6: 117–37.

Burstein, Paul, Rachael L. Einwohner, and Jocelyn A. Hollander. 1995. "The Success of Political Movements: A Bargaining Perspective." In *The Politics of Social*

Protest: Comparative Perspectives on States and Social Movements, ed. J. Craig
Jenkins and Bert Klandermans, 275–95. Minneapolis: University of Minnesota Press.

California Department of Social Welfare. 1940. *Biennial Reports* [for 1929–1949].
Sacramento, CA: State Printing Office.

———. 1943. *Public Assistance in California.* Sacramento: State Printing Office.

Cates, Jerry R. 1983. *Insuring Inequality: Administrative Leadership in Social Security, 1935–54.* Ann Arbor: University of Michigan Press.

Chong, Dennis. 1992. *Collective Action and the Civil Rights Movement.* Chicago:
University of Chicago Press.

Clemens, Elisabeth S. 1997. *The People's Lobby: Organizational Innovation and the Rise of Interest Group Politics in the United States, 1890–1925.* Chicago: University of Chicago Press.

Cohn, Samuel. 1993. *When Strikes Make Sense—and Why: Lessons from Third Republic French Coal Miners.* New York: Plenum.

Coll, Blanche D. 1995. *Safety Net: Welfare and Social Security, 1935–1979.* New
Brunswick, NJ: Rutgers University Press.

Cress, Daniel M., and David A. Snow. 2000. "The Outcomes of Homeless Mobilization: The Influence of Organization, Disruption, Political Mediation, and Framing." *American Journal of Sociology* 105: 1063–104.

Dahl, Robert. 1971. *Polyarchy: Participation and Opposition.* New Haven, CT:
Yale University Press.

Dalton, Russell. 1988. *Citizen Politics in Western Democracies: Public Opinion and Political Parties in the United States, Great Britain, West Germany, and France.*
Chatham, NJ: Chatham House.

———. 1995. "Strategies of Partisan Influence: West European Environmental Groups." In *The Politics of Social Protest: Comparative Perspectives on States and Social Movements,* ed. J. Craig Jenkins and Bert Klandermans, 296–323.
Minneapolis: University of Minnesota Press.

Earl, Jennifer. 2000. "Methods, Movements, and Outcomes: Methodological Difficulties in the Study of Extra-Movement Outcomes." *Research in Social Movements, Conflicts, and Change* 22: 3–25.

Gamson, William A. 1990. *The Strategy of Social Protest.* 2nd ed. Belmont, CA:
Wadsworth.

Ganz, Marshall Louis. 2000. "Resources and Resourcefulness: Strategic Capacity in the Unionization of California Agriculture, 1959–1966." *American Journal of Sociology* 105: 1003–62.

Giugni, Marco G. 1998. "Was It Worth the Effort? The Outcomes and Consequences of Social Movements." *Annual Review of Sociology* 24: 371–93.

Goldstone, Jack A. 1980. "The Weakness of Organization: A New Look at Gamson's *The Strategy of Social Protest.*" *American Journal of Sociology* 85: 1017–42.

Goodwin, Jeff. 2001. *No Other Way Out: States and Revolutionary Movements, 1945–1991.* New York: Cambridge University Press.

Hicks, Alexander. 1999. *Social Democracy and Welfare Capitalism: A Century of Income Security Politics.* Ithaca, NY: Cornell University Press.

Holtzman, Abraham. 1963. *The Townsend Movement: A Political Study.* New York: Bookman.

Huber, Evelyne, and John D. Stephens. 2001. *Development and Crisis of the Welfare State: Parties and Policies in Global Markets.* Chicago: University of Chicago Press.

Jasper, James M. 1997. *The Art of Moral Protest: Culture, Biography, and Creativity in Social Movements.* Chicago: University of Chicago Press.

Jenkins, J. Craig. 1983. "Resource Mobilization Theory and the Study of Social Movements." *Annual Review of Sociology* 9: 527–53.

Katznelson, Ira. 1981. *City Trenches.* New York: Pantheon.

King, Gary, Robert O. Keohane, and Sidney Verba. 1994. *Designing Social Inquiry: Scientific Inference in Qualitative Research.* Princeton, NJ: Princeton University Press.

Kingdon, John. 1984. *Agendas, Alternatives, and Public Policies.* Boston: Little, Brown.

Kitschelt, Herbert P. 1986. "Political Opportunity Structures and Political Protest: Anti-Nuclear Movements in Four Democracies." *British Journal of Political Science* 16: 57–85.

Klandermans, Bert, and Dirk Oegema. 1987. "Campaigning for a Nuclear Freeze: Grass-Roots Strategies and Local Governments in the Netherlands." *Research in Political Sociology* 3: 305–37.

Kousser, J. Morgan. 1974. *The Shaping of Southern Politics: Suffrage Restriction and the Establishment of the One-Party South, 1880–1910.* New Haven, CT: Yale University Press.

Kriesi, Hanspeter. 1994. "The Political Opportunity Structure of New Social Movements: Its Impact on Their Mobilization." In *States and Social Movements,* ed. J. Craig Jenkins and Bert Klandermans, 167–98. Minneapolis: University of Minnesota Press.

Kriesi, Hanspeter, Ruud Koopmans, Jan Willem Duyvendak, and Marco G. Giugni. 1995. *New Social Movements in Western Europe: A Comparative Analysis.* Minneapolis: University of Minnesota Press.

Lijphart, Arend. 1997. "Unequal Protection: Democracy's Unresolved Dilemma." *American Political Science Review* 91: 1–14.

Lipset, Seymour M., and Gary Marks. 2000. *It Didn't Happen Here: Why Socialism Failed in the United States.* New York: W. W. Norton.

Lipset, Seymour M., and Stein Rokkan. 1967. "Cleavage Structures, Party Systems, and Voter Alignments." In *Party Systems and Voter Alignments,* ed. Seymour M. Lipset and Stein Rokkan, 1–66. New York: Free Press.

Mayhew, David. 1986. *Placing Parties in American Politics: Organization, Electoral Settings, and Government Activity in the Twentieth Century.* Princeton, NJ: Princeton University Press.

McAdam, Doug. 1982. *Political Process and the Development of Black Insurgency.* Chicago: University of Chicago Press.

———. 1996. "Conceptual Origins, Current Problems, Future Directions." In *Comparative Perspectives on Social Movements,* ed. Doug McAdam, John D. McCarthy, and Mayer N. Zald. Cambridge: Cambridge University Press.

McAdam, Doug, John D. McCarthy, and Mayer N. Zald. 1988. "Social Movements." In *The Handbook of Sociology,* ed. Neil J. Smelser, 695–737. Beverly Hills, CA: Sage.

McAdam, Doug, Sidney Tarrow, and Charles Tilly. 2001. *The Dynamics of Contention.* New York: Cambridge University Press.

McCarthy, John D., and Mayer N. Zald. 2001. "The Enduring Vitality of the Resource Mobilization Theory of Social Movements." In *Handbook of Sociological Theory,* ed. Jonathon H. Turner, 533–65. New York: Kluwer Academic/ Plenum.

McKinley, Charles, and Robert W. Frase. 1970. *Launching Social Security.* Madison: University of Wisconsin Press.

Meyer, David S. 1993. "Institutionalizing Dissent: The United States Structure of Political Opportunity and the End of the Nuclear Freeze." *Sociological Forum* 8: 157–79.

———. 2002. "Social Movements and Public Policy: Eggs, Chicken, and Theory." Prepared for the workshop "Social Movements, Public Policy and Democracy," University of California, Irvine, January 11–13, 2002.

Orloff, Ann Shola. 1993. *The Politics of Pensions: A Comparative Analysis of Britain, Canada, and the United States, 1880–1940.* Madison: University of Wisconsin Press.

Pierson, Paul. 1994. *Dismantling the Welfare State? Reagan, Thatcher, and the Politics of Retrenchment.* New York: Cambridge University Press.

Pinner, Frank A., Paul Jacobs, and Phillip Selznick. 1959. *Old Age and Political Behavior: A Case Study.* Berkeley: University of California Press.

Piven, Frances Fox, and Richard A. Cloward. 1977. *Poor People's Movements: Why They Succeed, How They Fail.* New York: Random House.

———. 1989. *Why Americans Don't Vote.* New York: Pantheon.

————. 1993. *Regulating the Poor: The Functions of Public Welfare.* 2nd ed. New York: Vintage Books.

Polletta, Francesca. 2002. *Freedom Is an Endless Meeting: Democracy in American Social Movements.* Chicago: University of Chicago Press.

Putnam, Jackson K. 1970. *Old-Age Politics in California: From Richardson to Reagan.* Stanford, CA: Stanford University Press.

Schlesinger, Arthur M., Jr. 1960. *The Politics of Upheaval.* Boston: Houghton Mifflin.

Schwartz, Mildred A. 2000. "Continuity Strategies among Political Challengers: The Case of Social Credit." *American Review of Canadian Studies* 30: 455–77.

Skocpol, Theda. 1985. "Bringing the State Back In: Strategies of Analysis in Current Research." In *Bringing the State Back In,* ed. Peter B. Evans, Dietrich Rueschmeyer, and Theda Skocpol, 3–37. Cambridge: Cambridge University Press.

————. 1999. "How Americans Became Civic." In *Civic Engagement in American Democracy,* ed. Theda Skocpol and Morris P. Fiorina. Washington, DC, and New York: Brookings Institution and Russell Sage Foundation.

Tarrow, Sidney. 1996. "States and Opportunities: The Political Structuring of Social Movements." In *Comparative Perspectives on Social Movements,* ed. Doug McAdam, John D. McCarthy, and Mayer N. Zald. Cambridge: Cambridge University Press.

————. 1998. *Power in Movement: Social Movements, Collective Action, and Politics.* New York: Cambridge University Press.

Tilly, Charles. 1978. *From Mobilization to Revolution.* Reading, MA: Addison-Wesley.

————. 1999. Conclusion to *How Social Movements Matter: Past Research, Present Problems, Future Developments,* ed. Marco Giugni, Doug McAdam, and Charles Tilly. Minneapolis: University of Minnesota Press.

————. 2000. "Regimes and Contention." CIAO Working Paper.

Townsend National Weekly. 1936–1950. Chicago: Townsend National Weekly, Inc.

U.S. Bureau of the Census. 1975. *Historical Statistics of the United States: From Colonial Times to 1970.* Washington, DC: U.S. Government Printing Office.

U.S. CES (Committee on Economic Security). 1935. *A Report to the President.* Washington, DC: U.S. Government Printing Office.

————. 1937. *Social Security in America: The Factual Background of the Social Security Act as Summarized from Staff Reports to the Committee on Economic Security.* Washington, DC: U.S. Government Printing Office.

U.S. Congress. House of Representatives. 1936. *Hearings before the Select Committee Investigating Old-Age Pension Organizations.* 74th Cong., 2nd sess., vols. 1–2. Washington, DC: U.S. Government Printing Office.

U.S. Congress. Senate Committee on Finances. 1935. *Hearings on the Economic Security Act.* Washington, DC: U.S. Government Printing Office.

Valocchi, Steve. 1990. "The Unemployed Workers' Movement: A Reexamination of the Piven and Cloward Thesis." *Social Problems* 37: 191–205.

Witte, Edwin. 1962. *The Development of the Social Security Act: A Memorandum on the History of the Committee on Economic Security and Drafting and Legislative History of the Social Security Act.* Madison: University of Wisconsin Press.

2

Social Movements, the Rise of New Issues, and the Public Agenda

Frank R. Baumgartner and Christine Mahoney

The agenda of the U.S. government has changed dramatically in the period since World War II. Much of the impetus for this change has come from social movements and the organizations they have spawned. Any number of examples can demonstrate the truth of that assertion, from women's rights to the rights of the handicapped, environmental protection, and other areas. Similarly, there is no doubt that public policies channel the future participation and attitudes of established social movements and the organizations that spring from them. But how can we demonstrate these links systematically? To say that social movements often cause large policy changes is certainly not to say that social movements dictate public policy directions, or even that social movements are more important than other causes of policy change. After all, policy changes can be caused by many other sources including business activities, stochastic shocks, the preferences of policy makers, or public opinion. The relative importance of social movements compared to other possible causes of policy change is a large issue beyond the scope of any single chapter-length treatment. In this chapter, we explain an approach to the question and demonstrate its feasibility. The longer-term research agenda of demonstrating the links between social movements and public policy in many areas of interest may now be feasible because of newly available data resources.

This chapter presents an overview of the Policy Agendas Project (see Baumgartner and Jones 2002, 2003).[1] The data sets that comprise the Policy Agendas Project include comprehensive compilations of (1) all congressional hearings; (2) all public laws; (3) all stories in the *Congressional*

Quarterly Almanac; (4) a sample of abstracts taken from the *New York Times Index*; and (5) a consistently coded, inflation-adjusted time series of the federal budget. (Other data resources, including bill introductions, presidential papers, and executive orders, are being added to this resource, and links are also being established to the Spaeth Supreme Court database and the Poole and Rosenthal congressional roll-call voting database.) Each of the data sets covers the time period from 1947 to recent years. Most are coded according to a complex, highly detailed, and historically consistent set of 226 topic and subtopic codes. This allows one to trace government and media attention to such questions as water pollution, inflation, health insurance availability, defense appropriations, or any other topic of government activity over the entire second half of the twentieth century. This new data resource, which is freely available to all users, should be valuable to scholars of public policy and social movements alike.

The data collected as part of the Policy Agendas Project allow one to trace not only the growth of new issues but also the size, composition, and structure of the governmental agenda as a whole. As we will note, the size of the agenda and the areas of activity of the U.S. federal government changed dramatically over the fifty years following World War II. We document the growth of several sets of social movement organizations (SMOs) and their impact on the policy agenda by tracing the growth of women's movement groups, human rights organizations, minority and civil rights groups, environmental groups, and the membership of the American Association of Retired Persons (AARP). Then we demonstrate that the entire public agenda, the set of all issues attracting the attention of the U.S. government, has been transformed over the past five decades. Some issues have risen in concern and others have declined; overall the diversity of the public agenda has grown dramatically. We close with a discussion of the links between the demands and mobilization of social movements on the one hand and the activities and concerns of government on the other, showing that these are strongly interactive. As social movements of many types have grown, governmental response has been swift. At the same time, social movement organizations are affected by areas of governmental activity, especially after the creation of large new public programs affecting their interests.

Social Movements and Public Policy

What are the links between the growth of social movements and governmental attention? Social movements can be at the core of attracting initial attention and governmental activity in a new area of public life, but once established these governmental programs have strong impacts on the social movements themselves, especially on the organizations and interest groups related to them.

In *Agendas and Instability in American Politics,* Baumgartner and Jones (1993) argued that government activities and new programs are often the legacies of social movements and agenda-setting processes. In contrast to the Downsian view suggesting that issues rise onto and recede from the public agenda with little long-term impact on government (Downs 1972), they noted that a common reaction in government to the rise of new issues is to create a program, agency, or budget designed to deal with the new issue (or, perhaps more commonly, to create multiple programs, agencies, and budgets). Once these new programs are established they rarely disappear. Rather, they grow into established programs, generating their own constituencies and affecting professionals, service providers, contractors, and beneficiaries. Examples include the Medicare and Medicaid programs, various environmental and pollution control efforts (including the creation of the EPA itself in 1970), conservation and land-use initiatives, civil rights and nondiscrimination policies, and a great range of other programs that were created and cultivated with the encouragement of social movements or communities of professionals and others supporting and typically benefiting from the policy. (It is important to note that the permanence of government programs is by no means a given; many do shrink or disappear over time if they generate no constituency of support or if their constituency itself declines over time; see Baumgartner 2002.)

The American government grew dramatically during the second half of the twentieth century; this was partly due to the efforts of new social movements to place new issues on the federal agenda. These newly mobilized groups, such as women, environmentalists, civil rights workers, human rights activists, and the elderly, succeeded in gaining government attention to their causes. As new programs were established to deal with their concerns, the programs and spending associated with them generated new interests themselves, as affected constituencies, service providers, and others entered into long-term relations with the government officials responsible for these new programs. The result is self-perpetuating and helps explain not only the growth of government but also the growth in the diversity of government activities. At the same time, the increased importance of government in various areas of social life has also affected the organizational fields associated with each of these areas. Paul DiMaggio and Walter Powell (1983) describe several reasons why groups in a given organizational field become increasingly similar over time; one of these is the role of the state.

As we will discuss in greater detail, we can clearly see evidence of this in our several cases; groups affect the state, and the state affects the groups.

In this section we address these issues with a description of five of the most prominent social movements of the post–World War II period. Debra Minkoff (1995) has provided one of the most complete compilations of the growth and development of social movement organizations over time, relying on an analysis of entries listed in the *Encyclopedia of Associations* (EA). Her data set includes information, among other variables, on staff size, budget, membership size, tactics, and goals for all civil rights, minority, and women's groups in each year from 1955 to 1988. We use Minkoff's data to trace the growth of SMOs associated with the women's movement as well as those associated with civil rights and racial minorities.[2] Figure 2.1 shows the number of women's organizations active from the period of 1955 to 1989, as well as the number of congressional hearings on women-related issues from 1947 to 1998.[3]

In the early postwar period, congressional attention to issues specifically or particularly of concern to women was unusual, sporadic, and unsustained. Figure 2.1 shows that only sixty-one hearings on women's issues occurred prior to 1970, an average of fewer than three hearings per year. Since 1970, attention steadily increased, with an average of over twenty hearings each year, reaching a peak of forty-seven hearings in 1991.

Minkoff's data on the number of SMOs related to the women's move-

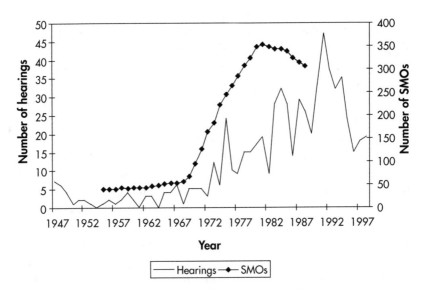

Figure 2.1. Congressional hearings and SMOs on women's issues.

ment show a dramatic increase during this same period, moving from just 57 organizations in 1968 to 165 groups in 1972, and increasing steadily in the years after this initial explosion. Certainly, the causes of increased attention in Congress to women's issues are not solely related to the growth of interest groups and social movement organizations concerned with these questions. Larger numbers of women were elected to the legislature; medical issues of concern to women rose in congressional interest; public opinion and public mores changed during this period. Still, there is no doubt that the growth in the numbers and resources associated with women's social movement organizations had a dramatic effect on the congressional agenda.

The example of the women's movement and its relation with congressional attention is no anomaly. Let us consider the case of the environment. Figure 2.2 shows the number of congressional hearings on environmental matters as well as a count of the number of active environmental interest groups, also taken from the EA. Baumgartner and Jones (1993, ch. 9) identified all groups focusing on environmental or conservation issues[4] listed in the EA at ten-year intervals beginning in 1960. Working from the creation dates of the organizations listed, they calculated estimates of the number of environmental SMOs active in 1961, 1970, 1980, and 1990.[5] Much as in the case of the women's movement, congressional attention to environmental issues was minimal during the period before roughly 1970. In fact, hearings averaged just sixteen per year until 1959 and only twenty per year from 1960 to 1968, and then began a dramatic and steady increase so that by the 1980s and 1990s there were regularly over one hundred hearings per year.

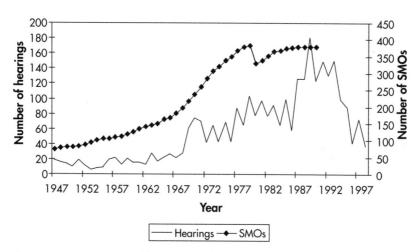

Figure 2.2. Congressional hearings and SMOs on environmental issues.

As the figure makes clear, the dramatic increase in congressional attention corresponds to a similarly striking increase in the number of interest groups active in pressing environmental demands. As in the case of women's issues, we would not want to assert a monocausal explanation of this increase in congressional attention. There were many reasons for increased congressional attention, not only social movement pressure. Still, it didn't hurt.

Debra Minkoff's study can be used again to trace the growth of organizations active in the area of civil rights and minority affairs; we use these data in Figure 2.3, comparing as before these numbers to a measure of congressional attention to civil rights and discrimination issues.

The timing of the increase of attention to civil rights is somewhat earlier than that of women's issues and, to a lesser extent, environmental issues, but the correspondence between the growth of the size of the interest-group population active in the area and the amount of congressional attention to the issue is just as striking. Groups focusing on civil rights and minority representation issues grew dramatically during the 1960s and 1970s. Congressional attention surged in the mid- to late 1960s, declined under the Nixon administration, then expanded again in the late 1970s through the late 1980s. The decline of congressional attention since 1987 to issues of discrimination and civil rights has been particularly dramatic; this may be related to the passage of legislation and to the increased controversy and courts-based activity surrounding affirmative action programs. In any case, throughout the period when we have data on both groups and agendas, we see that the growth of groups is strongly related to the growth of congres-

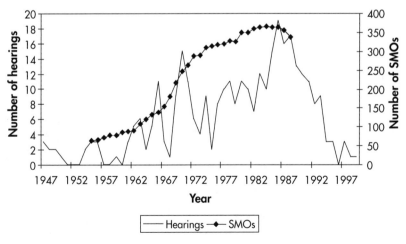

Figure 2.3. Congressional hearings and SMOs on civil rights and minority issues.

sional attention to the area.[6] Figure 2.4 shows equivalent data in the area of human rights.

Congressional hearings on human rights issues are virtually nonexistent until the mid-1960s and surge particularly in the mid- to late 1970s.[7] It is interesting to note that President Carter did not pull the issue of international human rights abuses out of a complete vacuum; as in other cases, the issue was partially "softened-up" by some preliminary attention to the topic (see especially Kingdon 1984 and Baumgartner and Jones 1993). Still, the Carter administration created an undeniably dramatic surge in attention as it made human rights an especially prominent aspect of its public rhetoric on international affairs. Finally, congressional attention to the issue of international human rights did not decline with the removal of Carter from office in 1980. Rather, attention stabilized at previously unprecedented levels, and the number of interest groups focusing exclusively or predominantly on human rights issues continued to rise throughout the period. While the president played a prominent role in placing international human rights on the congressional agenda in the 1970s, social movement organizations grew in the wake of this increased attention and in turn helped maintain the pressure to ensure that these issues did not disappear from the agenda when that president left office. Here we see, perhaps more strongly than in the other cases, the reciprocal nature of the relations between public policy and social movement organizations.

The ability of new public policies to create or promote the growth of

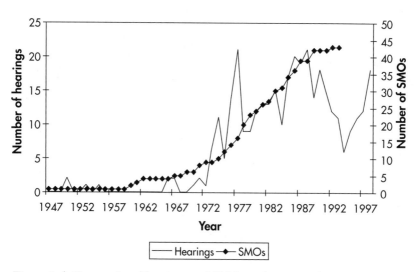

Figure 2.4. Congressional hearings and SMOs on human rights.

new social movement organizations can clearly be seen in the case of the elderly. Congressional attention to issues associated with the elderly began to grow in the early 1960s, especially with the Kennedy and Johnson administrations' focus on elderly and aging issues, as in their organization of the White House Conference on Aging (see Walker 1991). Many social organizations took an interest in issues relating to aging and the aged, but the number of interest groups focusing exclusively on representing this segment of the population was not large (perhaps because of the relative poverty of the elderly as compared to the general population at the time, a statistical fact that has long since reversed itself in the intervening years). With the creation of Medicare and the expansion of the Social Security program in the 1960s, government spending on pensions, health care, and other services for the elderly began to skyrocket. As congressional attention (and government spending) to elderly issues rose, so did the membership of the AARP. While a single SMO cannot be said to represent an entire social movement, the AARP is now the largest membership organization representing elderly interests in America; indeed, it is the largest membership group of any type in the country. The growth of the group's membership is therefore a useful indicator of the growth of the organizational component of the elderly movement. As Figure 2.5 shows, this growth clearly followed rather than preceded the growth of congressional attention to elderly issues.[8]

In the next section, we turn our attention to long-term trends and the overall effect of social movements on the government's agenda. As social

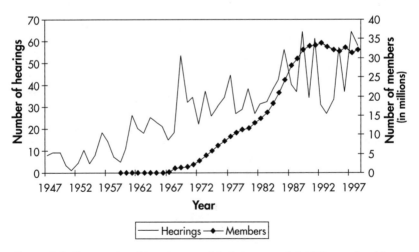

Figure 2.5. Congressional hearings on elderly issues and AARP membership.

movements have been successful in gaining attention, inevitably they have had to pay closer attention to the governmental allies (and opponents) that they helped to create.

The Transformation of the Policy Agenda of the Federal Government

During the period from World War II to the present, the federal government has been transformed. Many have noted these changes, in particular the size of government: we have moved from a minimalist government to a major social welfare state (even if the movement here has been less dramatic than in other Western countries). Employment by government has grown, the size of the federal budget has grown, the number of regulations has grown, the number of federal programs has grown, and all this is well known (see, for example, Light 1995). Of course, state governments employ many more people than the federal government, and their growth over the past fifty years has been even more striking than that at the federal level; further, tax expenditures, outside contracting, privatization of services, and tax subsidies have grown over the decades as federal policy makers have attempted to shield the true size of government (see Light 1999; Howard 1997). No matter how one considers it, government grew and diversified dramatically over the last half of the twentieth century.

Figure 2.6 shows an especially rapid rise in the numbers of hearings between 1960 and 1980; during this period the typical number of hearings in congressional committees of all types virtually doubled, from one thousand

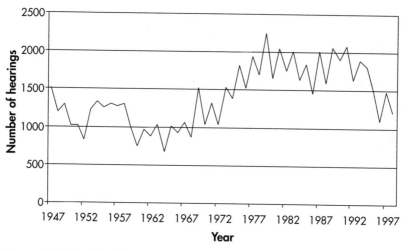

Figure 2.6. Number of congressional hearings by year.

to about two thousand hearings per year. (Note the saw-toothed pattern in the data; Congress typically holds a greater number of hearings in the first year of a two-year electoral cycle, and passes more legislation in the second year while holding fewer hearings.) This dramatic change in levels of congressional activity coincided with the decentralization of Congress; authority shifted from a few power barons chairing the major committees to hundreds of subcommittee chairs—almost every member of Congress was chair or ranking member on at least one subcommittee. This decentralization gave hundreds of members great autonomy within a particular area of public policy. Most important, this shift in congressional organization can be seen as a reaction to the increased workload. Congressional reforms aimed at decentralization were a logical consequence of the dramatic growth in the size and range of activities of the federal government in the period between 1947 and 1980. With more agencies to oversee, more programs to monitor, more money to allocate, more constituent demands to handle, and a greater number of distinct areas of governmental action, these reforms allowed Congress to adapt to a new environment of complexity.

Not only did government grow in size over the period discussed here, but, as many observers have pointed out, it has changed even more dramatically when we consider the diversity of government activities. The government has not only a larger number of activities but a more diverse portfolio of activities. This can be seen in Figure 2.7.

The Policy Agendas Project defines 226 areas of government activity,

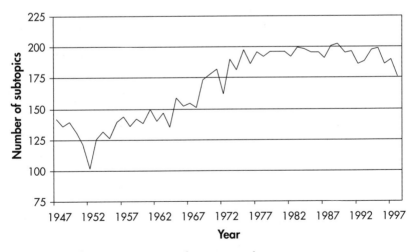

Figure 2.7. The increasing range of congressional attention.

ranging from macroeconomic policies focusing on the inflation rate to medical malpractice issues. Figure 2.7 displays the number of distinct subtopics in the Policy Agendas Project congressional hearings data set on which at least one hearing was held in each year from 1947 to 1997. During the early postwar period Congress was only attentive to an average of about 125 subtopics, but this number changed substantially over time, reaching and maintaining attention to nearly 200 issues from 1970 onward. Scores of activities that we now think of as natural and accepted areas of federal intervention are in fact relatively new areas of federal government activity. For example, in the early postwar period over 50 percent of congressional hearings were on just three topics: defense-related items; government operations themselves; and public lands, Interior Department issues, and water/irrigation projects. Other topics of attention, such as science and technology, housing and community development, foreign trade, transportation, social welfare programs, education, domestic commerce, environment, law enforcement, or health care, received less than 5 percent of attention each. Government under Eisenhower simply did not do very much in many areas of activity. The distribution of issues receiving attention shifted dramatically over time. Figure 2.8 demonstrates that those issues that dominated the agenda in the early postwar period dropped to being the object of only 30 percent of congressional hearings.

Congressional attention in the early postwar period was narrowly focused on just a few traditional areas of government activity, in particular

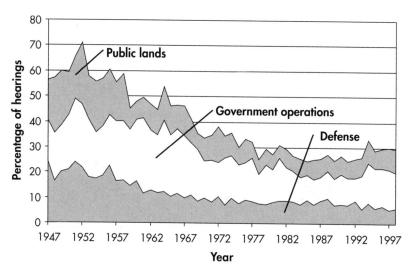

Figure 2.8. The decreasing attention of congressional hearings to old issues.

defense, Interior Department issues and public lands, and government operations themselves. (This last area concerns many "housekeeping" or "management" issues such as dealing with government properties and leases as well as District of Columbia affairs, nominations and appointments, and so on.) Many areas of considerable current attention were simply not on the radar screen at the time: health care before the creation of the Medicare program; environmental issues before the creation of the EPA; space, science, and technology policy before the creation of NASA; foreign trade before the more recent expansion of our integration into the world economy—all these are areas where Congress simply did not pay much attention. Combined, the three areas with greatest attention in the early period declined from a peak of constituting 70 percent of the hearings in 1952 to only about 30 percent during the period since the late 1970s. Congressional hearings in the last three decades show considerable attention to many issue areas virtually absent from the congressional agenda in the early years. Figure 2.9 shows the explosion of attention to five issue areas.

Congressional hearings on environment; health issues; law, crime, and family issues; international affairs and foreign aid; and space, science, technology, and communications burgeoned throughout the last five decades. Constituting less than 10 percent of the agenda space in the late 1940s, these areas together made up 35 percent in 1998. The late 1960s saw a spike

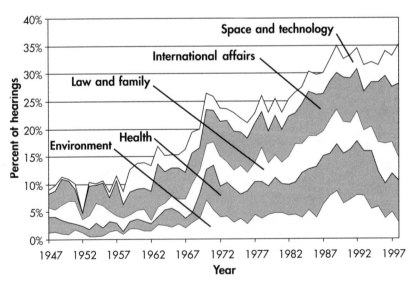

Figure 2.9. The increasing attention of congressional hearings to new issues.

in attention, and the 1970s and 1980s witnessed a steady increase in attention to all five areas as established federal programs demanded and justified continued congressional oversight of them. Together, Figures 2.8 and 2.9 show how great the changes in the nature of the political agenda have been. Though not apparent in this presentation of the data, it is also clear that congressional attention, once dominated by a small number of topics, increasingly is spread among many (on this question see Baumgartner, Jones, and MacLeod 2000; Baumgartner and Jones 2002). Many of the areas of greatest growth in government attention have been those with the most prominent social movements at their cores.

Social Movements and Policy Change

This chapter gives some idea of where we may look for the impacts of social movements on public policy. It also should make clear that social movements are neither the only sources of new public policies nor likely to have an impact on their own. When they have a long-term impact on public policy they interact closely with other groups within their organizational fields. Further, as government activities have grown, often in response to initial demands by social movements, different constituencies have been mobilized and organizational fields themselves have been transformed. Thus, the chain reactions of attention, spending, and vested interest that social movements may put into action can have long-lasting effects on public policy, social movements themselves, and other organizations such as professional and trade groups. The dynamics of public policy ensure that new sets of participants will become active in issue areas as these areas become the objects of considerable state activity, spending, and regulation (see DiMaggio and Powell 1983; Frank, Hironaka, and Shofer 2000). From health care to elderly issues to environmental causes of all kinds, we can see the tremendous impact of various social movements in American politics. Similarly, in the traditional areas of extensive government activity that have not been the objects of social movement mobilizations, we have seen a steady atrophy not only in attention but in spending as well. The agenda of the federal government has been transformed in the post–World War II period in large part (though not exclusively) by the rise of new social movements.

Our discussion of the linkages between organizational mobilization and congressional attention across five areas of social movement activity has shown some consistencies as well as some important differences. The most important consistent feature of the data is the long-term correspondence between the two trends: where social movement organizations develop in great numbers, so too does congressional attention rise. Clearly, social movements and the organizations they spawn are not the only cause of increased congressional concern with new issues. Public opinion, technological advance, demographic change, and presidential initiatives play a role, among other factors. No matter where the initial surge in attention comes from, however, our five cases all show a consistent pattern in which Washington-based interest groups associated with the social movement develop in great numbers (or with great membership) and act to focus attention on continued government involvement in that issue area. The links between social movements and public policy are not simple or unidirectional, but they are close.

These Washington-based advocates continue to push for congressional attention even when more traditional social movement activities have declined. Minkoff's (1997) research on the civil rights and women's movements shows that while protest events declined over time, SMOs continued to form until the advocacy communities reached a critical density, at which point the formal organizations grew more slowly in numbers, but maintained a high level of organizational presence. Tarrow's (1994) work on cycles of protest provides a model for understanding how the increased collective action of the civil rights movement spread to other issue areas and also how protest activity may decline. The civil rights movement is often seen as the catalyst for the mobilization of numerous subsequent movements including the four others we discuss here. Whether discussed in terms of a change in the opportunity structure or in the introduction of a master frame, the rise of civil rights and minority movements altered the political environment in a manner that facilitated the mobilization of women, peace activists, environmentalists, and antinuclear advocates, among others (McAdam 1996; Snow and Benford 1992). But it is the very nature of a cycle of protest that, over time, the intensity and frequency will decline for both the broader cycle and the specific movements operating within it. While the activity of the movements may ebb, the formalized institutions those movements spawned will go on. This is clearly demonstrated by our data; for all four social movements on which we have the number of SMOs, the number of viable groups that endure far outweighs the number of those that ceased to exist. Further, this growth and subsequent institutionalization far outlasted the period during which the social movements themselves were at their peak of activity and protest.

Traditionally there has been disagreement in the literature over the place of formalized social movement organizations, with some arguing that the challenging nature of social movements required an antisystem approach favoring the use of "outside" tactics. Efforts to alter government institutions preclude the use of institutionalized routes of influence, according to some.

This view has shifted to a general acceptance of the central role of formal SMOs in social movement communities, as seen in nearly all work from the resource mobilization perspective. Diani's (1992) review of numerous conceptualizations of the term "social movement" by some of the most influential scholars working in the subfield arrives at a consensual definition that clearly moves away from viewing social movements only as antisystem actors. It is important to recognize the critical role of formalized SMOs; as discussed, established institutions and organizations working in close relations with allied government agencies can sustain a movement that has lulled in the eyes of its constituents. In addition, as a large body of interest-group literature has shown, insider tactics do not preclude the use of outsider tactics, but the ability to use both offers social movements more opportunities for effective political action (see, for example, Schlozman and Tierney 1986; Walker 1991; Kollman 1998; Baumgartner and Leech 1998). As SMOs associated with a given movement are established, a certain number of these are likely to be institutionalized with staff resources in Washington and to become familiar with institutional processes. As these insider groups develop and grow, the movement also gains access to new and different information, becomes better skilled at using insider strategy, and ultimately more adept at influencing public policy. The establishment of an organization as a player in formal institutions of government does not prohibit the use of outsider tactics by it or by allied organizations drawn from the same general movement (see Minkoff 1995; Kollman 1998). In any case, our five examples make clear that where social movements are successful in gaining government attention, the growth and development of Washington-based interest groups is a logical consequence. This process may transform social movements, to be sure. But the development of a movement should clearly be studied in conjunction with the interest groups it spawns and supports. These groups, more than any unorganized or spontaneous parts of the movement, are likely to be closely tied to the development of government attention, spending, and programs. In turn, their growth helps sustain that government attention. The lasting impact of a social movement on public policy therefore is difficult to assess without careful attention to the formalized organizations that share the goals of the movement.

Many studies in political science and sociology report results similar or analogous to those we report here. Together, this growing body of literature suggests that social movements and the interest-group communities they generate should be studied in close connection with their interactions with government; clearly they are mutually dependent. Further, it appears that this is not peculiar to social movement organizations but can be generalized to organizations of many types ranging from educational groups to trade associations, business groups, engineering groups, health-care organizations, agriculture organizations, and others. Baumgartner and Beth Leech tracked the growth of different types of organizations in their discussion of changes in the nature of the national interest-group system over time (1998, Table 6.1). They showed that public affairs groups, health-care groups, social welfare organizations (especially service providers), and others that can be linked to many of the areas of growth in government activity were among the fastest growing sectors of the group system, as assessed by the numbers of groups listed in annual volumes of the EA. Veterans' groups and agricultural groups, among others, are among the categories with the slowest growth. Areas of growth and decline in the group system appear to be related to areas of growth and decline in the relative amounts of congressional attention to those same areas of public policy.

Jack Walker's analysis similarly showed different rates of growth among groups in the profit, nonprofit, and citizens' sectors, and he clearly saw these developments as tightly linked to the changing nature of the political agenda (1991; see also 1966). In his 1977 article on agenda setting, Walker explicitly linked new issues on the congressional agendas not only to social movements but also, and perhaps more strongly, to established communities of professionals working in Washington and elsewhere. Jeffrey Berry's (1999) recent analysis of the changing nature of the federal agenda, and the rise of postmaterial issues in particular, clearly points to the importance of new social movements and the institutionalization of the new-left citizens' organizations in Washington over the past several decades.

DiMaggio and Powell (1983) argued that organizational fields would become increasingly homogeneous to the extent that there was greater state involvement in the field, among other things. Our five cases clearly show an increased Washington-based presence that may be attributed to one of the three causes they identify: mimicry, where groups copy those innovations from others that appear to work; state involvement, most clearly; and professionalization (see also McCarthy, Britt, and Wolfson 1991; they discuss the tendency toward structural uniformity resulting from institutional channeling mechanisms). David John Frank, Ann Hironaka, and Evan Shofer (2000) note the tight interdependencies between the growth of environmental NGOs at the international level and state involvement in environmental issues. As we have noted in the U.S. case, they show how environmental protection has become a normal, bureaucratized, and expected part of the policy portfolio of all governments. A great range of studies therefore point to findings and processes similar to those we describe here.

Another recent project linking group activity with government attention shows that variations in activity levels by lobbyists in Washington as
reflected in lobby registration reports in Congress, available over six-month
reporting periods and in seventy-four different areas of congressional activity, can best be explained by the long-term congressional interest in
that area (see Leech et al. forthcoming). Leech and colleagues conducted a
detailed pooled-time-series analysis of the areas in which lobbyists register
over time to show that government attention drives lobbying activity and
that this relationship is stronger than that for government spending or for
indicators of the level of activity in the relevant economic sector. That is to
say, public policy creates the demand for lobbying as much as lobbying and
social movement activity creates a demand for public policy.

Social movements are clearly at the center of much policy change. However, social movements are not the only sources of new issues; there are many
other sources of new topics of attention. Further, there is nothing inevitable
about the processes described here. Even when social movements do rise to
prominence and achieve government attention, they may or may not spawn
well-financed SMOs active in keeping their issues in the limelight. (Berry
notes in particular the failure of the conservative organizations of the 1980s
to establish the same kind of powerful Washington presence as the liberal
groups of the 1960s and 1970s did to great effect.) Perhaps the greatest long-
term impact of social movements, among the scenarios that seem apparent
here, is that as SMOs develop, they must interact more closely over time
with established professional communities, especially among service providers, be they social workers, medical researchers, environmental engineers,
or the manufacturers of pollution abatement equipment. Eventually, most
groups then become much more closely a part of the Washington policy process, in spite of their "pure" social movement roots. While this trend toward
increased bureaucratization is not the only possible transformation, it is a
common one. Hanspeter Kriesi discusses this process of institutionalization
as including "stabilization of an SMO's resource flow, the development of
its internal structure, the moderation of its goals, the conventionalization of
its action repertoire, and its integration into established systems of interest
intermediation" (1996, 156). Rucht (1996) describes the process as a shift
in the type of movement structure over time, from a traditional grassroots
model characterized by loose, decentralized structure, engaging in protest
activities and dependent on committed adherents, to an institutionalized
interest-group or party-oriented model, characterized by reliance on formal
organization. Increasing institutionalization, however, need not suggest negative undertones of co-optation and concession.

Becoming part of a Washington policy community, reaching compromises with businesses or service providers seeking to profit from government spending programs, and dealing with questions of policy implementation may seem like the worst fate for a group of idealistic and often ideologically committed activists in their later years. It is apparent from the data presented here, however, that such an outcome may be one of the most important and influential in the long term. As movements or other sources have success in establishing continued government attention to their issues, new programs are often established. Whether these are pension and health insurance programs, environmental protection or antidiscrimination laws with their attendant enforcement mechanisms, or human rights bodies continuously working over the years, these programs and activities spawn and perpetuate further relations with nonprofit organizations, businesses, and other interests concerned with the new policy and the social problem it is designed to address. Thus, social movements, their organizational representatives, and public policies are intertwined in a complex web of mutual interdependence.

More systematic research on these linkages is clearly needed. Certainly much of it will come from detailed analysis of particular policy areas such as those built up around particular social movements. Some of it may also ask the broader question of where new issues come from; some come from social movements, but some do not. In his introduction to this volume, David Meyer makes reference to the "chicken and egg question" concerning the links between social movements and public policy. There can be no doubt about the tight linkages between social movements, social movement organizations, and government, at least in the cases discussed here. We have argued that these links are so strong and their cumulative effect has been so great that the very nature of American government was transformed during a period of active social ferment, from the 1960s to the 1970s. Whether looking at particular policy areas or at the entire federal government, scholars of public policy are well advised to pay close attention to the rise and roles of social movements and the organizations they spawn in constructing theories of public policy. By the same token, we hope to have shown that students of social movements cannot understand the development or impact of the movements they study without also incorporating information about public policy and government response to the movement. While social movements may develop at first in areas far removed from public policy and government agencies, if successful they later find that their activities are tightly linked with the continuation and development of new public policies.

Notes

1. Research for the original data collection was supported by grant SBR–9320922 from the National Science Foundation and continues under grant SBR–0111611. Bryan Jones is codirector with Baumgartner on this larger project; we acknowledge and appreciate the support of Penn State University and the University of Washington, as well as that of NSF. Thanks to John McCarthy and Erik Johnson for comments.

2. We express our appreciation to Professor Minkoff for graciously sharing her data set.

3. To select women-related congressional hearings in the Policy Agendas Project database, we first identified hearings on three topics particularly related to women's issues: gender and sexual orientation discrimination (topic 202); parental leave and child care (508); and family issues, including such things as domestic abuse (1208). These three topics included a total of 417 hearings. Reading through the short descriptions allowed us to discard 58 of these that were related to things other than women (for example, discrimination against homosexuals in topic 202 or abuse against the elderly in topic 1208), leaving 359 women-related hearings in these three topic areas. In addition, we scanned the short descriptions of each hearing for the following words: women, woman, female, girl, pregnan*, mother, maternal, infant, wife, breast, mammo*, domestic violence, sexual harassment, abortion, rape, equal pay, birth, pornography, homemaker, prostit*, cervical, and fertilization. This procedure identified 651 additional hearings. Deleting false hits (e.g., hearings on the "birth" of the nuclear age) and duplicates left us with a total of 944 women-related hearings from 1947 to 1998.

4. Baumgartner and Jones explain their selection procedures as follows: All groups indicating a concern with environmental questions and listed in the EA were included. This included those listed under the keywords "environmental quality," "environmental protection," "wildlife conservation," and "conservation," as well as selected groups listed under "water resources," "ecology," "environmental law," "fishing," "forestry," and "ornithology." In addition, each entry in the entire EA was read to determine if some other groups should be included, even if they had not been listed under the appropriate keyword. Finally, those groups that were clearly tied to industry, such as chemical company consortia conducting environmental research, were deleted. The resulting data set therefore contains all groups primarily concerned with environmental issues in each edition of the EA studied (1961, 1970, 1980, and 1990). See the codebook description and data available at http://polisci.la.psu.edu/faculty/baumgartner/.

5. The number of groups was calculated separately from those groups listed in 1970, 1980, and 1990, and the figure reports the cumulative totals by creation

date, using only those groups still in existence (as reflected by their listing in the EA) at the end of the decade. This explains the decline in 1980; a similar decline in 1970 does not appear because more groups were created in that year than went defunct in the entire previous decade. A total of 461 groups were listed at some point during this period; 378 were still in existence in 1990. Hearings are taken as the full set of hearings on topic 7, environmental issues. There are 2,966 hearings from 1947 to 1998.

6. For civil rights we use Minkoff's data on minority groups and congressional hearings on topic 201, ethnic minority and racial group discrimination; there are 327 hearings in the series.

7. Data on human rights organizations come from the 1996 edition of the EA. Forty-six groups were listed under the subject heading of human rights; forty-four of these listed their creation dates, and these were used to calculate the number of groups in existence each year. This number therefore excludes those groups that merged or went defunct during the period before 1996. Congressional data are from topic 1925, international affairs/human rights. There were 353 such hearings during the period.

8. Data on AARP membership were provided directly by the AARP; we appreciate their cooperation. Data on congressional hearings about elderly issues were identified in a manner similar to our method for women's issues. First, we gathered data on the following topics: age discrimination (204); Medicare and Medicaid (303); elderly health issues (311); elderly assistance programs/social services for the elderly (1303); and elderly and handicapped housing (1408). Then we searched for the following words in our summaries: elder*, geriatric, Medicare, aging, older, nursing home, retire, social security, senior, and hospice. Deleting false hits (174 cases) and duplicates (2,790 cases) left us with 1,510 hearings on elderly issues from 1947 to 1998.

References

Banaszak, Lee Ann. 1996. *Why Movements Succeed or Fail: Opportunity, Culture, and the Struggle for Woman Suffrage.* Princeton, NJ: Princeton University Press.

Baumgartner, Frank R. 2002. "Social Movements and the Rise of New Issues." Paper presented at the Conference on Social Movements, Public Policy, and Democracy, University of California, Irvine, January 11–13.

Baumgartner, Frank R., and Bryan D. Jones. 1993. *Agendas and Instability in American Politics.* Chicago: University of Chicago Press.

———, eds. 2002. *Policy Dynamics.* Chicago: University of Chicago Press.

———. 2003. The Policy Agendas Project. Databases distributed through the University of Washington Center for American Politics, http://www.policyagendas.org.

Baumgartner, Frank R., Bryan D. Jones, and Michael C. MacLeod. 2000. "The Evolution of Legislative Jurisdictions." *Journal of Politics* 62: 321–49.

Baumgartner, Frank R., and Beth L. Leech. 1998. *Basic Interests: The Importance of Groups in Politics and in Political Science.* Princeton, NJ: Princeton University Press.

Berry, Jeffrey M. 1999. *The New Liberalism: The Rising Power of Citizen Groups.* Washington, DC: Brookings Institution.

Costain, Anne. 1992. *Inviting Women's Rebellion: A Political Process Interpretation of the Women's Movement.* Baltimore, MD: Johns Hopkins University Press.

Diani, Mario. 1992. "The Concept of Social Movement." *Sociological Review* 40, no. 1: 1–25.

DiMaggio, Paul J., and Walter W. Powell. 1983. "The Iron Cage Revisited: Institutional Isomorphism and Collective Rationality in Organizational Fields." *American Sociological Review* 48 (April): 147–60.

Downs, Anthony. 1972. "Up and Down with Ecology: The Issue Attention Cycle." *Public Interest* 28: 38–50.

Frank, David John, Ann Hironaka, and Evan Shofer. 2000. "The Nation-State and the Natural Environment over the Twentieth Century." *American Sociological Review* 65 (February): 96–116.

Freeman, Jo. 1975. *The Politics of Women's Liberation.* New York: McKay.

Gamson, William, and David S. Meyer. 1996. "Framing Political Opportunity." In *Comparative Perspectives on Social Movements,* ed. Douglas McAdam, John McCarthy, and Mayer Zald. Cambridge: Cambridge University Press.

Howard, Christopher. 1997. *The Hidden Welfare State: Tax Expenditures and Social Policy in the United States.* Princeton, NJ: Princeton University Press.

Jones, Bryan D., Frank R. Baumgartner, and James L. True. 1998. "Policy Punctuations: U.S. Budget Authority, 1947–95." *Journal of Politics* 60: 1–33.

Katzenstein, Mary Fainsod, and Carol Mueller, eds. 1987. *The Women's Movements of the United States and Western Europe: Consciousness, Political Opportunity, and Public Policy.* Philadelphia: Temple University Press.

Kingdon, John W. 1984. *Agendas, Alternatives, and Public Policies.* Boston: Little, Brown.

Kollman, Ken. 1998. *Outside Lobbying: Public Opinion and Interest Group Strategies.* Princeton, NJ: Princeton University Press.

Kriesi, Hanspeter. 1996. "The Organizational Structure of New Social Movements in a Political Context." In *Comparative Perspectives on Social Movements,* ed. Douglas McAdam, John McCarthy, and Mayer Zald. Cambridge: Cambridge University Press.

Leech, Beth L., Frank R. Baumgartner, Timothy LaPira, and Nicholas Semanko.

Forthcoming. "Drawing Lobbyists to Washington: Government Activity and Interest-Group Mobilization." *Political Research Quarterly.*

Light, Paul C. 1995. *Thickening Government: Federal Hierarchy and the Diffusion of Accountability.* Washington, DC: Brookings Institution.

———. 1999. *The True Size of Government.* Washington, DC: Brookings Institution.

McAdam, Doug. 1996. "Conceptual Origins, Current Problems, Future Directions." In *Comparative Perspectives on Social Movements,* ed. Douglas McAdam, John McCarthy, and Mayer Zald, 23–40. Cambridge: Cambridge University Press.

McCarthy, John D., David Britt, and Mark Wolfson. 1991. "The Channeling of Social Movements in the Modern State." *Social Movements, Conflicts, and Change* 13: 45–76.

Miller, Lisa L. 2001. "The High-Cost of Symbolic Politics: Crime on the Public and Congressional Agendas, 1947–1992." Unpublished manuscript. Pennsylvania State University.

Minkoff, Debra. 1995. *Organizing for Equality: The Evolution of Women's and Racial-Ethic Organizations in America, 1955–1985.* New Brunswick, NJ: Rutgers University Press.

———. 1997. "The Sequencing of Social Movements." *American Sociological Review* 62 (October): 779–99.

Rucht, Dieter. 1996. "The Impact of National Contexts on Social Movement Structures: A Cross-Movement and Cross-National Comparison." In *Comparative Perspectives on Social Movements,* ed. Douglas McAdam, John McCarthy, and Mayer Zald, 185–204. Cambridge: Cambridge University Press.

Schlozman, Kay Lehman, and John T. Tierney. 1986. *Organized Interests and American Democracy.* New York: Harper and Row.

Snow, David, and Robert Benford. 1992. "Master Frames and Cycles of Protest." In *Frontiers of Social Movement Theory,* ed. Aldon Morris and Carol McClurg Mueller, 133–55. New Haven, CT: Yale University Press.

Tarrow, Sidney. 1994. *Power in Movement: Social Movements, Collective Action, and Politics.* New York: Cambridge University Press.

Walker, Jack L., Jr. 1966. "A Critique of the Elitist Theory of Democracy." *American Political Science Review* 60: 285–95, 391–92.

———. 1977. "Setting the Agenda in the U.S. Senate: A Theory of Problem Selection." *British Journal of Political Science* 7: 423–45.

———. 1991. *Mobilizing Interest Groups in America.* Ann Arbor: University of Michigan Press.

3

Velcro Triangles: Elite Mobilization of Local Antidrug Issue Coalitions

John D. McCarthy

Scholars of contemporary U.S. social movements vigorously debate the extent to which movements actually affect specific social policies. Nevertheless, there is a pretty broad consensus among these scholars that much of what citizens groups do as they try to bring about social change is aimed, directly or indirectly, at influencing the behavior of government actors and the content of public policies. Reflecting the key features of historical accounts of the emergence of national social movements in the nineteenth century, social movements have been conceived by most contemporary scholars as consisting of independent groups of citizens who join together to make contentious claims on governments. As a result, the primary relations between governments and citizen actors are seen in their contention over the contents of public policies. The image of independent social movements emerging out of local civil society is consistent with what we know of many U.S. social movements in recent years, resonating especially with accounts of the insurgent actors of the civil rights movement of the 1960s and 1970s (Jenkins and Eckert 1986). Indigenous social actors who heroically rise up against great odds to alter the social landscape are the embodiment of the romantic caricature of social movements.

In contrast to this image, however, extensive evidence exists to suggest that a great deal of local citizen collective action in recent decades in the United States has been sponsored and encouraged by government and elite actors (McCarthy and Zald 2002). Elites mobilize citizens groups to press for social policies they prefer, helping to generate grassroots policy claims on governments and reflecting an interpenetration of the state and civil society that is seriously at odds with the prevailing caricature of the origins of collective action. If we are to understand the full array of mobilization of local collective action, we must move beyond the automatic assumption that its origins are in indigenous, totally independent, and local collective actors.

Community antidrug coalitions provide a rich opportunity to explore the extent as well as the mechanisms of elite sponsorship of local mobilization around public policy issues. During the last fifteen years newly formed issue coalitions have become increasingly common across U.S. states and local communities. These coalitions seek to mobilize institutional actors as well as individual citizens to bring about social and public policy change. The coalitions are heavily sponsored by elites, including government at all levels, foundations, businesses, and nonprofit corporate actors as well as citizens from all walks of life. They appear to be heavily concentrated in particular social issue domains, such as public health (e.g., Healthy Community Coalitions and Substance Abuse Partnerships). New coalitions appear to be less common around class and ethnic conflict issue domains or in environmental and international conflict issue domains.

Community-level coalitions are *a historically specific institutional type* of collective action that has proliferated across U.S. communities and among issue domains in recent decades. The particular features of these coalitions make them especially effective vehicles of elite-sponsored mobilization. Substance abuse partnerships are the most common of the community coalitions, and they will be the primary focus of what follows. The availability of federal government and foundation financial support in recent years expanded the incentive for local actors to adopt the substance abuse community partnership template. These coalitions normally enroll a wide membership and seek to mobilize extensive group and individual citizen efforts. Membership in them, in contrast to membership in other coalition types, is relatively loose and unstructured. Unlike the highly institutionalized "iron triangles" of an earlier period that linked congressional committees, public agencies, and client industries (Gais, Peterson, and Walker 1984; Peterson 1993), the ties between members and these coalitions are often quite informal; membership may require little more commitment than attending coalition meetings. Members may become attached and unattached to these coalitions with an ease reminiscent of Velcro fasteners.

The dynamic community coalition type has displayed a particular vitality in recent years, one that privileges citizen mobilization around issues that are the focus of the new community coalitions. As a result these elite-sponsored community coalitions are important in shaping the local terrain of institutional and citizen mobilization and hence the demography of collective demands for social change in local communities. The emergence and spread of these coalitions, therefore, inevitably affects the public policy process in local communities, having made substance abuse one of the most prominent local social issues in communities across the United States.

I begin by considering the wide variety that exists among coalition forms that have been the object of attention by social movement scholars before I describe, in some detail, the recent emergence of local antidrug coalitions. This allows me to place these coalitions into broader theoretical perspective and to specify their most important features. I go on to discuss elite mobilization of citizen collective action in general and local antidrug coalitions in particular. I conclude with an analysis of the consequences of the rapid proliferation of these coalitions on the extent of local citizen mobilization around policy issues and its implications for local policy agenda setting.

Lessons from Research on Social Movement Coalitions

Social movement scholars have paid increasing attention to the emergence and dynamics of coalitions, paying greatest attention to explicating the conditions under which coalitions are likely to form and among whom (e.g., Staggenborg 1986; McCammon and Campbell 2002; Hathaway and Meyer 1997; Van Dyke 2003). In general, coalitions are more or less formally constituted agreements among preexisting groups, organizations, and, sometimes, individuals to cooperate in the pursuit of common purposes. In the modern context, such purposes or issues, more often than not, translate into policy goals. Coalitions vary along a number of important dimensions, including (1) the conditions that give rise to them, (2) their lifespan, and (3) the composition of their memberships.

A number of studies of coalition formation support the conclusion that *external threats* (McCammon and Campbell 2002; Rochon and Meyer 1997; Staggenborg 1986; Van Dyke 2003) can serve as an important impetus to the formation of coalitions. As well, the *availability of resources* is seen to facilitate coalition formation (Staggenborg 1986; Van Dyke 2003; Zald and McCarthy 1980).

Coalitions may be formed for shorter or longer periods, their permanence typically being the result of the specificity and achievability of their common goals. For instance, many times coalitions are formed to stage protest events and dissolve after an event is staged (Gerhards and Rucht 1992; Van Dyke 2003; Jones et al. 2001). Other coalitions are formed for the purpose of pursuing specific legislative goals and may not survive the success or failure of achieving them (Meyer and Rochon 1997; Laumann and Knoke 1987).[1] Long-term coalitions are more likely to be built around more diffuse issue and policy agendas.

Coalitions also differ in the strength of the ties that bind coalition participants together. The relations between coalition partners can vary from quite formal written agreements to informal working relationships that entail little more than agreeing to lend a group's name to a common effort. The strength of ties and their permanence can be related to the level of contribution of resources, including financial and human, along with the stability of those contributions, and to common efforts.

Finally, coalitions can be distinguished by the heterogeneity in the composition of their memberships. The heterogeneity among coalition partners' (1) constituencies, (2) issue goals, and (3) culture/identities have each been recognized as important in understanding the likelihood of coalition formation. Potential coalition partners who share issue goals and draw their constituents from similar pools of supporters are seen as likely to resist joining common efforts (Zald and McCarthy 1980; Hathaway and Meyer 1997). Such an argument suggests that coalitions are more easily formed among partners with diverse constituencies who share issue goals. In contrast to the argument concerning constituencies that stresses organizational interests is one that suggests that coalitions are more likely among partners who share common identities (Arnold 1995; McCammon and Campbell 2002). Such an expectation is consistent with concerns expressed by those who have called for broad progressive issue coalitions about the difficulties of creating common efforts across the divides of class and identities of other kinds (Rose 2000; Bystydzienski and Schact 2001).

Emergence and Growth of the Substance Abuse Community Coalition Movement

Many local antidrug coalitions had already come into existence during the first two decades of the U.S. "war on drugs." This ongoing war continues to be waged by the police on the streets and borders of the United States, in the U.S. Congress and in state legislatures, in the courts, in the press, and by presidents, governors, and mayors.[2]

> As wars will do, the War on Drugs escalated piecemeal, a product of the hopes and fears and ambitions of people with varying motives and disparate points of view. . . . the War on Drugs, in name and spirit, started during the 1968 presidential campaign, when the country discovered how drugs could stand in for a host of troubles too awkward to discuss plainly. The war metaphor worked for Richard Nixon that year. It continues to

work for politicians ranging from Jesse Jackson to Jesse Helms because nearly everyone has found a reason to enlist: parents appalled by their teens' behavior, police starved for revenue, conservative politicians pandering to their constituents' moral dungeon, liberal politicians needing a chance to look tough, presidents looking for distractions from scandals, whites—and blacks—striving to explain the ghetto, editors filling page one, spies and colonels needing an enemy to replace Communists . . . (Baum 1996, vii–ix)

One of the consequences of this war was the proliferation of local antidrug coalitions in communities across the United States. An attempt to enumerate all of these coalitions in 1992 and 1993 identified more than two thousand that claimed to be the "lead coalition against substance abuse" in their community (Join Together 1993). But while the war on drugs had provided the conditions for the proliferation of these coalitions, the majority of the coalitions have not shared its national leaders' strong emphasis on law enforcement and interdiction that has been reflected in the federal budget for the war. Instead these diverse coalitions have preferred to emphasize prevention and treatment, what they characterize as "demand" as opposed to "supply" solutions to drug problems. As well, their focus has been as much, if not more, on the legal drugs of alcohol and tobacco than on illicit drugs. This is seen in the fact that 75 percent of the coalitions reported extensive program activities aimed at alcohol use and 26 percent reported extensive activities aimed at tobacco use (Join Together 1993).

Beginning in the late 1980s and early 1990s, a series of national-level initiatives substantially expanded the opportunities for such groups, funding them, legitimating them, and providing enhanced technical assistance to them. One of the earliest came out of the private sector. "[In 1989] The Robert Wood Johnson Foundation (RWJF) launched Fighting Back, its largest demonstration program ever, to reduce demand for drugs through community coalitions. RWJF credits the Fighting Back concept as the origin of the federal initiatives" (Hallfors et al. 2002, 237). RWJF funded only a modest number of community coalitions directly (fourteen), but one account of the emergence of the movement suggests, "Not only did Fighting Back directly fund coalitions, its call for applicants also helped spark the movement. Many of the original applicants that did not receive grants were able to find funding elsewhere, and these coalitions formed a strong foundation for the coalition movement" (Drug Strategies 2001, 2).[3]

Starting in 1990 a new federal program began providing grants to local community antidrug coalitions through the Center for Substance

Abuse Prevention (CSAP), a division of the U.S. Department of Health and Human Services. Two hundred and fifty-one coalitions were funded between 1990 and 1996 at a cost of close to *one-half billion dollars*. On the heels of that initiative a new federal initiative was launched. "Since 1997, the Office of National Drug Control Policy [ONDCP] has funded 464 anti-drug coalitions with an additional $95 million, and the president's 2002 budget request would double funding for community anti-drug coalitions to $350 million over 5 years, including an $11 million increase in 2002" (Hallfors et al. 2002, 237).

Two national initiatives were launched in the early 1990s that resulted in ongoing sources of technical assistance and support for local coalitions. "In November 1990, the first national meeting of community coalitions in Washington, DC, drew 450 people from 172 cities. With guidance and support from the President's Drug Advisory Council, a new organization, the Community Anti-Drug Coalitions of America (CADCA), became the national public voice for these emerging coalitions" (Drug Strategies 2001, 2).

In 1992 the President's Drug Advisory Council (PDAC), under the guidance of Jim Burke, the former Chairman and CEO of Johnson and Johnson and the current Chairman of the Partnership for a Drug-Free America, encouraged the formation of CADCA to respond to the dramatic growth in the number of substance abuse coalitions and their need to share ideas, problems, and solutions. The organization was officially launched in October 1992 under the leadership of Alvah Chapman, the Director and retired Chairman and CEO of Knight Ridder, Inc. who became CADCA's first chairman. With their guidance, the organization has evolved to become the principal national substance abuse prevention organization working with community-based coalitions and representing their interests at the national level. (cadca.org)

CADCA now claims to represent more than five thousand community coalitions across the United States. CADCA's major financial support comes from the RWJF and the John S. and James L. Knight Foundation. The CADCA's vision statement is worth quoting at length:

Community coalitions—more than any other entity—are poised to connect multiple sectors of the community, including businesses, parents, media, law enforcement, schools, faith organizations, health providers, social service agencies, and the government. By acting in concert through the coalition, all of the partners gain a more complete understanding of the community's problems. Together, the partners organize and develop plans and programs to coordinate their anti-drug efforts. The result is a comprehensive, community-wide approach to substance abuse and its related problems.

At the same time, the Robert Wood Johnson Foundation funded Join Together, a national organization to support community-based programs working toward reducing, preventing, and treating substance abuse. Since 1991, Join Together, supported by $16 million from the RWJF, has provided technical assistance including online help with strategy development, funding, and operations for coalitions nationwide.

Community Coalitions against Substance Abuse

A survey was conducted of a subset of local community substance abuse coalitions that were identified in 1992 and 1993 (Join Together 1993). The researchers were able to identify more that 5,000 such groups, and surveyed the more than 2,100 coalitions that identified themselves as the "lead" substance abuse coalition in their community. Most of them were of recent origin, having been in existence for an average of 5.4 years when the survey was completed. I briefly summarize the results of the survey.[4]

The extent and diversity of membership. The membership of almost all coalitions included local schools (90 percent), law enforcement agencies (85 percent), and alcohol and drug prevention agencies (76 percent). Sixty-three percent included businesses, and 61 percent religious organizations. Thirty-four percent of the coalitions included civic/fraternal organizations as members, and citizen action groups were the fastest growing segment of membership in the coalitions, with 32 percent of them adding such groups between 1992 and 1993. Forty-one percent of the coalitions included media leaders and organizations. "Nearly 60 percent of the coalitions report having an equal representation of professionals, large organizations, citizens, lay people, activists, and government officials among their membership" (Join Together 1993, 14). Figure 3.1 provides a more comprehensive description of the composition of coalition membership.

Unfortunately, respondent coalitions were not asked the size of their membership, but we do have such membership reports for twenty-four coalitions funded by CSAP.[5] Those groups averaged 40 member partners in 1992, and the average size grew steadily to 120 by 1996 (Substance Abuse and Mental Health Services Administration 2000). These several sources of evidence, then, indicate that antidrug coalitions typically enroll a large number of member participants and that the members represent a broad range of community institutions and organizations.

Membership criteria. The Join Together survey, unfortunately, did not ask coalition respondents to describe how membership was determined.

Members	% of coalitions
Schools	90
Law enforcement	85
Prevention providers	76
Parents	72
Volunteers	71
Treatment providers	70
Local government	67
Youth	64
Private business	63
Government human services	62
Courts/probation	61
Government health services	56
Recovering people	55
Other concerned citizens	54
Private health services	48
Private human services	43
Universities	42
Mass media	41
Child protective services	40
Affected populations	38
Recreation departments	36
Civic/fraternal organizations	34
Citizen action groups	29
Organized labor	14
Alcohol beverage control	13
Alcohol industry	8

Figure 3.1. Characteristics of members participating in antidrug coalitions. N = 2,196. (Data from Join Together 1993.)

Descriptions of particular coalitions, however, suggest that for many of them membership is rather informal. For instance, for the SAFE 2000 El Paso, Texas, community partnership, "There was no formal process for becoming a partnership member: those who expressed an interest and desire were considered members. This lack of a formal process was intentional" (Substance Abuse and Mental Health Services Administration 2000). And in the Springfield, Missouri, Ozarks Fighting Back partnership, "membership . . . was less structured, being defined in de facto terms—actual participation in programs . . . [although] member agencies signed a written agreement" (ibid.). For the Aberdeen, South Dakota, Alcohol and Drug Abuse Council, "Membership in the coalition requires registration at two previous meetings, which entitles an individual or organization to vote on upcoming initiatives and the overall direction of the coalition" (Drug Strategies 2001, 25). An American Public Health Association handbook for coalitions recommends, "Let everyone who wants to join the coalition be a member" (Berkowitz and Wolff 2000, 40). The Campus Community Partnership United Against Dangerous Drinking, of which I am a member, has no formal membership criteria. The sum of this evidence reinforces the loosely coupled or Velcro-like nature of the ties that bind antidrug coalition members to these local efforts.

Mobilization of financial resources. One-third of the coalitions have budgets less than $50,000, but one-fourth have budgets greater than $500,000, as seen in Figure 3.2. Eighty percent of the respondent coalitions' aggregate funds come from some level of government, with the federal government being the most important source. Forty-one percent receive some federal funding, as seen in Figure 3.3. "This reflects the commitment by the federal

Budget size	% of coalitions
Less than $10,000	16
$10,001 to $50,000	17
$50,001 to $100,000	12
$100,001 to $250,000	16
$250,001 to $500,000	15
Greater than $500,000	24

Figure 3.2. Reported annual operating budgets of antidrug coalitions. N = 2,196. (Data from Join Together 1993.)

Source	% of total	% of coalitions completely dependent
Federal government	41	15
State government	27	6
Local government	12	2
Private sector	12	
Foundations	3	
Sales/dues	5	

Figure 3.3. Source of funds flowing to antidrug coalitions. N = 1,681. (Data from Join Together 1993.)

government in recent years to develop community coalitions through the Center for Substance Abuse Prevention (CSAP) Partnership Program, the Drug Free Schools and Communities Act, and the Bureau of Justice Assistance community demand-reduction grants" (Join Together 1993, 12). An additional 27 percent of the funds come from state government sources and 12 percent from local government. In spite of the lead role several foundations have taken in sponsoring and encouraging local substance abuse coalitions, described above, only 3 percent of the aggregate financial support reported by the survey respondents came from foundations. A significant minority (23 percent) of the coalitions are wholly dependent on government financial support of some kind.

Mobilization of volunteer labor. Together the respondent coalitions reported having more than 55,000 volunteers who helped in furthering their activities, or more than 25 volunteers per coalition. Consistent with this picture are the reports of the twenty-four CSAP-funded coalitions where more than two thousand hours of volunteer effort were reported, on average, for each six-month reporting period from late 1993 to early 1996 (Substance Abuse and Mental Health Services Administration 2000). So, beyond enrolling partner/members, who may do little more than attend regular coalition meetings, these groups also field collective action projects that engage many local citizens in antidrug projects. The expansion of antidrug partnerships within and across communities, therefore, has certainly served to mobilize collective action around substance abuse issues.

Local sponsorship. The coalitions take a variety of forms. "Miami's coalition [for instance] was started by the business community. One of its founders is chairman of Knight Ridder newspapers and its executive committee consists only of non-governmental leaders. The coalition in San Francisco is located in the mayor's office. And in Boston there are two coalitions—one based in the mayor's office and another led by people from both the public and private sectors" (Substance Abuse and Mental Health Services Administration 2000, 15–16). About a quarter of the coalitions are based in government health agencies. Another 22 percent of them are freestanding groups. These groups are smaller and are more likely to be focused on alcohol issues. Fifteen percent of the groups are formal nonprofits based, for instance, in community centers and YMCAs. So, beyond the financial support available to these coalitions, local institutional sponsorship is also commonly available to them.

Issue/policy goals. More than 70 percent of the coalitions supported the following policy changes: restrictions on alcohol advertising, lower blood alcohol limits for young drivers, lower blood alcohol limits for adult drivers, increased taxes on alcohol, increased financial grants to community coa-litions, increased law enforcement of drug and alcohol laws, and increased penalties for the sale and possession of drugs. The vast majority of them opposed decriminalization of drug sales and possession, but few of them pursued activities aimed at accomplishing these particular goals.

Antidrug Partnerships as a Coalition Type

In spite of the barriers that have been identified in creating them, issue coali-tions are a very common organizational form at national, state, and local lev-els. It is not at all unusual that local issue coalitions include both individual and organizational members, and the organizations included may range from those primarily interested in the issues that drew the groups together to those with only tangential concerns about those issues. The wide prevalence of social change coalition structures has been clearly documented for local groups in the peace movement (Edwards and Foley 2003), the environmen-tal movement (Andrews and Edwards 2003, 2004), and among local groups working to empower poor citizens (McCarthy and Walker 2004), ranging between 10 and 25 percent of them.[6] The new community antidrug partner-ships are not unusual in their basic organizational form. They are distinc-tive both in the incredibly broad community representation in membership that they are capable of achieving and in the typically loose attachment that many members have to the coalitions themselves.

Before presenting the argument for their distinctiveness, I describe two state-level issue coalitions in the drug policy domain that provide an instructive contrast with one another with respect to the extent of their sup-port and the inclusiveness of their membership, both key to understanding the strengths of the local antidrug coalitions. I conclude this section with a brief description of the proliferation of local community coalitions within and well beyond the substance abuse issue domain.

State-Level Antidrug Coalitions

Minnesota Smoke-Free Coalition. Mark Wolfson's (2001, 75–81) rich ac-count of the formation of the Minnesota Smoke-Free Coalition locates its origins in a meeting convened by representatives of the Minnesota Medical Association and the Minnesota Department of Health:

> The coalition has worked on institutional policy, such as an effort to en-courage hospitals to go smoke-free. . . . The coalition has also been active in changing public policy. In 1988 it convinced the Metropolitan Sports Facility Commission to make the Metrodome Stadium (home of the

Minnesota Twins and Vikings) smoke-free. In addition, the coalition's Public Policy Committee has been extremely active in state legislation, working to pull together a more-or-less-coordinated lobbying effort of its constituent groups. (78)

The coalition emerged with very strong ties to the Association for Nonsmokers-Minnesota (ANSR). "ANSR was the first single-issue tobacco control organization in Minnesota, and one of the first such groups in the United States. It began as a program of the Hennepin County office of the American Lung Association in 1973 when a staff person and a group of volunteers began working on the issue of second-hand smoke" (49).

The composition of the coalition illustrates the ways in which the movement has built on the rich reservoir of resources (including money, legitimacy, and expertise) contained within state and local health organizations. The members of the coalition—which are organizations not individuals—included the following in the mid-1990s:

1. Health voluntary associations (the branches of ACS, AHA, and ALA)
2. Health care provider and insurer organizations (including Blue Cross Blue Shield, Health Partners, Medica, the Park Nicollet Medical Center and Foundation, the Mayo Clinic, and the Minnesota Medical Group Management Association)
3. Health professional associations (including the Hennepin County Medical Society Foundation, the Minnesota Medical Association and Minnesota Medical Association Auxiliary, and the Minnesota Society for Respiratory Care)
4. Tobacco control advocacy organizations (ANSR)
5. The University of Minnesota School of Public Health
6. Government agencies (the Hennepin County Community Health Department and the Minnesota Department of Health) (77)

Partnership for a Drug-Free America State/City Alliances. The Partnership for a Drug-Free America (PDFA) was begun in 1986 with a grant from the American Association of Advertising Agencies (Buchanan and Wallack 1998). By 1992 it was spending more than $350 million dollars on national and local media campaigns designed to reduce illicit drug use. The organization received support from a wide variety of businesses, including pharmaceutical, tobacco, and brewing companies. The group depended on pro bono contributions of media copy provided by advertising agencies, which were included in various media sources at either no cost or reduced cost.

In 1991 PDFA launched its

State/City Alliance Program [that] has grown to 55 member Alliances that reach more than 93 percent of all U.S. households. Working closely with the Partnership staff, each alliance creates a substance abuse prevention media campaign tailored to the specific needs of its communities. The objective of Alliance campaigns is to secure ongoing participation by every available media outlet. Partnership member Alliances deliver a depth of media penetration no national organization could ever hope to accomplish. Alliance efforts are strengthened by a corps of dedicated media volunteers, known as Key Market Coordinators (KMCs) in the top 50 media markets. These professionals, primarily senior executives of advertising agencies, serve as PDFA representatives in their cities and work closely with the media. The Partnership further supports its member Alliances with regional managers who oversee the nation's top 75 media markets.[7]

Surfing the Web sites of PDFA State/City Alliances suggests that many of them are housed in state and local public health substance abuse programs, although a significant minority appeared to be nested in freestanding substance abuse coalitions. It seems clear that PDFA has affiliated with preexisting community substance abuse prevention coalitions.

Drug Free Pennsylvania (DFP), for instance, is dedicated to using the power of the mass media and the strength of unions and businesses to reduce the demand for illegal drugs. DFP was begun in 1990, before the founding of the PDFA State/City Alliance program. The board of directors of DFP include the governor, attorney general, and physician general. They also include representatives of a bank, a number of businesses, the Pennsylvania Business Roundtable, the Pennsylvania Manufacturers Association, a U.S. attorney, Blue Cross Blue Shield, the Pennsylvania Medical Society, the Pennsylvania AFL-CIO, a judge, and members of the state legislature.

These two state-level antidrug coalitions differ, most obviously, in the diversity of their memberships. The Minnesota Smoke-Free Coalition includes primarily members who have a direct stake in the tobacco health issue,[8] while Drug Free Pennsylvania, judging from the affiliations of the members of its board of directors, includes representation from a far broader range of community institutions. This reflects, to some extent, the consensus surrounding public policy on these two issues. While almost no state-level organizations, institutions, or prominent individuals are likely any longer to speak out in favor of "substance abuse," an organized remnant, mostly composed of tobacco manufacturers and tobacco retailers, can and does continue to provide a public opposition (Wolfson 2001). To the extent that an issue threatens conflict in a state or a local community, the likelihood that a broad-based coalition will form to promote it is substantially reduced (see the *New York Times* archive for articles on local pro-tobacco advocacy).

Key Elements of the Local Antidrug Coalition Form

The most important organizational features of the local antidrug coalitions, and their public health cousins, are (1) the loose and informal nature of membership, (2) their large and extremely diverse memberships, and (3) the elite sponsorship and support they receive. The first two features are discussed here, and the third is discussed in the next section.

These coalitions are, typically, relatively weak organizational structures in that coalition partners have few formal requirements for attaining membership and there are few, if any, comprehensive expectations of membership behavior beyond attending coalition gatherings. A coalition partner usually allows his, her, or its name to be used by the coalition, thereby lending to the coalition, at least in part, whatever public legitimacy that name may possess. Membership also may imply that an organizational partner is willing to lend some of its people (employees and/or members) to the efforts of the coalition, might provide it other resources, especially including in-kind resources (such as meeting space and supplies), and might detail individuals to the coalition for temporary leadership roles. It is this looseness in the definition of membership of the coalitions that accounts for the fact that almost all of them include both individual and organizational members and gives membership in them its Velcro-like quality.

Many coalitions employ professional staff—recall that about a quarter of the substance abuse coalitions surveyed by Join Together reported annual budgets of over $500,000. It is typical, nevertheless, even if coalitions are staffed, that top leaders and highly involved board members serve as volunteers. This feature of coalitions advantages the best-resourced members in shaping a coalition's activities and issue foci.

The relatively nondemanding nature of membership means that coalitions may include members with widely varying strengths of commitment to its core issue, ranging from single-issue community organizations to businesses and governmental agencies that are only marginally concerned with much of the agenda of the coalition. This feature of coalitions means that their makeup is constantly shifting from year to year. At the same time, the composition of the constituent organizations that devote the most resources to coalition organizational maintenance and goal accomplishment is likely to be unstable from year to year. These shifting resource commitments are the result of a combination of the changing correspondence between the interests of constituent organizations and the coalition as well as changes in the ability of constituent organizations to lend resources to the coalition.

It is quite remarkable how large and incredibly diverse the memberships of these coalitions appear, based on the limited evidence we have available. As an organizational form, these coalitions seem to have been able to overcome the difficulties of uniting individuals and groups with diverse interests and cultures in common efforts. This achievement stems from a combination of loose membership requirements and the fact that the groups seek diffuse goals around the consensus issue of substance abuse. The strongly prosecuted war on drugs has turned the reduction of substance abuse into one that almost no group is prepared to challenge.

The looseness of membership attachment to coalitions—in contrast, for instance, to the tightness of attachment (through bureaucratic control as well as contractual relationships) of chapters to a national organization such as MADD—can be seen as a weakness of the coalition form giving it a transitory, more fragile character. On the other hand, coalitions appear to mirror the network form of organization identified by firm researchers (Powell 1990; Scott 1998). The strengths of that form are its greater flexibility and adaptability to changing environmental circumstances as compared with more traditional hierarchal forms.

The Broad Proliferation of Community Coalitions

Beyond the efforts to spawn coalitions by CSAP and RWJF that have been described, an additional "hundreds of millions of dollars are being invested in coalition development as a prevention and health promotion intervention" (Wandersman et al. 1996, 300). Other notable programs aimed at spawning local community issue coalitions include:

- SAFEKIDS—local, state, and national coalitions to prevent childhood injuries, supported by Johnson and Johnson
- The Kellogg Foundation's Community-Based Public Health Initiative funds consortia of schools of public health, local health case agencies, and community-based organizations to promote community-based public health training and service
- The National Cancer Institute's COMMIT and ASSIST community tobacco-control programs funded by the National Institutes of Health

- The PATCH cardiovascular health-promotion program granted by the U.S. Centers for Disease Control and Prevention
- Native-American tribe health-promotion efforts sponsored by the U.S. Office of Minority Health
- Health-promotion grant initiatives by the Henry J. Kaiser Family Foundation
- The Community Consortium Demonstration Project sponsored by the Centers for Disease Control and Prevention (ibid.)

In addition to these many efforts are those aimed at developing local healthy community coalitions. "The U.S. Department of Health and Human Services formally embraced the Healthy Communities concept in 1989, asking the National Civic League to help launch the U.S. Healthy Communities Initiative. . . . Since then, hundreds of community partnerships . . . and community-based organizations have adopted the Healthy Communities approach to community building" (Norris and Pittman 2000, 119–20). Further, Communities That Care coalitions have proliferated in recent years. These groups seek to organize local communities to promote health development of young people and families, focusing especially on substance abuse prevention (Hawkins and Catalano 1992). There are currently twenty-eight Communities That Care networks in Pennsylvania, for instance (Tammy Genzel, personal communication, 2003).

This extensive proliferation of local community issue coalitions has resulted in high densities of them in many communities. Enumerating partnerships across communities is quite difficult, but the director of the Penn State Prevention Research Center has done so for my own community (Mark T. Greenberg, personal communication, 2003). In State College, Pennsylvania, and its surrounding county, Centre County, there are at least thirteen community partnerships. These include the Tobacco Coalition, Centre County Communities That Care, Centre Region Communities That Care, Stand for Children, Smart Start–Centre County Child Care and Education Initiative, Interfaith Coalition, the Safety Net, Healthy Communities, GIN (Geriatric Interest Network), the Domestic Violence Coalition, the Housing Coalition, Workforce Coalition (PICCC, Career Links), the Partnership: United Against Dangerous Drinking.[9]

Elite Facilitation of Local Collective Action

Scholars of collective action have traditionally conceived of it as independent insurgent challenges that target and make claims on the state (Tilly 1978; Oberschall 1973; Gamson 1990; Oliver and Marwell 1992; McAdam,

McCarthy, and Zald 1988). While some analysts stress the indirect role of the state in facilitating collective action through the creation of opportunities and openings, there has been less attention by scholars of social movements to the direct role of the state in facilitating the emergence and expansion of collective action. This is true in spite of widespread evidence of such state facilitation. Even less attention has been paid to corporate facilitation, both direct and indirect, of social movements (see Useem and Zald 1982 and Pichardo 1995 for exceptions).

The extent of such facilitation comes as no surprise to those familiar with the work of scholars of interest groups, however. Jack Walker's Washington, DC, surveys (1991), for instance, showed extensive financial support being provided to facilitate the founding of citizens groups by both government (20 percent of the groups formed between 1960 and 1983) and corporations (35 percent of the groups formed during the same period). And the extensive funding of social movement organizations by private foundations, such as civil rights, environmental, and women's, has been well documented (Jenkins and Halci 1999). So the pattern of elite sponsorship we see for the antidrug coalitions is not a new one, although the sheer magnitude of it as revealed in the sponsorship of coalitions across local communities may represent a break from past experience in the United States. The thick interpenetration of the governmental, business, and nonprofit sectors in conceiving and spawning coalitions as well as participating in their ongoing operations at the local level may represent an important new trend, what Mark Wolfson calls "state-movement interpenetration" (2001). Evidence of this trend is illustrated in the conclusions reached by a group of scholars and nonprofit executives convened by the Aspen Nonprofit Sector Research Fund. The Nonprofit Sector Strategy Group calls attention to a rapidly increasing trend it calls "corporate citizenship," a new model of business-nonprofit engagement. "One outgrowth of this new approach is a new pattern of corporate engagement with the nonprofit sector, including . . . Broader 'community partnerships' in which corporations join with nonprofit organizations, and often government agencies, in long-term, multi-pronged efforts to address complex societal issues" (Nonprofit Sector Strategy Group 2001, 5). While wary of the risks entailed in such cooperation between sectors, the group also calls for additional investment in such cross-sector coalition forms.

What we see in the mobilization of community coalitions is a widespread effort to mobilize citizen engagement. Citizens typically do not get engaged unless they are provided opportunities to do so, and these organizational vehicles are a key mechanism for providing those opportunities

(McCarthy and Zald 2002). Consequently, facilitation of coalitions by governmental agencies, firms, foundations, and other nonprofit groups indirectly facilitates widespread citizen mobilization.

Facilitating Mechanisms

Provision by sponsors of collective action templates. One of the most important ways in which elite groups have mobilized these new coalitions is to generate and widely disseminate the template for creating one of them. The direct funding of local coalitions, of course, carries with it guidelines for creating them, but there now exist extensive written materials that provide the outlines of the coalition template for any group interested in starting one. Examples include *Community-Based Public Health: A Partnership Model* (Bruce and McKane 2000), published by the Kellogg Foundation and the American Public Health Association, and *The Spirit of Coalition* (Berkowitz and Wolff 2000), which is a manual for how to organize a coalition, how to raise funds for it, and how to run its meetings, develop its leaders, and recruit and retain members.

The assistance by elite sponsors in the creation of the Mothers Against Drunk Driving (MADD) chapter template provides another example of this mechanism. Soon after Candy Lightner held a press conference in Sacramento, California, to announce the formation of MADD, a public health consultant approached her to give the benefit of his wide experience in advocacy. He had soon facilitated the award of a grant from National Highway Traffic Safety Administration (NHTSA) that allowed him and Lightner to develop a set of materials that became the "chapter starter kit." Further support from NHTSA, supplemented with foundation support, helped disseminate these materials to local activists, first in California and then more widely across the United States. The development and dissemination of this collective action template greatly facilitated the rapid formation of local groups (McCarthy et al. 1988; McCarthy and Harvey 1989). The MADD template has been widely emulated since then. For instance, ACES, a group that works for more stringent child support enforcement, chose the MADD template after a systematic search prior to its founding. ACES crafted its own chapter startup materials on the MADD model, facilitating the founding of more than three hundred local chapters of the group in the late 1980s.

The provision of resources. Once coalitions have gotten organized, they may receive all kinds of resources contributed by local sponsors. Dan Cress and David Snow (1996, 1095), in their study of the mobilization of local homeless groups, developed a quite useful categorization of resource types, each of which had been made available by outside sponsors to at least some of the groups they studied.[10] In the extensive facilitation of coalitions we can find evidence of resource subsidies from elite sponsors for each of the types of resources they enumerate.

Moral resources include endorsements by external organizations and public figures of the aims and actions of a group. Beginning with the appointment of William Bennett as the first drug czar in the Reagan administration, accompanying its escalation of the war on drugs with the extensive involvement of First Lady Nancy Reagan, and continuing through the Bush and two Clinton administrations, the federal executive branch in the United States provided unstinting rhetorical and moral support to those citizens and groups who might wish to become engaged around the issue of drug abuse in their own communities (Baum 1996). With minor exceptions state authorities reinforced these messages.

We have already seen evidence of the extensive financial support of local coalitions by national, state, and local governments. In addition, many local institutional members, such as universities, law enforcement agencies, schools, and religions, may provide *material resources,* through grants as well as the provision of tangible goods and services such as supplies, meeting space, office space, and transportation.

Informational resources, including the provision of strategic support and technical support, are important to the functioning of local coalitions. As we have already seen, direct technical support to local coalitions are provided by CADA and Join Together, and extensive written materials, and now Web sites, created by foundations and other national groups, are available to them.

Human resources constitute one of the most important resources for local citizens groups, most of which, in contrast to these coalitions, have few material resources. Human resources consist of the provision of time and energy to a coalition. The diversity of membership in these coalitions, as seen in Figure 3.1, means that the motives for joining are quite varied. Individual members represent demographic groups including youth, people recovering from drug addictions, and concerned citizens, for instance. Their involvement should reflect a combination of the typical forces that generate social movement participation, including network connections, solicitations to potential members to participate, and enthusiasm on the part of those who are asked to participate for the coalition goals (Klandermans 1997). The vast majority of coalition members, however, are representatives of organizations, associations, as well as public and private agencies. Since these members are usually delegated to the coalition by their respective institutions, their membership may represent an organizational decision to affiliate rather than an individual one. The motives for these organizations may include enthusiasm for the diffuse goals the coalition pursues but probably also include at least the public relations value of involvement and the desire to shape the activities of the coalition in the organization's interests. Constituent coalition partner organizations vary extensively in the procedures employed in deciding to become a coalition member. These range from authoritative CEO choices in more hierarchical firms, through delegation based on technical divisions of labor in many agencies, to consensus processes of delegation among some citizens groups. In any case, many representatives are delegated, and, as a result, their participation is not fully voluntary and is normally considered part of their employment obligation.

To the extent that broad support within coalition partner organizations is necessary for membership, more controversial issues will limit the likelihood of developing broad coalition memberships. It is this process that led Gary Delgado (1986) to notice that community organizations consisting of coalitions of religious congregations were quite restricted in the kinds of issues they were able to agree to pursue together. Co-opting a wide range of organizations into an issue coalition is probably only feasible around the framing of issues that find wide community support (McCarthy and Wolfson 1992; McCarthy and Walker 2004).

How Antidrug Coalitions Shape the Mobilization of Local Collective Action

The historically situated coalition template that has been created around the substance abuse issue and other similar public health issues in recent years appears to have been effective as a tool to mobilize extensive and far-reaching collective action in local communities. What are the implications of this success for the landscape of citizen collective action in communities across the United States? And what are the consequent implications for local public attention and policy agendas?

Antidrug coalitions have succeeded in mobilizing vast numbers of individuals and groups in communities across the United States during the last decade. The coalition form, in general, has advantages for mass mobilization over social issue organizations that recruit citizen members one by one. Most important is the efficiency of "bloc recruitment" (Oberschall 1973). Recruiting an organization to join a coalition is similar to recruiting an African-American congregation to join a civil rights campaign. If successful, such a strategy can produce large numbers of supporters far more efficiently than recruiting isolated individuals one by one. This is true, of course, only to the extent that the leaders of coalition partner organizations can deliver the support of their organizational members and/or employees.

These coalitions generate opportunities for citizen engagement for the individuals who participate in them, even if many of those participants are involved only as a result of having been detailed to the coalition by the organization that employs them. Many other participants come representing citizens groups, and others only themselves. And these coalitions, as we have seen, mobilize extensive volunteer efforts. This is a form of citizen engagement that has not been noticed, or accounted for, by those who have lamented its ostensible decline and attempted to chronicle its extent and form in the recent period (Putnam 2000; Skocpol 1999: Wuthnow 1998). Even if they had noticed this burst of citizen engagement, those observers would most likely not have been heartened by it. Those who lament the decline of citizen participation, like those who analyze insurgent collective action, imagine citizen collective action as a process that aggregates citizen preferences from the bottom up. Elite social construction of issues and top-down mobilization of citizen preferences is unlikely to be viewed as a solution to the atrophy of citizen engagement.

Elite sponsorship of local collective action, when it is as successful as the antidrug campaign has been in mobilizing local actors, has important consequences in shaping the aggregate issue focus of local collective action. These consequences occur through the related mechanisms of channeling and crowding.

Channeling occurs when environmental factors narrow and direct either the form or the substance of collective action. Channeling effects have been identified in at least two important environmental mechanisms, state regulation of organizational form and elite financial support. State regulation of collective action in the United States operates primarily through federal rules governing nonprofit organizations and has its greatest impact on organizational form and tactics. Regulated collective actors display remarkable homogeneity in organizational form and extreme moderation in their choice of tactics (Cress 1997; McCarthy, Britt, and Wolfson 1991). And although large proportions of social movement groups who receive no elite funding do register, elite financial support almost always carries with it the requirement that a group register, usually as a 501(c)3 entity.[11]

The channeling mechanism of elite financial support operates, as well, by facilitating some subset of collective actors who are thereby privileged in their efforts to mobilize around their chosen issues (Jenkins and Eckert 1986). In this way the substantive mix of collective action is shaped. Channeling citizen collective action to substance abuse has certainly had the effect of privileging the set of issues subsumed under its broad frame in local communities across the nation. Elite funding has manufactured what appears to be widespread grassroots mobilization in support of the war on drugs. Recall that the Join Together survey found overwhelming support among antidrug coalitions for a number of specific policy changes, such as increased law enforcement and penalties for drug possession. It is quite clear that this elite-sponsored mobilization has had a direct impact on local policy attention cycles as well as the setting of priorities on local policy agendas.

In addition to channeling, there is another related mechanism that may have an even more important impact in local communities, *mobilization crowding*. Most scholarly attention to these channeling mechanisms, as well as to policy attention and policy agenda setting for that matter, focuses on the national level. At that level it is implicitly assumed that there is an unlimited supply of collective actors, so even if some of them are privileged in receiving elite support and thereby are able to mobilize more extensively, other collective actors pursuing different and competing substantive agendas are likely to slog on in any case. But at the local level it is more reasonable to believe that issue mobilization is more finite, at the extreme limited by the available time of individual and collective actors. While not completely a zero-sum game, widespread local mobilization around one substantive issue agenda has a high likelihood of crowding out mobilization around other substantive agendas. Elite funding for issues agendas in local communities, then, not only has the effect of privileging some collective actors over others, it may actually inhibit the emergence of collective actors around competing issue agendas. It remains to be seen whether the emergence and growth of the many coalitions discussed, those spawned by the war on drugs and their public health cousins, have crowded out other efforts to mobilize citizen action in local communities. If this is the case, then the enormous elite penetration of local communities described here may itself bear some responsibility for the ostensible atrophy of citizen engagement by absorbing the efforts of many potential "individual" community activists into collective action projects that focus their energies through their professional locations rather than their personal values.

The community coalition form, with its loose, Velcro-like membership features, is particularly well suited as a vehicle for extensive and diverse issue mobilization in local communities. Its rapid diffusion across issue arenas provides evidence of both its perceived effectiveness as well as its institutional legitimacy. Because the template is a public good, activists pursuing different causes can easily adapt it to their own purposes. My analysis suggests, however, that its appropriateness should be limited to local issues that have been successfully framed as ones with wide community support.

Finally, my speculations on the local impact of the elite-sponsored prolif-eration of antidrug coalitions on local social policy processes remain that—just speculation. Researchers of social movement emergence and activities as well as researchers of public policy processes have mostly ignored local communi-ties. As a result, we know very little about either domain in local communities and, as a result, almost nothing about how social movement mobilization at the community level affects local issue attention, policy attention, or policy-setting and implementation processes. The almost universal penetration of local communities by the antidrug coalition movement continues to provide an excellent opportunity to explore these questions.

Notes

Thanks go to Andrew Martin, David Meyer, and Mark Wolfson who provided me valuable feedback on earlier drafts of this paper.

1. These short-term coalitions are also often labeled "policy networks" (Lau-mann and Knoke 1987; Helco 1978; Peterson 1993).

2. The scholarship on this war is quite modest. Most of it is oppositional, but very little of it makes an attempt to describe and analyze its strategy and structure and how it affects local communities (e.g., Baum 1996; Betram et al. 1996; Mass-ing 2000).

3. See Jellinek and Hearn (1991) and Spickard and Sarver (1994) for more detail on the background of the Fighting Back initiative.

4. Little systematic evidence is available about the full array of commu-nity substance abuse coalitions beyond the results of the Join Together survey (see Couto 1998 and Butterfoss, Goodman, and Wandersman 1993 for exceptions). On the other hand, we know more about drinking and driving coalitions (e.g., McCarthy and Wolfson 1996; McCarthy and Harvey 1989) and tobacco control coalitions (e.g., Rogers et al. 1993) that emerged in the 1980s and 1990s. Informa-tion garnered from descriptions of coalitions as well as anecdotal evidence will, therefore, also be introduced in this account of the modal patterns of substance abuse coalitions. More often, the accumulating body of research on coalitions attempts to assess their impact on local communities without first attempting to describe variations in exactly how they are organized and what they do (e.g., Saxe et al. 1997; Yin et al. 1997).

5. These coalitions were chosen to be part of a systematic evaluation of the impact of substance abuse partnerships (Substance Abuse and Mental Health Ser-vices Administration 2000).

6. A study of local protest events in Tucson, Arizona, found that eleven of

the fourteen events were fielded by coalitions of groups rather than a single group (Jones et al. 2001).

7. From the Partnership for a Drug-Free America's Web site, at http://www.drugfreeamerica.org/About-us.

8. This is also the case for the state-level Wisconsin victims coalition described by Weed (1995).

9. I am a member of the Partnership: United Against Dangerous Drinking. This coalition is touted as an exemplary anti–substance abuse partnership (Drug Strategies 2001, 24) and receives financial support from the Pennsylvania Liquor Control Board, Pennsylvania State University, the State College School District, and the State College Borough Police Department.

10. Earlier scholarship on collective action that stressed the importance of resources had not, however, paid close attention to operationalizing the key concept of resources (see McCarthy and Zald 2002). For an exception, see Oliver and Marwell (1992). Gary Marx developed a similar category scheme for describing the facilitation of social movements (1979, 96), although his primary interest was in the flip side of the dimensions, the repression of movements. His substantive analysis centered on the FBI "Cointelpro" program aimed at hindering the activities of social movement groups.

11. A group that registers with the U.S. Internal Revenue Service as a 501(c)3 receives certain beneficial tax advantages, but also agrees to abide by certain regulations governing its operations, including, most importantly, restrictions on its freedom to engage in partisan political activity.

References

Andrews, Kenneth T., and Bob Edwards. 2003. "The Impact of Political, Social, and Human Resources on the Spatial Distribution of Local Environmentalism." Paper presented at the annual meeting of the American Sociological Association, Atlanta.

———. 2004. "Advocacy Organizations in the American Political Process." *Annual Review of Sociology* 30: 479–506.

Arnold, Gretchen. 1995. "Dilemmas of Feminist Coalitions: Collective Identity and Strategic Effectiveness in the Battered Women's Movement." In *Feminist Organizations: Harvest of the New Women's Movement,* ed. Myra Marx Ferree and Patricia Yancey Martin, 276–90. Philadelphia: Temple University Press.

Baum, Dan. 1996. *Smoke and Mirrors: The War on Drugs and the Politics of Failure.* Boston: Little Brown.

Berkowitz, Bill, and Tom Wolff. 2000. *The Spirit of Coalition.* Washington, DC: American Public Health Association.

Bertram, Eva, Morris Blachman, Kenneth Sharpe, and Peter Andreas, eds. 1996.

Drug War Politics: The Price of Denial. Berkeley: University of California Press.

Bruce, Thomas A., and Steven Uranga McKane. 2000. *Community-Based Public Health: A Partnership Model.* Washington, DC: American Public Health Association.

Buchanan, David R., and Lawrence Wallack. 1998. "This Is the Partnership for a Drug-Free America: Any Questions?" *Journal of Drug Issues* 28: 329–56.

Butterfoss, Frances Dunn, Robert M. Goodman, and Abraham Wandersman. 1993. "Community Coalitions for Prevention and Health Promotion." *Health Education Research* 8: 315–30.

Bystydzienski, Jill M., and Steven P. Schact. 2001. Introduction to *Forging Radical Alliances across Difference: Coalition Politics for the New Millennium,* ed. Jill M. Bystydzienski and Steven P. Schact, 1–20. Boulder, CO: Rowman and Littlefield.

Couto, Richard A. 1998. "Community Coalitions and Grassroots Policies of Empowerment." *Administration of Society* 30: 569–94.

Cress, Daniel M. 1997. "Nonprofit Incorporation among Movements of the Poor: Pathways and Consequences for Homeless Social Movement Organizations." *Sociological Quarterly* 38: 343–60.

Cress, Daniel M., and David A. Snow. 1996. "Mobilization at the Margins: Resources, Benefactors, and the Viability of Homeless Social Movement Organizations." *American Sociological Review* 61: 1089–109.

Delgado, Gary. 1986. *Organizing the Movement: The Roots and Growth of ACORN.* Philadelphia: Temple University Press.

Drug Strategies. 2001. *Assessing Community Coalitions.* Washington, DC: Drug Strategies.

Edwards, Bob, and Michael Foley. 2003. "Social Movement Organizations beyond the Beltway: Understanding the Diversity of One Social Movement Industry." *Mobilization* 8: 85–107.

Gais, Thomas L., Mark A. Peterson, and Jack L. Walker. 1984. "Interest Groups, Iron Triangles, and Representative Institutions in American National Government." *British Journal of Political Science* 14: 161–81.

Gamson, William A. 1990. *The Strategy of Social Protest.* 2nd ed. Belmont, CA: Wadsworth.

Gerhards, Jurgen, and Dieter Rucht. 1992. "Mesomobilization: Organizing in Two Protest Campaigns in West Germany." *American Journal of Sociology* 98: 555–95.

Hallfors, Denise, Hyunsun Cho, David Livert, and Charles Kadushin. 2002. "Fighting Back against Substance Abuse: Are Community Coalitions Winning?" *American Journal of Preventive Medicine* 23: 237–45.

Hathaway, Will, and David S. Meyer. 1997. "Competition and Cooperation in Movement Coalitions: Lobbying for Peace in the 1980s." In *Coalitions and Political Movements: The Lessons of the Nuclear Freeze,* ed. Thomas R. Rochon and David S. Meyer, 61–79. Boulder, CO: Lynn Rienner.

Hawkins, J. David, and Richard F. Catalano Jr. 1992. *Communities That Care: Action for Drug Abuse Prevention.* San Francisco: Jossey-Bass.

Helco, Hugh. 1978. "Issue Networks and the Executive Establishment." In *The New American Political System,* ed. Anthony King, 87–124. Washington, DC: American Enterprise Institute.

Jellinek, Paul. S., and R. P. Hearn. 1991. "Fighting Drug Abuse at the Local Level: Can Communities Consolidate Their Resources into a Single System of Prevention, Treatment, and Aftercare?" *Issues in Science Technology* 7: 78–84.

Jenkins, J. Craig, and Craig M. Eckert. 1986. "Channeling Black Insurgency: Elite Patronage and Professional Social Movement Organizations in the Development of the Black Movement." *American Sociological Review* 51: 812–29.

Jenkins, J. Craig, and Abigail Halci. 1999. "Grassrooting the System? The Development and Impact of Social Movement Philanthropy, 1953–1990." In *Philanthropic Foundations: New Scholarship, New Possibilities,* ed. Ellen C. Lagemann, 229–56. Bloomington: Indiana University Press.

Join Together. 1993. *1993 Report to the Nation: Community Leaders Speak Out against Substance Abuse.* Boston: Boston University School of Health.

Jones, Andrew W., Richard N. Hutchinson, Nella Van Dyke, Leslie Gates, and Michelle Companion. 2001. "Coalition Form and Mobilization Effectiveness in Local Social Movements." *Sociological Spectrum* 21: 207–31.

Klandermans, Bert. 1997. *The Social Psychology of Protest.* Cambridge, MA: Blackwell.

Laumann, Edward O., and David Knoke. 1987. *The Organizational State: Social Choice in National Policy Domains.* Madison: University of Wisconsin Press.

Marx, Gary T. 1979. "External Efforts to Damage or Facilitate Social Movements: Some Patterns, Explanations, Outcomes, and Complications." In *The Dynamics of Social Movements,* ed. Mayer N. Zald and John D. McCarthy, 94–125. Cambridge, MA: Winthrop.

Massing, Michael. 2000. *The Fix.* Berkeley: University of California Press.

McAdam, Doug, John D. McCarthy, and Mayer N. Zald. 1988. "Social Movements." In *Handbook of Sociology,* ed. Neil J. Smelser, 695–737. Newbury Park, CA: Sage.

McCammon, Holly J., and Karen E. Campbell. 2002. "Allies on the Road to Victory: Coalition Formation between the Suffragists and the Woman's Christian Temperance Union." *Mobilization* 7: 231–51.

McCarthy, John D., David W. Britt, and Mark Wolfson. 1991. "The Channeling of Social Movements in the Modern American State." *Social Movements, Conflict, and Change* 13: 45–76.

McCarthy, John D., and Debra S. Harvey. 1989. "Independent Citizen Advocacy: The Past and the Prospects." In *The Surgeon General's Workshop on Drunk Driving: Background Papers,* Office of the Surgeon General, U.S. Public Health Service, 247–60. Washington DC: Department of Health and Human Services.

McCarthy, John D., and Edward T. Walker. 2004. "Alternative Organizational Repertoires of Poor People's Social Movement Organizations." *Nonprofit and Voluntary Sector Quarterly* 33, no. 3: S97–S119.

McCarthy, John D., and Mark Wolfson. 1992. "Consensus Movements: The Dynamics of Mobilization and Growth." In *Frontiers in Social Movement Theory,* ed. Carol Mueller and Aldon Morris, 273–97. New Haven, CT: Yale University Press.

———. 1996. "Resource Mobilization by Local Social Movement Organizations: The Role of Agency, Strategy, and Structure." *American Sociological Review* 61: 1070–88.

McCarthy, John D., Mark Wolfson, David P. Baker, and Elaine M. Mosakowski. 1988. "The Founding of Social Movement Organizations: Local Citizens Groups Opposing Drunken Driving." In *Ecological Models of Organizations,* ed. Glenn R. Carroll, 71–84. Cambridge, MA: Ballinger.

McCarthy, John D., and Mayer N. Zald. 2002. "The Enduring Vitality of the Resource Mobilization Theory of Social Movements." In *Handbook of Sociological Theory,* ed. Jonathan H. Turner, 533–65. New York: Kluwer Academic/Plenum.

Meyer, David S., and Thomas R. Rochon. 1997. "Toward a Coalitional Theory of Social and Political Movements." In *Coalitions and Political Movements,* ed. Rochon and Meyer, 227–52.

Nonprofit Sector Strategy Group. 2001. *The Nonprofit Sector and Business: New Visions, New Opportunities, New Challenges.* Washington, DC: Aspen Institute.

Norris, Tyler, and Mary Pittman. 2000. "The Healthy Communities Movement and the Coalition for Healthier Cities and Communities." *Public Health Reports* 115: 118–24.

Oberschall, Anthony. 1973. *Social Conflict and Social Movements.* Englewood Cliffs, NJ: Prentice-Hall.

Oliver, Pamela E., and Gerald Marwell. 1992. "Mobilizing Technologies for Collective Action." In *Frontiers in Social Movement Theory,* ed. Aldon D. Morris and Carol McClurg Mueller, 251–72. New Haven, CT: Yale University Press.

Peterson, M. A. 1993. "Political Influence in the 1990s—From Iron Triangles to Policy Networks." *Journal of Health Politics, Policy, and Law* 18: 395–438.

Pichardo, Nelson A. 1995. "The Power Elite and Elite-Driven Counter-Movements—The Associated Farmers of California during the 1930s." *Sociological Forum* 10: 21–49.

Powell, Walter W. 1990. "Neither Market nor Hierarchy: Network Forms of Organization." *Research in Organizational Behavior* 12: 295–336.

Putnam, Robert D. 2000. *Bowling Alone: The Collapse and Revival of American Community.* New York: Simon and Schuster.

Rochon, Thomas R., and David S. Meyer, eds. 1997. *Coalitions and Political Movements: Lessons of the Nuclear Freeze.* Boulder, CO: Lynn Rienner.

Rogers, Todd, Beth Howard-Pitney, Ellen C. Feighery, and David G. Altman. 1993. "Characteristics and Participant Perceptions of Tobacco Control Coalitions in California." *Health Education Research* 8: 345–57.

Rose, Fred. 2000. *Coalitions across the Class Divide: Lessons from the Labor, Peace, and Environmental Movements.* Ithaca, NY: Cornell University Press.

Saxe, Leonard, Emily Reber, Denise Hallfors, Charles Kadushin, Demos Jones, David Rindskopf, and Andrew Beveridge. 1997. "Think Globally, Act Locally: Assessing the Impact of Community-Based Substance Abuse Prevention." *Evaluation and Program Planning* 20: 357–66.

Scott, W. Richard. 1998. *Organizations: Rational, Natural, and Open Systems.* Upper Saddle River, NJ: Prentice Hall.

Skocpol, Theda. 1999. "Advocates without Members: The Recent Transformation of American Civic Life." In *Civic Engagement in American Democracy,* 461–510. Washington, DC: Brookings Institution/Russell Sage Foundation.

Spickard, A. G. Dixon, and F. Sarver. 1994. "Fighting Back against America's Public Health Enemy Number One." *Bulletin of the New York Academy of Medicine* 71: 111–35.

Staggenborg, Suzanne. 1986. "Coalition Work in the Pro Choice Movement: Organizational and Environmental Opportunity and Obstacles." *Social Problems* 33: 374–90.

Substance Abuse and Mental Health Services Administration. 2000. *Prevention Works through Community Partnerships: Findings from SAMHSA/CSAP's National Evaluation.* Rockville, MD: National Clearinghouse for Alcohol and Drug Information.

Tilly, Charles. 1978. *From Mobilization to Revolution.* Reading, MA: Addison-Wesley.

Useem, Bert, and Mayer N. Zald. 1982. "From Pressure Group to Social Movement: Efforts to Promote the Use of Nuclear Power." *Social Problems* 30: 144–56.

Van Dyke, Nella. 2003. "Crossing Movement Boundaries: Factors That Facilitate Coalition Protest by American College Students." *Social Problems* 50: 226–50.

Walker, Jack. 1991. *Mobilizing Interest Groups in America: Patrons, Professions, and Social Movements.* Ann Arbor: University of Michigan Press.

Wandersman, Abraham, Robert Valois, Leslie Ochs, David S. de la Cruz, Erica Adkins, and Robert M. Goodman. 1996. "Toward a Social Ecology of Community Coalitions." *American Journal of Health Promotion* 10: 299–306.

Weed, Frank. 1995. *Certainty of Justice: Reform in the Crime Victim Movement.* New York: Aldine de Gruyter.

Wolfson, Mark. 2001. *The Fight against Big Tobacco: The Movement, the State, and the Public's Health.* New York: Aldine de Gruyter.

Wuthnow, Robert. 1998. *Loose Connections: Joining Together in America's Fragmented Communities.* Cambridge, MA: Harvard University Press.

Yin, Robert K., Shakeh J. Kaftarian, Ping Yu, and Mary A. Jansen. 1997. "Outcomes from CSAP's Community Partnership Program: Findings from the National Cross-Site Evaluation." *Evaluation and Program Planning* 20: 345–55.

Zald, Mayer N., and John D. McCarthy. 1980. "Social Movement Industries: Competition and Cooperation among Movement Organizations." *Research in Social Movements, Conflicts, and Change* 3: 1–20.

Zald, Mayer N., and Bert Useem. 1987. "Movement and Countermovement Interaction: Mobilization, Tactics, and State Involvement." In *Social Movements in an Organizational Society,* ed. Mayer N. Zald and John D. McCarthy, 247–72. New Brunswick, NJ: Transaction Press.

II
The Social Movement–State Nexus: The Structure and Consequences of Interpenetration

Valerie Jenness

Social movement scholars and scholars of public policy have traditionally divided the social-political world between "insiders" and "outsiders" in order to develop an understanding of the complex relationship between social movements, the state, and public policy. Insiders are those located firmly within governmental institutions; by virtue of being most proximate to the policy-making process, they are most strategically located to determine the contours of public policy. Insiders are state bureaucrats, politicians, and others who, quite literally, write public policy. In sharp contrast, outsiders are those at least one step removed from the formal governing process; nonetheless, they try to influence the formulation, content, and implementation of public policy by engaging in contentious politics. To do so, grassroots activists, associations of all sorts, and the networks that surround them engage in what Best calls "outsider claimsmaking" (1990).[1]

They do so in response to extant public policy and/or to shape the formulation of new policy. With these key players in place, understanding the development and implementation of public policy has most often required examining when and how outsiders mobilize to pressure insiders to write some types of public policies and not others.

Although convenient for analytic purposes and certainly capable of yielding important theoretical insights, this traditional formulation of the relationship between social movements and the state is increasingly problematic. Recent empirical research reveals complicated social structures and processes that, in one way or another, render the boundaries between insiders (i.e., policy makers) and outsiders (i.e., social movement actors and organizations) fuzzy at best and completely misleading at worst. A more nuanced understanding of the interpenetration between social movements and the state is required. The next three chapters focus on very different empirical referents and historical eras in an effort to theorize the structures and processes through which the social movement–public policy nexus comes into being and proves consequential for policy.

In "Creating Credible Edibles: The Organic Agriculture Movement and the Emergence of U.S. Federal Organic Standards," Mrill Ingram and Helen Ingram focus on the passage of the Organic Food Production Act of 1990 to examine how regulatory law emerges and changes over time. Treating the passage of this federal law as "a major policy achievement for an effort long sidelined in mainstream agricultural politics," they draw on rich archival, interview, and media data to trace the origins and evolution of regulatory standards contained in this landmark legislation as well as the concept of organic itself. Doing so enables them to reveal the changing contours of a "public conversation" among key stakeholders, including organic farmers, retailers, scientists, environmentalists, certifiers and agency representatives, consumer groups, and politicians. The political dialogue and attendant policy trade-offs made between these stakeholders were shaped by rising public concern over food safety, longstanding resistance to federal agricultural policy, and a fast-growing market for organic products that represented both opportunity and risk for the development of public policy related to "creating credible edibles." This work offers a number of theoretical lessons about the interactive and mutually constitutive nature of the social movement–state nexus: social movement reliance on markets as a source of political opportunity can lead back to government; the content of proposed and enacted policy shapes the strategies of social movements and vice versa, and both change over different stages in the policy process; and, over the course of the policy-making process, social movements can move "inside" the state and the government can move "outside" the state even as the basic distinction between the two is reinforced.

Consistent with the arguments laid out in the chapter by Ingram and Ingram, in "Inside and Outside the State: Movement Insider Status, Tactics, and Public Policy Achievements," Lee Ann Banaszak argues we must re-examine the boundaries drawn between a social movement and "others," especially the state. Focusing on the case of the modern women's movement and public policy designed to enhance the status and welfare of women, especially equal employment policy, Banaszak draws on interview and demographic data to direct analytic attention to what she calls the "state-movement intersection." Departing from those who examine how institutional activists and movement institutionalization influence public policy, Banaszak compellingly argues that the state-movement intersection "consists of self-identified members of the movement who hold recognizable positions within the state." Accordingly, movements can be more or less located within state structures, especially along three measurable dimensions: the number of movement activists within the state, type of movement outsider status held by those inside the state, and type of location occupied within the state. Offering an empirical analysis of the first dimension—the number of women in state structures over time—Banaszak nonetheless hypothesizes that empirical work on all of these dimensions of the state-movement intersection advances our understanding of how public policy affects the development and composition of the state-movement intersection via the creation of new locations for movement activists within the state as well as new operating rules and norms; and, in turn, the structure of the state-movement intersection affects the development of both social movement tactics and public policy inspired by social movements.

Finally, Ryken Grattet continues the pursuit of a more nuanced view of the relationship between movements and states in his chapter on "The Policy Nexus: Professional Networks and the Formulation and Adoption of Workers' Compensation Reforms." By examining the social movement whose goal was to ensure that workers receive financial compensation for work-related injuries and attendant disabilities, Grattet explains how a constellation of political actors who constituted the policy nexus "pulled off a string of legislative victories in a short period of time." Arguing that movements that orientate toward social change via legislative reform and involve professionals rather than aggrieved persons might have different engagement processes with the state than other types of movements, Grattet skillfully demonstrates the ways in which movement professionals were uniquely situated to affect policy formation, in this case the passage of state-level workers' compensation laws throughout the United States in the early part of the twentieth century, insofar as they constitute social networks that tie actors together across organizations and space. Using both qualitative and quantitative data, Grattet shows how these ties were crucial to the timing, content, diffusion, and institutionalization of workers' compensation reform. Specifically, he demonstrates that the policy nexus in this case was composed of a network of relationships that linked state officials, researchers, and insurance men, but not labor or management, victims, or company owners. Moving away from the particulars of this case, Grattet argues that the policy nexus shapes policy making in three ways: it is critical for the development of policy templates that summarize abstract ideas for reform, which can emanate from diverse sectors of the nexus; it is an arena in which competing interests can be managed, which includes the development of justifications that can mute grounds for opposition; and it can be consequential for what policy proposals emerge as modal and diffuse across geopolitical units. These analytic arguments serve as the basis from which Grattet theorizes how a policy nexus can resolve the "problem of uniformity of action" via state-movement interpenetration that facilitates coordination of action.

Note

1. Joel Best, *Threatened Children: Rhetoric and Concern about Child-Victims* (Chicago: University of Chicago Press, 1990).

4

Creating Credible Edibles: The Organic Agriculture Movement and the Emergence of U.S. Federal Organic Standards

Mrill Ingram and Helen Ingram

When the U.S. Department of Agriculture released its proposed rules on organic food production for public comment in 1997, the response was very large—and largely negative. In the months following the release and invitation to comment, over a quarter of a million letters, postcards, and e-mails poured in from individuals, farmers, traders, environmentalists, scientists, and consumers, marking the largest public response ever to any USDA proposed regulations. What captured the attention of so many who commented on the draft rule was the inclusion of the use of genetically modified organisms (GMOs), irradiation, and sewage sludge as acceptable organic practice. The majority of the quarter of a million commentators voiced a decidedly negative reaction to these three aspects of the draft regulation. People wrote that they were "shocked" and "outraged," that the USDA had offered a "fatally flawed" proposal, an "insult to the intelligence of the organic community," and was trying to "hijack organic agriculture." Edward Brown, produce manager at Wedge Co-op in Minneapolis, summed it up for many when he said, "They have no interest in providing our organic community with a historically significant and correct rule. . . . they erase the lines that divide conventional and organic agriculture. We didn't realize the USDA language would benefit corporate agriculture and give them a beachhead into the organic movement" (Schmelzer 1998, 28).

The USDA got the message, or at least part of it, and responded to many of the comments, removing the offending three provisions and making other requested revisions to the proposed rule. A new draft rule moved through another round of comment in 2000 (the second version received almost forty-five thousand comments), and a final rule was published in the *Federal Register* in December 2000. Ten years after the Organic Food Production Act (OFPA) of 1990 authorized federal organic regulation, the alternative agriculture community achieved a set of federal standards for organic agriculture—standards that not only establish unified rules for the production and handling of all organic food in the United States, but also legitimize a once-alternative mode of food production as an established sector of the contemporary food system.

Alternative agriculture embraces a great diversity of farming practices. The new federal regulations focus on organic production, which is defined in the law as "management practices that foster the cycling of resources, promote ecological balance and conserve biodiversity." Organic management practice eschews the application of synthetic chemicals, particularly pesticides and fertilizers. For many consumers, "organic" has come to signify cleaner, safer, and more healthful food and an alternative to the conventional system of food production. The comment period was a significant event in the evolution of the alternative agriculture movement and in the emergence of the organic food industry, and marks a major policy achievement for an effort long sidelined in mainstream agricultural politics. This chapter examines the emergence of the organic regulations and uses them as a focal point for entering into the discussion of how social movements influence policy formation and the evolution of social movements trying to effect political change.

Theoretical Implications

Recent literature on public policy and social movements emphasizes the way in which policy and citizen movements influence each other, pointing to the need to examine the "multidimensional connections" and "iterative interactions" between social movements and the policy process (Meyer, introduction to this volume; also see McAdam, McCarthy, and Zald 1996; Tarrow 1998). In their work on the emergence of new institutions, Rao, Morrill, and Zald examine organizational "field conditions" that "set many of the political constraints and opportunities that social movements and new organizational forms face as they emerge and attempt to sustain themselves" (2000, 249). Within this context, the authors examine how new institutions and new policies arise as activists construct boundaries around, and validate, new activities and organizations (2000, 241).

This case study attempts to contribute to our understanding of the interactive relationships between social movements and public policy by examining both the "field conditions" for the emergence of organic agriculture and the processes by which activists established new institutional forms and validated them. Our case study sheds light on credibility seeking in social movements, how marginal groups strategize and frame their arguments in order to establish themselves as experts to be included within the boundaries of legitimate discourse (Brulle 2000; Rochon 1998). At the federal level, U.S. agricultural policy has long been a classic example of policy stasis in which an "iron triangle" of agency personnel, agricultural commodity interest groups and agribusiness, and members of congressional subcommittees set budget and spending priorities to serve the interests they represent (Batie 1985). How the organic agriculture movement was able to turn a modest opportunity presented in the Organic Food Production Act of 1990 into a site and forum for mobilization is instructive about the ways in which movements can affect policy change even in hostile environments.

While there has been a great deal of scholarly attention directed to the ways in which social movements affect public policy, less attention has been given to the relationships between social movements and economic forms. Cultural institutional scholars have theorized about the social embeddedness of markets and the extent to which new organizational forms, including economic institutions, emerge in the context of actions taken by governmental institutions and social mobilization of networks around shared ideas and cultural frames (Davis and McAdam 2000; Lounsbury, Ventresca, and Hirsch 2002). Fligstein (1996) goes so far as to adopt a "markets as politics" approach. The organic movement has received tremendous support and affirmation in the marketplace, and the ability of activists to develop new institutions and policies, especially around organic certification, were critical building blocks in the construction of federal-level organic regulation. The legitimacy they gained through this process gave them a foothold in an unfriendly federal agricultural establishment, forcing the government into a contradictory position in which it attempted to both support status quo agricultural interests and agency positions and also to respond, and appear legitimate to, growing civic interest in alternative food production (O'Connor 1998). The marketplace also generated widespread consumer support for the movement, enabling it to push for a different kind of construction of the food system from that prevailing in mainstream agriculture. Just how different this construction is now that the regulations are in place—the extent to which organics addresses resource inequalities or represents a redistribution of access and privilege—remains to be seen, a point we return to later.

The organic movement evolved dramatically as a result of its involvement in the market and policy spheres. This case provides an opportunity to examine not only cultural aspects of the marketplace and shifts in economic organization as a result of social movement action (Lounsbury, Ventresca, and Hirsch 2002), but also how successful involvement in the market fed back to affect the relative strength of different components of the social movement, even the concept of organic itself (Jenness and Grattet 2001). As we will make clear, the commercial adherents in the organic movement gained ground by capitalizing on widespread and increasing consumer concern over food safety. Imperatives of the market, such as the need to distinguish the organic agricultural product from competitors, encouraged the social movement to pursue some strategies rather than others in its efforts in the public policy arena.

The organic regulations have been lauded as a tremendous accomplishment in establishing in the mainstream a way of farming that only two decades ago was considered the turf of back-to-the-land cranks (Youngberg, Schaller, and Merrigan 1993). Even with the changes made by the USDA in response to public comment, however, the regulations have also been described as a failure for the organic movement, particularly because they increase the challenges faced by smaller farmers and ease entry for large agribusinesses and others who do not embrace core values of the movement (Gershuny 2002; Goodman 2000; Guthman 1998; Lilliston and Cummins 1998; E. Lipson 1998; Sprinkle 2002; Vos 2000). The discourse around the regulations reflects anticipation and dread as a once sidelined movement merged into the mainstream. Involving the original farm groups who pushed for organic certification at the state level, the commercial interests who lobbied Congress for federal legislation, and the quarter of a million interested consumers who commented on the draft organic rule, the organic regulations are a product of what has been called a "public conversation" (Robinson 2002). With the ongoing role of the National Organic Standards Board in implementation (about which we say more later), appeals for changes to and exemptions from the rule, and participation of diverse groups with explicit expectations about the goals of the law, this is clearly a continuing conversation.

The newness of the legislation makes difficult any final pronouncement on success or failure or the extent to which associated new forms represent strong "speciation." Rao, Morrill, and Zald classify new organizations in terms of strong or weak speciation depending on the distinctions between new and old "core features," including goals, authority relations, technology, and served markets (Rao, Morrill, and Zald 2000; Scott 1995). Success, as scholars of both social movements and policy have pointed out, is not easy to establish (Ingram and Mann 1980; Meyer 2000). The debates about whether or not the regulations are a victory or a defeat raise the issue of co-optation, for example, a concept that has marked studies of social movements and their relationship to government agencies since Philip Selznick's study of how a progressive social agenda in the Tennessee Valley Authority was sacrificed to achieve a political and organizational victory (Selznick 1966). William Gamson in *The Strategy of Social Protest* defined the notion of co-optation to mean the acceptance of a social movement as a legitimate policy actor but without fundamental gains in policy action (1975). More recently, scholars have looked past a black-and-white definition of co-optation in order to better understand the trade-offs social movements make in order to achieve political goals or wider social appeal (Campbell 2001; Meyer 2000). We also wish to move beyond an all-or-nothing concept of co-optation and to examine the policy process as it illuminates how social movements strategize and frame their arguments in order to achieve political victory and wider appeal and how this process influences the choice of policy tools and, ultimately, the makeup of the social movement itself. This dynamic is essential to understanding the ongoing national "conversation" about the organic rule.

Information and evidence for this case study comes from many sources, as we sought to track the discourse of organic agriculture over time and across institutional arenas (Hajer 1995; Jenness and Grattet 2001; Lounsbury, Ventresca, and Hirsch 2002). Analysis of minutes from National Organic Standards Board meetings, ongoing since the drafting of the original rule, has been complemented with interviews with people involved. Organic farmers, certifiers, and agency representatives were also interviewed about their perspectives on the evolution of the regulations. Besides examination of governmental and trade reports about the progress of the industry and attendance at organic farming workshops and meetings, our research included a content analysis of public comments made to the USDA about the draft rule, a sample of which was made available on the USDA's National Organic Program (NOP) Web site. We also conducted a content analysis of newspaper articles on organic agriculture in the *New York Times* and the *San Francisco Chronicle* between 1989 and 2000, which allowed us to track changes in the level of mainstream media attention, the tone of the stories, sources of authority identified, and the continuity of specific goals and issues, including human health, environmental health, and agricultural economics.[1]

Field Conditions: The Traditional Agricultural Policy Monopoly

We begin with the fate of early attempts to introduce concepts related to alternative and organic agriculture into mainstream political circles, and focus on the policy monopoly tying the Department of Agriculture to commodity groups and agribusiness. Public policy scholars have taught us that policy stasis is more common than policy change, and that networks of interests sharing common core beliefs and orientations to problems come to dominate not only policies, but the institutions that make and implement policy (Baumgartner and Jones 1991; Jenkins-Smith and Sabatier 1994). As noted, agricultural politics is a quintessential example of this kind of stasis, an example of an iron triangle of commodity groups, district representatives, and federal bureaucracy that has maintained itself for decades. Since the Progressive era in the early twentieth century, the Department of Agriculture has been broadly involved in agricultural research and education. Most pre–New Deal programs were built from the bottom up in response to agrarian demands (Sanders 1999). This strong clientele-service orientation of the Department of Agriculture was institutionalized in the passage of the New Deal's Agricultural Adjustment Act of 1933, which prescribed parity prices for the commodities that farmers produced and initiated vast agricultural programs administered by the federal Department of Agriculture.

Over time, farmers' political access gravitated from the traditional lobby group, the Farm Bureau, toward constituency groups reflecting the predominant commodities grown in particular congressional districts (Hansen 1991). By the 1950s, commodity interests were structured into the organization of Congress. The House Committee on Agriculture was dominated by ten commodity subcommittees that drew membership from congressional representatives whose districts grew mainly those particular crops. It was rare for legislators to serve on subcommittees where there was not a specific benefit to their particular districts. Informal rules of specialization and reciprocity dictated that subcommittee recommendations related to particular commodities were seldom challenged in committee or even on the floor of Congress (Jones 1961, 1962). The constituency orientation of the House Agricultural Committee has persisted, despite the declining numbers of farmers and strong challenges mounted by consumer and environmental groups (Hurwitz, Moiles, and Rohde 2001).

This commodity agriculture domination of Congress and the USDA extends beyond price supports to include research. Through its "competitive" grants programs, the agricultural establishment has strong links to production-oriented researchers at land-grant universities (Marcus 1994; NRC 2001). These researchers are closely tied to large agribusiness firms that supply seeds, chemical fertilizers, pesticides, and, increasingly, genetically modified agricultural products (Kloppenburg 1988). The resilience and persistence of this network is remarkable, especially in the face of shrinking numbers of farmers and relative contribution to national economic welfare.

During the 1960s and the 1970s, organic agriculture bore a highly negative connotation in political circles. The rejection of synthetic pesticides and fertilizers by organic practitioners was ridiculed as belonging to an antiquated era in production agriculture, and critics discounted it as regressive and unscientific (Youngberg, Schaller, and Merrigan 1993). In a 1971 statement on organic farming, former secretary of agriculture Earl Butz said, "We can go back to organic farming if we must—we know how to do it. However, before we move in that direction, someone must decide which 50 million of our people will starve" (Butz 1971, 19). In the 1980s, proponents and lobbyists attempted to defuse the damaging organic image by adopting new terminology, such as "low-input agriculture" and "sustainable agriculture." The new labels did little to ensure legislative success, however. Attempts in 1982 and 1985 by the few friends of organic agriculture in Congress to introduce legislation to facilitate and promote the scientific investigation and understanding of methods of organic farming and to assist family farmers and others to use organic methods, got nowhere. The 1985 farm bill shunned the use of the term "sustainable," let alone "organic" (Youngberg, Schaller, and Merrigan 1993, 302). It was not until 1988 that Congress initiated a low-input sustainable agriculture research and education program with the tiny appropriation of $3.8 million. Hundreds of millions, in comparison, were allocated for conventional farming research and education programs to produce commodities that were also price supported by government. The new program was misinterpreted by some to be not a new approach to farming, but business as usual, just with fewer inputs. Proponents of alternative agriculture who tried to redirect federal farm policy learned from these experiences that Congress and the USDA were not interested in providing them with the same kind of distributive benefits, such as research and education, as was provided to conventional agriculture.

Despite numerous pledges of Democratic and Republican administrations to put an end to costly agricultural programs benefiting the few, the traditional policy monopoly has persisted—as the passage of the 2002 farm bill exemplifies. Modest efforts on the part of the Bush administration's secretary of agriculture Ann Veneman to redirect how government gives out $20 billion each year in farm subsidies, were brought to a swift halt in 2001. Her predecessor, Dan Glickman, who served as agricultural secretary for six years during the Clinton administration, was not surprised. He remarked, "By and large we went along with Congress on farm programs. Agricultural committees are very parochial but very powerful. I worked on things like food safety where I could make a difference, and stayed away from farm subsidies where I couldn't make much difference" (Becker 2001, 14).

Veneman's experience and Glickman's comment contribute to our understanding of the "field conditions" for the emergence of new forms in agriculture. The arena of federal agricultural policy is characterized by the domination of a few groups of influential actors who resist changes to the status quo (Rao, Morrill, and Zald 2000, 260). At the same time, however, the larger field of agricultural policy is broad and diverse, extending beyond production and subsidies to include a whole galaxy of issues such as international trade, the development of new technologies, nutrition, rural development, migrant labor, food security, and food safety. As we will review in the next section, recurrent problems and institutional failure in a number of these overlapping areas provided opportunities for the organic movement. Morrill has discussed this as the "interstitial emergence" of new institutional forms, which he describes as the result of activists and other players in "overlapping fields" who critique existing practices and innovate and create new forms, gaining legitimacy as their causes and ideas resonate across multiple overlapping fields (Morrill 2003).

Roots and Branches of the Alternative Agriculture Movement

Despite its policy dominance, production-oriented commodity agriculture has had long-standing critics. In fact, ever since the application of synthetic chemicals in farming began to emerge as a solution to soil fertility and pest problems, farmers and others were voicing concerns over the environmental sustainability of such practices and critiquing the social implications and perceived collusion of government and industry in the support of the "chemical" approach to growing food. Sir Albert Howard expressed his dismay at the current state of agriculture in Britain in 1940: "The amalgamation of the artificial manure industry, the Ministry of Agriculture, the experiment stations, the agricultural colleges, the agricultural press, and the country agricultural committees is complete. All urge upon the farmer and the gardener the use of more and more chemicals almost as a moral duty" (1940, 7).

Howard's critique was echoed many times during the ensuing decades, as proponents of organics continued to voice skepticism and mistrust of the science and government involvement in agriculture, skepticism fueled by the reality of government's exclusive support for a commodity and production orientation in agriculture. Publisher J. R. Rodale imported and fostered many of Howard's ideas in the United States, and despite the hostile atmosphere in land-grant universities and university extension programs toward alternative farming practices, the movement continued to grow (Youngberg, Schaller, and Merrigan 1993). Often the people who chose to pursue alternative farming methods were those who were consciously turning their backs on mainstream practice, such as independent-minded farmers suspicious of government-funded advice in the first place or "back-to-the-landers," who had not grown up farming but turned to an agricultural way of life explicitly as an avenue to move away from mainstream culture and government (Youngberg 1978).

It is worth emphasizing that the new federal organic standards represent a narrow slice of what is a very diverse arena of thoughts and actions about agriculture. The alternative agriculture movement has always included both a critique of conventional agriculture and agricultural science as well as diverse innovations in growing food and fiber (M. Ingram 2004). It has been built through the on-farm research of individual farmers and also through long-lived institutions including publishing houses and research institutes, such as Rodale and Acres U.S.A., and supported by "critical communities" of farmers, crop consultants, university scientists, publishers, journalists, gentleman farmers, gardeners, health officials, and others—the very definition, perhaps, of "organic intellectuals" (Epstein 1996; Gieryn 1999; Rochon 1998).

In the organic sector, the development of a growing market niche during the 1970s and 1980s necessitated means to verify or guarantee to consumers that products were in fact grown without chemicals. Farmers organized themselves into organic growers' associations, created educational and certification programs, and sponsored their own organic labels. The programs were self-regulatory: like beauticians, barbers, real estate brokers, construction contractors, and other professionals who set their own standards for practice, organic farmers performed inspections, served on certification boards, and set the bar blocking entrance to competitors who did not conform to standards defined as organic—much of this work on a volunteer basis. Organic activists have been described as a "resilient and self-reliant group of individuals, who do their own research, their own teaching, their own extension, develop their own companies . . . craft their own organizations in a complete vacuum of institutional support or government funding" (Clark 2001, 30).

A profusion of different labels and concern over fraud soon encouraged advocates in some states to seek state government involvement and certification. As early as 1974, Oregon passed a law defining "organic." California farmers established California Certified Organic Farmers in 1973 and followed Oregon's lead in writing a state law that passed in 1980 (E. Lipson 1998). By the mid-1990s over half the states had laws or rules, many of them substantially different from one another, regulating the production and marketing of organically grown food and fiber (Greene 2001). These

early efforts "trickled up" to the federal level, and as part of increasing interest in alternative approaches to food production, the USDA funded a report
published in 1980 on organic farming (USDA 1980).[2]

Trouble in the Mainstream, Opportunity in the Market

Although the government report was well received by many, it did little to
change existing policy. The impetus for more radical change only occurred
as economic, environmental, and social ills in conventional agriculture
began to accumulate throughout the 1980s (Adams 2003) and as the organic product gained success in the marketplace. In the mid-1980s more
than two hundred thousand farms went bankrupt. The EPA identified
agriculture as the largest nonpoint source of water pollution. Pesticides and
nitrates from fertilizers and manures were identified in the ground waters
of most states. Pesticide and other chemical residues and antibiotics in food
became major issues, exemplified by the Alar apple scare of 1989. Alar,
Uniroyal Chemical Company's trade name for the compound daminozide,
is a synthetic growth promotant and was sprayed on apples so that entire or-
chards would ripen at the same time. Growing evidence of Alar as a human
carcinogen fueled a *60 Minutes* story based on a Natural Resources Defense
Council report on the toxicity of Alar and its particular risks for children.
Public outcry, including support from actress Meryl Streep, caused the
chemical to be removed from the market. Food safety and the dangers of
pesticides were on the public agenda for the long term. Interest grew in
"chemical-free" food, and organic food began to appear in supermarkets
like Wegmans and Safeway. "Don't Panic, Eat Organic" became the catch-
phrase for an emerging organic industry capitalizing on widespread consumer concern about food safety.[3] Continuing public concern about the
impacts of chemical residues on produce, especially for children, helped
pass the comprehensive Food Quality Protection Act in 1996. Organic
dairy products, especially milk, which form such a large percentage of
children's diets, saw some of the earliest and most explosive market growth,
especially in the wake of concerns about the use of the growth hormone
rBGH (DuPuis 2000).

As Rao, Morrill, and Zald have noted, organizational and market
failures create new possibilities. Opportunities for change arise "when
problems or issues persistently spill over from one organizational field to
another" (2000, 242). Although most consumers purchase organic food
out of concern for their own or their children's health, consumer surveys
have found environmental protection to be a significant motivating factor
(Greene 2001). In response to increased economic pressures and technologi-

cal "advances," much of the farming sector has for decades experienced increased concentration and integration, resulting in more and larger factory-type farming operations. This trend has supported dramatic changes in rural areas, including shifts in labor demographics, working conditions, and new environmental problems. Rural residents have found themselves living near huge livestock operations, holding thousands, even millions, of animals. Problems with smell, noise, and air and water pollution have created an increasingly critical public view of agriculture, reflected to some extent in increasing legislative and regulatory attention, such as the U.S. EPA's rules on "Confined Animal Feeding Operations" and many state and county government attempts to restrict livestock operation expansion. For multiple reasons and in many places, conventional agriculture has become a new environmental frontier.

Many activists in the organic movement have long bemoaned the lack of emphasis paid by the organic movement to the environment (Gussow 1991). Certainly, the environmental movement has historically paid little attention to agriculture. However, there has been increasing attention to environmental abuses in agriculture and corresponding interest in the ecological emphasis in organic agriculture. In 1989, the National Research Council published a report illustrating some environmental benefits of alternative farming (NRC 1989). These issues represented tremendous opportunity for the organic movement, helping to provide critical masses of supporters and developing a resonant "frame" for organics (Snow and Benford 1992).

An Initial Victory: The 1990 Organic Food Production Act

By the end of the 1980s, the hodgepodge of state regulations and inconsistent practices were increasingly problematic for interstate commerce. In addition, problems with fraudulent claims of organic, and a rumor that the FDA wanted an outright ban on the organic label, helped push a diverse group of supporters to work together for wider-spread legislation (E. Lipson 1998). By that time the organic market was already enjoying the 20 percent annual growth rate that it sustained throughout the following decade (Greene 2001). Its potential was clear to anyone involved in the emerging industry, and a federal standard promised to facilitate interstate and international trade, promote consumer confidence, and protect the organic product from being absorbed by existing agribusiness. Besides organic farmer groups, who were often represented by certifying agencies, state governments were increasingly interested in promoting economic development around organics. Sponsors of bills during the late 1980s for federal organic legislation included senators Peter DeFazio of Oregon, Gary Condit of California, Wyche Fowler of Georgia, and Richard Lugar of Indiana. Consumer groups provided another significant source of support. According to some, the Alar scare was the pivotal event that led to federal-level involvement in organic regulations (E. Lipson 1998; Pollan 2001). Certainly it provoked a surge of interest from consumers. The event caused the Center for Science in the Public Interest to expressly support national organic legislation, gathering a petition of 236,000 signatures asking for a bill.

Much of the impetus and financial backing for the push for federal-level organic legislation came, however, from the commercial sector. As organic marketing moved beyond the food stands where local farmers sold produce to city dwellers, a complex network of packers, wholesalers, processors, and retailers emerged and institutionalized itself in a number of trade associations with avowedly political goals. Representing the largest of the organic trade interests, the Organic Trade Association (OTA) made the passage of the 1990 Organic Foods Production Act a major target. The OTA (then known as the Organic Foods Production Association of North America) was part of the Organic Food Alliance, a group formed explicitly to support an umbrella set of guidelines for use of the term "organic." As Mark Retzloff, a founder of Horizon Organic Dairy and past president of the OTA board put it, "Many of us had seen the term 'natural' become diluted and meaningless, and we didn't want to see that happen to 'organic'" (E. Lipson 1998, 4). The successful takeover of health and natural foods by profit-seeking agribusinesses is a common story among those who support and practice organic agriculture, and the shared history encouraged diverse proponents of organics to seek strict and comprehensive legislation (Belasco 1989). While it might seem hypocritical for Retzloff, founder of a $127 million public corporation, to critique the profit strategizing of other large and successful food industry enterprises, Retzloff characterizes many interested in the commercial success of organics. These supporters believed in the need for food system reform and yet felt comfortable pursuing those goals within what many have critiqued as a corrupt existing food system (Allen and Sachs 1993; Goodman and Redclift 1991; Pollan 2001). Issues that concerned many social justice, farmers', and environmental groups were downplayed in favor of the commercial sector's agenda of government oversight and legitimization of the agricultural production of a cleaner, safer product. The relative influence of the commercial agenda and the tremendous public support for organics as a safe food influenced the policy process. The markets for chemical-free products were what monopolized the attention of the organic industry advocates. The demand for a certifiably "pure" product dominated their vision for organics and their influence on the rule-drafting process as well.

With intense lobbying and support from these groups, the 1990 Organic Food Production Act passed Congress. This act passed as an amendment to the farm bill and circumvented the House Agricultural Committee by being brought by Senator Patrick Leahy directly to the floor of the House to be included as Title XXI (E. Lipson 1998). The amendment included no support for any organic research or extension. Leahy's and others' previous failures at passing federal organic legislation made them "wary of using the [organic] label to advance the research and education agenda" (Youngberg, Schaller, and Merrigan 1993). The 1990 farm bill as a whole included many initiatives for environmental protection and sustainable agriculture research and education, yet most of those lacked the clarity and necessary backing that would see them through implementation—an agreed-upon definition of "sustainable agriculture," for example, was elusive (Bird 1991; Youngberg, Schaller, and Merrigan 1993).

Creating Organic Expertise: The National Organic Standards Board

A notable feature of OFPA was the creation of the National Organic Standards Board (NOSB), a diverse fifteen-member board to be composed of four farmers, two handlers/processors, one retailer, one scientist (with expertise in toxicology, ecology, or biochemistry), three consumer/public interest advocates, three environmentalists, and one certifier. The NOSB was charged with collecting information from stakeholders around the country and drafting a set of organic rules. The board was also to be responsible for a final list of allowable substances in organic farming. OFPA did not have the full approval of the House Agricultural Committee, and congressional support for organic agriculture remained at a low level. Indeed, the two years following the passage of the 1990 act have been called the "lost years" due to federal foot-dragging on implementing the act and providing funding for the NOSB so it could get to work on draft regulation (Gershuny 2002). After two years, the funding for the NOSB materialized, members were appointed, and the board proceeded to undertake an arduous process of drafting a set of federal standards for organic agriculture and gathering feedback from farmers and the organic industry around the nation.

While the NOSB constituted a site for mobilization and an opportunity to register policy preferences closely linked to the governmental process, the group was not fully supported by all involved, many of whom felt the board's representation was skewed against full expression of the core social agenda of mainstream organic farmers. Farmers were upset that the fifteen-member board included only four farmers, and that those four included people representing large organic businesses like Craig Weakley of Muir Glen and Gene Kahn of Cascadian Farms—people whom other organic farmers viewed as lacking in deep farming experience and representing a strong industry interest (E. Lipson 1998).

The NOSB also encountered numerous challenges in drafting a set of recommendations that would be generally acceptable to the fragmented organic community—finding agreement between different state programs, for example, or pleasing both food processors and consumer representatives (E. Lipson 1998; Gershuny 2002). Food processors and handlers insisted on the allowance of certain synthetic additives and stabilizers that they felt were imperative in order to bring more processed foods with longer shelf lives to mainstream outlets. Farmer representatives wanted a rule that would require newcomers to understand a larger philosophy of alternative farming, one that worked not only to avoid harming the environment but went beyond that to enhance it. Commercial and consumer interests, on the other hand, wanted a rule that would guarantee an absolutely pure product, with less attention paid to the overall production process.

In June 1995, the NOSB submitted a draft proposed organic rule to the secretary of agriculture for final review and passage. However much farmers' voices were muted in negotiating with the NOSB, their lines of communication with the political process were virtually cut when the recommendations moved from the board to the interior of the USDA. Organic advocates had little experience in the process of interagency review of proposed legislation since their legislative achievements were so limited. Maintaining the original integrity of alternative agriculture programs and keeping them funded and operational once they enter the twin "black boxes" of USDA and appropriations has been very problematic (Marshall 2000). Administrative rule making greatly advantages the established interests in policy monopolies (Baumgartner and Jones 1991). As officials within the USDA exercised the opportunity to review the proposed regulations, they spoke on behalf of the perspectives of their long-term constituencies. Agencies outside the USDA expressed their own mission and clientele interests in asking the secretary of agriculture for changes. According to NOP staff member Grace Gershuny, people involved knew that there would be trouble in getting the rule past the Office of Management and Budget, the Environmental Protection Agency (EPA), and the Food and Drug Administration (FDA). The EPA and FDA, for example, had both previously issued statements about the scientific evidence supporting the safety of genetically engineered organisms, the use of which was restricted in the drafted organic standards (Gershuny, personal communication; Conover 1998).

One persistent critique of organic farming is that its claims of environmental and human health benefits have not been clearly established by mainstream peer-reviewed scientific research (Trewavas 2001). Advocates quote multiple reasons for this, including lack of funding, low research status for organic issues, no "organic" land at experiment stations on which to do research, and research methodologies geared toward measuring yield rather than capturing the complexity and effectiveness of a holistic production system (M. Lipson 1997; Sooby 2001). Despite this lack of scientific evidence, organics has thrived on its reputation for producing healthier food—both for the human body and for livestock and the environment. While there is an expanding body of peer-reviewed published "science" on the issues, its paucity makes it a frequent target of critics.[4] Both the EPA and the FDA, however, based their decisions during the agency review process on evidence produced by peer-reviewed risk assessment science, the same science that informed previous decisions about the safety of GMOs and sewage sludge. This led to changes in the draft rule, some of them radical enough to fuel significant public reaction.

The proposed rule emerged from the USDA in 1997, after more than two years of administrative makeover. There were not only substantial changes but also the loss of what some saw as clarity of purpose and flexibility in the rules. The most egregious changes, which became known as the "Big Three," were the inclusion of practices that the NOSB had placed outside of proper organic practice: irradiation of food, the use of genetically modified organisms, and applications of sewage sludge. In the maelstrom that followed, it was usually overlooked that, while these issues were indeed reintroduced by the USDA, they were inserted in the preamble to the rules along with an invitation to comment. This subtlety was lost as the Big Three became the rallying cry for what was portrayed as a government move to take over, undermine, hijack, and co-opt the emerging industry for big business and destroy choice in the marketplace. People were upset about the Big Three, upset about big business, and upset about Big Brother.

The lessons the organic agriculture social movement was taught in the rule-making process were those implementation scholars know well. Despite the imposition of advisory bodies and administrative procedures intended to make bureaucratic processes more transparent, democratic, and open, insiders are greatly advantaged (Pressman and Wildavsky 1979; Mazmanian and Sabatier 1983; Montjoy and O'Toole 1984; H. Ingram 1989). While a social movement might establish a beachhead in a commission or advisory board, such as the NOSB, the interior of the bureaucratic landscape is populated by long-term residents who have their own established ways of doing things and are quite isolated from social movements attempting nonincremental change. Moreover, the diffusion of responsibility in the rule-making process provides any particular administrative official with cover should an adverse reaction occur. Under certain circumstances, agency officials might try to anticipate adverse public reaction and adjust their actions accordingly. However, agency insiders clearly felt, as did the House Committee on Agriculture, that the organic movement lacked any real political power or wider appeal. They were mistaken.

The Comment Period: A Right to Choose

The USDA's misreading of the public landscape had dramatic implications, especially through uniting and galvanizing the organic movement and also opening up a whole new opportunity for public comment on the larger food system (Gamson and Meyer 1996; Gershuny 2002). Activists realized that the protest of organic lobbyists and farmers would not be sufficient to substantially modify a rule that had already undergone much revision. Allies were needed. Ordinarily, transaction costs for citizens to participate in public comment in rule making are prohibitively high. Thousands of proposed rules appear in the *Public Register* every year, and massive public reaction is rare. The marketplace proved friendly ground for the organic movement, as activists were able to rally consumers in food co-ops and health food stores and through consumer organizations such as Working Assets, which was the single largest source of individual comments, some thirty-five thousand. Postcards and petitions were available near the checkout counters of foodstores, and Working Assets and other organizations provided customers with form letter e-mails to be sent to the USDA. Form letters, of course, shaped many of the comments, and were one reason why the Big Three received such consistent focus. In addition, the Big Three had enormous symbolic appeal, although these issues only scratched the surface of problems that advocates found in the USDA's proposed rule. One key explanation for the magnitude of the protest that occurred was the seriousness of the perceived threat. The presence of the Big Three was especially upsetting. According to one author, genetically engineered organisms, the use of municipal sludge, and irradiation were highly controversial subjects even in mainstream agro-food systems: "That they could be thought to be appropriate to a set of standards for organic production and handling indicates the most profound kind of cognitive dissonance" (Vos 2000, 249). Cleavages within the movement disappeared. As David Meyer has observed, "When public attention to an issue is growing, and resources are relatively available, groups are more likely to cooperate" (Meyer, introduction to this volume).

The challenge for the movement was framing the issue in a way that would move it even further into the public arena (McCarthy, Smith, and Zald 1996, 293). Successful protest involves cooperation and coordination among groups and also the framing of appeals that unify the social movement and have broad public resonance. Mistrust of government, suspicion of big business or corporate control, and individual rights to choose are all larger themes in the history of American protest. A decade earlier, alternative food advocates had watched helplessly when agribusiness expropriated the image of "healthy foods" and slapped it on everything from cupcakes to sugared cereal. This experience informed the strategies of movement leaders. Form protest letters and press releases were drafted portraying the U.S. government and agribusiness as threatening to take away the basic right to choose. Our survey of the representative comments posted online by the USDA National Organic Program reveals that lack of trust in government and the right to choose were two bass notes in the symphony of responses generated to the proposed rule (also see Shulman 2000).

The right to choose is what Tarrow might call a master frame, a successful framing that is copied from one movement by others (Tarrow 1998, 117; Snow and Benford 1992). The right to have a choice about food resonated with the larger American notion of individual rights and a more recent construction of the rights of the "reflexive consumer" (DuPuis 2000). Food and drugs are a particular focus for the reflexive consumer since it involves a personal choice about what a person will or will not let into her body. Like "not in my backyard," "not in my body" begins with a refusal. Traditional authority is challenged, and the reflexive consumer asserts the right to choose not only between commodities but also which authority to believe. In this case, the authority was not the government but the NOSB, a group from "inside" organics and "outside" the tainted halls of government and money. "Listen to the NOSB!" protesters cried.

The comment period did more than wake up members of the public to the idea of general choice. Perhaps even more important, organics became the alternative to food containing genetically modified organisms. Although the American public has been consuming GMOs on a regular basis for years, the issue had never before found its way into a large public discussion. By asking for public comment about allowing GMOs in organics, the government gave people a policy arena to speak about a topic that had never before been so widely aired (Gershuny, personal communication). The mainstream press had repeatedly reminded Americans that, contrary to Europeans, they do not care about their food (e.g., Whitney 1999;

Economist 1999). Clearly, however, when provided with an opportunity to speak, Americans will insist that they do care indeed.

The Rule Gets Real

Some quarter of a million comments later, the Big Three were disallowed, and the USDA responded extensively to many other comments and requests made about the rule. The policy process encouraged people to overcome differences, so much so that some even said the movement had matured to the point of being capable of self-regulation (E. Lipson 1998). At the same time, the very forces that made the protest such a success sowed the seeds of future problems. While the broader coalition of interests supporting organic labeling laws was critical to legislative success, it diminished the relative influence of the core group of organic farmers and activists. In the eyes of some, the consumer focus skewed the movement, co-opting it away from basic values of reinventing the food system toward business as usual and providing a "purer" product.[5] Many farmers wanted stricter and more explicit regulations in order to protect the organic process from those who would take false advantage of the label—large, industrial-type farms, which might try to profit from the higher prices brought by the label without undertaking any of the process and philosophy of organic practice. The regulations were also a tool to facilitate trade. Commercial interests focused on the "highest possible standards" so that they could guarantee consumers the best possible product. These goals, and the groundswell of public interest in organics as a safe haven from food safety scares, brought the two groups together and encouraged them both to push for stringent and detailed language in the legislation.[6] As a driving force in the shape of legislation, however, consumer demand for safe food meant that in the policy-making process attention was focused on delineating and protecting a definitive organic process rather than on supporting new innovation. The policy tools embedded in legislation have a large effect on whose interests are best served (Schneider and Ingram 1997). "Capacity-building" tools, for example, target programs for research, training, experimentation, and education. Certification, a regulatory tool, establishes barriers to those who would commit fraud but fails to provide avenues for newcomers and new directions. In some respects, the federal organic legislation exemplifies the limitations of green consumerism and the marketplace as an arena for social change (DuPuis 2000; Goodman 2000; Guthman 2000).

As one example of compromises made in the administrative rule-making process, the guidelines for compost making are very specific, even including the temperatures piles must reach and how often they must be turned.[7] This not only raises the issue of how such a detail will be policed but also ignores other avenues for generating safe, effective compost. Other aspects clearly favor larger, more diversified operations. The amount of paperwork and bureaucracy involved in certification is a burden that is certainly felt more by those unable to hire a consultant or pay someone else to stay on top of details. Antibiotics are another example. When faced with a sick milk cow that has not responded to homeopathic or herbal remedies, a farmer may turn to antibiotics to save her. According to the new rule, the use of antibiotics puts this cow out of organic milk production for life. If a farmer is large and diversified, he or she can move the cow to a conventional part of the operation, which is not an option for a small organic farmer.[8]

As a new organizational form, federal organic policy may illustrate what Rao, Morrill, and Zald have defined as "weak speciation" (2000, 240). That is, in considering the form's goals, authority relations, technology, and served markets, there are few radical differences from existing policy. For example, the policy does not guarantee anything about the size of the operation that produced an organic product or anything about the working conditions and wages of the operation's labor force or conditions for the sale of the product. A significant amount of organic produce originates from operations that run conventional and organic operations side by side (Greene and Kremen 2003). The strongest difference lies in the technological and management changes insisted on by the policy, supported by the development of new ideas about agriculture. Sustaining soil fertility and managing pests and plant diseases without synthetic chemicals requires learning, thought, and foresight on the part of the farmer, as well as sensitivity to the environment of the farm. There is little doubt that organic practice will be an environmental boon and a health benefit, especially for field laborers.

Advocates at the core of an alternative agriculture movement, who envisioned a locally based food system, new financial, educational, and research support for smaller farmers, or improved food security for underserved consumers, will not find much support in this policy. Perhaps the largest impacts will be felt, ironically enough, by the conventional agriculture system that sought to deny the importance of organics. If enough of the consuming public insists on affordable, available, and organic produce, then many more conventional farmers will be encouraged to take the plunge and will have to learn a new way of growing food—one that requires agriculture to "foster the cycling of resources, promote ecological balance and conserve biodiversity."[9] In and of itself, this is a radical and positive change. If organic policy fell short in many aspects, it may well have succeeded in providing strict-enough guidelines so that the technology of business as usual but with fewer inputs is no longer an option.

In addition, the ongoing role of the NOSB to determine allowable substances, to clarify the rule, and to develop guidelines for practices deserves continued attention. The advisory group has the potential to provide a rare conduit for new and diverse voices of authority in the policy implementation process. The implementation of the rule left much to be desired in the eyes of many, and legal action followed quickly.[10] Mainstream press attention around October 21, 2002, when the act went into effect, did not hesitate to focus on the small farmers not well served by the organic policy (Fromartz 2002). In addition, it has been pointed out that larger agricultural reform is a goal of increasing numbers of conventional farmers reeling from successive waves of financial crises, some of whom are looking to new constituents—consumers, environmentalists, even animal rights advocates—for support in resisting corporate domination and changing a government policy that continues to insist: get big or get out (Greider 2000).

Conclusion

The case of organic product certification offers a number of lessons about the interactive and mutually constitutive nature of social movements, governmental institutions, and markets. The alternative agriculture movement was for decades prohibited entry into the agricultural establishment and denied any subsidy, research, or education benefits. The marketplace, however, provided financial support for growth and technological innovations and encouraged the movement to establish and institutionalize certification programs. A whole new set of production relationships and networks grew around organics, supporting growers, processors, packers, co-ops, health food stores, and others involved in alternative commodity chains. Reliance on markets led inevitably back to government, however, as organic farmers and traders encountered problems with proliferation of labels and product quality control. State certification of organic products to meet these concerns led, in turn, to demand for federal regulations. Support for certification was also heavily supported by consumer groups and commercial interests. The extended process of developing organic legislation and interest from consumers and industry clearly focused the movement on organic product certification, and less was said about creating better distributive benefits like research and education for alternative agriculture or larger food policies that affect the political and economic structure of agriculture.

This chapter reinforces the message that the content of policy shapes the strategies of social movements and that the influence of social movements on policy may vary substantially across different stages of the policy process. In general, the implementation phase of policy maximizes the influence of established interests and minimizes the access of social movement actors. The study also sheds light on how to address the issue of co-optation and the benefits of examining social movements in more nuanced, interactive terms. A great deal of interpenetration took place between the organic agriculture movement and the state apparatus for standard setting and monitoring. The movement moved "inside" through the NOSB and carved itself a place within the agricultural policy establishment; the government also moved "outside" through the certification process to influence the practice of organics on the ground.

While the Department of Agriculture clearly placed organic agriculture as a low priority, it did this in denial of recurrent and diverse crises and failures in the larger agricultural domain. These issues, especially food safety, resonated with a large number of people. The organic movement was able to mobilize critical support from consumers concerned about contamination of the food supply by chemical pesticides and fertilizers and concerned with the collusion of government and big business that would cost a consumer her or his ability to choose a product, especially one guaranteed free of GMOs.

This story may serve to emphasize the importance of the right to choose as a master frame. While rights and justice are widely recognized as frames that bridge differences and bring people together in the civil rights, women's, indigenous peoples', and gay rights movements, among others, the right to choose has an individual rather than a group identity appeal. Like the "not in my backyard" movements, they tend to be parochial and particular to one's neighborhood or, in this case, body. However, as this case shows, the frame has great symbolic appeal. The potential for the reflexive consumer to support sustained reformative action in agriculture is part of an unfinished story.

Finally, this chapter speaks to the processes by which social movements claim authority and legitimize new boundaries. Although the alternative agriculture movement has always appealed to science in making claims about its benefits to human health and the environment, establishment science has not been supportive of these efforts. People in the organic movement who were making claims about the superiority of organic produce downplayed the use of establishment science. Furthermore, when mainstream agricultural science stood squarely behind the use of GMOs in the rule-making process, the majority of organic consumers chose to take the word of the NOSB that they should be prohibited, despite federal government reassurance that they were safe. Appeals to scientific authority had a rather low profile in the public discourse, scientific uncertainty was underscored, and concerns about freedom to choose and confidence in food safety dominated the debate. While it may be important for the long-term credibility of alternative agriculture to offer a "peer-reviewed" scientific rationale, that rationale is clearly not decisive in building a public constituency. This finding may reflect a growing skepticism among the public about the independence and integrity of science in areas of critical public concern including health and the environment, as well as concern over decision making in public institutions based on risk assessments rather than precaution. The ongoing responsibility of the NOSB as it guides the regulation, especially its process of decision making, makes it an excellent site to watch for the emergence of new ideas about science, risk, and agriculture.

Notes

1. We are indebted to Leah Fraser and Bryan McDonald for the collection and analysis of newspaper data.

2. As an indication perhaps of the speed of new ideas in Washington, it was almost a decade later that the National Research Council published a study on the scientific, economic, and environmental viability of alternative agricultural systems, helping to officially sanction alternative agricultural practices (NRC 1989).

3. The contentious issue of food safety deserves more attention than we can give here (see Nestle 2003). Much can be said about the ongoing efforts to define the issue and to develop standard definitions of problems and solutions. Organics, while offering a solution to concerns over pesticides, has also been attacked as a source of E. coli contamination from the use of manure as fertilizer (Trewavas 2001). Organics has received the majority of its negative publicity from attacks on the use of manure as a threat to food safety. This is ironic since both conventional and organic farms use manure as a source of soil fertility, and there is far more oversight of the use of manure for soil fertility in organic farming.

4. Relatively little voice was given to the scientific community in the mainstream press during the years around the passage of the regulation. Our content analysis of coverage of organics in the *New York Times* and the *San Francisco Chronicle* between 1989 and 2000 reveals that despite the persistence of scientific issues like pathogens in manure, scientists were not given much voice, and the representation of scientists and scientific organizations in articles on organic farming actually dropped during this period. Attention to the issues of human health remained high, increasing over time. Instead of relying on the scientific establishment as a final voice of authority, the public, as we will explain, came to see the NOSB as an alternative, grass-grown authority on the organic product, one free from the compromising interests of government, agribusiness, and conventional science.

5. As Garth Youngberg pointed out in his 1980 report on organic farming, this was not a new concern for the movement (USDA 1980, 8).

6. At the same time, it was important for organic food processors to be able to use some additives like xanthan gum and ascorbic acid. There were heated debates within the organic community over whether these synthetics should be allowed— or any processing of organic food at all. In the end, many of the demands of the food processors ruled.

7. According to some, this language was copied from the EPA requirements for large-scale municipal composting operations and was adopted in order to ease the passage of the draft rule through the administrative process (Gershuny, personal communication).

8. In arguing against such a strict rule about antibiotics, it has been pointed out that consumers who would not hesitate to turn to antibiotics to heal their children or themselves would likely have no problem with a farmer who used antibiotics as a last resort in order to keep an organic milk cow healthy (Gershuny 2002).

9 "7 CFR Part 205 National Organic Program; Final Rule," *Federal Register* 65, no. 246 (December 21, 2000).

10. On October 16, 2002, the Center for Food Safety and other advocates filed a legal petition to force the USDA to establish a peer review panel to oversee the accreditation of organic certifiers, as was required in the regulation.

References

Adams, Jane. 2003. *Fighting for the Farm: Rural America Transformed.* Philadelphia: University of Pennsylvania Press.

Allen, Patricia, and Carolyn Sachs. 1993. "Sustainable Agriculture in the United States: Engagements, Silences, and Possibilities for Transformation." In *Food for the Future: Conditions and Contradictions of Sustainability,* ed. Allen, 139–68. New York: Wiley.

Batie, Sandra. 1985. "Soil Conservation in the 1980s: A Historical Perspective." In *The History of Soil and Water Conservation,* ed. Douglas Helms and Susan Flader. Washington, DC: Agricultural History Society.

Baumgartner, Frank, and Bryan Jones. 1991. "Agenda Dynamics and Policy Subsystems." *Journal of Politics* 53, no. 4 (November): 1044–74.

Becker, Elizabeth. 2001. "Agriculture Secretary vs. Sacred Cow." *New York Times,* December 11, A14, col. 3.

———. 2002. "Big Farms Making a Mess of U.S. Waters, Cities Say." *New York Times,* February 10, sec. 1, 20, col. 1.

Belasco, Warren. 1989. *Appetite for Change: How the Counterculture Took on the Food Industry, 1966–1988.* New York: Pantheon Books.

Bird, Elizabeth. 1991. "Research for Sustainability? The National Research Initiative's Social Plan for Agriculture." Walthill, NB: Center for Rural Affairs.

Brulle, Robert, J. 2000. *Agency, Democracy, and Nature: The U.S. Environmental Movement from a Critical Theory Perspective.* Cambridge: MIT Press.

Butz, Earl. 1971. "Crisis or Challenge." *Nation's Agriculture* (July–August): 19.

Campbell, David. 2001. "Conviction Seeking Efficacy: Sustainable Agriculture and the Politics of Co-optation." *Agriculture and Human Values* 18, no. 4: 353–63.

Clark, Anne. 2001. "A Passion for Pasture, an Alternative to Bulk-Commodity Agriculture." *Acres, U.S.A.* 31, no. 11: 28–31.

Conover, Kristen A. 1998. "Public Groundswell Sways Organic Guidelines." *Christian Science Monitor,* May 14.

Davis, Gerald, and Doug McAdam. 2000. "Corporations, Classes, and Social Movements after Managerialism." *Research in Organizational Behavior* 22: 237–82.

DuPuis, Melanie. 2000. "Not in My Body: rBGH and the Rise of Organic Milk." *Agriculture and Human Values* 17: 285–95.

Economist. 1999. "Seeds of Discontent." Editorial, February 20, 75–77.

Epstein, Steven. 1996. *Impure Science: AIDS, Activism, and the Politics of Knowledge.* Berkeley: University of California Press.

Fligstein, Neil. 1996. "Markets as Politics: A Political-Cultural Approach to Market Institutions." *American Sociological Review* 61: 656–73.

Fromartz, Samuel. 2002. "Small Organic Farmers Pull Up Stakes." *New York Times,* October 14.

Gamson, William A. 1975. *The Strategy of Social Protest.* Homewood, IL: Dorsey Press.

Gamson, William A., and David Meyer. 1996. "Framing Political Opportunity." In *Comparative Perspectives on Social Movements,* ed. Doug McAdam, John McCarthy, and Mayer Zald. Cambridge: Cambridge University Press.

Gershuny, Grace. 2002. "The Organic Revolution." Unpublished manuscript, Institute for Social Ecology.

Gieryn, Thomas. 1999. *Cultural Boundaries of Science: Credibility on the Line.* Chicago: University of Chicago Press.

Goodman, David. 2000. "Organic and Conventional Agriculture: Materializing Discourse and Agro-ecological Managerialism." *Agriculture and Human Values* 17, no. 3: 215–19.

Goodman, David, and Michael Redclift. 1991. *Refashioning Nature: Food, Ecology, and Culture.* London: Routledge.

Greene, Catherine. 2001. "U.S. Organic Farming Emerges in the 1990s: Adoption of Certified Systems." Agriculture Information Bulletin 770. Washington, DC: U.S. Department of Agriculture, Economics Research Service, Resources Economics Division.

Greene, Catherine, and Amy Kremen. 2003. "U.S. Organic Farming in 2000–2001: Adoption of Certified Systems." Agriculture Information Bulletin, no. 780. Washington, DC: USDA-ERS.

Greider, William. 2000. "The Last Farm Crisis." *Nation,* November 2. At http://www.thenation.com (accessed October 26, 2002).

Gussow, Joan. 1991. *Chicken Little, Tomato Sauce, and Agriculture.* New York: Bootstrap Press.

Guthman, Julie. 1998. "Regulating Meaning, Appropriating Nature: The Codification of California Organic Agriculture." *Antipode* 30, no. 2: 135–54.

———. 2000. "Raising Organic: An Agro-Ecological Assessment of Grower Practices in California." *Agriculture and Human Values* 17, no. 3: 257–66.

Hajer, Michael. 1995. *The Politics of Environmental Discourse: Ecological Modernization and the Policy Process.* Oxford, UK: Clarendon Press.

Hansen, John. 1991. *Gaining Access: Congress and the Farm Lobby, 1919–1981.* Chicago: University of Chicago Press.

Howard, Sir Albert. 1940. *An Agricultural Testament.* London: Oxford University Press.

Hurwitz, Mark, Roger Moiles, and David Rohde. 2001. "Distributive and Partisan Issues in the 104th House." *American Political Science Review* 95, no. 4: 911–22.

Ingram, Helen. 1989. "Implementation: A Review and Suggested Framework." In *Public Administration: The State of the Discipline,* ed. N. B. Lynne and A. Wildavsky. Chatham, NJ: Chatham House.

Ingram, Helen M., and Dean E. Mann, eds. 1980. *Why Policies Succeed or Fail.* Vol. 8 of *Sage Yearbooks in Politics and Public Policy.* Beverly Hills, CA: Sage.

Ingram, Mrill. 2004. "Fertile Ground: Geographies of Knowledge about Soil Fertility in the Alternative Agricultural Movement." PhD diss., University of Arizona.

Jenkins-Smith, Hank, and Paul Sabatier. 1994. "Evaluating the Advocacy Coalition Framework." *Journal of Public Policy* 14, no. 2: 175.

Jenness, Valerie, and Ryken Grattet. 2001. *Making Hate a Crime: From Social Movement to Law Enforcement.* New York: Russell Sage Foundation.

Jones, Charles. 1961. "Representation in Congress: The Case of the House Agriculture Committee." *American Political Science Review* 87, no. 3: 657–71.

———. 1962. "The Role of the Congressional Subcommittee." *Midwest Journal of Political Science* 6, no. 4: 327–44.

Kloppenburg, Jack R. 1988. *First the Seed: The Political Economy of Plant Biotechnology, 1492–2000.* Cambridge: Cambridge University Press.

Lilliston, Ben, and Ronnie Cummins. 1998. "Organic vs. 'Organic': The Corruption of a Label." *Ecologist* 28, no. 4 (July/August): 195–200.

Lipson, Elaine. 1998. "A Brief History of the National Organic Standards." *California Certified Organic Farmers Newsletter* (Spring): 4–11.

Lipson, Mark. 1997. *Searching for the "O-Word": Analyzing the USDA Current Research Information System for Pertinence to Organic Farming.* Santa Cruz, CA: Organic Farming Research Foundation.

Lounsbury, Michael, Marc Ventresca, and Paul Hirsch. 2002. "Social Movements, Field Frames, and Industry Emergence: A Cultural-Political Perspective on U.S. Recycling." Institute for Policy Research working paper, Cornell University. At http://www.northwestern.edu/ipr/publications/papers/2002/WP-02-27.pdf (accessed November 2002).

Lowi, Theodore J. 1964. Review of *American Business and Public Policy: The Politics of Foreign Trade* (New York: Atherton, 1963), *World Politics* 16, no. 4 (July): 677–715.

Marcus, Alan. 1994. *Cancer from Beef: DES, Federal Food Regulation, and Consumer Confidence.* Baltimore, MD: Johns Hopkins University Press.

Marshall, Andrew. 2000. "Sustaining Sustainable Agriculture: The Rise and Fall of the Fund for Rural America." *Agriculture and Human Values* 17: 267–77.

Mazmanian, Daniel, and Paul Sabatier. 1983. *Implementation and Public Policy.* Glenview, IL: Scott Foresman.

McAdam, D., J. D. McCarthy, and M. N. Zald. 1996. *Comparative Perspectives on Social Movements.* Cambridge: Cambridge University Press.

McCarthy, John D., Jackie Smith, and Mayer Zald. 1996. "Accessing Public, Media, Electoral, and Governmental Agendas." In *Comparative Perspectives on Social Movements.* Cambridge: Cambridge University Press.

Meyer, David. 2000. "Claiming Credit: The Social Construction of Movement Success." Research Monograph 42. Irvine: Center for the Study of Democracy, University of California, Irvine.

Montjoy, Robert, and Laurence J. O'Toole. 1984. *Regulatory Decision Making: The Virginia State Corporation Commission.* Charlottesville: University Press of Virginia.

Morrill, Calvin. 2003. "Institutional Change through Interstitial Emergence: The Growth of Alternative Dispute Resolution in American Law, 1965–1995." In *How Institutions Change,* ed. Walter Powell and Daniel Jones. Chicago: University of Chicago Press.

Nestle, Marion. 2003. *Safe Food: Bacteria, Biotechnology, and Bioterrorism.* Berkeley: University of California Press.

NRC (National Research Council). 1989. *Alternative Agriculture.* Washington, DC: National Academy Press.

———. 2001. *Publicly Funded Agricultural Research and the Changing Structure of U.S. Agriculture.* Washington, DC: National Academy Press.

O'Connor, James. 1998. *Natural Causes: Essays in Ecological Marxism.* New York: Guilford Press.

Pollan, Michael. 2001. "The Organic-Industrial Complex: All about the Folks Who Brought You the Organic TV Dinner." *New York Times Magazine,* May 13, 30–65.

Pressman, Jeffrey, and Aaron Wildavsky. 1979. *Implementation: How Great Expectations in Washington Are Dashed in Oakland.* Berkeley: University of California Press.

Rao, Hayagreeva, Calvin Morrill, and Mayer Zald. 2000. "Power Plays: How Social Movements and Collective Action Create New Organizational Forms." *Research in Organizational Behaviour* 22: 237–81.

Robinson, Barbara. 2002. Interview with deputy administrator, Transportation and Marketing Programs, USDA. *Diane Rheme Show,* October 24.

Rochon, Thomas R. 1998. *Culture Moves: Ideas, Activism, and Changing Values.* Princeton, NJ: Princeton University Press.

Salamon, Lester, and Odus Elliott. 2002. *The Tools of Government: A Guide to the New Governance.* Oxford: Oxford University Press.

Sanders, Elizabeth. 1999. *Roots of Reform.* Chicago: Chicago University Press.

Schmelzer, Paul. 1998. "Label Loophole: When Organic Isn't." *Progressive* 62, no. 5 (May): 28.

Schneider, Anne, and Helen Ingram. 1997. *Policy Design for Democracy.* Lawrence: University of Kansas Press.

Scott, W. R. 1995. *Institutions and Organizations.* Newbury Park, CA: Sage Press.

Selznick, Phillip. 1966. *TVA and the Grass Roots: A Study in the Sociology of Formal Organization.* New York: Harper and Row.

Shulman, Stuart. 2000. "Citizen Agenda Setting, Digital Government, and the National Organics Program." Paper presented at the annual meeting of the American Political Science Association, Washington, DC, August 31–September 3.

Snow, David, and R. Benford. 1992. "Master Frames and Cycles of Protest." In *Frontiers in Social Movement Theory,* ed. A. Morris and C. McClung Mueller, 133–55. New Haven, CT: Yale University Press.

Sooby, Jane. 2001. *State of the States: Organic Farming Systems Research at Land Grant Institutions, 2000–2001.* Santa Cruz, CA: Organic Farming Research Foundation.

Sprinkle, Steve. 2002. "Transitions Certified Organic Industry News." *Acres U.S.A.* 32, no. 2 (February): 6–7.

Tarrow, Sidney. 1998. *Power in Social Movements: Social Movements and Contentious Politics.* Cambridge: Cambridge University Press.

Trewavas, Anthony. 2001. "Urban Myths of Organic Farming." *Nature* 410 (March 22): 409–10.

USDA. 1980. *Report and Recommendations on Organic Farming.* Washington, DC: U.S. Department of Agriculture.

Vos, Timothy. 2000. "Visions of the Middle Landscape: Organic Farming and the Politics of Nature." *Agriculture and Human Values* 17, no. 3: 245–56.

Whitney, Craig. 1999. "Europe Loses Its Appetite for High-Tech Food." *New York Times,* June 27, 3.

Youngberg, Garth. 1978. "Alternative Agriculturists: Ideology, Politics, and Prospects." In *The New Politics of Food,* ed. Don F. Hadwiger and William P. Browne, 227–46. Lexington, MA: Lexington.

Youngberg, Garth, Neill Schaller, and Kathleen Merrigan. 1993. "The Sustainable Agriculture Policy Agenda in the United States: Politics and Prospects." In *Food for the Future: Conditions and Contradictions of Sustainability,* ed. Patricia Allen, 295–318. New York: Wiley.

5

Inside and Outside the State: Movement Insider Status, Tactics, and Public Policy Achievements

Lee Ann Banaszak

The forces that led to its [one branch of the women's movement] forma-tion were set in motion in 1961 when President Kennedy established the President's Commission on the Status of Women at the behest of Esther Petersen *[sic]*, then director of the Women's Bureau. Operating under a broad mandate, its 1963 report, *American Women,* and subsequent com-mittee publications documented just how thoroughly women are still denied many rights and opportunities. . . . The activity of the federal and state commissions laid the groundwork for the future movement. (Freeman 1975, 52)

Equal employment opportunity for women began its development as a national policy during John F. Kennedy's presidency. Support for the principle was among the recommendations of the President's Commission on the Status of Women, which, from 1961 to 1963, investigated women's position in American society and drew up an agenda of desirable reforms. The Commission marks the beginning of governmental recognition of women's status as a legitimate matter for policy consideration. The Kennedy years also witnessed the first legislative recognition of federal re-sponsibility toward working women, the Equal Pay Act of 1963. . . . Both the initiatives . . . resulted from Kennedy's delegation of responsibility for women's affairs to Esther Peterson. (Zelman 1982, 23)

These two renditions—one oriented toward the movement and one toward the policy—tracing the beginnings of the second wave of the women's movement, highlight the role of the Kennedy administration, particularly the assistant secretary of labor, Esther Peterson, as crucial in aiding and inspiring future mobilization. However, there are two very different views on how to interpret this event from a social movement perspective. The first and more common view is to see the Kennedy administration's action as an opening in the structure of political opportunities. Kennedy, in an attempt to woo and keep women supporters for the Democratic party, especially in the face of rising support for the Equal Rights Amendment, provides an opening in the state, which mobilizes women into a new emerging movement. This view, accepted by both authors above, portrays the establishment of the President's Commission on the Status of Women as an action of a politically motivated government, separate from a not-yet-existent women's movement.

However, an alternative interpretation, examining the important role of Esther Peterson, begins with a focus on the continuity in the first and second waves of the women's movement (Rupp and Taylor 1987; Ryan 1992). In this interpretation, Esther Peterson is not just a lackey of the Kennedy administration; she is an activist in a preexisting women's movement, albeit one that is divided (Banaszak 1996a; Harrison 1988) and in abeyance (Rupp and Taylor 1987). One group of women's organizations that developed from the old suffrage coalition advocated protective legislation for women workers (Harrison 1988, 7–8; see also Banaszak 1996a; Ryan 1992). Prior to the development of the second wave, movement organizations such as the Women's Trade Union League had influence in the Women's Bureau (Stetson 1995, 267). As a part of this tradition, Esther Peterson, the woman who developed and promoted the idea of a presidential commission to Kennedy, had long been an advocate for women workers. Viewed this way, the creation of the President's Commission on the Status of Women becomes not just a political opening created by a separate state and distinct political allies *external* to the movement, but an outcome of the movement molding its own opportunities as well. However, it is a movement tactic that can be performed only by a particular type of movement activist, one who straddles the borders between the state and the movement, or between a movement and its allies.

This chapter argues that to understand the tactics, strategies, and outcomes of a social movement, particularly decisions to undertake moderate tactics or to take to the streets, we must reexamine the boundaries we draw between a movement and "others," especially the state. Social movement and public policy literatures both draw strict lines between the state and social movements. In contrast, I argue that the degree to which movements have activists or organizations located within the state varies, both at the emergence of the movement and over time. This claim contradicts the views of social movement scholars who argue that for social movements to challenge the political order they must be located completely outside the polity (see, for example, Banaszak, Beckwith, and Rucht 2003a; Jenkins and Klandermans 1995; Tilly 1978). While the movements discussed here exist outside the state, they may have overlapping memberships with the state. The overlap occurs because states, as sets of institutions, may have members who also are movement activists either through social movement organizations or by being "occasional contributors" or participating in "nonorganized, spontaneous activities" (della Porta and Rucht 1995, 232). I label this overlap the state-movement intersection. Furthermore, I argue that the size, location, and historical context of this state-movement intersection influence the larger movement's development, strategies, and outcomes.

I will first discuss previous analyses of the interactions between states and movements within the social movement literature and develop some initial hypotheses that argue that movements can be located more or less within the state. I differentiate my concept of state-movement intersection from previous discussions of institutional activists and movement institutionalization. In the next section, I examine how public policy affects the development of the state-movement intersection, shaping the fundamental character of the movement. The state-movement intersection cannot be understood without exploring how public policy, in part movement achieved, creates new locations for movements within the state. In the final substantive section, I argue these intersections are important because they produce different mixes of tactics within social movements. I illustrate this with examples from the U.S. women's movement.

The State and the Social Movement in Social Movement Theory

Although the state and its relationship to social movements has become an increasing focus of the social movement literature (Banaszak, Beckwith, and Rucht 2003b; Birnbaum 1988; Flam 1994; Jenkins and Klandermans 1995; Tarrow 1998), such elaborations follow Tilly (1978) by firmly locating movements as independent actors outside the state. As a result, social movement scholars typically discuss the state and a social movement as two separate entities engaged in largely conflictual interactions. Views of the state and its role in interacting with social movements differ. Some authors discuss the state largely as a coherent entity that does not change over time (Kitschelt 1986; Birnbaum 1988); others recognize that the state is an amalgamation of actors with potentially different relationships to social movements that also change over time, particularly as they interact with other actors (Flam 1994; della Porta and Rucht 1995; Tarrow 1998). Moreover, the state can play many roles in relationship to social movements; it can be the target of social movement demands for change, the facilitator/repressor of social movement protest, the enforcer of social movement outcomes, or an ally/opponent in the struggle for social movement change. In all of these cases, the state is divided sharply from the movement; it is part of the political environment that movements encounter.

However, once we concede that states and movements are composed of actors, collective and individual, that may behave in diverse and sometimes conflictual ways, we open up the possibility that some actors may be members of both the state and a social movement.

Some scholars of social movement have begun to acknowledge the existence of this intersection between movements and the state.[1] Santoro and McGuire (1997) explicitly challenge the idea that members of the state and social movement activists are separate by arguing that institutional or insider activists significantly increase the likelihood of achieving policy outcomes desired by the social movement. Mary Katzenstein's analyses of movements within the church and the military (1998a, 1998b), although not focused on the state per se, show how movement actors may exist and act within established institutions and how they can undertake protest within the established boundaries of institutional action (see also Moore 1999, 99). While Katzenstein does not expressly address the intersection of institution and movement, because the movements she studies exist solely within institutional boundaries, her analysis goes far to establish the possibility of such an overlap. Finally, Smith and Lipsky (1993) specifically examine the process by which nonprofit groups become part of the state through the contracting out of state functions.

Each of these analyses is limited in its usefulness. Neither Katzenstein nor Moore focuses on the institution of the state. Given the unique characteristics of the state as an institution[2] and its large role in social movement contention, it is necessary to explore the specific intersection of the state and social movements. Both Smith and Lipsky and Santoro and McGuire challenge the traditional boundaries of state and movement. Yet Smith and Lipsky examine only a specific part of the state-movement intersection—the incorporation of nonprofits into state activities. Although Santoro and McGuire develop the theoretical concept of institutional activists, in the end they do not necessarily view these individuals as part of the movement but rather as institutional (or insider) resources for social movements (see Santoro 1999). In talking about the state-movement intersection, I am arguing that movement activists who are part of the state should be recognized as part of the movement as well.

The women and politics literature has gone much further in recognizing and exploring the intersection between women's movements and the state, although much of this literature has received little attention within the larger social movement literature. Within the literature on "state feminism" there have been a number of individuals who have concentrated on "femocrats" (Eisenstein 1996; Mazur 1995a, 2001, 2002; Outshoorn 1994, 1997; Pringle and Watson 1992; Sawer 1995; Stetson and Mazur 1995; Vargas and Wieringa 1998). These authors recognize that the state is not a uniform actor and that parts of the state may indeed harbor feminists who may influence movement tactics and related policy outcomes (Mazur 2001; Outshoorn 1994; Sawer 1995; Stetson and Mazur 1995). Within this field, the term "femocrat" has various meanings, ranging from all women who occupy policy-making positions in "women's policy machineries"[3] (see Outshoorn 1994 or Watson 1990) to feminists within any part of the bureaucracy (see, e.g., Eisenstein 1990) to feminists within women's policy machineries (see, e.g., Sawer 1995).

Despite its depth, the literature on femocrats still leaves several holes in terms of our understanding of the state-movement intersection. First, by focusing solely on the intersection of women's movements and the state, the literature loses the chance to examine the way other social movements intersect with the state and how variations in state-movement intersections play a differential role in movement development. In particular, many of the authors within the femocrat literature argue that the patriarchal nature of the state and society largely determine the effects of femocrats (see, for example, Mazur 2001, ch. 1; Pringle and Watson 1992). I wish to separate the effects of patriarchy from those that result from the effect of the state as a unique and powerful institution in its own right.

Although much of the literature investigates policy outputs, where the movement has been the center of attention, authors have tended to conflate the existence of movement activists within the state with debates on the choice of insider/outsider tactics (see, for example, Eisenstein 1990; Outshoorn 1994, 1997). The presence of feminists within the state is assumed to indicate the use of insider or institutional tactics, and therefore any significant state-movement intersection is considered synonymous with insider tactics. In this view, only supporters of insider tactics become femocrats, or individuals who take such jobs are completely molded by bureaucracies.[4] Yet feminists may take positions in government while maintaining outside activism (particularly if they hold positions outside of women's policy machineries). In addition, as some of the examples will indicate, movement activists within the state may even use their position to encourage extra-institutional or protest tactics by the movement. While it seems likely that larger state-movement intersections encourage the use of insider tactics, this should be a hypothesis that undergoes examination.

Even those individuals who have gone the furthest in recognizing the existence of feminists in the state have tended to implicitly characterize femocrats as separate from the movement. For example, Outshoorn, in interviewing women in women's policy positions, separates them into allies of the movement and professionals. Yet, she notes, several of the feminist bureaucrats she interviewed "denied the implicit dichotomy of my question by pointing out resolutely that they themselves were part of the movement (or by saying 'you belong to both')" (1994, 152). Similarly, Vargas and Wieringa (1998) note that feminists have become both politicians and civil servants. Yet when they start to analyze the creation of public policy they refer to "iron triangles," implicitly separating feminist politicians and femocrats from the women's movement.

Placing femocrats outside the movement distorts the view of the women's movement in two ways. First, it reduces the diversity of the movement. In a time when scholars are increasingly emphasizing the diverse and different opinions within the movement itself, labeling femocrats as the "other" excludes their voices from our understanding of the movement. Second, to the extent that femocrats are associated with particular tactical choices, defining them as outside actors produces distorted views of the women's movement by tending to make the movement seem more unified around extra-institutional tactics than it is in reality.

If we are to comprehend the interactions between movements and states, we need a theoretical perspective that incorporates an understanding of both movements and states as diverse entities that may have multiple points of intersection. Such a perspective must acknowledge the intersection of states and movements and analyze the effect of state-movement intersections on the development and tactics of the movement as well as on state-movement interactions and their outcomes.

Conceptualizing State-Movement Intersections

To begin with, we need to define the concept of the state-movement intersection so that it can be clearly identified for any social movement. The state-movement intersection consists of self-identified members of the movement who also hold recognizable positions within the state. Like the researchers of femocrats, I am interested primarily in those movement activists within the state in positions that allow them to influence policy outputs. On the other hand, like Eisenstein (1990), I prefer not to identify primary locations within the state that movement activists must occupy. Rather, the state-movement intersection (in the form of movement activists within the state) may be located in multiple locations within the state, not just in those agencies that are considered primary policy makers in the area of interest to a particular movement.[5] In the discussion that follows I utilize this definition when I refer to the state-movement intersection.

In addition to a conceptual definition, we need to create a way of measuring or characterizing state-movement intersections. These intersections can be measured along three different dimensions. First, one can simply talk about the *number of movement activists* within the state. For example, on one extreme, the South African antiapartheid movement represents one movement that had few if any activists located within the state. On the other hand, movements such as the environmental movement may have many members within the ranks of the state. It is also important to remember that movement activists in the state may be drawn from specific parts or wings of a movement. For example, Freeman divided the women's movement into "older" and "younger" wings. In talking about the creation of the National Organization for Women, one of the premier movement organizations of the older wing, she notes that the founders "were primarily from the professions, labor, government and the communications industry" (1975, 55), while the younger wing came largely out of "social-action projects of the 1960s" and had little connection to government (56). Thus, a movement's representation within the state may not reflect the character of the movement as a whole.

Second, movements can be characterized by the *type of movement outsider status* that occurs. Returning to Tilly (1978), social movement scholars have viewed movements as challengers, existing outside of the state or "polity." However, I argue that this outside existence can vary quite a bit from movement to movement. Consider, for example, the civil rights movement and the environmental movement. In the case of the civil rights movement, blacks were explicitly and completely excluded from the polity in most southern states. These exclusions included legal prohibitions that disenfranchised them as well as social norms and repression that excluded African-Americans from any form of participation. The environmental movement faced a different kind of exclusion. Legally, members could vote and hold office; no norms excluded them from holding offices of power. Yet many of their ideas were unacceptable to established political parties so that they largely were not adopted or supported by government actors.

Figure 5.1 arrays different types of exclusion along a continuum. An

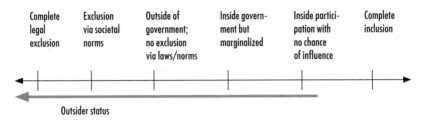

Figure 5.1. Theorizing types of outsider movement status as a continuum.

important part of this continuum of outsider status for my purposes is the several ways that movements may be outsiders even while existing within the state. Movement actors can be inside the government, but they may not be established members/players in the polity. For example, movement actors can be marginalized in parts of the bureaucracy that are ignored by key players; even with official positions within the state they may have little or no ability to influence policy. Indeed, Mazur (1995b) describes the Ministère des Droits de la Femme in France as a women's policy machinery that was highly marginalized within the state. It is even possible to go one step further and have movement activists as full and equal partners in policy *discussions*. However, if this represents a norm of access to the discussion without the possibility of affecting the final policy decisions, the activists in the state are still ultimately outsiders since there is no hope of effecting the changes desired by the movement.

Third, state-movement intersections can occur at different *locations within the state*. There may be very different ways of characterizing state locations. In liberal democracies, one may examine whether movement activists enter the bureaucracy, parliament, and the judiciary as well as institutions of interest mediation such as political parties and parapublic institutions (P. Katzenstein 1987).[6] In federal countries, one can examine state-movement intersections at national and subnational levels.

For specific movements, there may be different ways to categorize locations within the state. One important distinction is between locations of government recognized as related to the movement and those that are not. Some parts of the state may be more open to participation by movement actors than others. For example, bureaucratic agencies created as a result of movement action may be more accessible to movement actors than other bureaucratic agencies. As Eisenstein (1996) and others have noted, we might expect to find governments more accepting of feminist activists within women's policy machineries. However, the interests of movement activists do not always coincide with the agencies created by the state to address movement demands. We might also expect to find movement activists in other arenas related to their interests. For example, feminists in the United States interested in violence against women are unlikely to enter the Women's Bureau, located in the Department of Labor, which does not have jurisdiction over this policy problem. Similarly, environmentalists are as likely to be drawn to the Department of Energy and the Department of Agriculture as to the Environmental Protection Agency. Location within the state is likely to be important since some places may be better for movement activists to achieve policy ends. For example, Bonastia (2000) has argued that affirmative action policies failed in the Bureau of Housing and Urban Development (HUD) but fared better in the Equal Employment Opportunity Commission (EEOC) because HUD was divided by multiple purposes and independent agencies, served multiple constituencies, and suffered from a scandal in one part that tainted the entire agency. As a result, issues of constituency, purpose, and history may all come to bear on whether a particular location within the state is more or less useful to movement activists.

Although this conceptualization of the intersection of states and social movements suggests that three different dimensions are important, I will look at the size of this intersection and discuss why large intersections between the state and social movements might be important for our understanding of social movements and the role that public policy plays in influencing such intersections.

Theorizing the Effects of State-Movement Intersections

If the existence of the state-movement intersection has been ignored by social movement theorists, this is only problematic if these intersections influence the development, tactics, or outcomes of social movements. In this section, I present some initial hypotheses relating the size of the state-movement intersection to movement tactical choices.

Many of the theories about the dynamics of social movements suggest that movements may become more conventional in their tactics, particularly when encouraged by governments to do so (Piven and Cloward 1977; Meyer and Tarrow 1998; Tarrow 1998). In particular, Piven and Cloward argue that the state may incorporate some movement elites into the political system, thereby moderating their demands and demobilizing protest. The unflattering stereotype behind this claim is of the bureaucrat who believes that only institutional paths lead to change. This view is predicated either on the idea that those individuals who choose jobs within the state do so because they already believe that institutional paths to change are the best way or on the idea that once individuals become insiders their views become completely molded by their careers.

One need not rely solely on these premises to assert that insiders will tend to choose insider tactics. Insiders may also choose insider tactics because they have a wider array of such tactics available to them (Tilly 1978). Because they learn insider tactics in the course of working in government, they are more likely to employ such tactics than those who have less knowledge of and facility with insider repertoires. Following any of these lines of argument would lead to the hypothesis that a large state-movement intersection increases the likelihood of insider tactics.

On the other hand, political opportunity theories offer a more nuanced view of the connection between the state-movement intersection and insider tactics. Movement activists within the state do have a closer perspective on the political opportunities afforded by insider tactics and therefore are likely to be better informed about the actual political opportunities that exist. This increase in information is important since several theorists have suggested that social movements must recognize the existence of political opportunities in order for these to affect social movement activities (Banaszak 1996b; Sawyers and Meyer 1999). If movement activists within the state are most likely to be aware of the array of political opportunities within the state, we might see these activists utilizing more insider tactics. Yet this perspective implies that where they have information that inside opportunities really are closed, we would expect movement activists within the state to pursue extra-institutional tactics.

As the size of state-movement intersections increases for any particular movement, we might expect the use of insider tactics to increase as well unless all avenues are closed, when we would expect to see movement activists in the state also encouraging outside tactics. If true, insider status and insider tactics need not be synonymous; under some circumstances we should see insiders perpetrating outsider tactics. Before we examine the connection between insider tactics and movement activists in the state, we need a better understanding of how and why state-movement intersections develop.

The Development of State-Movement Intersections

The factors that lead to the creation or transformation of state-movement intersections can be categorized in terms of supply and demand.[7] On the one hand, there may be reasons that social movement activists become drawn into the state. Some of those reasons may relate to the specific characteristics of the individuals themselves (and the corresponding distribution of those characteristics across movements); others may relate to the movement activists' experiences within the movement (e.g., activists may develop an increasing expertise through interaction with the state that leads them to desire a career in the state). Factors that lead activists to enter the state are considered *supply* factors, that is, they increase the supply of activists in the state.

On the other hand, the state may seek to encourage movement activists to enter the state by providing differential opportunities. They may alter such opportunities over time as their desire to have movement input waxes and wanes. For example, less than two months after the Kennedy assassination, Lyndon Johnson publicly vowed to follow the Commission on the Status of Women's suggestion by hiring fifty women in top government jobs. The scramble for qualified appointees led to women's organizations as varied as the Business and Professional Women's Organization to the Lucy Stone League nominating qualified candidates (Harrison 1988; Zelman 1982). The government's encouragement of women activists provides a *demand* reason for the increase in the state-movement intersection. While there are potentially many factors that contribute to the state providing such opportunities, I will focus on the role that public policies play, giving examples from the women's movement.

The Role of Public Policies

While public policy may affect movement activists' interest in working with the state indirectly, policies are more likely to influence the state-movement intersection by increasing and decreasing opportunities for movement activists to enter the state. The literature on social movement outcomes recognizes that access to the state can be one type of positive outcome (Banaszak 1996b; Burstein 1985; Gamson 1990; Schumaker 1975). However, this form of social movement success usually is conceived much more broadly than mere opportunities for increasing the size of the state-movement intersection. Gamson, for example, in discussing four indicators of "acceptance," mentions "inclusion" as the fourth indicator.[8] "Inclusion" is defined as the most extreme form of acceptance where challenging group members are given "positions of status or authority in the antagonist's organizational structure" (1990, 32). As I have already suggested, Piven and Cloward (1977) have most explicitly focused on the specific form of acceptance implied by movement activists entering the state.

I describe three ways that public policies make opportunities for movement activists to gain entrée to state positions: change in organizations, personnel, and operating rules and norms. I provide examples of each by looking at the changes wrought by the early demands made by the U.S. women's movement for equal opportunity in employment. While particular public policies may create more than one of these changes at a time (for example, a new operating rule also creates changes in personnel), they each represent different mechanisms by which policies may create opportunities for movements to enter the state.

Organizational change. Public policies often result in the creation, combination, or elimination of specific organizations (i.e., departments, agencies) that can open or close opportunities for movement activists to enter the state. Policies that mandate new governmental activities sometimes create new organizations to implement those policies, or more often they assign new tasks to existing organizational entities. When the policy change is pursued by a social movement, the organization in charge of the new policy may seek to utilize movement expertise in administrating the new programs. While this may happen both when organizations are created and when the existing competencies of an organization are expanded, new organizations are more likely to create opportunities for movement activists to enter the state. In part, this reflects the lack of incumbent personnel to take up the existing tasks and the attraction to movement activists of being able to build the organization from the ground up.

In the case of the women's rights movement, the passage of the Civil Rights Act of 1964 and the creation of the Equal Employment Opportunity Commission provided opportunities for entrée into the state. The EEOC created one hundred initial openings for staff whose job it was to deal with complaints of sexual and racial discrimination (EEOC 2000, 5). While most of these positions were filled by personnel from other parts of the federal bureaucracy, others entered the government for the first time. Furthermore, although the women's movement had not yet experienced resurgence, those with an interest in discrimination sought positions there because it appeared to be an exciting place to work (author's interview with former EEOC lawyer, May 11, 2002).

Personnel changes. Government policies may also result in fundamental changes in the people occupying particular positions, granting greater (or in other cases limiting) access to state positions for movement activists. For the women's movement, the creation of the Equal Employment Opportunity Commission was not the only factor. Indeed, because Title VII did not apply to federal employees, the creation of the EEOC did not alter many personnel decisions within the federal government.[9] However, in 1967, under pressure from women's organizations and the President's Commission on the Status of Women, President Johnson signed executive order 11375, which added a ban on sexual discrimination to the previous executive order that outlawed racial discrimination in federal employment (Zelman 1982, 116). Because the previous executive order also called for affirmative action, the Civil Service Commission immediately instituted the Federal Women's Program, which was designed to improve women's position within the civil service (Harrison 1988, 202). Although the order created no new agencies (outside of a Federal Women's Program coordinator), the growing opportunities for women as a whole increased the supply of positions available to feminist activists.

The legislation and executive orders that banned discrimination in hiring for women and minorities had a lasting effect on equal employment policies for both groups. However, it is worth noting that policies that create personnel changes may also be administration specific. Particular governments may choose to increase the number of movement activists or make other personnel changes that create opportunities for movement activists. Lyndon Johnson's 1964 decision to appoint fifty women to high-level positions represents such an opportunity. Similarly, Richard Nixon named Barbara Hackman Franklin as his staff assistant responsible for recruiting women to high-level positions in the federal government. Indeed, changes in the size of the state-movement intersection may be one of the results of the traditional political opportunity that occurs when allies come to power in government.

Changes in operating rules and norms. Finally, policies may influence the degree to which movement activists enter the state even when organizational charts remain unchanged and there is no attempt to alter government personnel. The operating rules and norms of government organizations can make government positions more attractive or make particular locations within the state more or less hospitable to movement activists. In the case of the EEOC, the executive director often informally affected the norms of the commission. The first two executive directors of the EEOC discouraged the enforcement of the sex provision of Title VII, even though one-third of the complaints filed in the first year cited sex discrimination (EEOC 2000, 7). Indeed, Herman Edelsberg, the second executive director, was quoted in the press as saying, "There are people on this Commission who think that no man should be required to have a male secretary—and I am one of them" (Harrison 1988, 187). The hostility toward enforcing the sex provision of Title VII was so explicit in the first years of the EEOC that it became the motivating force behind the creation of the National Organization for Women (NOW) and provoked the resignation of Aileen Hernandez, the five-member commission's only woman (Harrison 1988, 196). This example illustrates how particular leaders can influence the operating rules and norms of state institutions, making entrée into the state more difficult (or attractive) to movement activists.

When should we see these sorts of policy changes? I have used a fairly specific and narrow example (equal employment policy and the women's movement) to illustrate how policy changes the organization, personnel, and operating rules and norms of the state in ways that alter the state-movement intersection. I suspect that such examples are ubiquitous. Anytime the state adopts policies (even informal ones) that affect the movement or its goals (and perhaps even in some other cases), it alters the state-movement intersection.

Such policies are not likely to be evenly distributed over time or states. As Baumgartner and Jones note, policy change can occur both incrementally and in bursts, when "old ways of doing things are swept aside, to be replaced by new organizational forms" (1993, 235). Burstein (1999, 17–18) argues that smaller changes, like the turnover of administrations, also provide opportunities for movements to influence policy implementation because there is wider discretion at these times. The examples I have described involve both the sweeping transformations chronicled by Baumgartner and Jones (the passage of Title VII) and the more ubiquitous change described by Burstein (Johnson's fifty-women campaign). Both forms of policy transformation inspire changes in movement actors within the state as the public policies that create or close opportunities for entrée are first implemented and then altered.

Similarly, some states and some parts of each state will be more vulnerable to state-movement intersection than others. Moore (1999, 101) argues that institutions like the state are more open to challenge (and therefore change) when the clients that are served determine institutional support, especially when those clients are organized. This suggests that states that are more open to movements (see, for example, Kitschelt 1986) are likely to have greater intersections with social movements. The state institutions that deal with issues of importance to the movement—like the EEOC in the United States—are also likely to have larger numbers of movement activists for both demand and supply reasons.

The State-Movement Intersection and Insider Tactics

Examining the connection between insider tactics and U.S. women's movement activists within the state requires two steps. Because the state-movement intersection has not been examined in great detail, I first describe the size of the intersection between the state and the women's movement. I then bring some evidence to bear on the questions of whether and how this state-movement intersection influences the choice of insider tactics by the movement. For each of these steps, I utilize both quantitative and qualitative evidence. The quantitative data are drawn from existing sources and as such provide at best a hint about the general overview of the intersection between state and women's movement. The qualitative data are drawn from archival research on the early years of the second wave of the women's movement, oral histories drawn from the Schlesinger Library's Women in the Federal Government collection, the Pennsylvania State University's A Few Good Women collection, and a small number of interviews with women's movement activists who held positions in the U.S. bureaucracy. I identified these "insider" activists by their clear and sustained activism within feminist oganizations as documented in the historical record. The fourteen women interviewed were active in the early phase of the second wave (1964–72), and the qualitative examples are all drawn from this period. These interviews were conducted as part of an ongoing project on the effects of the state-movement intersection on the U.S. women's movement.

Describing the Intersection between the U.S. Women's Movement and the State

Determining the number of movement activists within the state is difficult because there are no consistent statistical data on the movement (or even organizational) membership of U.S. bureaucrats. I rely here on several different measures that might provide some insight.

While not all women are feminists, knowing the number of women in the civil service provides a theoretical upper bound in measuring the degree of intersection between the state and the women's movement.[10] The percentage of women in bureaucratic positions with the government is a statistic that has been collected over time and so provides a sense of how the potential size of the state-movement intersection could change over time. Figure 5.2 presents the percentage of women employed in upper GS pay

Year	% of women in GS13–15 jobs
1966	3.64
1977	5.16
1981	8.55
1985	11.10
1989	15.48
1993	19.84
1996	22.17

Figure 5.2. Percentages of GS13–15 jobs held by women, 1966–96. (Data from Naff 2001, 41, for 1977–96; U.S. Civil Service Commission 1968, 11, for 1966.)

grades of the federal government over three decades. The figure suggests that there has been considerable growth in the proportion of women in the U.S. bureaucracy. In the ten years between 1966 and 1977, the percentage of women in these midlevel pay grades grew by over 40 percent. Nonetheless, in 1977 women still constituted a small percentage of the workforce in these pay grades; by 1996 they had grown to a larger percentage, although they were still underrepresented compared to their proportion in the working population. Interestingly, much of that growth occurred between 1981 and 1993, under the Reagan and Bush administrations, when the number of women in higher GS grades almost doubled. Thus, there was tremendous growth in the number of women in higher-level governmental positions over the three decades of the women's movement, providing the potential for greater state-movement intersections.

Figure 5.2 represents only the upper limit of movement activists within the state; many of the women in those high-level GS grades are not feminist activists.[11] It is more difficult to uncover whether these numbers represent an influx of movement activists into the state, particularly over time. I found only one survey, conducted in 1977, that asks women bureaucrats to identify whether they are active in women's organizations. The Center for the American Woman and Politics (1978) surveyed women appointees to the federal executive branch in 1977. That survey suggests that during the Carter administration, women's movement activists were quite common in this group. Of the twenty-two women who completed the survey and answered this question, 36 percent stated that they were members of feminist social action organizations such as the National Organization for Women (NOW) or Women's Equity Action League (WEAL). Over half of the respondents mentioned belonging to other sorts of women's organizations, including groups like the National Federation of Business and Professional Women, that sought greater opportunities for women. However, the survey suffered from a low response rate, both for the entire survey (only 40 percent returned the questionnaires) and for the particular question (of the thirty-five individuals who answered the survey, only twenty-two—62 percent—completed this question). Thus, we have information for only 25 percent of the total female federal appointees surveyed, and it is possible that individuals who responded were more likely to be feminists. Nonetheless, the numbers suggest that the percentage of activists at the highest levels of the bureaucracy may be fairly large under the right circumstances. Even if we assume that all nonrespondents are nonfeminists, we would still conclude that at least 9 percent of the women appointees were members of feminist organizations. Given the small proportion of the general population that ever becomes active in social movements, this number is significant.

My qualitative interviews with early feminist activists who were employed by the federal government and the oral histories I consulted mirror the survey during the Carter administration. None of the women I interviewed were political appointees during the early years of the women's movement, and none of them served in the same agency of government, yet all mentioned that there were relatively few women above GS-13 in government and that they were usually the only woman at this level in their own offices.[12] As a result, they tended to form networks with women at the same levels in other offices, departments, and agencies, particularly with those already supportive of a feminist agenda. In the years prior to the revitalization of the women's movement, feminist networks developed through interdepartmental or interagency cooperation on issues, external organizational membership, or the few government training programs where women could go. For example, the President's Commission on the Status of Women resulted in a number of midlevel bureaucrats (particularly those who were attorneys) being assigned tasks that brought them into contact with the committee. Most of these women were also members of women's professional organizations (such as the Business and Professional Women's Organization and the National Woman's Party) where they met other women with similar interests. Finally, while women were largely excluded in the 1960s from advanced training courses for midlevel bureaucrats, the Department of Agriculture's Graduate School offered such a course for women where feminists from different offices met each other.

Thus, there is both qualitative and limited statistical evidence that the U.S. women's movement did have a presence within the federal government from the beginnings of the second wave through the mid-1970s. Many of the women I interviewed were working in the federal government as the second wave of the women's movement began, and many of them considered themselves feminist activists even in these early years. Given the existence of an intersection between the U.S. women's movement and the state, I now turn to an exploration of how that intersection influenced the tactics of the U.S. women's movement.

Insider Activists and Insider Tactics

Given the lack of any systematic information about state-movement intersections, it is difficult to say anything about how movement activists in the state affect the movement. To take a first cut at whether employment within the state influences movement activists' activity, I examined feminist activists in the Verba et al. (1990) American Citizen Participation Study data. Because I have selected only activists in organizations who said that they were most active in women's organizations, the number of movement activists is very small. Nonetheless, Table 5.1 shows that there is little relationship between use of protest as a tactic and movement activists' location vis-à-vis the state. Movement activists who were also government employees were less likely to state that they had engaged in protest activity in the past two years, but the connection between tactics and insider status is not statistically significant.[13]

These data hint that movement activists located within the state may not utilize tactics different from those used by activists outside the state. Although we can take this analysis only as suggestive, there does not appear to be a "linkage of location, form, and content" (M. Katzenstein 1998b, 195). Freeman's categorization of old and new movement activists may explain one reason for the lack of difference among feminist activists in government. Freeman argues that movement activists in government are located in the older wing of the women's movement. They may not differ in their tactics or beliefs from other members of that wing, but the different wings, drawn from different groups of women, each have radically different emphases in terms of content and tactics (Freeman 1975; Ferree and Hess 1985; Ryan 1992). Without more information on the activists and their characteristics,

Table 5.1. Cross-tabulation of feminist activists in and out of the state by protest activity.

		Nongovernmental employee	Governmental employee	Total
Engaged in protest in past two years	No	6 (46%)	5 (83%)	11 (58%)
	Yes	7 (54%)	1 (17%)	8 (42%)
Total		13 (100%)	6 (100%)	19 (100%)

Source: These data were taken from the American Citizen Participation Study conducted by Verba et al. (1990) (ICPSR data set 6635).

Note: Feminist activists are women who state that they are most active in women's organizations. To make sure that this category does not include women working in antifeminist or other women's organizations, women were asked a number of questions about attitudes toward equal opportunity, gender roles, and abortion. Those giving nonfeminist answers were excluded (as was the lone male who was most active in women's organizations). Fisher's exact method produces a $p = .1366$.

we cannot conclude that the employment in the state is the cause of the small and insignificant difference among activists in Table 5.1.

Moreover, knowing that feminist activists within the state are engaging in protest less than those activists outside the state does not provide conclusive information that this group is more conservative or moderate than other activists. We are faced with a paucity of information about the sorts of activities in which such movement activists engage. The qualitative evidence from existing oral histories and my own qualitative interviews with early feminist activists help to fill this void. Although not providing systematic evidence about all feminist activists within the state, these data illustrate the activities of a number of feminists who were employed by the federal government.

One thing that becomes clear from my interviews is that feminist activists within the state had a wide array of nonprotest tactics available to them and that participation in protest appears to have been chosen primarily when other inside tactics were ineffective. Two examples illustrate tactical decisions made by feminist insiders within the bureaucracy.

First, many of the feminist activists I interviewed (or who have left oral histories) were lawyers. In the late 1960s, a number of them—many among the founding members of NOW—represented women suing employers in court for employment discrimination. This legal work was done off the job, but their place in the federal government gave these feminist activists considerable insight into the initial workings of the EEOC, including the knowledge that it ultimately had no compliance mechanism, and information (through grapevines of feminist activists in government) about which plaintiffs needed legal help (Paterson 1986; Pressman Fuentes 1999; author's interview, March 25, 2002). Many of these equal employment cases became the biggest early successes for the rising women's movement.

Although feminist activists within the state often acted within institutions, as Katzenstein (1998a) and McAdam, Tarrow, and Tilly (2001) argue, this by no means made their tactics moderate or conventional. There is evidence in the early women's movement to support the unconventional nature that institutional tactics may take. For example, because the Equal Employment Opportunity Commission had no enforcement powers before 1972, its feminist lawyers turned to other institutional means to encourage compliance. In the case of AT&T, a company that accounted for about 7 percent of the commission's workload, attempts to use conciliation to change policies were unsuccessful. One EEOC lawyer, who was also active in NOW's Legal Defense Foundation, found out in 1970 that AT&T was petitioning the Federal Communications Commission (FCC) for a rate hike. This lawyer developed a strategy to have the EEOC attempt to block the rate increase (Freeman 1975, 189; Shapiro 1973). As this lawyer told the story, the EEOC's argument was molded to present a "really revolutionary view of sex discrimination . . . We wanted to present the whole sociology and psychology of sexual stereotypes as it was inculcated into the Bell System structure" (*Washington Post,* May 20, 1973). Thus, despite using an institutional approach, the activities of this insider feminist were neither conventional in tactics nor moderate in ideology.

Second, feminist activists employed by the federal government did not limit their activities to institutional activities; many organized or participated on the front lines of very public protests. In 1967 several women from the Washington, DC, chapter of NOW organized a picket of the EEOC to protest its ruling that permitted separate help wanted ads. The protests occurred when the EEOC was ignoring sex discrimination cases and some leaders of the EEOC had made very discriminatory statements. Feminist activists within the federal government were aware that the EEOC was essentially closed to issues of sex discrimination, and it was these activists who encouraged and organized the pickets. The press coverage in the *Washington Post* (December 15, 1967, B3) included a photograph of one of the picketers, who was identified by name—but not by the fact that she was employed in a different federal agency. In fact, of the approximately dozen women who marched on the picket line in Washington, DC, that day, two or three of them were employees of the federal government. A few other feminist activists within government supported and helped to organize the pickets but had serious concerns that their jobs might be in jeopardy, which kept them from actually participating in the pickets.[14] Feminists inside the state did participate in and support extra-institutional protest, but they chose this particular tactic only when working within the system (in this case the EEOC) did not seem possible.

The emphasis on the moderation of movements by insiders represents a major thesis within social movement theory. The preliminary evidence on feminist activists presented here suggests that there is little to indicate that a larger state-movement intersection will produce less protest. The small sample of feminist activists from the American Citizen Participation Study does not allow us to say with certainty that state-movement intersections contribute to either growing moderation or a demobilization of the movement. There are also at least some examples of insiders choosing protest activities when other opportunities are closed. Yet, the anecdotal evidence suggests that the size and character of the state-movement intersection influences the movement's tactical decisions.

Conclusion

In 1975, Jo Freeman, looking at a vibrant and active women's movement, concluded:

> There is clearly a symbiotic relationship between feminists within our governmental institutions, feminists operating in the private sphere, and even feminists who are openly opposed to and/or alienated from the American political system. (230)

In this chapter, I have focused on those portions of the movement and the state that overlap, particularly the "feminists within our governmental institutions" that Freeman mentions. That feminist activists, civil rights activists, and environmental activists sometimes take jobs within the state is no secret to any social movement scholar or movement activist. Yet social movement scholars ignore these activists when they define social movements as necessarily outside the state and characterize movements and states as separate entities interacting with one another. In fact, both movements and states are more complicated than such an analysis suggests. I argue that we must redefine movements and states as institutions that have the potential for overlapping memberships.

The call for a more nuanced view of movements and states is more than a trivial conceptual redefinition. These state-movement intersections can have important effects on the development and outcomes of social movements. In this chapter, I have examined one particular aspect of social movement development—the decision to take to the streets or work the air-conditioned halls of government. This dichotomy is often complicated by the belief that working within the state means moderating the movement. Social movement and feminist scholars have often (with some important exceptions) assumed that when movement activists choose to work within the state they are tempering their goals and moderating their tactics. The preliminary evidence presented in this chapter suggests that the connection between the state-movement intersection and insider tactics is more tenuous. Feminists working in the state often chose insider tactics—but not always. When they perceived that opportunities within the state were closed, they were willing to take to the streets. Moreover, some of the actions that occurred within the halls of government were by no means moderate, as the EEOC's attempt to block AT&T's rate hike suggests.

The women's movement presence within the state also provided additional opportunities, which might have been absent if the movement had existed solely outside the state. Networks of feminists in the federal bureaucracy in

the late 1960s gave the movement access to information about women pressing equal employment claims against corporations. This information allowed
the women's movement to press for social change using the courts (often
using lawyers whose day jobs were in the federal bureaucracy). It also helped
the movement identify opportunities within government (i.e., an EEOC ignoring its mandate to protect women) that directly led to protest politics.

Not all social movements will have as large an intersection with the
state as the U.S. women's movement seems to have had. I am arguing for
increased attention on state-movement intersections because this may be
one important variable that distinguishes different social movements, and
even the same social movement, over time. I have also tried to explore
some of the factors that might explain variations in the size and character
of state-movement intersections. Public policy is a vital link in our understanding, accounting for many of the dynamic changes in state-movement
intersections, which in turn may affect the choice of tactics, the type of outcomes, or the mobilization and demobilization of the movement. The formation, modification, or elimination of particular public policies changes
the organization of government, moves people in and out of institutions,
and creates a web of operating rules and norms that determines the functioning of the state. These types of changes, whether profound or minute,
sometimes even in areas far removed from the social movement's primary
issue, may alter the state-movement intersection by changing the supply of
movement activists interested in positions within the state or by altering the
demand of the state for movement activists.

Notes

This essay was initially prepared for the workshop on "Social Movements and Public Policy," January 11–13, 2002, Laguna Beach, California. The author thanks
Karen Beckwith, David Kirchner, Amy Mazur, Dieter Rucht, Jennifer Schoonmaker, Dorothy McBride Stetson, and the editors of this volume for comments
given in the course of developing this chapter. I also thank Chad Lavin for an
insightful question that led to this essay.

1. There is a very large literature on the use of insider tactics and strategies as
opposed to traditional extra-institutional tactics (see, for example, Amenta, ch. 1
this volume; Banaszak 1996b, ch. 7; Bernstein 2001; Rochon and Mazmanian
1993). However, the decision to utilize insider or outsider tactics is a separate concept from the overlap in groups and individuals of movements and states, as I will
discuss more fully later.

2. These unique features of the state include a monopoly on the legitimate use
of force and its position as regulator, in liberal democracies, of the mechanisms

that allow outsiders to directly influence the institution, such as elections (Moore 1999, 100; Poggi 1990).

3. Women's policy machineries are defined, following Stetson and Mazur (1995), as the bureaucratic institutions within the state responsible for policies specific to women. The names of these institutions and the specific types of policies that fall under the rubric "specific to women" vary quite substantially across countries. In this chapter, I also include in my discussion of women activists within the state those individual bureaucrats making women's policy in departments or agencies that have other primary concerns.

4. Outshoorn (1994, 144) is an exception in recognizing this underlying assumption.

5. One reason for not pre-associating particular locations with the movement is that the identification of specific agencies with individual issues is often the result of considerable conflict, and even if seemingly stable in the short term may undergo rapid change in some periods (Baumgartner and Jones 1993).

6. As we move away from government institutions and into other parts of the state, it becomes more difficult to speak as clearly about state institutions. Institutions of interest mediation present a problem since they begin to overlap more completely with elements of social movements such as social movement organizations. In this chapter, I avoid this conundrum by keeping my discussion largely on the bureaucracy.

7. The supply-demand analogy used here is inspired by Randall (1987) and McCarthy (ch. 3 this volume).

8. Gamson defines acceptance as "acceptance of a challenging group by its antagonists as a valid spokesman for a legitimate set of interests" (1990, 28).

9. In any case, the EEOC's leadership was initially openly hostile to enforcing the sexual discrimination clause (see, for example, Harrison 1988, 187–91).

10. It is also possible that men may count themselves among feminist activists. The qualitative interviews turned up the names of several male bureaucrats who were active members of feminist organizations. However, they are likely to be fairly rare.

11. It seems more plausible that the women in high GS grades during the Reagan and Bush administrations are more likely to be countermovement activists.

12. The exceptions were the Woman's Bureau, the Children's Bureau, the Bureau of Home Economics, and the Office of Education, all of which had higher concentrations of women in the mid- and upper levels of the bureaucracy (Kiplinger 1942, 303–4).

13. Because chi-squared tests can be unreliable when the expected cell counts are less than 5, I also used Fisher's exact method for calculating probabilities, which is not subject to the same concern (see McNemar 1969, 272–75). The result

using chi-squared and Fisher's was the same (p = .1366), indicating that there was not a significant difference between activists and nonactivists.

14. Given that the 1937 Hatch Act forbids federal employees from taking "an active part in political management or in political campaigns" (U.S. Civil Service Commission 1949, 11), the danger to the jobs of these participants was very real. For example, the boss of one of the picket participants expressed concern that the activist's presence in public demonstrations might adversely affect their office. From then on, that particular activist wore a disguise when participating in public demonstrations (private communication, July 15, 2002).

References

Banaszak, Lee Ann. 1996a. "When Waves Collide: Cycles of Protest and the Swiss and American Women's Movements." *Political Research Quarterly* 49 (December): 837–60.

———. 1996b. *Why Movements Succeed or Fail: Opportunity, Culture, and the Struggle for Woman Suffrage.* Princeton, NJ: Princeton University Press.

Banaszak, Lee Ann, Karen Beckwith, and Dieter Rucht. 2003a. "When Power Relocates: Interactive Changes in Women's Movements and States." In *Women's Movements Facing a Reconfigured State,* ed. Lee Ann Banaszak, Karen Beckwith, and Dieter Rucht, 1–29. Cambridge: Cambridge University Press.

———, eds. 2003b. *Women's Movements Facing a Reconfigured State.* Cambridge: Cambridge University Press.

Baumgartner, Frank, and Bryan Jones. 1993. *Agendas and Instability in American Politics.* Chicago: University of Chicago Press.

Bernstein, Anya. 2001. *The Moderation Dilemma: Legislative Coalitions and the Politics of Family and Medical Leave.* Pittsburgh: University of Pittsburgh Press.

Birnbaum, Pierre. 1988. *States and Collective Action: The European Experience.* Cambridge: Cambridge University Press.

Bonastia, Chris. 2000. "Why Did Affirmative Action in Housing Fail during the Nixon Era? Exploring the 'Institutional Homes' of Social Policies." *Social Problems* 47, no. 4: 523–42.

Burstein, Paul. 1985. *Discrimination, Jobs, and Politics: The Struggle for Equal Employment Opportunity in the United States since the New Deal.* Chicago: University of Chicago Press.

———. 1999. "Social Movements and Public Policy." In *How Social Movements Matter,* ed. Marco Guigni, Doug McAdam, and Charles Tilly, 3–21. Minneapolis: University of Minnesota Press.

Center for the American Woman and Politics. 1978. *Women in Public Office: A Biographical Directory and Statistical Analysis.* 2nd ed. Metuchen, NJ: Scarecrow Press.

della Porta, Donatella, and Dieter Rucht. 1995. "Left-Libertarian Movements in

Context." In *The Politics of Social Protest: Comparative Perspectives on States and Social Movements,* ed. J. Craig Jenkins and Bert Klandermans, 229–72. Minneapolis: University of Minnesota Press.

EEOC (Equal Employment Opportunity Commission). 2000. *The Story of the United States Equal Employment Opportunity Commission: Ensuring the Promise of Opportunity for 35 Years.* Washington, DC: Equal Employment Opportunity Commission.

Eisenstein, Hester. 1990. "Femocrats, Official Feminism, and the Uses of Power." In *Playing the State: Australian Feminist Interventions,* ed. Sophie Watson. Boston: Allen and Unwin.

———. 1996. *Inside Agitators: Australian Femocrats and the State.* Philadelphia: Temple University Press.

Ferree, Myra Marx, and Beth Hess. 1985. *Controversy and Coalition: The New Feminist Movement.* Boston: Twayne.

Flam, Helena, ed. 1994. *States and Anti-Nuclear Movements.* Edinburgh: Edinburgh University Press.

Freeman, Jo. 1975. *The Politics of Women's Liberation.* New York: Longman.

Gamson, William. 1990. *The Strategy of Social Protest.* 2nd ed. Belmont, CA: Wadsworth.

Harrison, Cynthia. 1988. *On Account of Sex: The Politics of Women's Issues, 1945–1968.* Berkeley: University of California Press.

Jenkins, J. Craig, and Bert Klandermans. 1995. "The Politics of Social Protest." In *The Politics of Social Protest: Comparative Perspectives on States and Social Movements,* ed. J. Craig Jenkins and Bert Klandermans, 3–13. Minneapolis: University of Minnesota Press.

Katzenstein, Mary Fainsod. 1998a. *Faithful and Fearless: Moving Feminist Protest inside the Church and Military.* Princeton, NJ: Princeton University Press.

———. 1998b. "Stepsisters: Feminist Movement Activism in Different Institutional Spaces." In *The Social Movement Society,* ed. David S. Meyer and Sidney Tarrow, 195–216. Boulder, CO: Rowman and Littlefield.

Katzenstein, Peter. 1987. *Policy and Politics in West Germany: The Growth of a Semisovereign State.* Philadelphia: Temple University Press.

Kiplinger, W. M. 1942. *Washington Is Like That.* New York: Harper and Brothers.

Kitschelt, Herbert. 1986. "Political Opportunity Structures and Political Protest: Anti-Nuclear Movements in Four Democracies." *British Journal of Political Science* 16, no. 1: 57–85.

Kranz, Harry. 1976. *The Participatory Bureaucracy.* Lexington, MA: Lexington Books (D. C. Heath).

Mazur, Amy. 1995a. *Gender Bias and the State: Symbolic Reform at Work in Fifth Republic France.* Pittsburgh: University of Pittsburgh.

———. 1995b. "Strong State and Symbolic Reform." In *Comparative State*

Feminism, ed. Dorothy McBride Stetson and Amy Mazur. Thousand Oaks, CA: Sage.

———, ed. 2001. *State Feminism, Women's Movements, and Job Training.* New York: Routledge.

———. 2002. *Theorizing Feminist Policy.* Oxford: Oxford University Press.

McAdam, Doug, Sidney Tarrow, and Charles Tilly. 2001. *Dynamics of Contention.* Cambridge: Cambridge University Press.

McNemar, Quinn. 1969. *Psychological Statistics.* 4th ed. New York: John Wiley.

Meyer, David, and Sidney Tarrow. 1998. *The Social Movement Society.* Boulder, CO: Rowman and Littlefield.

Moore, Kelly. 1999. "Political Protest and Institutional Change." In *How Social Movements Matter,* ed. Marco Guigni, Doug McAdam, and Charles Tilly. Minneapolis: University of Minnesota Press.

Naff, Katherine. 2001. *To Look Like America: Dismantling Barriers for Women and Minorities in Government.* Boulder, CO: Westview Press.

Outshoorn, Joyce. 1994. "Between Movement and Government: 'Femocrats in the Netherlands.'" *Schweizerisches Jahrbuch für Politische Wissenschaft* 34: 141–63.

———. 1997. "Incorporating Feminism: The Women's Policy Network in the Netherlands." In *Sex Equality in Western Europe,* ed. Frances Gardiner, 109–26. New York: Routledge.

Paterson, Judith. 1986. *Be Somebody: A Biography of Marguerite Rawalt.* Austin, TX: Eakin Press.

Piven, Francis, and Richard Cloward. 1977. *Poor People's Movements: Why They Succeed, How They Fail.* Random House: New York.

Poggi, Gianfranco. 1990. *The State: Its Nature, Developments, and Perspectives.* Stanford, CA: Stanford University Press.

Pressman Fuentes, Sonia. 1999. *Eat First—You Don't Know What They'll Give You.* Philadelphia: Xlibris.

Pringle, Rosemary, and Sophie Watson. 1992. "'Women's Interests' and the Post-Structuralist State." In *Destabilizing Theory: Contemporary Feminist Debates,* ed. Michèle Barrett and Anne Phillips. Stanford, CA: Stanford University Press.

Randall, Vicki. 1987. *Women and Politics: An International Perspective.* Chicago: University of Chicago Press.

Rochon, Thomas, and Daniel Mazmanian. 1993. "Social Movements and the Policy Process." *Annals of the American Academy of Political and Social Science* 528: 75–87.

Rupp, Leila J., and Verta Taylor. 1987. *Survival in the Doldrums: The American Women's Rights Movement, 1945 to the 1960s.* New York: Oxford University Press.

Ryan, Barbara. 1992. *Feminism and the Women's Movement.* New York: Routledge.

Santoro, Wayne A. 1999. "Conventional Politics Takes Center Stage: The Latino Struggle against English-Only Laws." *Social Forces* 77, no. 3: 887–909.

Santoro, Wayne A., and Gail M. McGuire. 1997. "Social Movement Insiders: The Impact of Institutional Activists on Affirmative Action and Comparable Worth Policies." *Social Problems* 44, no. 4: 503–20.

Sawer, Marian. 1995. "'Femocrats in Glass Towers?' The Office of the Status of Women in Australia." In *Comparative State Feminism,* ed. Dorothy McBride Stetson and Amy Mazur, 22–39. Thousand Oaks, CA: Sage.

Sawyers, Traci M., and David S. Meyer. 1999. "Missed Opportunities: Social Movement Abeyance and Public Policy." *Social Problems* 46, no. 2: 187–206.

Schumaker, Paul. 1975. "Policy Responsiveness to Protest-Group Demands." *Journal of Politics* 37 (May): 488–521.

Shapiro, Harvey D. 1973. "Women on the Line, Men at the Switchboard." *New York Times Magazine,* May 20, 1973, 26ff.

Smith, Steven Rathgeb, and Michael Lipsky. 1993. *Nonprofits for Hire: The Welfare State in the Age of Contracting.* Cambridge, MA: Harvard University Press.

Stetson, Dorothy McBride. 1995. "The Oldest Women's Policy Agency: The Women's Bureau in the United States." In *Comparative State Feminism,* ed. Dorothy McBride Stetson and Amy Mazur, 254–71. Thousand Oaks, CA: Sage.

Stetson, Dorothy McBride, and Amy Mazur. 1995. *Comparative State Feminism.* Thousand Oaks, CA: Sage.

Tarrow, Sidney. 1998. *Power in Movement: Social Movements and Contentious Politics.* 2nd ed. Cambridge: Cambridge University Press.

Tilly, Charles. 1978. *From Mobilization to Revolution.* Reading, MA: Addison-Wesley.

U.S. Civil Service Commission. 1949. *Hatch Act Decisions (Political Activity Cases) of the United States Civil Service Commission.* Washington, DC: U.S. Government Printing Office.

U.S. Civil Service Commission. Bureau of Management Services. 1968. *Study of Employment of Women in the Federal Government.* Washington, DC: U.S. Government Printing Office.

Vargas, Virginia, and Saskia Wieringa. 1998. "The Triangle of Empowerment: Processes and Actors in the Making of Public Policy for Women." In *Women's Movements and Public Policy in Europe, Latin America, and the Caribbean,* ed. Geertje Lycklama à Nijeholt, Virginia Vargas, and Saskia Wieringa. New York: Garland.

Verba, Sidney, Kay Lehman Schlozman, Henry E. Brady, and Norman Nie. 1990. *American Citizen Participation Study* [computer file]. ICPSR version. Chicago: University of Chicago, National Opinion Research Center (NORC) [producer], 1995. Ann Arbor, MI: Inter-university Consortium for Political and Social Research [distributor], 1995.

Watson, Sophie. 1990. "The State of Play: An Introduction." In *Playing the State: Australian State Interventions,* ed. Sophie Watson. Boston: Allen and Unwin.

Zelman, Patricia G. 1982. *Women, Work, and National Policy: The Kennedy-Johnson Years.* Studies in American History and Culture no. 33. Ann Arbor, MI: UMI Research Press.

6

The Policy Nexus: Professional Networks and the Formulation and Adoption of Workers' Compensation Reforms

Ryken Grattet

Social Movements and Public Policy Making

Scholarship on social movements and public policy exist as largely isolated enterprises (Meyer, introduction to this volume). They rely on different theoretical languages, concepts, and motivating questions, and individual studies in one field of scholarship rarely cite work in the other field (some exceptions are Burstein 1998, 1999; Amenta 1998; Amenta and Halfmann 2000). This is surprising given that social movements frequently focus on public policy to define some set of putative conditions as a social problem and given that public policy is frequently the product of social movement activism. In many ways, this gap represents the linchpin of this volume. What is needed is a common theoretical vocabulary for describing how social movements and government are connected to one another and how policy is shaped by the nature of that connection.

In this chapter, I propose some concepts and an analytic strategy for unpacking movement–public policy relationships, and I use these tools to investigate the Progressive era movement for workmen's compensation. Compensation reform provides an illustrative case because it reveals how focusing either on extra-state social movements or on intragovernmental public policy dynamics can be misleading. At first glance, compensation reform appears to be a case where "outsiders," business and labor groups, successfully lobbied for a policy change; however, a closer analysis reveals that a third group, professionals—some of whom were located "inside" the state—were significantly involved in formulating the systems that were ultimately adopted by states. As such, the case points out the limits of the conventional understanding of states and social movements as conceptually separable entities (see also Wolfson 2001; Banaszak, ch. 5 this volume). The case is also useful because it is not a clearly "positive" case of reform.[1] Although compensation reform was one of the first American social insurance policies, it passed here well after it did in many other industrialized nations, and successful passage was preceded by several years of failed attempts. How the movement subsequently pulled off a string of legislative victories in a short period of time reveals much about the ways movements and governments are intertwined and the consequences for policy such entanglements produce. The following section introduces the concepts and analytic strategy.

Movement Types, Movements of Professionals, and Movements as Networks

Any discussion of the relationship between movements and policy must begin by delineating types of movements on the basis of their policy orientation. Movements focused on litigation, movements focused on legislative change, and movements focused on policy implementation each may have quite different effects on public policy. Some movements develop reputations for prioritizing one policy strategy over others. For example, it is commonly understood that the trade union movement of the nineteenth century was primarily oriented toward changing policy through the courts (Urofsky 1980). Likewise, until the 1960s the NAACP was mainly oriented toward promoting civil rights through litigation (Rosenberg 1990). Policy is made in several different "access points" within the state, and each context places somewhat different constraints on what can be done (Jenness and Grattet 2001). Much more could be said about this; the main implication I want to draw here is that the lessons learned about movement-government connections in the workers' compensation movement, which was devoted to changing policy through the legislature, are most relevant to other movements similarly oriented to legislation.

It is also important to delineate movements based on the types of actors involved. In particular, movements involving professionals rather than victims or aggrieved persons might be thought to have different engagements with policy processes. If nothing else, movements of professionals tend to be oriented "upward" toward changing policy rather than "downward" toward mobilizing citizens and changing public opinion, and from this difference in orientation flow different organizing dynamics and obstacles. Movements in which professionals play central roles may also have a tendency toward coalition forms (McCarthy, ch. 3 this volume; Sabatier and Jenkins-Smith 1993). This is because professionals approach social problems from the standpoint of the impartial expert. Their strength lies more in their ability to formulate technical solutions than in constructing problems in ways that attract the attention of legislators. The critical distance professionals have, which is a source of authority, can actually be a liability when legislators are moved—as they frequently are—by emotional appeals from victims or directly affected parties. Getting victims' groups or partisans or state officials to form a coalition and endorse the professional diagnoses and treatment of a problem can be enormously beneficial for getting the movement goals on the legislative agenda. Put another way, professional input may be less critical to the issue creation phase, when some set of conditions are constructed as a problem, and more critical to the policy formulation phase, when solutions are crafted. Composed of what Skocpol calls "reformist professionals" (rather than strictly labor and business forces, as one might assume), the workmen's compensation movement offers an example of some of the ways that movements of professionals can affect policy formation and some of the limits on their ability to do so.

In addition, while it is common to view social movements as rooted in organizations (e.g., SMOs) I suggest it is equally important to view them as social networks that tie actors together across organizations and social space (see Rosenthal et al. 1985). This shift in attention underlies the analytic approach employed in this chapter, which uses qualitative and quantitative methods to examine the structure and history of the compensation reform network. The existence of a reform network, its formation and structure, who is central, who is marginal, how it is distributed across space—all may be relevant considerations in accounting for the timing, content, and diffusion of reform. By movement networks, I mean both connections among activists and connections among activists, experts, and state officials. Together, these linkages are what I call the policy nexus.[2]

The policy nexus is where the state and social movements intersect. As state actors come to occupy positions of authority in the network and as movement actors come to occupy positions in government (Banaszak, ch. 5 this volume), the boundary between the state and the movement can become blurry. Contrary to much work on social movements, recognition of the interpenetration of movements and the state makes problematic the degree of autonomy from the state that movements are conventionally understood to have. Movements are not so easily classified "independent actors outside the state" (see ibid.). But how does the policy nexus matter?

The policy nexus shapes policy making in potentially three ways. First, a policy nexus is critical for connecting abstract ideas (reform models and templates) to the specific legislative campaigns for reform. The connections represented by the policy nexus link experts, labor and management groups, and state administrative officials with governors and legislators who can initiate the legislative process. Without a policy nexus in place, lawmakers may be less aware of the theoretical bases for reform proposals and therefore less likely to act. The reason for this is that a big part of what a policy nexus does is provide an arena for the dissemination of rhetoric that policy makers can use to justify a reform. Thus, the policy nexus provides communication channels to key officials that allow for legitimated models of reform to be presented to lawmakers. The absence of a policy nexus may impede the timing of reform and shape the kinds of alternatives legislators consider.

A second role for a policy nexus is that it provides an arena where conflict between competing interests can be managed. How the policy nexus is structured, who is allowed a major role, and who is allowed a minor role can serve to mute extreme proposals from entering the discussion, narrowing the range of alternative proposals presented to policy makers. In this way, the structure of the policy nexus may impact on the content of the reform proposals that come out of it.

Finally, the geographic structure of a movement network may have implications for the policy diffusion process (Burt 1987; Coleman, Katz, and Menzel 1966; Rogers 1995). States that have greater representation in the network may be expected to adopt the reform earlier than those that are less well represented. Thus, the geographic structure of the network may affect the timing of adoption of reforms across the states.

The remainder of this article unfolds as follows. First, I describe the historical context that preceded the compensation movement, including the origins of compensation principles and the early attempts to reform the employer's liability system. Next, I discuss the formation and structure of the compensation reform network in qualitative and quantitative terms. I then turn to a discussion of the effects of the policy nexus: how the structure of the policy nexus reduced conflict between groups, how it influenced the diffusion of compensation reform across states, and how it provided a set of justifications for countering the major grounds for opposition.

Open Windows: Unexploited Opportunities for Policy Innovation

If widespread dissatisfaction about the existing system and the availability of institutional models provide sufficient impetus for reform, then compensation should have passed sometime between 1890 and 1909. Both elements were in place at the time. By the late 1880s, the question of how to distribute the costs of industrial accidents had become one of the most contentious issues in labor-management relations. Over the prior six decades, the doctrines expounded by U.S. courts, which placed the burden of those costs on workers, steadily lost support from both labor and management. Labor disliked the system because it provided few remedies for injured workers, and business was dissatisfied because, under the old system, they faced unpredictable juries that occasionally gave out huge awards to sympathetic victims of accidents. The question for both groups was, "Do we continue to push for revisions to the existing system of employer's liability, or do we try an entirely new approach?"

European ideas about social insurance, including workmen's compensation systems, were available to American policy makers as early as 1893 with John Graham Brooks's publication of *Compulsory Insurance in Germany* by the U.S. Department of Labor. A few years later, in 1898, William F. Willoughby, also an employee of the Department of Labor and Commerce, published *Workingmen's Insurance.* Both publications surveyed the existing methods for dealing with industrial safety and insurance in use by European countries. The Brooks report was requested three years prior when President Benjamin Harrison urged Congress to change the safety and compensation rules governing interstate commerce. "It is a reproach to our civilization that any class of American workmen should in the pursuit of a necessary and useful vocation be subjected to a peril of life and limb as great as that of a soldier in time of war" (quoted in Minnesota Employees' Compensation Commission 1911, 100). Thus, politicians at the highest level were focused on the issue of industrial accidents, and senior Department of Labor officials were well informed about the alternatives that America might consider in changing its approach to the problem. Despite the availability of models of compensation represented in the Brooks report, nothing was accomplished regarding the issue of compensation for industrial accidents.[3]

The need for a change in the existing industrial accident law was expressed in other arenas. Between 1900 and 1909, popular magazines and professional periodicals published a steady, but small, stream of articles dealing with the issue of industrial accidents and possible remedies. One measure of this trend can be seen in Figure 6.1. The *Readers' Guide to Periodical Literature* underrepresents trade, professional, and academic periodicals, but nonetheless the graph reveals an unmistakable increase in the media attention to the issue. Muckraking journalists like William H. Hard published scathing evaluations of the system for dealing with accidents. With titles like "The Law of the Killed and Wounded" (Hard 1909), "Making Steel and Killing Men" (Hard 1907), "Our Murderous Industrialism" (Mark 1907), and "Slaughter of the Innocents by Commercialism Juggernaut

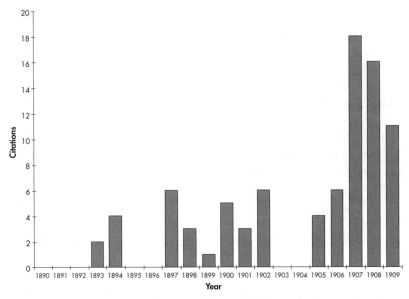

Figure 6.1. Citations to articles on employer's liability and industrial accidents, 1890–1909. (Data from the Readers' *Guide to Periodical Literature.)*

in Pennsylvania" (*Arena* 1906), these articles were designed to dramatize the plight of injured workers. Curiously, this attention arose during a time when industrial injuries and deaths were leveling off in some major industries, if not declining (Figure 6.2).[4]

Other information sources emerged at this time too. Departments of Labor in New York State and Massachusetts (see Minnesota Employees' Compensation Commission 1911, 113) and the federal government published reports on the operation of the employer's liability system, statistics on accident frequencies, and the safety procedures installed in some industries (U.S. Bureau of Labor 1901, 1902, 1905, 1907, 1908, 1909). All of this material accumulated during the period prior to 1909, contributing to the growing body of informational resources on the subject but eliciting little in the way of a public policy response.

After the turn of the century a few scattered companies like U.S. Steel and later International Harvester began to offer private insurance plans to provide relief for their injured workers. These programs tended to require contributions by workers and the company to a mutual insurance fund. Trade associations like the National Metal Trades Association and the National Cotton Manufacturers Association also offered accident insur-

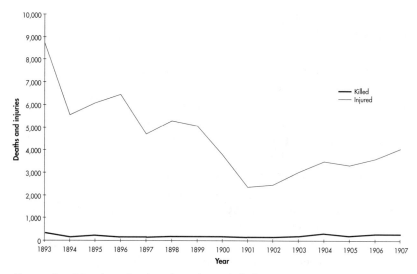

Figure 6.2. Number of railroad employees killed or injured in work accidents, 1893–1907.

ance. Although both types of programs were created in response to the problems associated with the employer's liability system, they were never envisioned as substitutes for that system. For example, a worker covered under a private plan was not forbidden from taking his employer to court under the existing employer's liability law. Companies that created programs often also supported reform of the law (Ramsey 1909, 58), if for no other reason than because legal reform held the promise of imposing an insurance system on their competitors. Thus, the notion of providing some kind of insurance-like option, albeit a private one, for dealing with industrial accidents was already present within some industries and a few progressive companies.

Signals that reform was possible were emerging on the legal front as well. Between 1860 and 1900, state legislatures modified industrial accident doctrine by expanding employer duties or abrogating one or another of the employer's common law defenses (Grattet 1997). Between 1902 and 1908, however, four states and the federal government broke stride with the strategy of modifying one part or another of their employer's liability system. In 1902 the Maryland legislature created a cooperative insurance fund for certain "perilous" occupations. This program was organized in much the same way as some of the private insurance plans, with joint contributions made by both workers and their employers. It was a voluntary system; as an inducement to employees for joining, legislators removed the employer's defense of "contributory negligence," meaning that under the plan a worker could not have the question of whether his actions contributed to the accident scrutinized in the disposition of the case. However, this law was declared unconstitutional on the grounds that it gave judicial powers to an administrative officer, the state insurance commissioner (Lord 1911, 26). In 1905, a commission appointed by the Illinois legislature reported a pair of bills: one simply permitted employers and employees to contract out of the existing employer's liability laws if they entered a mutual insurance arrangement, and the other was compulsory compensation law. Neither bill was adopted, and the commission was disbanded. In addition, Massachusetts and Connecticut set up legislative commissions to explore various reform options, but neither produced any legislation. Finally, the U.S. government established a compensation system for its own employees in 1908. This system, however, was more like the private schemes at International Harvester and U.S. Steel than the later forms of public compensation in that it was an initiative undertaken by a single employer to provide for its employees. Nevertheless, some reformers hailed it as an important declaration of support for the "essential justice of the principle of compensation" (Judson 1909, 84).

Next Montana (1909) and New York (1910) adopted different forms of compensation, but both were subsequently declared unconstitutional. The Montana law instituted an elective compensation system for its coal mining industry. The Montana high court declared the law unconstitutional because it violated the employer's right of equal protection of the laws. Basically, employers who paid into the accident fund could also be sued under the employer's liability laws and, therefore, could be compelled to pay twice for the same injury.[5] The New York legislature passed a compulsory law in 1910 for extra-hazardous industries, but it was ruled unconstitutional by the New York Court of Appeals—the state's highest court—because it took the property of employers without due process of law.[6] Naturally, the fact that the Maryland, Montana, and New York laws were each declared unconstitutional for different reasons left lawmakers and policy experts scratching their heads about which form of compensation would "work" and which would be constitutional.

Prior to 1910, activity on the issue of accident law reform occurred within a variety of different societal sectors. States and the federal government produced and disseminated reports and summaries of European systems. A few companies and industries experimented with private insurance programs. Some states and the federal government experienced fits and starts in the area. Activities in these sectors, however, were isolated and uncoordinated and show that, while there was a demonstrated appetite for reform by policy makers and other officials and a wide range of informational resources on the nature of the problem and how other countries were responding, successful policy action was lacking. In theoretical terms, the absence of such action shows that despite availability of a discursive foundation, ideological resources, institutional models, and a receptive policy-making audience that was concerned about finding a solution to the issue—all of which provided an opportunity for reform—reform itself was not forthcoming. What was missing?

The Policy Nexus: Structure and Effects

The major obstacle faced by these early reform attempts was the general problem of uniformity of action. Especially in the area of industrial policies, states are typically reluctant to attempt bold reforms that may increase business costs for fear of driving business to neighboring states. Such conditions create a "comparative disadvantage" for adopting states. In the short run, compensation would raise insurance costs for business, although most of its supporters contended that the overall economic gains of compensating injured workers would, in the long run, benefit the economic health of a state and its industries. If compensation was going to make it onto the policy agenda in America, the effort had to be coordinated across states, and that could only be done by the formation of an interstate network of supporters who were able to push compensation through more or less simultaneously.

With available historical and archival sources, we can reconstruct in some detail the process by which this interstate network was formed. The idea of coordinating compensation reform across state lines occurred to the employer's liability commissions in New York and Minnesota at roughly the same time in 1909. The Minnesota and New York commissions differed from earlier state commissions in Massachusetts and Connecticut in that, from their inception, both sought to build an interstate coalition rather than focus narrowly on reform in their own state. The Minnesota Employees' Compensation Commission was formed by the governor on May 11, 1909, at the request of the Minnesota Department of Labor, the state bar, and the Minnesota Employer's Association via the governor. It consisted of three men: H. V. Mercer, president of the Minnesota State Bar; George M. Gillette of Minneapolis Steel and Machinery Company and the Minnesota Employer's Association; and W. E. McEwen, the Minnesota commissioner of labor. Each of these men would soon become central players in the national movement for compensation reform. Two of them—Mercer and

Gillette—were Republicans, and McEwen was a Democrat (Minnesota Employees' Compensation Commission 1911). The first thing this group did was to compile the various European laws. Despite the work of earlier writers and the U.S. Department of Labor and Commerce bulletins and reports, few English translations of the European laws existed. In one of its initial actions, the commission contacted the U.S. Bureau of Labor asking for the translations to be made. The bureau agreed to do it; moreover, it provided the Minnesota commission with an advanced copy of the report, which was eventually published in 1911 (Minnesota Employees' Compensation Commission 1911). Mercer, chairman of the Minnesota commission, through these contacts with the federal government, met Miles M. Dawson. Dawson was a government actuary who, along with Lee K. Frankel, another actuary, was hired by the Russell Sage Foundation to travel to Europe in 1908 to investigate the forms of workmen's insurance currently operating there. Their findings were later published by the Russell Sage Foundation as *Workingmen's Insurance in Europe* (Frankel and Dawson 1910). The Minnesota commission report indicates that Mercer traveled with Dawson through Europe—although it is not clear that it was during the investigation for the Russell Sage Foundation—and that they "discussed the various systems daily" (Minnesota Employees' Compensation Commission 1911, 31). Each of the Minnesota commission members eventually made similar research trips to Europe.[7] In addition, Mercer corresponded with Frankel and Dawson throughout 1909, and through contacts with the federal government Mercer became acquainted with Charles P. Neill, secretary of the U.S. Bureau of Labor. Neill oversaw the publication of the Bureau of Labor's *Summary of Foreign Workmen's Compensation Acts* (1908). These contacts with federal government officials and leading researchers on European systems initiated the rudiments of an interstate network of social reformers interested in exploring various forms of workers' compensation.

While Mercer, the lawyer on the commission, made connections with federal government officials and experts on the European laws, McEwen, the Democrat and the Minnesota state labor commissioner, cultivated ties with the American Association for Labor Legislation (AALL). The AALL was a national organization devoted to the advancement of labor legislation and was composed mostly of academics, like Henry Farnam, Henry R. Seager, Richard T. Ely, and Adna F. Weber (see Skocpol 1992, 176–203). It also included state labor department officials and some social workers. McEwen attended a meeting of the City Club in Chicago, along with Farnam, the president of the AALL and an economist from Yale University, and both spoke about the question of industrial accidents and workmen's compensation reform. The AALL's 1909 annual report states that as a result of this meeting "a public effort was made to pave the way for a conference" (19). This meeting opened up another set of connections between the Minnesota commission and members of the scholarly and academic community interested in accident law reform. After this contact the AALL secretary John R. Commons, an economist and labor historian from the University of Wisconsin, visited with members of the Minnesota commission to plan a national conference.

A few months before Minnesota's commission was established, a similar commission was established in New York State. As with the Minnesota commission, a complex pattern of interorganizational linkages is evident. The American Association for Labor Legislation was the chief sponsor on behalf of the bill for the establishment of the commission, and members of the New York branch of the AALL worked in close collaboration with the governor of New York and the state's labor department prior to that time (Wesser 1971, 351). Ultimately, Henry R. Seager, president of the New York State branch of the AALL, became the vice chairman of the New York commission. The commission also included Crystal Eastman, who, like Frankel and Dawson, was funded by the Russell Sage Foundation to investigate the industrial accident problem. Her study of industrial accidents in Allegheny County, Pennsylvania, was published by the Russell Sage Foundation and titled *Work Accidents and the Law* (1910). Eastman also had connections with the AALL. She was secretary of the New York branch and had given an important address—"The American Way of Distributing Industrial Accident Losses"—at the 1908 AALL conference. As a result of that presentation, she was asked to write a pamphlet on the subject of employer's liability that was published by the AALL and distributed to its membership. The history of the New York commission, like that of the Minnesota commission, reflects a strategy of working with the AALL, government officials, and compensation experts rather than labor and business leaders.

While initially the contact between state commissioners was indirect, mostly via the AALL, this soon changed.[8] Shortly after meeting with the Minnesota commission, John R. Commons, AALL secretary, spoke to several members of the New York commission stressing "the importance of uniformity of investigation" (AALL 1909, 19). During June, less than a month after the formation of the Minnesota commission, Commons wrote to Mercer asking him to call an "Interstate Conference on Workmen's Compensation" (ibid., 10). Mercer sent out the following invitation on July 14:

To . . .

You are invited to be present at the The Marlborough-Blenheim, at Atlantic City, July 29–31 and take part in a conference with the various State and Government officials and others interested in legislation changing the basis of recovery for injuries received in the course of employment from that of negligence or fault of the employer, to that of risk of the industry or insurance; at which conference the persons whose names appear under the several subjects will be asked to lead the discussions along the respective lines appearing in the program herein.

You are requested to extend this invitation to such persons as can contribute knowledge on the subject.
Yours truly,

H. V. Mercer
Chairman Minnesota Employees' Compensation Commission
Minneapolis

Referred to as the "Atlantic City Conference," the meeting included participation of members of the Wisconsin, New York, and Minnesota commissions, Lee Frankel and Miles Dawson, Charles Neill, and representatives of seven major insurance companies. Mercer admitted that he expected to find resistance from the insurance people to changing the existing system. One insurance representative, however, informed him that the insurance companies knew some kind of reform was inevitable. They were simply happy to be asked to participate in shaping it (Minnesota Employees' Compensation Commission 1911, 142).[9] The participants in the conference addressed both the broad outlines of the issue of workers' compensation—its "desirability," its "possibility," and its "practicability"—and more specific topics such as the problems associated with the present system, the operation of the foreign systems currently in place, possible insurance rate increases that might attend the adoption of compensation, and the constitutionality of various compensation plans. Much of the Atlantic City Conference, however, was devoted to further organizing rather than substantive policy. The conference participants voted to establish the National Conference upon Compensation for Industrial Accidents (NCCIA) and appoint an executive committee, and planned for subsequent meetings.

These connections formed the basis for an emerging policy nexus—a network of relationships that linked state officials, researchers, and insurance men. It is notable that, at this point, the network contained no direct representatives of labor or management, no accident victims, and no company owners financially impacted by the employer's liability system. These were professional reformers in the sense that they sought to remake the administrative capacity of the state for the public good, based on the application of expertise in broad areas of knowledge and by virtue of their neutrality relative to the economic interests at stake (Brint 1994, 6–8). Professionals would continue to dominate the formation of the compensation policy nexus. Labor and management officials were brought in later and remained marginal to the interstate movement.

The initial Atlantic City NCCIA conference was a model of organizational networking. As a result of the conference, members of the Minnesota commission rose to near-celebrity status within the growing circle of reformers. One member was asked to address an insurance group in New York City, and his speech generated a lengthy debate in an insurance trade journal (Minnesota Employees' Compensation Commission 1911, 147). Mercer, initially secretary and later chairman of the NCCIA, described the views of the Minnesota commission regarding the constitutionality of compensation at the third annual American Association for Labor Legislation meeting in December 1909 in a paper titled "Constitutional Problems in Workmen's Compensation." Mercer, McEwen, and Gillette all gave speeches at the National Civic Federation (NCF) conference in November 1909, a meeting devoted entirely to the issue of industrial accidents, safety, and workers' compensation (NCF 1910). The NCF was a kind of omnibus progressive organization bringing together a diverse collection of progressives from a variety of movements (e.g., urban reformers, charities and settlement house workers, politicians, labor, employers).

The NCF conference was an important forum as it brought members of the Minnesota network into the orbit of more mainstream labor and business leaders. In particular, it furthered contacts between members of the Minnesota commission and high-ranking American Federation of Labor (AFL) officials. Mercer had corresponded with AFL president Samuel Gompers and vice president John Mitchell during his investigations of the legal aspects of compensation while he was president of the Minnesota State Bar. At that time, late 1908 and early 1909, Gompers and Mitchell admitted in letters to Mercer that they knew little about the issue (Minnesota Employees' Compensation Commission 1911, 125–26). Although Mitchell was not particularly knowledgeable about the issue of compensation, he provided another set of connections, and by 1909 he had become the epitome of a well-networked progressive. He had been the president of the United Mine Workers of America, was currently vice president at the AFL, a member of the executive councils of both the NCF and the AALL, and later in 1909 was appointed to the New York State Employer's Liability Commission. Thus, Mitchell, a well-credentialed "labor" man, provided a link between the community of commissioners, organized labor, and intellectuals. The same year Mitchell joined the New York Employer's Liability Commission, his colleague at the AFL, Samuel Gompers, revised his initial opposition and announced support for workmen's compensation. Although there is no factual record about what exactly changed his mind, it is plausible to conjecture that his contacts with the emerging compensation policy nexus may have influenced his decision to shift commitments. Mitchell became active in the NCCIA, attending its second and third meetings in January and June 1910. Big labor had become a part of the network, and the labor representatives were now steeped in expert literature on compensation and social insurance and ensconced in the interstate community of reformers.

When the by-laws of the NCCIA—renamed the National Conference on Workmen's Compensation for Industrial Accidents (NCWCIA) in 1910—were adopted, their purpose was "to bring together the members of the commissions and committees of the various States and of the National Government, representatives to be appointed by the governors of the different States, and other interested citizens, to discuss plans of worker's compensation and insurance for industrial accidents" (NCWCIA 1910a, 3). The name change was significant in that, unlike the old name, it explicitly identified workmen's compensation as the central focus of the group. Between the first and third meetings of the organization, four additional states appointed industrial accident commissions (Massachusetts, Illinois, New Jersey, and Ohio). By the fourth meeting in late 1910, Connecticut and Montana delegates were participants. The emergence of the national forums seemed to encourage a number of states to step up their interest and activity on the issue of compensation. The conferences offered hope that compensation could be coordinated across states and thereby reduce the comparative disadvantage of a single state operating in isolation.

As the preceding discussion indicates, the formation of the compensation policy nexus took place relatively quickly between 1909 and 1911. The central figures in the network were state commissioners and professionals, and conferences were understood to be forums that aided the "uniformity of action" that was key to mounting such a significant change in industrial policy.

A Quantitative Depiction of the Policy Nexus

In addition to the conferences mentioned thus far, other organizations were beginning to hold meetings during the 1905 to 1909 period as well. The American Federation of Labor conferences in 1905 and 1906 contained a few general speeches on the industrial accident problem. The American Association of Labor Legislation, formed in 1906, included papers on the subject during its 1907 to 1909 conferences. The National Civic Federation conference in 1909 was completely devoted to the issue of industrial accidents, safety, and worker welfare. The National Association of Manufacturers conferences took up the issue in 1910 and 1911. Together with the NCCIA/ NCWCIA, these arenas provide another way of assessing the structure of the emerging interstate network. From the proceedings of sixteen national conferences held by these organizations—all of the national conferences in which the issue was discussed—I constructed a network database that tracked participation. Participation is coded very generally as having spoken at the conference regarding some aspect of the industrial accident problem. The list of participants reads like a Who's Who of progressive civic leaders and includes former U.S. president Theodore Roosevelt, industrialist Andrew Carnegie, settlement house leader Jane Addams, U.S. senator Elihu Root, and representatives from business, labor, insurance, charities, and the legal profession.

Many of those participating in these conferences were only peripherally involved with the compensation movement: three-quarters of the participants were involved in only one of the sixteen conferences, 16 percent participated in two, and 8 percent participated in three or more. To identify the core actors in the national network, I reduced the original incidence matrix from 192 to 47 individuals by removing the participants that attended only one conference. This reduction removes the most marginal actors and, conveniently, also makes the data set more manageable for analysis in UCINET IV (Borgatti, Everett, and Freeman 1992). Centrality measures for each individual participant in the conferences were computed using the Freeman degree-based method (Freeman 1978–79). This approach simply measures the number of times an individual attended a conference in common with each other individual in the network.

Degree-based centrality is a measure of the amount of direct contacts an individual has made; it ignores any indirect connections. The centrality rankings are reported in Figure 6.3 and point to a handful of individuals who possess a number of notable attributes. Eight are commissioners, assigned by their respective state legislatures to investigate the industrial accident problem and propose legislative reforms, although only four state commissions are represented (Minnesota, New York, Massachusetts, and Wisconsin). The occupational background of this group is relatively mixed; it includes lawyers, insurance experts, state legislators, academics, labor, and business representatives. The business participants occupy statuses and affiliations that suggest they might be more moderate than extreme. For

Name	State	Freeman degree	Occupation/organizational affiliation
H. V. Mercer	MN	81	Minnesota State Bar president; Minnesota commissioner
John Mitchell	NY	63	AFL second vice president; Mine Workers Union; New York commissioner; executive committee NCF
Amos Saunders	MA	55	Ingersoll Rand Company; NCCIA secretary; Massachusetts commissioner
Lee K. Frankel	NY	53	Metropolitan Life Insurance Company; coauthor *Workingmen's Insurance in Europe* (with Dawson)
George Gillette	MN	53	Minnesota commissioner; Minnesota Employer's Association; Minneapolis Steel and Machine Company; NAM member
Miles Dawson	NY	52	Actuary; coauthor *Workingmen's Insurance* (with Frankel); Sage Foundation Fellow
Paul Watrous	WI	52	Wisconsin commissioner and state delegate
Wallace Ingalls	WI	50	Wisconsin commissioner and state delegate
Henry Seager	NY	44	Professor; New York Commissioner, founder of AALL; president of AALL New York branch
Henry Farnam	CT	41	Economics professor; AALL president
Frederick Hoffman	NJ	41	Statistician, Prudential Life Insurance Company
W. E. McEwen	MN	41	Commissioner of labor; Minnesota commissioner
William Moulton	MI	41	Sociological Department, Cleveland Cliffs Iron Company
George A. Ranney	IL	41	Chair of Advisory Board on Welfare Work, International Harvester Company

Figure 6.3. Ranked centrality scores for the most-central participants in national conferences on industrial accidents, 1905–11.

example, the company representatives were not owners or board members of corporations but were employed in the sociological and welfare departments of their respective firms. Aside from the two academics concerned with labor legislation and a state labor commissioner, there was only one individual from a trade union background in this core group (AFL vice president John Mitchell, previously discussed). These data suggest a focus on experts, moderate elements of business, and employer's liability commissioners, particularly those in New York, Minnesota, Massachusetts, and Wisconsin.

Figure 6.4 plots a multidimensional scaling analysis of individual participation in all of the conferences and provides a visual depiction of the similarities and differences between individuals in the network based on which conferences they attended. Specifying a two-dimensional solution gives a fit at the .052 stress level, which is a good fit (Scott 1991, 164).[10] The two dimensions that seem to structure the results are, on the x-axis, whether or not an individual participated in employer or labor conferences. Participation of National Association of Manufacturers (NAM) officials correspond to low values of x, whereas individuals associated with the AFL

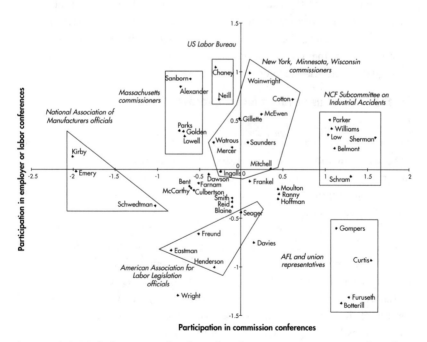

Figure 6.4. Multidimensional scaling plot of participation in national conferences on industrial accidents, 1905–11.

and other unions possess high values. The y-axis distributes participation based on whether or not an individual participated in conferences sponsored by the commissions, the NCCIA conferences. Note that most of the individuals that are assigned high scores are commissioners or individuals that became involved in the interstate arenas through contacts with commissioners in New York and Minnesota. Those who scored low on this dimension are individuals associated with the AALL. There are, however, a number of individuals who "crossed over" and participated in different kinds of conferences. These individuals appear in the middle of the plot. Those with the highest centrality scores tend to cluster around the participants in the NCCIA conferences, suggesting that these conferences were especially important. Participants in labor and employer conferences did not interact much with those in other arenas, signaling that those groups were marginal in the network.

The quantitative analysis confirms the findings of the historical narrative. With perhaps the exception of one man, AFL vice president John Mitchell, labor and business officials were relatively marginal players in forums that formulated compensation. The professionals, and the conferences they attended, were the most central. The peripheral location of labor and business does not mean that their involvement was irrelevant. Getting them involved but keeping them in relatively peripheral roles may have given the movement legitimacy without having to be exclusively concerned with balancing labor and management interests.

The Policy Nexus as an Arena for Compromise

A strength of coalition movements—that they incorporate a diverse array of collective actors—can also be a weakness. The more diversity a coalition encompasses, the more potential for division and conflict. In fact, earlier state campaigns in Massachusetts had collapsed as a result of divisions between groups that supported reform but could not agree on strategy. Similarly, the interstate movement was threatened by two kinds of conflict.

The first issue was whether the employer's liability system should be replaced with workmen's compensation or whether the reform efforts should continue to liberalize the employer's liability system. Initially, conservative industrialists and some labor groups, including the American Federation of Labor, were opposed to compensation. The National Association of Manufacturers, a conservative businessmen's association, and other more local groups like the Arkwright Club in Massachusetts (Asher 1969) had stridently opposed compensation as "socialist policy" and because employers feared that insurance costs under compensation would surpass the amounts they were already spending. The AFL was also reluctant to endorse compensation. Asher reports that the AFL leadership was hostile to "legislation deeply involving the administrative machinery of government in labor problems, as well as the psychological difficulty of abandoning agitation for stronger employer's liability law" (457). Schattschneider wrote, "the definition of alternatives is the supreme instrument of power" (1960, 68). This was true in the case of compensation reform, as the fiercest opponents to displacing the old system were not invited to participate in the discussion. Conflicts about whether or not compensation was a viable solution was minimized by the creation of arenas like the NCCIA, in which the vast majority of participants already endorsed some sort of compensation system. John Mitchell, the AFL vice president and New York commissioner, participated in the NCCIA conferences, but in the latter conferences only after the AFL leadership had converted to compensation. None of the NAM representatives participated in the NCCIA conferences.[11] The initial conflict was overcome by creating discursive arenas in which the most contentious elements of the labor and business communities were excluded.

The second issue was whether the compensation system should be elective or compulsory. Compulsory plans required participation in the compensation system by eliminating the employer's liability laws, whereas the elective plan retained some elements of the old system and allowed workers or employers to choose between systems. With a few exceptions, employers favored the compulsory plan (with a loophole built in for accidents caused by the gross negligence of the employee) because it promised to control costs by removing the possibility of unpredictable and large damage awards. Labor was split, with some groups seeing benefits in the security of a compulsory law and others reluctant to trade away common law rights and accept limitations on damages. The lawyers, state officials, and remaining professionals represented were also divided, often couching opposition to the compulsory plan in terms of constitutionality. Supporters felt the constitutional objections could be overcome, whereas the opposition believed the only solution was to make the law elective and therefore more readily compatible with the principles of due process of law and liberty of contract.

The final, NCCIA conference, held in Chicago in late November 1910, provides an example of how the conferences created opportunities for surmounting such conflicts. It culminated with a series of ballots on specific elements of a model compensation act. A committee was established to draft two different kinds of codes: a compulsory compensation scheme and an elective system. Over the course of the NCCIA conferences the elective plan had taken on a specific meaning. While it included the idea that employers could choose between systems, it contained strong incentives for participating by eliminating the common law defenses employers had historically enjoyed. It could have been more appropriately named the coercive-elective plan since it made the choice of not accepting the compensation plan highly undesirable. One participant regarded it as "compulsory in form, elective in fact" (Dickson 1910, 260). Because the plan retained the principle of election, its proponents claimed that it could surmount constitutional objections based on liberty of contract. In this way, the elective plan was constructed close to the compulsory plan, yet it would not, in principle, interfere with employers and workers to freely contract the terms of the employment relation through state imposition of compensation.

The closing of the gap between the two forms also allowed the reform community to overcome the imperative of uniformity. Originally, the participants saw the two forms as quite different in terms of practices and philosophies; by the end, they agreed that the differences were not significant. The controversy about uniformity shifted to the details, such as how much would be paid out for certain types of injuries. The Wisconsin commission wrote, after participating in the conferences,

> This committee does not believe that it is important for economic reasons that neighboring states or states far removed should adopt similar bills as regards compulsory or optional [elective] features; it is, however, the conclusion that Wisconsin and other states, particularly neighboring states, should adopt uniform or nearly uniform, scale of compensation. (Wisconsin Committee on Industrial Insurance 1911, 40)

After the conferences, questions of uniformity centered not on the compulsory/elective issue, but on the scale of compensation. The NCCIA conferences gave a green light for states to proceed toward compensation, but in ways that balanced the prerogatives of the various constituencies. While the conferences did not prompt exact uniformity on all the details, they did serve to limit the range of legitimate alternatives.

The conferences provided arenas where conflict between segments of the reform community was managed and a consensus about two general compensation models was forged. Additionally, it makes sense to consider whether or not participation in the conferences affected the next stage in the policy-making process—the adoption of compensation by state legislatures. Using the conference participation data described earlier, this time aggregated from the individual level to the state level, I calculated estimates of the centrality of each state in the reform network. I combined the centrality measures with event-history data gathered by Eliza Pavalko for her 1989 study of the timing of compensation reform. Pavalko found that more industrialized states (measured in terms of manufacturing productivity), fewer agricultural states, and states that had experienced high levels of litigiousness regarding work injury cases (measured by the number of state supreme court cases) were likely to adopt compensation earlier than states that did not have these characteristics. After replicating Pavalko's event-history findings in relation to macroeconomic and legal variables, I added the state centrality measure to see if it affected her results. It did not produce significant effects and did not add to or alter Pavalko's original findings (Pavalko 1989).[12] This means that states that were central to the network were no more likely to adopt compensation early than those that were not. Put another way, even though nine out of the ten states with the highest centrality scores passed compensation laws early (i.e., prior to 1914), several other states that did not participate in the reform network (and thus had centrality scores of zero) also passed early. These states were mostly western states like California, Montana, Oregon, Washington, Nevada, and Arizona for whom the travel distances may have prohibited participation in the conferences.

While centrality does not appear to affect timing, there is evidence that it affects the content of the laws passed. Based on a coding of the content of the laws in terms of features representing more or less progressive approaches, I found that states that participated in the network were more likely to have adopted progressive forms of the laws.[13] For example, the most central states in the network were more likely than the others to possess plans that replaced 60 percent or more of workers' wages; their plans also covered a greater percentage of the state workforce and were more likely to rely on centralized insurance in a state fund rather than private or self-insurance. The evidence found here suggests that the structure of the policy nexus may influence the content rather than the timing of adoption.

The Policy Nexus as a Forum for Legitimating Compensation

Besides the management of conflict and the achievement of a general consensus that the elective plan was the most strategic way of pursuing reform, the most important consequence of the conferences was the development of an elaborate repertoire of justifications for compensation. Both elective and compulsory systems were said to provide greater justice and efficiency than the old system. The elective system proponents argued that their model fit best with the American tradition of freedom of choice—which was especially central to the legal and cultural conception of the employment relation; it would be the least objectionable to the courts, and it would permit workers to sue for unlimited damages in cases where employers were grossly negligent. Advocates of the compulsory model argued that it was the only solution that would truly eliminate the waste and rancor created by the old system, and that while it removed the ability to sue, it worked "prompt average justice" (Sherman 1911, 14) for industrial accidents. The latter feature provided security for workers and prevented them from being manipulated by ambulance-chasing lawyers. While these arguments seem geared toward winning support from business, labor, and the populace, reformers also were deeply concerned with making compensation constitutional (Grattet 1998). It was precisely because of the marginal position of labor and management that the discussion could prioritize the question of how the courts would respond to legislation.

Partly because the compulsory plan raised more constitutional issues, its proponents worked out a set of arguments designed to surmount constitutional challenges. The first and most important of these was a long legal brief by Mercer on the "Legal Possibility of Workmen's Compensation Acts" (Atlantic City Conference 1909, 54–216) presented at the initial NCCIA conference in Atlantic City. Mercer, a lawyer, was the most central individual in this network, and it is likely that his ideas would have been substantially less influential had he been a more marginal player. This brief was an early attempt to find a constitutional basis for workers' compensation laws, and it laid the groundwork for what would eventually be called the Minnesota theory. The theory contained three different kinds of arguments designed to negotiate major constitutionality questions raised in relation to the more progressive compulsory compensation law. First, Mercer argued that any intrusions such a law might have on the "liberty of contract" principle could be justified by the police power doctrine—the legal power of states to legislate on matters of the public interest and safety, even when that legislation breaches the liberty of contract or due process principles. Second, the system could be made compatible with the equal protection of laws by eliminating the possibility that an employer would have to pay the same injured worker twice. Finally, Mercer argued that satisfying the employer's right to due process did not necessarily require a jury trial; thus, he attempted to pave the way for administrative adjudication of accident claims. Although not everyone agreed with the methods Mercer advanced to surmount constitutional impediments, his brief became a kind of template for justifying compulsory compensation in the face of constitutional objections. It provided a veritable sourcebook, fully annotated with cases, for constructing a constitutionally valid account for compensation reform. Roughly 1,500 copies of the proceedings of the Atlantic City

Conference, which included Mercer's brief, were published and distributed to members of the legislature in Minnesota, other state commissions, attorney generals and governors of various states, judges of record in the Eighth Circuit Court of the United States, "bigger" newspapers and journals, and "bigger" libraries across the country (Minnesota Employees' Compensation Commission 1911, 144). Mercer introduced his constitutional theory at an opportune moment, when it seemed to many that serious constitutional impediments obstructed the reform movement.

The Minnesota theory provided a legitimating framework that was directed at what the reform community felt was the greatest threat: that opponents would use constitutionality issues to reject policy change. As a framing strategy it was not designed to mobilize participation in a reform movement, it was not designed to appeal to victims of industrial accidents, and it was not designed to persuade business leaders. Frankly, it might not have been a focus at all if the policy nexus was dominated by labor and business. It was a reflection of the dominance of the network by professionals and professional discourse. The policy nexus not only provided a forum for the theory to be developed, it distributed it to the audiences that needed to be convinced.

Conclusions: Professionals, Opportunities, and Policy Reform

The archival and network data I have discussed suggest that the relationship between social movements, structural conditions, political opportunities, and policy reform is complex. Widespread dissatisfaction with the old system and the appearance of discursive resources like intellectual treatises, papers, and books on social insurance were insufficient to inspire reform of the industrial accident system. Social insurance ideas reached American soil in the late nineteenth century, but there were few mechanisms to disseminate these principles and to permit them to enter the state policy-making arena. Only the rudiments of these facilitating structures existed prior to 1909; attempts at compensation-like reform before that date were rare and ineffectual. During 1909 a set of social relationships began to emerge between newly formed commissions and a few preexisting reform organizations. These relations were formalized in the creation of the NCCIA. The national conferences held under NCCIA auspices provided the central forums for sharing knowledge about the issue and for working out differences between segments of the reform community. While gradual changes in the industrial economy were certainly a background force shaping general dissatisfaction with the employer's liability system and the increasing desirability of social insurance, such factors are incapable of adequately accounting for the abruptness with which compensation systems were constructed. Reforms began to sweep across the country only after the rapid formation of a policy nexus. As a case of legislative reform brought on by social movement activity, the compensation policy nexus highlights that the boundaries between the state and social movements can be quite blurry. The policy nexus was interstate, although regionally concentrated, and put experts from private research foundations, the academic world, and the federal government in contact with state commissioners—individuals uniquely positioned to influence the scope of legislation within particular states.

I found that the policy nexus affected compensation reform in three ways. First, the relatively marginal location of labor and management meant that reformers did not have to concentrate their efforts on aligning their rhetoric and building compromises with those interests. The reform production process evident in these conferences suggests that reformers sought first and foremost to align compensation with the U.S. Constitution and American governmental traditions. This fact has implications for recent work on framing, including work on compensation (Go 1995). As an elite network, compensation reformers did not seem particularly interested in aligning their movement with broad cultural themes for the purpose of mobilizing mass participation, as is often the focal concern in research on framing processes, but instead were largely interested in satisfying the technical legal requirements for reform. This feature of the reform discourse must be seen as a consequence of the way the compensation policy nexus was organized. In other words, we could expect that if labor and management had played more central roles, the central preoccupation of the conferences would have been the costs of compensation and justice and fairness for the workingman. While these themes certainly emerged, reformers—as professionals and experts—saw the courts as the principal obstacle to enacting compensation.

Second, the geographical structure of the policy nexus had a small effect on the adoption of reform. While states that were central to the reform network did not necessarily adopt compensation earlier, they did tend to adopt more progressive forms. Other pressures may be responsible for *when* policy makers act on an issue, but *how* they choose to act may be shaped by the network linkages within the broader policy nexus.

Third, the networks and discursive spaces created by the policy nexus were important in managing conflict among competing groups and compensation models. Probably the most important effect of the conferences and the broader networks they reflected is the marginalization of the most extreme elements, which minimized the range of alternative proposals that emerged, and meant that from an early point the question was not whether compensation should be enacted, but which precise form.

The formation of a policy nexus may not always resolve conflicts. It is possible to imagine that in some circumstances it might actually escalate conflict. Exactly what quality of network reduces or enhances conflict is beyond the empirical scope of this case study. It is possible to suggest a few factors that may have reduced conflicts between compensation reformers: the frequency and duration of the meetings, the ability of professionals to claim a monopoly on the issue and thereby exclude truly radical perspectives from entering the debate, the strong desire on the part of everyone involved to make some kind of change in the existing system, and the ethic of "uniformity" and interstate cooperation that provided the backdrop to reformers' conversations. To evaluate these variables requires cross-movement analyses of not only campaigns that succeeded but those that failed as well.

It is important to point out that the kinds of networks found here are a historically contingent phenomenon. During the Progressive era, mail correspondence and conferences were a mainstay of social movement organizing. While they remain an important feature among professionals today, they have been joined by other discursive mediums such as telephones, faster mail service, and computer networks—connections that make the reconstruction of the policy nexus more difficult than tabulating attendance at conferences. Nonetheless, the message might be the same: where there is conflict between segments of the reform community, the creation of some kind of forum may enable resolution. Inversely, it is doubtful that lack of discursive spaces will lessen conflict.

Finally, the problem confronting American social insurance enthusiasts was that there was really no prefigured discursive community ready to promote compensation ideas. In Europe, public civil service bureaucracies provided a natural medium through which social insurance principles could flow and an organizational apparatus to campaign for reforms. In order to accomplish similar goals, American reformers needed to find a substitute. The policy nexus described here provided that substitute. Unfortunately, the connections forged between these elements were short-lived. After compensation began to sweep across the country, the national networks fragmented. Perhaps it was this failure to construct a durable network of professionals that made compensation such an anomaly and doomed other Progressive era social insurance movements.

Notes

For comments on earlier drafts, I thank William T. Bielby, William L. F. Felstiner, Laura Grindstaff, John Hall, Helen Ingram, Valerie Jenness, Connie McNeely, David Meyer, John Mohr, Belinda Robnett, Wesley Shrum, Mark Suchman,

John R. Sutton, and Marc Ventresca. I also wish to thank Eliza Pavalko for sharing her event-history data with me. Direct all correspondence to Ryken Grattet, Department of Sociology, University of California, Davis, CA 95616. E-mail: rtgrattet@ucdavis.edu.

1. A tendency in work on social reform is to select cases where a policy change succeeded rather than failed. Focusing on these so-called positive cases is problematic insofar as it presents an incomplete comparison. In order to know that some set of causal conditions resulted in policy change requires looking at the presence or absence of those conditions when a policy change didn't happen (Skocpol 1979, 37).

2. For a discussion of how relations between state and nonstate entities have been characterized theoretically in political science and political sociology, see Burstein 1991.

3. Instead, the legislation that did emerge in the mid-1890s dealt with the industrial accident problem from the standpoint of prevention (e.g., Safety Appliance Act of 1893) rather than compensation.

4. The data reported here are from the railroad industry, which historically accounted for the most significant accident cases. Although comprehensive comparative data are unavailable, Bergstrom (1992) argues that total accidents continued to increase as mechanization spread to other industries.

5. *Cunningham v. Northwestern Improvement Co.,* 44 Mont. 180 (1911), 209.

6. *Ives v. South Buffalo Ry.,* 201 N.Y. 271 (1911).

7. As Daniel T. Rodgers has recently documented in his book *Atlantic Crossings,* such trips were common among Progressive era reformers and reflected a transnational circuit through which policy ideas could circulate. "Americans in the Progressive Era between the 1890s and the First World War did not swim in problems—not more so, at any rate, than Americans who lived through the simultaneous collapse of the economy and the post–Civil War racial settlement in the 1870s. It would be more accurate to say that they swam in a sudden abundance of solutions, a vast number of them brought over through the Atlantic connection" (1998, vii).

8. During 1909, the Wisconsin legislature formed a committee to examine the industrial accident problem, but in terms of the emerging national network it did not take a leadership role. This may have been a result of the composition of the committee, which included assemblymen and state senators rather than professionals. Assemblymen and state senators had more diverse constraints on their time and attention that prevented them from becoming leaders in the emerging national network.

9. The insurance men may also have seen a business opportunity in the reforms since at least some of the states that adopted compensation did so with a provision that employers could provide insurance from a private insurance company. Legally mandated insurance was no doubt a great boon for the insurance industry.

10. Three-, four-, and five-dimensional solutions yield slightly better fits; however, the same clustering patterns remain.

11. The NAM leadership eventually converted to compensation after 1910. During that year, Miles Dawson gave a speech at the NAM national meetings about his and Frankel's research on the European plans, and the NAM established the Industrial Indemnity Committee to analyze the situation and provide recommendations.

12. By this I mean that the results were the same in terms of direction, magnitude, and significance. Moreover, the goodness of fit of the model was not improved. I also considered the possibility that the effects of centrality in the network might be limited to the early adopters, which I tested by estimating an interaction effect between a dichotomous time period variable (with 1913 as the break point) and centrality. Again, the effects were not significant. Replication results and results including the centrality variable and the interaction terms are available on request from the author.

13. Sixteen states had centrality scores of 15 or higher. A centrality score of 15 means that a state had one participant at fifteen conferences or had fifteen participants at one conference or any combination of conferences and participants adding up to fifteen. This seems like a reasonable cut point to delineate states that had significant involvement in the conferences from those that did not. The sixteen states are referred to as "the most central states" in the succeeding passage.

References

AALL (American Association for Labor Legislation). 1909. *Proceedings, Reports, Addresses. Third Annual Meeting.* New York City, December 28–30. Princeton, NJ: Princeton University Press.

Amenta, Edwin. 1998. *Bold Relief: Institutional Politics and the Origins of Modern American Social Policy.* Princeton, NJ: Princeton University Press.

Amenta, Edwin, and Drew Halfmann. 2000. "Wage Wars: Institutional Politics, WPA Wages, and the Struggle for U.S. Social Policy." *American Sociological Review* 65, no. 4: 506–28.

Arena. 1906. "Slaughter of the Innocents by Commercialism Juggernaut in Pennsylvania." *Arena* 35 (April): 424–26.

Asher, Robert. 1969. "Business and Workers' Welfare in the Progressive Era: Workmen's Compensation Reform in Massachusetts, 1880–1911." *Business History Review* 43: 452–75.

———. 1983. "Failure and Fulfillment: Agitation for Employers' Liability Legislation and the Origins of Workmen's Compensation in New York State, 1876–1910." *Labor History* 24: 198–222.

Atlantic City Conference on Workmen's Compensation Acts. 1909. *Report.* Atlantic City, New Jersey, July 29–31. Secretary H. V. Mercer.

Bergstrom, Randolph E. 1992. *Courting Danger: Injury and Law in New York City, 1870–1910.* Ithaca, NY: Cornell University Press.

Borgatti, Stephen, Martin Everett, and Linton Freeman. 1992. *UCINET IV Version 1.0.* Columbia: Analytic Technologies.

Brint, Steven G. 1994. *In an Age of Experts: The Changing Role of Professionals in Politics and Public Life.* Princeton, NJ: Princeton University Press.

Brooks, John Graham. 1893. "Compulsory Insurance in Germany, Including an Appendix Relating to Compulsory Insurance in Other Countries in Europe." U.S. Department of Labor, Special Report of the Commissioner no. 4. Washington, DC: U.S. Government Printing Office.

Burstein, Paul. 1991. "Policy Domains: Organization, Culture, and Policy Outcomes." *Annual Review of Sociology* 17: 327–50.

———. 1998. *Discrimination, Jobs, and Politics: The Struggle for Equal Opportunity in the United States since the New Deal.* 2nd ed. Chicago: University of Chicago Press.

———. 1999. "Social Movements and Public Policy." In *How Social Movements Matter,* ed. Marc Guigni, Doug McAdam, and Charles Tilly. Minneapolis: University of Minnesota Press.

Burt, Ronald S. 1987. "Social Contagion and Innovation: Cohesion versus Structural Equivalence." *American Journal of Sociology* 92: 1287–1335.

Coleman, James S., Elihu Katz, and Herbert Menzel. 1966. *Medical Innovation.* New York: Bobbs-Merrill.

Dickson, William B. 1910. "Remarks at the National Conference on Workmen's Compensation for Industrial Accidents." In *Proceedings of Conference of Commissions on Compensation for Industrial Accidents,* 260. Chicago, November 10–12.

Eastman, Crystal. 1908. "The American Way of Distributing Industrial Accident Losses." Address to the American Association for Labor Legislation. In *Proceedings of the Second Annual Meetings,* 43–58. Atlantic City, New Jersey, December 29–30.

———. 1910. *Work Accidents and the Law.* New York: Russell Sage Foundation.

Frankel, Lee K., and Miles M. Dawson. 1910. *Workingmen's Insurance in Europe.* New York: Russell Sage Foundation.

Freeman, Linton C. 1978–79. "Centrality in Social Networks: Conceptual Clarification." *Social Networks* 1: 215–39.

Go, Julian, III. 1995. "Inventing Industrial Accidents and Their Insurance." *Social Science History* 20: 3401–38.

Grattet, Ryken. 1997. "Sociological Perspectives on Legal Change: The Role of the Legal Field in the Transformation of the Common Law of Industrial Accidents." *Social Science History* 21: 359–97.

———. 1998. "Substantiating a Worker's Right to Compensation." In *Public*

Rights, Public Rules: Constituting Citizens in the World Polity and National Policy, ed. Connie L. McNeely. New York: Garland.

Hard, William 1907. "Making Steel and Killing Men." *Everybody's* 12: 97–99.

———. 1909. "The Law of the Killed and the Wounded." *Everybody's* 14: 361.

Jenness, Valerie, and Ryken Grattet. 2001. *Making Hate a Crime: From Social Movement to Law Enforcement.* New York: Russell Sage Foundation.

Judson, Frederick N. 1909. "The Problems of Labor Legislation under Our Federal Constitution." Address to the American Association for Labor Legislation, New York, December 28–30. In *Proceedings of the Third Annual Meeting,* 108–20.

Lord, J. Walter. 1911. "An Argument for Compulsory Compensation." Address to the National Civic Federation, Department on Compensation for Industrial Accidents and Their Prevention, December 8. In *Proceedings of Winter Meeting,* 25–33.

Mark, C. H. 1907. "Our Murderous Industrialism." *World To-Day* 12: 97–99.

Minnesota Employees' Compensation Commission. 1911. *Report.* Minneapolis.

NCF (National Civic Federation). 1910. *Proceedings of Tenth Annual Meeting.* New York, November 22–23, 1909.

NCWCIA (National Conference on Workmen's Compensation for Industrial Accidents). 1910a. *Proceedings of the Third National Conference.* Chicago, June 10–11.

———. 1910b. *Proceedings of Conference of Commissions on Compensation for Industrial Accidents.* Chicago, November 10–12.

Pavalko, Eliza K. 1989. "State Timing of Policy Adoption: Workmen's Compensation in the United States, 1909–1920." *American Journal of Sociology* 95: 592–615.

Ramsey, F. W. 1909. "Employer's Obligation to Safeguard Machinery and the Compensation Plan of the Cleveland Foundary." Address to the National Civic Federation, New York, November 22–23. In *Proceedings of Tenth Annual Meeting,* 58–67.

Rodgers, Daniel T. 1998. *Atlantic Crossings: Social Politics in a Progressive Age.* Cambridge, MA: Harvard University Press, Belknap Press.

Rogers, Everett M. 1995. *Diffusion of Innovations.* 4th ed. New York: Free Press.

Rosenberg, Gerald. 1990. *Hollow Hope.* Chicago: University of Chicago Press.

Rosenthal, Naomi, Meryl Figrutd, Michele Ethier, Roberta Karant, and David McDonald. 1985. "Social Movements and Network Analysis: A Case Study of Nineteenth-Century Women's Reform in New York State." *American Journal of Sociology* 90, no. 5: 1022–54.

Sabatier, Paul A., and Hank C. Jenkins-Smith. 1993. *Policy Change and Learning.* Boulder, CO: Westview Press.

Schattschneider, Elmer E. 1960. *The Semisovereign People.* New York: Holt.

Scott, John. 1991. *Social Network Analysis: A Handbook.* Newbury Park, CA: Sage.

Sherman, P. Tecumseh. 1911. "Compulsory Compensation v. State Insurance." *Proceedings of Winter Meetings.* National Civic Federation, Department on Compensation for Industrial Accidents and Their Prevention.

Skocpol, Theda. 1979. *States and Social Revolutions: A Comparative Analysis of France, Russia, and China.* New York: Cambridge University Press.

———. 1992. *Protecting Soldiers and Mothers.* Cambridge, MA: Harvard University Press.

Tolbert, Pamela, and Lynne G. Zucker. 1983. "Institutional Sources of Change in the Formal Structure of Organizations: The Diffusion of Civil Service Practices." *Administrative Science Quarterly* 28: 22–39.

Tomlins, Christopher. 1985. *The State and the Unions: Labor Relations, Law, and the Organized Labor Movement, 1880–1960.* Cambridge: Cambridge University Press.

Tripp, Joseph F. 1976. "An Instance of Labor and Business Cooperation: Workmen's Compensation in Washington State." *Labor History* 17: 530–50.

Urofsky, Melvin. 1980. "State Courts and Protective Legislation during the Progressive Era: A Reevaluation." *Journal of American History* 72: 63.

U.S. Bureau of Labor. 1901. *The British Workmen's Compensation Act and Its Operation.* Bulletin 32. Washington, DC: U.S. Government Printing Office.

———. 1902. *Workmen's Compensation Acts of Foreign Countries.* Bulletin 40. Washington, DC: U.S. Government Printing Office.

———. 1905. *The New Russian Workmen's Compensation Act.* Bulletin 58. Washington, DC: U.S. Government Printing Office.

———. 1907. *British Workmen's Compensation Acts.* Bulletin 70. Washington, DC: U.S. Government Printing Office.

———. 1908. *Summary of Foreign Workmen's Compensation Acts.* Bulletin 74. Washington, DC: U.S. Government Printing Office.

———. 1909. *24th Annual Report: Workmen's Insurance and Compensation Systems in Europe.* Washington, DC: U.S. Government Printing Office.

Wesser, Robert F. 1971. "Conflict and Compromise: The Workmen's Compensation Movement in New York, 1980s–1913." *Labor History Review* 12 (Spring): 345–72.

Willoughby, William Franklin. 1898. *Workingmen's Insurance.* New York: Thomas Y. Crowell.

Wisconsin Committee on Industrial Insurance. 1911. "Report of Committee on Industrial Insurance." Wisconsin Legislative Reference Library, Madison.

Wolfson, Mark. 2001. *The Fight against Big Tobacco: The Movement, the State, and the Public's Health.* New York: Aldine de Gruyter.

III
The Nature of the Field: Impacts on Participation, Mobilization, and Identity

Helen Ingram

If the reciprocal relationships between public policy and social movements are like that of kettle drums whose separate voices roll together in overlapping waves of sound, then the theme of the three chapters in this part of the book is like the rumbling reverberations of such drumming that spread over time and distance. The interacting consequences of policy and social movements are both immediate and remote. For example, the opportunity structures or lack of them provided by policy for social movements are the most proximate of the reciprocal relationships. These are explored in parts II and III. As the three chapters in the latter suggest, the contents of policy reaches beyond the instigation and action of movements to affect the attitudes and behaviors of potential group members. Policy shapes the identity of individuals and their conception of themselves as citizens who have obligations to participate and who deserve the protection of the state.

Policy messages that isolate and demean citizens have a chilling effect on the inclination toward collective action and blight the possibility of social movements before organizers can even get started.

As previous chapters have demonstrated, public policies can be sources of critically important resources for social movements. Further, public policies construct broad or narrow categories or target groups toward whom policy is directed, thus providing more or less favorable platforms for movements in their attempt to frame inclusive issues. Public policy wields different kinds of tools, some establishing privileged, clientele relationships with government and some that lead recipients to expect only sanctions from government. These expectations shape whether the individual members of target groups perceive social movements as having any likelihood of success. This section suggests it is important to look beyond short-term consequences to long-term effects. Policies that consistently stigmatize certain categories of people encourage the individual members of those categories to distinguish themselves as better than the others and disassociate themselves from other stigmatized persons. The fellow feeling and shared identity basic to social movements is undercut.

Part III begins with a chapter that tells a positive story of a well-crafted policy that resulted in encouraging more citizens to participate in politics. Suzanne Mettler distinguishes between the resource, interpretive, and participatory effects of veterans' benefits, and argues that the GI Bill benefits offered at the end of World War II provided an exemplary mix of all three. Policy raised the levels of education and skills of a whole generation of young men, many who could not have gone to college or pursued vocational training without the subsidy provided by policy. Furthermore, the program treated beneficiaries with dignity and respect, as honored citizens, and they widely perceived it to be an effective turning point in their lives. Through such generous distribution of resources, and by conveying affirming messages, the GI Bill produced a long-term positive effect on political participation. Based on an extensive study of the subsequent behavior of the program's beneficiaries, Mettler concludes that programs that extend liberal benefits with high value can stimulate civic capacity and political involvement of policy recipients.

The lessons of Mary Katzenstein's chapter on prison reform take the message about policy repercussions further and in a less cheerful direction. She distinguishes between policies that target narrowly circumscribed human rights versus policies that build capacity and provide standing as citizens. Prison reformers have succeeded in providing prisoners the rights related to humane treatment that place the state in a favorable light, but other support is limited. Even the corrective rights policies of the 1970s were paternalistic and had disempowering implications with the increasing isolation of prisoners in high security facilities and with the channeling of protest into the courts. Draconian criminal penalties, including those that permanently deprive felons of the right to vote, marginalize an ever-expanding criminal class. In this situation collective action becomes virtually impossible for felons, and restrictive legislation has greatly circumscribed even their opportunities to petition on their own behalf. The resource, interpretive, and participatory implications for the incarcerated are all unfavorable. Further, the demonizing nomenclature and divisive categories of policy discourse and choice of tools deepen the chasm between those convicted of crimes and everyone else.

The capacity of policies to adversely construct target groups and discourage participation is limited and sometimes backfires, as Ellen Reese demonstrates in the case of California's campaign to restore welfare rights to legal immigrants. While, like prisoners, immigrants are often negatively constructed in policy discourse, a coalition of welfare advocates, groups concerned with hunger, and groups representing a variety of racial and ethnic groups combined to restore welfare rights threatened by federal and state laws. According to the author, the key to coalition building was the broad scope of the policy threat to groups who might not otherwise have had much in common. Instead of marginalizing and disempowering target groups, a series of policies that had a very wide spectrum of legal and illegal targets motivated and activated a broad array of groups. At the same time, the lessons of the chapter by Mary Katzenstein are reinforced in that illegal immigrants are excluded as beneficiaries of the policies of the welfare rights restoration movement. Undocumented workers gain no new protections from the movement and are left to struggle with their illegal status, which clearly impedes their ability to mobilize.

7

Policy Feedback Effects for Collective Action: Lessons from Veterans' Programs

Suzanne Mettler

The prospect of analyzing veterans and social movements in a single essay might strike many readers as paradoxical. Social movements are understood as "contentious politics," politics oriented toward change, typically in the direction of expanding democracy. By contrast, veterans are often associated, at least by younger generations, with "politics as usual," protection of the status quo, and the inherently hierarchical institutions of the military.

Such stereotypes of veterans are historically contingent, deeply influenced by the legacy of veterans' status within public policies. This essay explores programs geared toward veterans over time and suggests that policy designs have been highly consequential in shaping the form of their engagement in civic and political life. Some policies have treated beneficiaries as rightful dependents, while others have regarded them as contenders, and still others as advantaged, independent citizens. While recent scholarship has focused primarily on the dynamics through which policies stratify the citizenry and marginalize less advantaged social groups, this chapter illuminates how policy designs can also unify citizens, including the less fortunate, with salutary effects for their subsequent civic involvement.

To the extent that scholars have probed the effects of social movements for social policy and vice versa, the focus has been predominantly on social insurance and public assistance programs. Veterans have received relatively little attention. Yet, as Theda Skocpol shows in *Protecting Soldiers and Mothers* (1992), while European nations developed social insurance programs for working men and their dependents, the United States extended "equally extensive—and sometimes more financially generous" benefits to those who had "earned aid" through military service. Indeed, the United States had a long history of benefits for veterans, extending back to the Revolutionary War. After World War II, the United States once again pursued an exceptional course, granting—through the GI Bill—far more generous and extensive benefits to former soldiers than comparable nations. How have such programs affected veterans' inclination to participate in public life? Have they stimulated or thwarted social movements, and through what kinds of dynamics? In grappling with such questions, this chapter investigates a theoretical lacuna in the relationship between public policy and social movements.

The Social Movement—Public Policy Nexus

Social movement theorists who advocate a "political opportunity structure" approach offer more attention than their forebears to the role that states play in repressing or facilitating collective action (Tilly 1978; Tarrow 1998). As articulated by Peter Eisinger, "the incidence of protest is related to the openness of the structure of opportunities in a curvilinear fashion," with protest increasing as structures become somewhat less repressive and disappearing in instances in which government is highly responsive (1973, 28). Nonetheless, the effects of public policy for civic participation remain relatively neglected by students of "contentious politics" (Meyer 2002a, 2002b). Scholars offer considerable attention to the ways in which movements contribute to issue definition and agenda setting (Kingdon 1995; Stone 1988; Baumgartner and Jones 1993; Rochefort and Cobb 1994), but little to how policies may influence the possibilities for and shape of subsequent collective action.

Those studies that do consider public programs as an independent variable typically depict the state as a conservative force that co-opts movement goals or diffuses the momentum for protest. The classic treatment appears in Frances Fox Piven and Richard Cloward's book *Regulating the Poor: The Functions of Public Welfare* (1971), which interprets relief arrangements as tools of social control to quell social disorder. Several scholars have argued that American political history has consisted of cycles that begin with social protest aimed at expanding democracy, only to be followed by government responses that expand bureaucratic authority and state autonomy and, as such, remove power from ordinary citizens (Huntington 1981; Nelson 1982; Morone 1990). Offering such an example, Janet C. Gornick and David S. Meyer argue that the antirape movement fell into decline when government responses institutionalized the issue and undercut the movement's more radical goals (1998).

Must the interaction between social movements and government yield such tragic ends? Do government responses necessarily limit democracy by undermining the participation of citizens? Certainly some scholars have offered examples to the contrary. Doug McAdam's study of black insurgency highlighted the role of pro–civil rights Supreme Court decisions in the 1930s and 1940s in providing greater opportunities for movement success (McAdam 1982, 83–86). Both Anne Costain (1992) and Mary Katzenstein (1998) have shown that policy developments opened possibilities for feminist mobilization. Yet the dynamics through which public programs affect civic engagement remain undertheorized, leaving us with little understanding of how they affect citizens' inclination to participate and the form such participation takes. Why might some policies prompt citizens to become involved, and why might others disempower them? Why might some foster "contentious" or protest politics, while others lead to more conventional forms of participation?

I will argue that policy design functions as the key to such dynamics. As Helen Ingram and Anne Schneider have suggested, variation in the rules and tools of policy design convey critical messages to citizens about their role, place, and identity in the polity, with implications for collective action (Schneider and Ingram 1997). Joe Soss (1999) has probed such interpretive or cognitive effects, showing how clients of different welfare programs perceived the agency with which they interacted as a microcosm of government itself and extrapolated lessons about their own role in the political system. Soss's work (2001) has been especially useful in illuminating how stigma is instilled through social programs aimed for particular targeted groups, stymieing opportunities for collective action. My effort here is to offer a broad framework that allows us to examine both resource and interpretive effects of policy design and to consider consequences for advantaged groups as well as stigmatized groups. Toward that end, I draw on two additional theoretical approaches.

How Policy Design Affects Political Action

I build on the policy feedback approach, which views public policy as an independent variable with consequences for politics (Skocpol 1992, 57–60; Pierson 1993). Paul Pierson has noted that policy feedback analysis to date has focused primarily on effects for organized interests or political elites and called for more attention to effects for "mass publics," meaning citizens generally. He proposed analyzing two dynamics: (1) resource effects, how the resources and incentives policies provide shape patterns of behavior; and (2) interpretive effects, how policies convey meanings and information to citizens (1993). In order to make Pierson's approach more applicable to explaining the effects of policy for participation, I draw on Verba, Schlozman, and Brady's civic voluntarism model, with its attention to the impact of resources (free time, money, and civic skills) and psychological predisposition (attributes such as political efficacy, a sense of civic duty, or a group consciousness of having one's fate linked to others) (1995, 270–72). Attention to the tools and rules of policy design, as highlighted by Schneider and Ingram, is especially important for analyzing causal effects of public policy (1997, 93–99) other than resource effects.

The resulting theoretical framework extends policy feedback theory to specify how policy may affect citizens' civic involvement (Mettler 2002a, 353). First, the resources bestowed on citizens through policy, whether in the form of payments, goods, or services, have distinct *resource effects* for individuals' material well-being and life opportunities and directly affect their *capacity* (meaning ability, aptitude, or faculty) for participation. Second, features of policy design, including the administrative rules and procedures and the form and scope of eligibility and coverage, have *interpretive effects* for citizens. Through such features, individual citizens acquire perceptions of their role in the community, their status in relation to other citizens and government, and the extent to which a policy has affected their lives. As a result, policy design shapes citizens' psychological *predisposition* to participate in public life. In addition, the resources offered through a policy have interpretive effects, inasmuch as citizens perceive those aspects of government programs to affect their life circumstances. Finally, resource effects influence civic predisposition: education, for example, promotes attitudes of civic duty (Wolfinger and Rosenstone 1980, 36).

The question is, *how* do these relationships operate? In order to understand them, it is necessary to consider specific features of policy design. In this essay, I will assess two design features that likely determine the resource effects of the program. The *scope of eligibility* refers to the extent to which the program is available to all veterans or restricted to those with particular characteristics such as disability or financial need. The *value of resources* means the worth of the actual payments and/or program services provided for individual veterans. I will also consider two aspects of the administrative character of the program, both of which may yield interpretive effects. Policies' *procedures for determining eligibility* vary from particularistic, in which administrators yield considerable discretion, to standardized, with clear, uniform rules applied to all veterans. Given the forms of administration commonplace in the United States during the period in question, *procedures for benefit delivery* range from the patronage style that was commonplace in the late nineteenth and early twentieth centuries to more bureaucratic, routinized procedures that emerged with the growth of the federal government in the early twentieth century and especially during and after the New Deal.

A program's design features may promote resource and interpretive effects that in turn shape recipients' civic involvement in terms of both degree and form. Some programs might have negative resource and/or interpretive effects, thus failing to increase citizens' capacity for involvement and making them psychologically disinclined to be involved. Alternatively, others might have salutary effects, encouraging citizen involvement. This framework could be used to explain why, as scholars of political participation have noticed, recipients of social insurance programs or agricultural subsidies become more active in politics than those who share more common characteristics, while recipients of public assistance beneficiaries become less active (Verba, Scholzman, and Brady 1995; Rosenstone and Hansen 1993; Wolfinger and Rosenstone 1980; Campbell 2000). For our purposes here, it is especially interesting to consider the form that enhanced involvement takes: conventional or contentious. I expect that the most generous, inclusive, and standardized programs might promote conventional engagement, since citizens' demands are likely to be fairly well satisfied and they are likely to be assured of routinized procedures for exercising their political voice. Programs that are less inclusive, less generous, and more discriminating might be more likely to stimulate either passivity or contentious activism, depending on the particular mix of features and their timing in individual lives relative to other experiences of government.

In the next section, I offer an overview of veterans' policies over time, considering how different policy designs for benefit programs might have influenced civic and political activity among veterans of different wars. Then I consider the consequences of a policy that treated beneficiaries as advantaged citizens, focusing on the educational provisions of the GI Bill of Rights for World War II veterans. This examination, which permits consideration of the theoretical framework I have sketched, draws on new survey and interview data. We shall see that policy design features shape citizens' capacity for and inclination to be involved and the extent and form of their engagement in civic and political activity.

Veterans' Policies and Activity Prior to World War II: Policy Feedback Cycles

As it had in the development of public education, the United States granted more generous social provisions in veterans' benefits and did so far earlier than comparable nations. The American "citizen-soldier" became entitled to social benefits long before the celebrated "citizen-worker" in European nations acquired such rights (Skocpol 1992, 102–51). In 1818, three decades after the Revolutionary War, the U.S. government granted pensions to veterans who had served for at least two years if they were disabled or destitute; similar benefits were extended to veterans of the War of 1812 and the Mexican War.

By the late nineteenth century, as European nations extended social rights to their citizens as employees or their dependents, the United States developed increasingly ample policies for veterans and their dependents. The initial policy for Civil War veterans, established in 1862, offered strictly war-related pensions: they were granted only to veterans who had suffered a disability in military service and to widows whose husbands had war-related deaths. Veterans were also granted preferred status to acquire land under homestead legislation. By 1890, pressured by the Grand Army of the Republic (G.A.R.), Congress expanded the benefits to veterans who suffered from any infirmities, regardless of need or whether such disabilities were incurred during military service, and to widows of veterans regardless of whether their husbands' deaths were service related (Kato 1995, 2037–40; Dearing 1952). The only eligibility requirements were that the veteran had served at least ninety days and was too incapacitated to perform manual labor (McConnell 1992, 152–53). By the turn of the century, such pensions had become fairly large and widespread. As a result, the U.S. government granted social provision more than adequately to men who had proven their civic duty to the nation through military service, but not to others, even though most fulfilled another obligation historically deemed to be essential for men: participation in the workforce.

The Civil War pensions were designed to be what Theodore Lowi terms "patronage" or "distributive" policies, which are necessarily particularistic—aimed at a specific group to reward particular behavior (Lowi 1964). This feature was exacerbated through program administration, since pensions were delivered through the patronage system of party politics, permitting a high degree of discretion to local politicians who could in practice control the timing and targeting of benefits for political purposes (Skocpol 1992, 143–48). The program design features are summarized in the first column of Table 7.1.

How would Civil War pensions affect the political system? Scholars have recognized that they earned a poor reputation among Progressive reformers, who associated their delivery with widespread corruption, and that this made public officials wary of creating analogous benefits subsequently (Skocpol 1992). Yet the benefits shaped political activity not only via elites but also through citizens, particularly beneficiaries themselves. Among veterans, the design of the original pensions appears to have mobilized in-

Table 7.1. Comparison of policy design features of three versions of veterans' benefits, and subsequent resource, interpretive, and participatory effects among beneficiaries.

Program design features	Civil War benefits	World War I benefits	World War II benefits (GI Bill)
Scope of eligibility	Partially restricted	Highly restricted	Universal
Value of resources	High	Low	High
Procedures for determining eligibility	Particularistic	Standardized procedures	Standardized procedures
Procedures for benefit delivery	Patronage	Routinized, bureaucratic	Routinized, bureaucratic, automatic
Resource effects	Positive but restricted	Negative	Highly positive
Interpretive effects	Mixed	Negative	Highly positive
Participatory effects	Not contentious; likely to promote conventional political involvement	Involvement in contentious politics	Involvement in conventional civic and political activities

volvement in the conventional politics of the day, through the decentralized electoral system and party politics as well as in the G.A.R. veterans' organization (Crowley and Skocpol 2001). The pensions served as an "entering wedge," such that, as Stuart McConnell explains, "when arrears were paid, agitation for dependent pensions was begun; when those were paid, service pensions were demanded; when almost every veteran was on the rolls, calls for rate increases were heard; when the increases were forthcoming, demands for public land and other bonuses materialized" (1992, 157). Amid the highly competitive electoral politics of the post–Civil War era, public officials actively pursued veterans' votes in order to gain the margin of victory (Dearing 1952). Notably, although social movement activity soared during the late nineteenth and early twentieth centuries, the active groups did not include veterans (Sanders 1999; Hahn 1983; Hattam 1993; Clemens 1997). Veterans had already captured the attention of political officials and did not need to resort to contentious politics to make their voices heard.

Given the maligned image of Civil War pensions, policy makers sought a new policy design approach for World War I veterans. They pursued a system that they believed would be less expensive, less open to corruption, and more oriented toward the promotion of self-reliance. The resulting program covered a far smaller group of veterans and offered them considerably less than its predecessor. Rather than providing disability pensions, the new readjustment programs offered veterans only the option of purchasing low-cost insurance akin to that in workmen's compensation laws. Congress authorized medical and hospital care for veterans and, for the first time in history, vocational training (Kato 1995, 2038–39), but both such provisions were limited to the narrowly defined disabled.

Veterans found the new approach to be unsatisfactory. Few elected to purchase the insurance, which meant that they had no recourse in times of need. They deemed the vocational programs to be poorly administered, and the medical provisions insufficiently funded (Dillingham 1952, 131–44). As dissatisfaction grew widespread, veterans mobilized and began to pressure Congress for compensation in the form of a "bonus." In 1924, over presidential vetoes, Congress enacted such legislation and promised first payments in 1945. In 1931, after the Depression hit, policy makers conceded that veterans could begin to borrow against future bonuses. Yet a year later, with economic conditions still worsening, a "Bonus Army" of twenty thousand veterans, most of them jobless, descended on Washington to demand immediate payment of their benefits. They established a shantytown on the Anacostia Flats, and when no space was left, occupied some vacant buildings on Pennsylvania Avenue as well. Hoover demanded that the White House be put under guard and the streets vacated. Ultimately, he called in federal troops under General Douglas MacArthur to drive the veterans out. As historian William E. Leuchtenburg tells the story:

> The Army . . . carried out its mission with few casualties, but with a thoroughness that the situation scarcely required. Four troops of cavalry with drawn sabers, six tanks, and a column of steel-helmeted infantry with fixed bayonets entered downtown Washington. After clearing the buildings on Pennsylvania Avenue, they crossed the Anacostia Bridge, thousands of veterans and their wives and children fleeing before them, routed the bonusers from their crude homes, hurled tear gas bombs into the colony, and set the shacks afire with their torches. That night, Washington was lit by the burning camps of Anacostia Flats. (1963, 15)

Thus, in the case of World War I benefits, the policy design for veterans' benefits effectively stimulated social mobilization and protest. After the Civil War, veterans had enjoyed an advantaged position as the most privileged citizens in America's emergent welfare state. Under the new policy design, by contrast, they were treated more as stigmatized or second-class citizens, whose "dependence" on government was to be discouraged. The interpretive effects of such design features were likely exacerbated by historical context, inasmuch as veterans perceived themselves to be mistreated relative to an earlier generation of veterans. Consequently, veterans organized and engaged in contentious political struggle.

The Roosevelt administration responded to veterans' protests more graciously than the Hoover administration, but simultaneously sought to diffuse their claims through a new policy approach (Schlesinger 1959, 15). Rather than treating veterans differently from other citizens through targeted programs, officials aimed to incorporate them into broad-based social programs for citizens. Roosevelt made his position clear when he addressed the American Legion in 1933, stating, "no person, because he wore a uniform, must thereafter be placed in a special class of beneficiaries over and above all other citizens" (U.S. Congress 1934, 16). He followed up his rhetoric with action: the 1933 Economy Act repealed existing veterans' legislation and authorized the president to issue new regulations; through forty-one subsequent executive orders, the president eliminated pensions for nonservice disabilities, reduced compensation rates, dropped nearly 700,000 from the rolls, and introduced a means test (Kato 1995, 2039). Instead, his administration made jobs available to thousands through the Civilian Conservation Corps and later the Federal Emergency Relief Administration (Best 1992). Then the New Deal proceeded, through its core pieces of social and labor legislation, to expand American social citizenship by bestowing rights primarily on citizen-workers (Mettler 1998).

During World War II, however, the nation once again turned to policies geared toward veterans alone, this time through the Servicemen's Readjustment Act of 1944, otherwise known as the GI Bill of Rights. The Roosevelt approach became marginalized as the American Legion marshaled grass-roots support and pressured Congress to enact the generous readjustment program. Like the World War I program, the GI Bill avoided pensions for veterans and was geared to promote self-sufficiency. But unlike the prior policy, the GI Bill was not limited to disabled veterans, and its benefits were extensive and widely available, guaranteeing additional higher education or sub-college training paid at government expense, low-interest mortgage loans, and up to one year of standardized employment benefits to World War II veterans (Olson 1974; Ross 1969).

Fifty-one percent of all returning veterans—7.8 million—took advantage of the education and training benefits. By 1947, veterans on the GI Bill accounted for 49 percent of students enrolled in American colleges. Within ten years after World War II, 2.2 million veterans had attended college and 5.6 million had participated in trade and vocational training programs on the GI Bill (U.S. Congress 1973, 174; U.S. President's Commission on Veterans' Pensions 1956, 287).

The GI Bill was designed as a broad-based, universal program, with generous education and training benefits that were widely accessible to returning veterans (Skocpol 1997). To be eligible, veterans needed only to have an "other than dishonorable" discharge and to have served at least ninety days of active duty (Brown 1946, 13). The policy granted one year of education or training to all veterans who had served for ninety days, with an additional month of education for each additional month of service up to a maximum of forty-eight months. All tuition and fees were covered up to a total of $500 per year, and veterans received monthly subsistence payments of $75 if single, $105 with one dependent, and $120 with two or more dependents (U.S. Congress 1973, 20).

These important shifts in policy design meant that relative to earlier veterans' programs, the GI Bill granted broader access to its benefits and extended them in a more standardized form. Because Civil War pensions fit the model of distributive policies and were implemented through the patronage party system, they had been limited in their ability to promote broad and effective social citizenship (Skocpol 1992, 82–87, 120–24, 143–48; Lowi 1964; Mettler 2002b). Much less generous and inclusive, the World War I benefits sparked a social movement among veterans who realized that they were receiving treatment far inferior to that enjoyed by an earlier generation of veterans. By contrast, the GI Bill offered a social bill of rights, fixed and clear in statutory form. Unlike the pensions of the past, the new benefits were not contingent on subsequent appropriations. Also, whereas educational programs for World War I veterans had been limited to the disabled and pensions had been tied to more stringent requirements regarding length of service (Kato 1995, 2037–38), the GI Bill extended more universalistic rights with its lenient eligibility requirements.

Might inclusion in the GI Bill's generous education and training provisions affect beneficiaries' inclination and capacity for political activity? If so, how would such dynamics operate? And would the effect be the stimulation of social movement activity or participation in conventional politics? We proceed to examine this question in the next section.[1]

The GI Bill's Effects for Civic Involvement

Data

This section is based on a survey of in-depth, open-ended interviews with World War II veterans. Many survivors from World War II military units have formed their own veterans' organizations, groups that typically have mailing lists, generate newsletters, and hold reunions. I contacted several such organizations in an attempt to locate a few that were sufficiently different from each other and large enough to include veterans with a wide range of personal backgrounds, military ranks, and wartime experiences. For the study, I used lists from four military units: two from the U.S. Army (Eighty-Seventh Infantry Division, Eighty-Ninth Infantry Division) and two from the U.S. Army Air Force (379th Bomb Group; 783rd Bomb Squadron, 465th Bomb Group).[2] These units included only men; also, because the World War II military was still segregated, African-Americans served in separate units, none of which were included in this version of the survey.[3] Concerns that using organizational lists might bias the findings toward effects for highly active veterans were unfounded: the organizations include veterans who exhibit a wide array of activity levels.[4]

The quantitative component of the research design consisted of a mail survey of one thousand veterans. The survey investigated such topics as family background, civic and political activities, military service, education and training, the GI Bill, occupational history, and demographics. The survey subjects were randomly selected from four thousand names on the World War II military unit organizations' lists. In August 1998, each subject received a cover letter, a twelve-page survey booklet, and a reply envelope, followed by a reminder postcard one week later. Two subsequent packets were sent to nonrespondents four weeks and eight weeks later, in order to limit bias from early respondents. The survey yielded 716 completed surveys, a 73.5 percent response rate.

The qualitative component of the research consisted of twenty-eight semi-structured, open-ended interviews with veterans in all regions of the United States. Their names were drawn from the same lists as those used for the survey.[5] The interview covered the same basic topics as the survey, but while the survey data allows for systematic comparisons between groups, the interviews offer the opportunity to probe responses in greater depth and to understand their meaning in the context of individual lives (Hochschild 1981). Each interview lasted between one and a half and three hours.

Bonus Army No Longer

While many World War I veterans had turned their swords into placards and left marching in the Armed Forces for marching in the streets, non-black veterans of World War II pursued a different course.[6] No parallel activism analogous to the "Bonus Army" emerged among them. Only five percent reported that they "ever participated in a protest, march, or demonstration on some national, state, or local issue." Across time, such activism grew from a low of 1.6 percent in the 1950 to 1964 period, to 3.6 percent in 1965 to 1979, and leveled off at 2.7 percent in 1980 to 1998. The most common reasons for protest among World War II veterans involved labor issues, the Vietnam War, civil rights and school desegregation, abortion, and—lastly—veteran's issues. Although slightly larger numbers of GI Bill users were among those engaged in protest in each period, the relationship was not significant.

World War II veterans should not be considered unusually quiescent: indeed, protest is infrequent among the general population. Only 6 percent of those responding to a national survey of citizens in 1989 reported any protest activity in the previous twelve months (Verba, Schlozman, and Brady 1995, 51–52). It is unlikely that veterans were any less likely to engage in protest than other Americans. The point here is that they did not mobilize and protest *as veterans,* as had their World War I predecessors. To understand how World War II veterans did participate in public life, we will now examine how their inclusion in the GI Bill influenced them to become involved in more conventional forms of civic and political activities.

Effects for Civic and Political Involvement

Elsewhere, I have tested the effects of the GI Bill for memberships in civic organizations during the immediate postwar period, 1950 to 1964 (Mettler 2002a). The organizations included in that analysis are fraternal groups (e.g., Rotary, Lions, Elks); neighborhood or homeowners' associations; Parent-Teacher Associations (PTA) or school support groups; and a category titled "any other civic or community organization."[7] To isolate the effects of the GI Bill, it was necessary to control for several variables, including level of education, parents' level of education, standard of living during their childhood in the 1920s,[8] standard of living during the 1960s, and parents' civic activity. I conducted ordinary least-squares (OLS) regression to test these relationships.

This analysis reveals that use of the GI Bill's education and training provisions was highly significant in determining the degree to which veterans joined civic organizations in 1950–64.[9] GI Bill use had a positive effect: individuals who benefited from it were significantly more likely to be members of civic organizations than those who did not benefit from the program. The level of education a veteran had completed was also a significant determinant of civic activity, but GI Bill use was not reducible to this factor, given that it remained a significant determinant even when educational level was held constant. Not surprisingly, given the well-known connection between socialization in childhood and subsequent participation, veterans whose parents had been active in civic life were significantly more likely to join organizations (Jennings and Niemi 1981, ch. 4; Verba, Schlozman, and Brady 1995, 418–20, 437–38). Veterans' standard of living during the 1960s also proved to be a positive determinant of joining organizations, though at a lower level of significance than the aforementioned factors. The inclusion of this variable suggests that GI Bill use was not simply a proxy for the achievement of middle-class status. Neither childhood socioeconomic indicator—standard of living during the 1920s nor parents' level of education—appeared to bear a significant relationship to civic memberships.

I consider as well the GI Bill's role in relationship to political participation. For this analysis, I operationalize the dependent variable as a composite of individuals' memberships in political organizations (political clubs or political party committees) and participation in a range of political activities between 1950 and 1964. The types of political activities considered include contacting a political official to communicate concerns about some problem or issue; working on a campaign for a candidate running for national, state, or local office; serving on any official local government board or council that deals with community problems or issues; and contributing money to an individual candidate, party, or other organization that supported candidates. In this analysis, I substituted parents' political activity for parents' civic activity.

Once again use of the GI Bill for education or training proved to be a significant positive determinant of participation.[10] Parents' political activity had a significant, positive effect on veterans' political activity. The GI Bill made a marked difference, even independent of educational level, in promoting participation in a wide range of political organizational memberships and activities during the 1950s and early 1960s (Mettler 2002a).[11]

Resource Effects Promoting Conventional Political Involvement

The GI Bill yielded strongly positive resource effects; these emanated from design features that established the scope of eligibility and the actual value of goods and services. In practice, the eligibility requirements proved to be broadly inclusive. Among survey respondents, 10 percent failed to qualify for benefits.[12] The majority of program users were likely, furthermore, to qualify for the maximum amount of educational benefits, given that 75.3 percent had served in the military for three or more years. Some scholars have suggested that benefit usage is likely to have been biased on socioeconomic background, reasoning that veterans from more privileged backgrounds were likely to have been most able to take advantage of the benefits (Cohen 2003). I conducted logistic regression analyses using the survey data and found such presumptions to be inaccurate. In the case of use of the GI Bill for vocational training and other sub-college programs, the most highly significant variable was level of education prior to military service, which bears a negative relationship to GI Bill use, meaning that less well-educated veterans were most likely to use those benefits. Conversely, that same variable was a highly significant, positive determinant of veterans' use of the GI Bill for higher education. Year of birth proved to be a highly significant predictor of use of the GI Bill for higher education, with younger veterans more likely to use the benefits. A socialization factor, having been encouraged to pursue an education during childhood, also served as a highly significant determinant of the higher education provisions. The socioeconomic factors proved of some significance in determining program usage, but they did not predominate.[13] And while socialization experiences are typically expected to vary with socioeconomic background, this was not the case, as illuminated by the interviews: many veterans from lower socioeconomic backgrounds emphasized that their parents had encouraged them to pursue an education in order to get ahead. Similarly, high school graduation rates had increased during the 1930s, benefiting individuals across the socioeconomic spectrum in terms of premilitary education (Goldin 1998, 371). In sum then, the GI Bill offered broadly universal benefits among veterans of World War II, and little bias appeared in program usage.

How might we assess the value of the resources conveyed by the program? It is useful, first, to consider the actual dollar value of the benefits in current dollars. Based on the consumer price index, the purchasing power of 1948 dollars in 2000 would be as follows: $500, the amount paid per year for tuition and fees, would be worth $3,573; a $75 monthly living stipend for a single veteran worth $536; a $105 stipend for a veteran with one dependent worth $750; and $120 for a veteran with more dependents worth $857.[14] While the tuition coverage appears low by contemporary standards, tuition and fees at universities and colleges have risen much faster than the consumer price index over time. In 1948–49, the average cost of tuition and books and supplies amounted to only $234 at a four-year public institution and $418 at a four-year private institution; two-year colleges and vocational programs cost substantially less (U.S. Congress 1973, 29).

As another means of considering the value of program resources, we can assess their socioeconomic effects for veterans' lives. The most fundamental effect of the higher education provisions was to increase veterans' educational attainment. Controlling for important factors, scholars have found that these benefits likely boosted educational attainment among recipients by nearly three years (Behrman, Pollak, and Taubman 1989; Fligstein 1976). Vocational training provisions did not elevate formal educational levels, but did provide recipients with valuable training in a wide range of technical fields, enabling them to enter fields they would not otherwise have considered or to gain promotions more quickly in their chosen field. Both programs leveled the playing field by making education—a good that is viewed as synonymous with social opportunity—within reach of veterans of a wide range of backgrounds.

How did veterans themselves, retrospectively, assess the resource value of the GI Bill in their lives? Several questions in the World War II Veterans Survey that were directed to GI Bill users investigated whether they would have attained the same education if the program had not existed. Veterans were asked the extent to which they agreed with statements such as, "If the G.I. Bill or Public Law 16 had not existed, I could not have afforded the education or job training that I acquired after military service," indicating responses from strongly disagree to agree (1–4). The results revealed that over three-quarters of those who used the sub-college provisions and half of those who used the higher education provisions agreed or strongly agreed that if the GI Bill had not existed, they could not have afforded the education or job training they received after military service. While it is possible that the retrospective nature of the survey used here made some veterans answer differently than they would have fifty years ago, I found in interviews that veterans appeared to answer this question very thoughtfully. When I asked veterans whether they could have afforded additional education had the GI Bill not existed, some veterans who grew up in middle-class homes responded like George Josten, "Well, let me put it this way. I would have gotten a college education without the GI Bill. Whatever it would have cost I would somehow have paid for it, whether I committed myself to a job for several years after, or a loan, or something, because I was going to get that education."[15] But those who had grown up fairly poor were more likely to respond like Richard Werner, "I doubt it; I doubt very many kids in my school ever considered college because in those days you had to be very well off to go to college. And at the time America was still in the web of the Depression so I looked upon a college education about as likely as my owning a Rolls Royce with a chauffeur." Similarly, Stanley Soloman, who used the vocational training benefits, answered, "Definitely not. I couldn't afford it. I was only working part-time. We were married and had a child. I had to quit a job working for my uncle at a machine shop to go back to TV school."

A higher proportion of program beneficiaries felt that they would still have acquired education or training without the GI Bill, but it would have taken them longer: majorities of both sub-college and higher education beneficiaries agreed with this statement. As several veterans explained in the interviews, had the GI Bill not existed they would have had to attend night school or go to school part-time so that they could work a regular job and provide for their dependents. Majorities of both groups also agreed that while they would have obtained education or training without the GI Bill, they would have done so in a different program "of lesser cost, quality, or reputation." Some veterans noted in the interviews that because the GI Bill paid for tuition at any institution to which they were accepted, they were able to attend more expensive and prestigious universities than they would ever have imagined. Isaac Gellert grew up in a middle-class family that fell on hard times during the Depression when his father struggled to keep his small business afloat and subsequently died prematurely. He explained:

> I had the opportunity to go to Columbia University for the simple reason that the GI Bill paid everything. I probably would have—in the absence of any financial support—gone off to City College. But Columbia was essentially free; the GI Bill paid for most of my expenses. The support lasted even into graduate school. The first year of graduate school at Harvard was paid for by the GI Bill.

These results show that veterans perceived the GI Bill to have made an important difference in their ability to attain additional education after the war and in the form of education they received.

The highly universalistic scope of eligibility for GI Bill educational benefits and the impressive value of the benefits combined to produce strong, positive resource effects. By improving citizens' skills and network connections, these effects, in turn, increased citizens' civic capacity, making them more likely to be involved in public life. Education generally is known to increase individuals' capacity for civic engagement (Verba, Schlozman, and Brady 1995), but the GI Bill had independent effects, separate from educational level, in promoting such ends. Resources also produced interpretive effects, as evidenced by veterans' beliefs that the GI Bill made a difference in their lives. In addition, advanced education is reputed to increase citizens' sense of civic duty and inclination to participate.

Interpretive Effects Promoting Conventional Political Involvement

In order to prove their eligibility for the GI Bill, veterans simply had to present their discharge papers to a local office of the Veterans' Administration when they commenced their studies and again at the start of each semester. Most characterized the procedures as highly standardized and, for the most part, unobtrusive and efficient. Those who used the program for higher education were often astonished at how easily they qualified for the benefits. Said George Josten, a University of Illinois alumnus, "We had to apply . . . it was processed through some regional office that we lived near and then we simply got a check. I got a check for $75.00 and the school was paid [for tuition] directly. It was an extremely convenient arrangement." Similarly, Anthony Miller, who attended Xavier and Fordham, noted, "All of my expenses were paid, including books; all I ever had to do was sign something." The availability of the program was well publicized. Said Ross Flint, who graduated from Ohio State, "We all knew about it and said, hey, this was the way to go." Among vocational training beneficiaries, James Johnson, who worked for a gas company, recalled that his employer directed him toward the appropriate courses. Sam Marchesi credited Red Cross nurses in the hospital where he was recuperating from battle wounds with encouraging him to use the opportunity to further his education; he acquired vocational training that enabled him to become a custom builder.

Similarly, veterans praised program delivery, typically calling it "very well administered." The higher-education provisions were administered through the nations' vast array of well-established colleges and universities. Early on, some veterans felt that administrators and faculty were skeptical about whether they belonged on campus. Richard Werner, for instance, reported:

> I remember some of the [professors] talking and saying, "Why should we take these veterans in, their marks aren't as good as some of the other kids; their performance is horrible compared [to the others]." . . . But when it came to all the awards when I graduated, most of them were veterans.

For the most part, veteran college students felt that they were treated well. Josten commented,

> The professors liked us very much because we demanded them to give us very, very substantial answers and responses to our questions. We didn't buy off, let's say, with the pacifiers, we wanted some meat and potatoes with our education. They had to respond because they all felt we were sort of pushing them, we were urging them, we had to hurry up and get done and get on with our life. We were trying to make up for times gone by. I think they liked us because in a way we made them measure up and perform. Administration-wise, I think they liked the numbers we gave their organization. You know, I don't even remember any kind of a differentiation of age, veterans or non-veterans attendees.

The vocational provisions necessitated the instantaneous creation of numerous new programs, making implementation somewhat more complicated (U.S. Congress 1950, 9, 44–50) and cumbersome. Some interviewees remarked that they had to take frequent exams to pass to the next level of training. Said Stanley Soloman, who attended the DeVry School in Chicago to become a television repairman, "there was a lot of paperwork" involved in administering the program. None implied, however, that beneficiaries were stigmatized in any way, and most spoke highly of the quality of the courses they took.

Through the program's administrative procedures, GI Bill beneficiaries experienced a program in which they were treated with dignity and respect. Regardless of their socioeconomic background, they were regarded as having a right to pursue advanced education. Those who were eligible for the program were provided with ready access to benefits and regarded well throughout the course of their studies. As such, they experienced themselves as being more fully incorporated into the political community, as privileged citizens. This perception was strengthened, especially for those from low to moderate socioeconomic backgrounds, by veterans' assessments that the resources from which they had benefited were extremely valuable. In addition, some veterans, even those who could have attended college at their own expense, gained a sense of reciprocity, feeling that they owed something back to society for the valuable resources bestowed on them through the program. Through such dynamics, both administrative procedures and resources rendered beneficiaries not only more capable but also more inclined to participate in public life. They proceeded to participate in civic organizations and political activities at high levels, acting as a leaven for civic life in the mid-twentieth century and beyond.

From Policy to Politics

The development of the American administrative state over the twentieth century presents new conceptual challenges to social movement theorists. Especially from the New Deal onward, government expanded not only in size but, more important perhaps, in scope, becoming far more involved in the lives of individual citizens and in civil society than it had been previously. Public programs assumed a critical role in defining individuals' roles and identities in society and as citizens. The challenge remains to understand what such development means for collective action and democratization.

Social movement scholars, including those who utilize a "political opportunity structure" approach, still conceive of state/society relations in a late nineteenth- and early twentieth-century framework. They portray collective action as emerging predominantly in a "bottom-up" fashion, and depict activists as striving toward goals that are oppositional to those of state actors, operating through "contentious" politics, and typically losing power when the end goal—public policy—is achieved. Government programs have been portrayed, overwhelmingly, as necessarily antithetical to democratic participation. Yet over the twentieth century, the boundary between the state and social movements has often appeared to be more permeable and the relationship between the two more fluid and dynamic than this standard view allows. Interpenetration between the state and social movements has become the norm, and the role of markets looms large in the relationship between the two.

What does this transformed relationship portend for collective action? As other chapters in this volume have shown, some actors may move back and forth between official roles within the state and activity in social movements. Interest groups occupy a new terrain that often overlaps with state power, as well as the private sector. This essay demonstrates that public programs themselves may stimulate collective action and may do so in a variety of ways depending on policy design. As the state has become more powerful and infused in the everyday lives of citizens, it has gained greater capacity to exercise coercion. At the same time, however, it has also become involved extensively in the processes of democratization, as some groups that were previously outsiders gain status within the polity, and other groups become more fully incorporated as citizens through the extension of social rights.

The specifics of policy design make the difference, as effects vary with the rules and tools and resources assigned to programs. Programs may extend generous resources with high value, stimulating civic capacity and conventional involvement, or they may offer resources that actors perceive as less valuable than that given to other groups, spurring contentious responses. Administrative rules may convey positive messages to citizens by granting them status and including them in the polity, or they may extend the sense that recipients are second-class citizens, marginal to the state.

This analysis has examined patterns in the relationships between policy design and subsequent collective action among the targeted population. It suggests that public programs that offer direct cash benefits to individuals may prompt political involvement surrounding that particular issue. Judging by the post–Civil War experience compared to that of post–World War I, such participation may be channeled into electoral politics if such benefits are moderate in generosity and coverage, but may result in social protest if they are low and limited, especially when the historical precedent of more generous programs hovers in veterans' memories. By contrast, programs that offer services to individuals that enhance their social opportunity, such as the GI Bill, may have a general salutary effect on civic participation. Beneficiaries may become more fully incorporated as citizens and involved in a broad array of conventional civic and political activities rather than targeting their efforts to extending their benefits. In sum, public programs may have highly positive effects on civic engagement and may stimulate forms of action ranging from electoral participation focused on a single issue to protest or to broader involvement in a wide range of conventional civic and political activities.

The power of the theoretical framework offered here must be tested widely to assess its explanatory capacity for a wide array of public policies and their participatory effects. Case studies of various policy types might enable us to specify more clearly the types of policy design features that matter most and how they affect participation. Such studies must be attentive to historical context and the interpretive effects of prior policies on recipients' attitudes. Subsequent research might shed light on why some policies produce quiescence and others, mobilization. Analysis of how myriad public programs have shaped collective action is essential for explaining not only the politics of recent decades but also how future state action might expand democracy more fully.

Notes

1. Veterans' programs may, at the least, stimulate participation in veterans' organizations. These organizations are, on one level, like rent-seeking interest groups who seek to preserve and expand their members' benefits. The bulk of organizational activities, however, are civic in nature. The Grand Army of the Republic may be best remembered for its role in promoting Civil War pensions, but according to Stuart McConnell, its most fundamental task was for men who had fought the war on the Union side to explain "to themselves what it meant to be veterans" and to try to "tell civilians what it meant to belong to the nation the war had preserved" (McConnell 1992, 16). In other words, the organization's role was a discursive one that was intimately bound to tasks of defining a public, nation-building, and solidifying a citizenry. Advocacy for the GI Bill consumed less than a year of American Legion activities, while the organization worked for many decades to establish Babe Ruth Junior baseball teams in communities throughout the United States. As well, the organization sponsored Boys' State programs and Boy Scout camps; it assisted in building parks, playgrounds, and airfields; participated in care for orphans and emergency flood relief; and even helped promote the development of the National Archives. Veterans' organizations continue to make steadfast efforts, exercised through their participation in local parades and civic ceremonies, to pro-

mote patriotism by reminding other citizens of the duties and value of American citizenship (Pencak 1989, 278–301; Dearing 1952, 402–99).

2. An obstacle to obtaining mailing lists is that many veterans' organizations have by-laws that prohibit list circulation; efforts to attain lists from Navy and Marine units were thwarted by such restrictions.

3. Among the respondents, 98.5 percent described themselves as white.

4. Discussion of this matter and related methodological issues appear in Mettler 2002a.

5. To conduct these interviews, I traveled to all regions of the United States. Before each trip, I sent letters, requesting interviews, to about thirty individuals living within a two-hour radius of my base location. Among those who agreed to be interviewed, I selected five to seven individuals who lived in a variety of different neighborhoods and areas.

6. Outcomes were quite different among black GI Bill users, who became intensely involved in the civil rights movement, far more than black nonprogram users. See Mettler forthcoming.

7. From the qualitative data in the survey, I have deduced that this last category included several organizational types: service organizations, health-related organizations, alumni organizations and fraternities, cultural and educational organizations, commercial clubs, and local social, sports, or hobby clubs.

8. I chose to use the 1920s rather than the 1930s because it was a more "normal" time and would be likely to indicate more about the persistent socioeconomic status of families than the Depression era, when so many fell into worse living conditions than they generally experienced.

9. Results were as follows (standardized beta/significance): GI Bill use (0.16/0.01); parents' level of education (0.00/0.94); level of education (0.03/0.67); parents' political activity (0.17/0.00); standard of living 1920 (0.08/0.14); standard of living 1960 (0.03/0.54); R^2, 0.08; adjusted R^2, 0.06; sample size 379.

10. Results were as follows (standardized beta/significance): GI Bill use (0.14/0.01); parents' level of education (0.00/0.97); level of education (0.13/0.02); parents' civic activity, (0.21/0.00); standard of living 1920 (0.04/0.45); standard of living 1960 (0.09/0.06); R^2, 0.14; adjusted R^2, 0.13; sample size, 393.

11. In the essay cited here, I also included protest activities in the dependent variable. In a separate analysis for this chapter, however, I performed the same regression analysis with protest activities omitted from the dependent variable, allowing us to examine determinants of conventional involvement alone. The results are exactly the same. This is not surprising, given that, as noted earlier, the number of veterans participating in protest activities, especially during this period, was miniscule.

12. I am also including disabled veterans, who were covered by Public Law 16,

which extended education and training benefits comparable to those in the GI Bill. All survey questions were worded to include beneficiaries of both policies.

13. Among factors at the most modest level of significance, parents' level of education functioned as a negative determinant in relation to usage of the sub-college programs and a positive determinant of the higher education provisions. Standard of living in childhood also bore a positive effect on the latter.

14. These calculations are based on the Consumer Price Index, Urban Consumers, U.S. Department of Labor, Bureau of Labor Statistics, available at http://www.bls.gov/cpihome.htm.

15. Actual names are used for those interview subjects who have granted permission to do so; pseudonyms for those who have not.

References

Baumgartner, Frank R., and Bryan D. Jones. 1993. *Agendas and Instability in American Politics.* Chicago: University of Chicago Press.

Behrman, Jere R., Robert A. Pollak, and Paul Taubman. 1989. "Family Resources, Family Size, and Access to Financing for College Education." *Journal of Political Economy* 97, no. 2: 398–419.

Best, Gary Dean. 1992. *FDR and the Bonus Marchers, 1933–1935.* Westport, CT: Praeger.

Brown, Francis J. 1946. *Educational Opportunities for Veterans.* Washington, DC: Public Affairs Press.

Campbell, Andrea Louise. 2000. "The Third Rail of American Politics: Senior Citizen Activism and the American Welfare State." PhD diss., University of California, Berkeley.

Clemens, Elisabeth S. 1997. *The People's Lobby: Organizational Innovation and the Rise of Interest Group Politics in the United States, 1890–1925.* Chicago: University of Chicago Press.

Cohen, Lizabeth. 2003. *A Consumers' Republic: The Politics of Mass Consumption in Postwar America.* New York: Knopf.

Costain, Anne N. 1992. *Inviting Women's Rebellion: A Political Process Interpretation of the Women's Movement.* Baltimore, MD: Johns Hopkins University Press.

Crowley, Jocelyn Elise, and Theda Skocpol. 2001. "The Rush to Organize: Explaining Associational Formation in the United States, 1860s–1920s." *American Journal of Political Science* 45, no. 4: 813–29.

Dearing, Mary R. 1952. *Veterans in Politics: The Story of the G.A.R.* Baton Rouge: Louisiana State University Press.

Dillingham, William Pyrle. 1952. *Federal Aid to Veterans, 1917–1941.* Gainesville: University of Florida Press.

Eisinger, Peter K. 1973. "The Conditions of Protest Behavior in American Cities." *American Political Science Review* 67 (March): 11–28.

Fligstein, Neil. 1976. "The G.I. Bill: Its Effects on the Educational and Occupational Attainment of U.S. Males: 1940–1976." CDE Working Paper 76-9, Center for Demography and Ecology, University of Wisconsin–Madison.

Goldin, Claudia. 1998. "America's Graduation from High School: The Evolution and Spread of Secondary Schooling in the Twentieth Century." *Journal of Economic History* 58, no. 2: 345–74.

Gornick, Janet C., and David S. Meyer. 1998. "Changing Political Opportunity: The Anti-Rape Movement and Public Policy." *Journal of Policy History* 10, no. 4: 367–98.

Hahn, Steven. 1983. *The Roots of Southern Populism: Yeoman Farmers and the Transformation of the Georgia Upcountry, 1850–1890.* New York: Oxford University Press.

Hattam, Victoria C. 1993. *Labor Visions and State Power: The Origins of Business Unionism in the United States.* Princeton, NJ: Princeton University Press.

Hochschild, Jennifer. 1981. *What's Fair: American Beliefs about Distributive Justice.* Cambridge, MA: Harvard University Press.

Huntington, Samuel. 1981. *American Politics: Promise of Disharmony.* Cambridge, MA: Harvard University Press.

Jennings, M. Kent, and Richard G. Niemi. 1981. *Generations and Politics.* Princeton, NJ: Princeton University Press.

Kato, Kenneth T. 1995. "Veterans' Benefits: An Overview." In *The Encyclopedia of the United States Congress,* ed. Donald C. Bacon, Roger H. Davidson, and Morton Keller. 4: 2037–40. New York: Simon and Schuster.

Katzenstein, Mary. 1998. *Faithful and Fearless: Moving Feminist Protest inside the Church and Military.* Princeton, NJ: Princeton University Press.

Kingdon, John W. 1995. *Agendas, Alternatives, and Public Policies.* 2nd ed. New York: HarperCollins.

Leuchtenburg, William E. 1963. *Franklin D. Roosevelt and the New Deal, 1932–40.* New York: Harper and Row.

Lowi, Theodore J. 1964. "American Business, Public Policy, Case Studies, and Political Theory." *World Politics* 6: 677–715.

McAdam, Doug. 1982. *Political Process and the Development of Black Insurgency, 1930–70.* Chicago: University of Chicago Press.

McConnell, Stuart. 1992. *Glorious Contentment: The Grand Army of the Republic, 1865–1900.* Chapel Hill: University of North Carolina Press.

Mettler, Suzanne. 1998. *Dividing Citizens: Gender and Federalism in New Deal Public Policy.* Ithaca, NY: Cornell University Press.

———. 2002a. "Bringing the State Back In to Civic Engagement: Policy Feedback

Effects of the G.I. Bill for World War II Veterans." *American Political Science Review* 96, no. 2: 351–65.

———. 2002b. "Social Citizens of Separate Sovereignties: Governance in the New Deal Welfare State." In *The New Deal and the Triumph of Liberalism*, ed. Jerome Mileur and Sidney M. Milkis. Amherst: University of Massachusetts Press.

———. Forthcoming. "'The Only Good Thing Was the G.I. Bill': Program Effects on African American Veterans' Political Participation." *Studies in American Political Development*.

Meyer, David S. 2002a. "Opportunities and Identities: Bridge-building in the Study of Social Movements." In *Social Movements: Identity, Culture, and the State*, ed. David S. Meyer, Nancy Whittier, and Belinda Robnett, 3–21. New York: Oxford University Press.

———. 2002b. "Social Movements and Public Policy: Eggs, Chicken and Theory." Paper presented at the "Social Movements, Public Policy and Democracy" workshop, University of California, Irvine, January 11–13, 2002.

Morone, James A. 1990. *The Democratic Wish: Popular Participation and the Limits of American Government*. New York: Basic Books.

Nelson, Michael. 1982. "A Short, Ironic History of American National Bureaucracy." *Journal of Politics* 44: 474–79.

Olson, Keith W. 1974. *The G.I. Bill, the Veterans, and the Colleges*. Lexington: University of Kentucky Press.

Pencak, William. 1989. *For God and Country: The American Legion, 1919–1941*. Boston: Northeastern University Press.

Pierson, Paul. 1993. "When Effect Becomes Cause." *World Politics* 45: 595–628.

Piven, Frances Fox, and Richard A. Cloward. 1971. *Regulating the Poor: The Functions of Public Welfare*. New York: Vintage Books.

Rochefort, David A., and Roger W. Cobb, eds. 1994. *The Politics of Problem Definition: Shaping the Policy Agenda*. Lawrence: University Press of Kansas.

Rosenstone, Steven J., and John Mark Hansen. 1993. *Mobilization, Participation, and Democracy in America*. New York: Macmillan.

Ross, Davis R. B. 1969. *Preparing for Ulysses: Politics and Veterans during World War II*. New York: Columbia University Press.

Sanders, Elizabeth. 1999. *Roots of Reform: Farmers, Workers, and the American State, 1877–1917*. Chicago: University of Chicago Press.

Schlesinger, Arthur M., Jr. 1959. *The Coming of the New Deal*. Boston: Houghton Mifflin.

Schneider, Anne Larason, and Helen Ingram. 1997. *Policy Design for Democracy*. Lawrence: University Press of Kansas.

Skocpol, Theda. 1992. *Protecting Soldiers and Mothers: The Political Origins of Social Policy in the United States*. Cambridge, MA: Harvard University Press.

———. 1997. "The G.I. Bill and U.S. Social Policy, Past and Future." *Social Philosophy and Policy* 14 (Summer): 95–115.

Soss, Joe. 1999. "Lessons of Welfare: Policy Design, Political Learning, and Political Action." *American Political Science Review* 93, no. 2: 363–80.

———. 2001. "Spoiled Identity and Collective Action: Social and Political Consequences of Welfare Stigma." Unpublished paper in author's possession.

Stone, Deborah. 1988. *Policy Paradox*. 2nd ed. New York: W. W. Norton.

Tarrow, Sidney. 1998. *Power in Movement: Social Movements and Contentious Politics*. Cambridge: Cambridge University Press.

Tilly, Charles. 1978. *From Mobilization to Revolution*. Reading, MA: Addison-Wesley.

U.S. Congress. 1934. *Proceedings of the 15th National Convention of the American Legion, Chicago, Illinois, October 2–5, 1933*. H. Doc. 154, 73rd Cong., 2nd sess. Washington, DC: U.S. Government Printing Office.

U.S. Congress. Senate. 1950. *Report on Education and Training under the Servicemen's Readjustment Act, as Amended*. 81st Cong., 2nd sess. Washington, DC: U.S. Government Printing Office.

U.S. Congress. Senate. Committee on Veterans' Affairs. 1973. *Final Report on Educational Assistance to Veterans: A Comparative Study of Three G.I. Bills*. 93rd Cong., 1st sess. Washington, DC: U.S. Government Printing Office.

U.S. President's Commission on Veterans' Pensions. 1956. *Veterans' Benefits in the United States*. Washington, DC: U.S. Government Printing Office.

Verba, Sidney, Kay Schlozman, and Henry Brady. 1995. *Voice and Equality: Civic Voluntarism in American Politics*. Cambridge, MA: Harvard University Press.

Wolfinger, Raymond E., and Steven J. Rosenstone. 1980. *Who Votes?* New Haven, CT: Yale University Press.

8

Rights without Citizenship: Activist Politics and Prison Reform in the United States

Mary Fainsod Katzenstein

In an episode of life imitating art,[1] a Sing Sing corrections officer in New York State demanded that an inmate who had been shielding a cat and newborn kittens in his cell dispose of them in the trash compactor. When the inmate refused, the guard tossed the animals in the compactor himself. A New York county court judge sentenced the corrections officer to a one-year prison term. In another incident, this in Kansas, correctional officers were assessed $15,000 in compensatory and $30,000 in punitive damages after allegedly using excessive force to make a sixty-year-old prisoner stand rather than sit in the prison's medical clinic waiting area.[2] Following an Alabama incident, the U.S. Supreme Court recently held that guards were not protected by "qualified immunity" from being sued in a case that involved a chain gang inmate manacled to a "hitching post" for hours in the hot sun.[3] These are not typical prisoner rights cases in the sense that the overwhelming majority of such cases do not result in the claims of prisoners being upheld.[4] But prisoner rights litigation, despite its infrequently affirming results for prisoners' claims, is a fact of the civil rights landscape even in these generally post–civil rights times.

In 1995, prison and jail inmates were plaintiffs in forty thousand suits in the federal courts, close to a fifth of the federal civil docket.[5] This figure translated into 25 suits per 1,000 inmates in contrast to a rate of 0.7 suits per 1,000 filed by the population at large.[6] Filings in state courts varied from Iowa, where there were over 80 lawsuits per 1,000 inmates, to Massachusetts and North Dakota, where only 3 or 4 petitions per 1,000 inmates were filed. Although present-day prisoner litigation is reduced by

236

half due to the passage of the 1996 Prison Litigation Reform Act, suing in the courts continues to be the preeminent form, now much routinized, of prisoner activism.[7]

What the initial proliferation, subsequent routinization, and the current restriction on litigation reveals in a more general sense is the way that rights can both enable and disable. The institutionalization of prisoner rights, albeit important in continuing to secure protections for prisoners, successfully channeled prisoner claims into more narrowly defined concerns about conditions of confinement and away from broader questions about whether prisoners can claim in some more fundamental sense to have standing on a par with those society regards as citizens. As Suzanne Mettler's chapter on the GI Bill describes so well, the rights to social welfare subsidies created political capacity—affirming the identities of veterans to think of themselves as valued citizens and steering them toward a more active political life course. Prisoner rights created no such capacity. In the post-Attica decades, the rights extended to prisoners raised the standards of humane treatment in prisons but simultaneously did nothing to dismantle—in fact did much to heighten—the boundaries between those convicted of crimes and the "virtuous" citizen. If there is a Marshallian lesson to be stated here (Marshall 1950), it is that civil rights—the rights to religious liberty, freedom of speech, the right of access to the courts—should be seen as one distinct branch of democratic citizenship rather than as a sapling out of which a full flowering of democratic citizenship and political engagement will inevitably emerge.

I begin this chapter with the powerful distinction made by the late political theorist Judith Shklar between citizenship as rights and citizenship as "standing." In the chronological account of prison reform activism that follows, I propose that the more encompassing citizenship claims were channeled into a rights framework by a constitutionally bound judiciary quelling the advocacy work of both radical activists and liberal lawyers who were initially ready to push the framework of prison reform beyond the confines of "prison conditions." I end with a comment on the relationship between democratic citizenship and movement activism.

Citizenship and Rights

Since the central claim of this essay is that the policy response to prison reform activism favored rights over citizenship and since common parlance often elides rather than distinguishes the two terms, let me be clear about their usage here. The meaning of citizenship in America, the late Judith Shklar proposed in the 1989 Tanner lectures, must be understood largely against the backdrop of slavery. Citizenship in the United States, she states, is about respect (or "standing," her preferred term) based on the opportunity to earn and the opportunity to vote—both denied to those in bondage. Shklar writes:

> Even before Justice Taney announced that no black person had any rights that white people needed to respect, black chattel slavery stood at the opposite social pole from full citizenship, and so defined it. The importance of what I call citizenship as standing emerged out of this basic fact of our political history. (1991, 16)

What Shklar makes explicit, and that is only implicit in T. H. Marshall's analysis, is that abstract rights do not accord status on their own. Whether they do so or not depends on the historical and contemporary political context. Standing is shaped by the political place certain rights are given in a particular country context at a particular time. Shklar's idea of citizenship as standing elucidates even more directly than Marshall's argument the importance of citizenship *as relational.* Standing depends not just on having rights but on where the "ownership" of those rights places you in the social scheme of status relations in society.

The idea of citizenship as standing thus helps to broaden the discussion of prison reform activism. An emphasis on standing directs analysis beyond the question of which specific material rights prisoners lose on sentencing or might still have claim to while incarcerated, and toward the question of how those rights situate prisoners in relationship to their past, present, and future standing in society. The *Jailhouse Lawyers' Manual,* prepared by students from the *Columbia Human Rights Law Review,* is one of several remarkable texts made available for use by prisoners and prisoner advocates.[8] The manual details in its one thousand pages the case law on which rights claims can be advanced. An approach to citizenship that emphasizes standing would have students of criminal justice not simply master such a lexicon of rights but also attend to the significance that such rights accord to the rights-bearer in relationship to others more generally in society. Are there among such enumerated rights those that are fundamental to having status in society? As Shklar argues, would such rights emphasize eligibility to vote, the right to paid labor? What about the right to serve in the military, to have access to and control over property? Are there core signifiers that denote the minimal threshold signs of a group's acceptance as members of the American polity? In the discussion that follows, I present a narrative of how, even as a corpus of rights became institutionalized, prisoner claims to what might be more generally understood as the recognition of citizenship remained unrealized.

What is the significance of emphasizing citizenship as standing in the context of the last thirty years of incarceration policies in America? Introducing the concept of citizenship to a discussion of incarceration forces the question of whether punishment is intended to go beyond confinement—physical separation—to extend to the incapacitation of prisoners in other than geospatial terms. Are prison sentences intended to or do they result in the incapacitation of those convicted of crimes by also attaching to the physical penalty of separation from society the removal of other capacities—the ability to earn, the ability to vote, the ability to return to society free of a permanent handicap imposed by the sentence served?

The numbers at stake in such a discussion testify to its significance. There has been a massive rise in the prison population in the last thirty years. As of 2003, over 2 million inmates fill the prisons and jails in the United States. For most of the twentieth century the rate of incarceration remained fairly steady until the 1970s when a steep climb began. At the beginning of the 1970s, the United States was imprisoning about 93 per 100,000 of its population. The rate of incarceration in America (counting those in prisons and jails) is now about 700 per 100,000 in the population, surpassing Russia, which used to be the world leader in incarceration (Mauer 1999, 16). In 1980, 1.8 million people were under correctional supervision (in jail, prison, on probation or parole). In 2002, the number had grown to 6.7 million. At any one time, about 9 percent of the black population is under some form of correctional supervision.[9] Six percent of the American adult population has been convicted of a felony (Mauer and Chesney-Lind 2002, 18). Whether what is at stake is rights, citizenship, or both, the vast numbers so affected compel attention.

Overview

The narrative that elucidates the emergence of "rights without citizenship" is best set out chronologically. The 1970s were a defining decade. A movement of prisoners and prisoner advocates formed to demand rights to minimally decent conditions within prisons. But activism in this period sought to go beyond such rights claims as well. By an emphasis on racial identity and by assuming the self-description of "political prisoners," inmate activists sought self-respect, locating their lives as prisoners in the larger context of societal discrimination. Some voiced further demands for greater economic equality and political voice—thereby challenging society at large to recognize prisoners as—in Judith Shklar's terms—fellow citizens. Over the course of the 1970s and into the 1980s, the courts and legislatures reacted by pursuing an essentially bifurcated policy agenda. On the one hand, in response to the prisoner rights movement, the courts sought to force prisons to "professionalize"—to improve conditions of incarceration and to hold prisons accountable to more humane standards. On the other hand, lawmakers continuously repudiated demands that would have recognized prisoners as having present or future claims to the status of citizens. As policy discourse in the 1980s and 1990s increasingly demonized those convicted of crimes, lawmakers largely undermined the possibility that those either presently or previously in prison might become active citizens on their own or on others' behalf.

1970 to 1985: Recognizing Rights, Confining Citizenship Claims

Prisoner activism in the first part of the 1970s drew from the radical politics of the late 1960s. It targeted prison conditions, but its ideology encompassed a far larger agenda. The Black Muslims/black nationalists who were its core sought to assert themselves as self-regarding, radical agents of broader social change. For some, the vision was more than citizenship: it was revolution. By the end of the decade, this activism had been funneled into a much more professionalized legal corps of advocates—prisoner rights groups outside the prison and liberal judges as well as an increasingly active bar of *pro se* litigants. Citizenship claims, never mind the more radical vision of activist politics, had been largely derailed.

The prison movement began in the 1960s with Black Muslims organizing in the prison yard. The Nation of Islam brought into the prison two fundamental requisites of effective mobilization: an identity around which the disaffected could coalesce and a political method that was surprisingly, given its genuine spiritual mission, a wholesale, massive assault on the courts. Black Muslims in prison were invited to prove themselves as recruiters for and abiding defenders of the Nation of Islam.

Prisoners were not just potential converts; they were the backbone, in some ways, of the movement itself. Elijah Muhammad had spent time in prison having been convicted and briefly incarcerated for draft resistance during World War II. The connections forged between prisoners and the Nation of Islam were, as Eric Cummins elaborates, both ideological and organizational: Muhammad saw the black prisoner (according to Malcolm X) as the defining symbol of white racial exploitation. But the linkages were far more. The Nation of Islam saw the institution of the prison as a space in which networks and organizations could be established. Prisoners were invited to correspond personally with Muhammad, who sent literature and on occasion enclosed small amounts of money in his replies (1994, 69). Inside the prisons, Black Muslims sought to establish cohesive groups. It was not unusual, Eldridge Cleaver later wrote, to see "several Muslims walking around the yard, each with a potential convert to whom he would be explaining the *Message to the Black Man* as taught by Elijah Muhammad" (Cummins 1994, 70). Prisoners could be inmate ministers, captains, or members of the Fruit of Islam (the Muslim defense force in the prison).

Prisoners found in the Nation of Islam not only an identity, and with it a sense (in Shklar's terms) of standing, at least in their community of fellow believers, but also a method of representing a sense of themselves that could be heard outside their own community. That method was the "writ." As Cummins vividly narrates, in March 1963 a federal court judge turned down a writ brought by a group of Black Muslims in San Quentin seeking the right to practice their own religion. Anger with the judicial ruling intensified, and in August the San Quentin Mosque, on its own without professional legal assistance, submitted a $39 million lawsuit against the prison. By 1965 lawsuits from San Quentin were being filed at nearly three hundred per month. Habeas corpus petitions in the California prison system rose from 814 in 1957 to 4,845 in 1965 (Cummins 1994, 73, 80).

It was the Black Muslims who won, as James B. Jacobs describes it, "the first modern prisoners' rights case." Muslim prisoners had claimed the right to worship and to obtain the Koran. In *Cooper v. Pate* (1964), the Supreme Court acknowledged the legitimacy of Muslim prisoners challenging religious discrimination under Section 1983 of the Civil Rights Act of 1871, signaling to would-be claimants in the prison that the courts might now be reachable in a legal system that had long declared itself off-bounds to prisoners' civil rights claims. The importance of the Black Muslim movement was thus multidimensional: the movement probably helped to steer some prisoners away from violence because of the instructions to Muslim leaders in prison to keep black prisoners from the kind of trouble that would prolong their time behind bars. But the movement certainly also politicized large numbers of prisoners and became a flash point for prison violence, whatever its source. Without doubt, the movement helped to catalyze the litigation torrent that was to follow in the 1970s. Indeed, as Jacobs estimates, there were at least sixty-six reported federal court decisions involving Muslim issues in the prisons between 1961 and 1978 (1983, 36).

The greatest significance for black inmates of the Nation of Islam's presence in the prison was the conviction that came with conversion—that the black prisoner was somebody. On this issue, the rehabilitative model that had dominated penal thinking through the fifties was far less clear. Although the rehabilitation model sought to raise the prisoner's self-esteem so as to ease the reintegration of the prisoner back into the community, its ideological premise was that the prisoner was to "correct" ill-gotten ways and learn from the reigning norms of society. Whatever its intent, rehabilitation came to be seen as intently paternalistic and didactic.

The black nationalist movement saw the prisoner as an active agent of transformation, not as simply its object. It was the radical black nationalist movement with its writer-radicals like Eldridge Cleaver (once a minister in the Nation of Islam), George Jackson, and others, that clarified how inadequately the earlier liberal rehabilitation agenda had specified a route to citizenship defined not only in political but also in economic terms. The radical prison movement was an intermixing of Marxist class ideology and countercultural politics. As Cummins argues (partly through his analysis of Cleaver's *Soul on Ice*) the California radical prison movement was a denunciation of economic domination at the same time that it was an assertion of psychosexual masculinist politics that romanticized the convict-hero. Black nationalists in prison became the radically imagined members of an outlaw cult turned revolutionaries.[10]

Cummins writes in his introduction that these prisoners "were not revolutionary heroes of the coming struggle . . . but more rightly, simply the nation's beaten-down men" (1994, ix). His critique is acute, and yet his depiction fails to capture the way in which the radical prison movement insisted that ideas of agency and citizenship be taken seriously. Ironically, in some respect, these were as much liberal ideas as radical ones. The economic analysis called as much for the economic integration of the prisoner into the capitalist marketplace as it denounced capitalism itself.

Specifically, the prison activists demanded the right of prisoners to earn a wage. Black Muslims and others had raised issues about prison labor. In 1963, prisoners in Folsom went on strike for higher pay in prison industry jobs, joined by a sympathy strike at San Quentin (Cummins 1994, 79). But it was the infusion of Marxist analysis that gave the activism a leftist theoretical gloss. When the California Folsom prison rebellion broke out in 1970 (2,400 inmates declined to leave their cells to attend to the tasks of running the prison), the thirty-one demands enumerated by the prisoners included a set of concrete claims about prison jobs and wages that were much like those of any group attempting to organize a workplace and assert rights to bargaining power:

- We demand that industries be allowed to enter the institutions and employ inmates to work eight hours a day. . . .
- We demand that inmates be allowed to form or join labor unions.
- We demand that all institutions who use inmate labor be made to conform with state and federal minimum wage laws.

- We demand establishment of inmate workers insurance plan to provide compensation for work related accidents.
- . . . Many prisoners believe their labor power is being exploited in order for the State to increase its economic power and continue to expand its correctional industries . . . yet do not develop working skills acceptable for employment in the outside society and which do not pay the prisoner more than the maximum sixteen cents per hour wage. Most prisoners never make more than six or eight cents per hour. (Berkman 1979, 66)

The radical prison movement culminated in the Attica riot of 1971. Prisoners took over the main cell blocks, taking guards as hostages. One guard was killed shortly after the takeover. As the mood turned angry, and despite the efforts of some prison groups to protect the hostages, some of the guards were assaulted. In the general melee, widespread violence broke out among prisoners themselves. After four days, and when negotiations between the prisoners and the prison administration appeared to reach an impasse, state troopers and the National Guard unleashed a full-scale assault on the prison. Thirty-nine died (twenty-nine inmates, ten guards) and eighty-eight were wounded (Sullivan 1990, 106).[11] Governor Rockefeller's decision to send in troops to recapture the prison and the ensuing violence, fully covered as it was by television and other news media, had profound effects.

One effect was the impetus that Attica and prisoner unrest of the late 1960s and early 1970s created for legal activism. In New York State, Attica led the Bar Association to initiate the creation of a new office of prisoner's legal services to be funded by the state, hoping that this would help "defuse tensions in the state prisons" (Barletta and Kennedy 1998, 1). The National Prison Project of the ACLU was founded as well in 1972. This sharpened focus on prisons no doubt helped to bring pressure on the courts and, in turn, on the prisons. As the Prison Project's new executive director, Alvin J. Bronstein, commented: "When Attica exploded in September of 1971, it created an unmatched awareness of prisons and their nature. It was no longer true that prisons and prisoners were 'out of sight, out of mind.' The prisoners' rights movement began in earnest" (Bronstein 1977, 32).

The prisoner rights movement included local prisoner rights organizations, attorneys working for legal service offices, national organizations like the ACLU, and even some judges. Malcolm M. Feeley and Edward L. Rubin describe the widely known *Ruiz* case that led to the overhaul of the Texas correctional system (Feeley and Rubin 1993, 81–95; also DiIulio 1990). The case was initiated, in effect, by Judge William Wayne Justice, who sought out a lawyer for the prisoner complainants and asked his clerks to locate a "typical petition" in order to develop a test case "to see what a first-class lawyer could do with the state's contentions and what he could develop in favor of the inmates, because I wanted to find out if there was any substance to what [the prisoners] were saying."[12]

By the 1980s, prisoner rights claims making had become institutionalized. The prisoners' advocacy movement that took the form of litigation against statewide departments of corrections resulted in a proliferation of consent decrees. Feeley and Rubin report that, between 1975 and 1980, "federal courts held prisons in Mississippi, Oklahoma, Florida, Louisiana, and Alabama to be unconstitutional in whole or in part" (1999, 39–40). By 1985, twenty-eight more jurisdictions had been successfully sued. By the 1990s, "forty-eight of America's fifty-three jurisdictions have had at least one facility declared unconstitutional by the federal courts" (40).[13]

Gradually, the courts, the public, and even many prison officials came to see the reason for the reform of oppressive prison conditions. The lack of a post-Attica backlash in judicial circles was striking. Writing within a year of Attica, Chief Justice Warren Burger commented that it would be a mistake to "continue . . . to brush under the rug the problems of those who are found guilty and subject to criminal sentences. . . . It is a melancholy truth that it has taken the tragic prison outbreaks of the past three years to focus widespread public attention on this problem" (as quoted in Fliter 2001, 167). And indeed the Burger court in the early 1970s proved responsive to many prisoner claims. In 1972, in a case that involved a matter of prison discipline, Justice Burger wrote that the suit should not be dismissed unless it was beyond a "reasonable doubt that the plaintiff can prove no set of facts in support of his claim which would entitle him to relief"—thus easing the way, as John Fliter argues, to prisoner *pro se* appeals to the courts (2001, 97).

Many prison administrators, too, saw Attica as a goad to change in the prisons, a reason for initiating staff professionalization and securing additional funds from newly attentive legislators.[14] As the former director of the Minnesota Department of Corrections commented, "All authority was being challenged (by the unrest). As a result of that there was a general attitude of wanting to reform the prisons—to make them better. They—the elected officials—listened to you. There was a receptive climate for resources" (Riveland 1999, 173). Looking back on the 1970s, several prison officials recently emphasized the role the courts played in addition to the riots themselves, but the impulse to make changes in prison administration was clearly afoot.

The riots made us know that the old ways of doing things weren't working. Then the courts came in bringing the "due process movement." (James Spalding, director of the Idaho Department of Corrections)

In the seventies institutions were closed entities. "Out of sight—out of mind" was the norm. The internal focus was on the individual management of inmates, "changing the offender" and from the inmates' perspective "doing your own time." There was little interest or involvement by policy makers. . . . During the late seventies and early eighties, the courts took over as the major influence in prison administration. (Joseph Lehman, secretary of the Washington State Department of Corrections)

As the courts entered the prison administration arena from the mid-1970s through the mid-1980s, setting new standards of acceptable physical and operational conditions (or in some cases describing nonacceptable conditions), conditions in many prisons across the country improved. (Frank Wood, former director of the Minnesota Department of Corrections)[15]

State legislatures, too, fell behind the reform spirit. Changes came immediately to Attica itself, starting with the reduction of inmates from the previous population of 2,200 to 1,158 and the hiring of a number of black and Spanish-speaking corrections officers. One hundred and fifty bills related to prison reform were introduced in the New York State legislature in 1972 (Benjamin and Rappaport 1974, 211). Significantly, governors in both California and New York called for funds to build super-maximum facilities intended, it was argued, to contain the most vicious of the prison rioters, but the legislatures in both states voted the proposals down (Cummins 1994, 270).[16]

But activism that went beyond issues of prison conditions met with far less success. Liberal reformers had devoted much of their activism to bringing the courts in to hold prisons accountable for oppressive conditions, but they had not limited themselves to issues of prison rules, regulations, and the prison itself. In the 1970s, groups of lawyers, individual law faculty, and prisoner rights groups addressed the issue of felony disenfranchisement and the civil disabilities attendant to time spent behind bars. By the early 1970s, legal scholars had developed considerable expertise on issues of civil disabilities and were turning out articles and law review notes urging the courts to end ex-felon disenfranchisement. There was a flurry of law review articles and special issues published between 1970 and 1975 with titles like "Disenfranchisement of Ex-Felons: A Reassessment" (Rebeck 1973; *Yale Law Journal* 1974; Tims 1975).[17]

But while the legislatures and courts had been responsive to claims about prison conditions, provisions to respond to broader claims met with a firm rebuff, particularly at the federal level. In 1966, the California Supreme Court opened the way for litigation on voting rights in a case that involved the disenfranchisement of two people convicted of violating the Selective Service Act twenty years earlier.[18] The court's decision held the California provisions to be excessively broad in that its exclusion of those convicted of "infamous" crimes applied to those convicted of felonies not evidently related to election fraud or violations. The ruling no doubt encouraged others, and a number of challenges to the disenfranchisement laws of other states soon followed.[19]

In 1974, the issue finally reached the Supreme Court in *Richardson v. Ramirez* (418 U.S. 24)[20] where, in an opinion written by Justice Rehnquist, the Court upheld the California disenfranchisement laws as consistent with the provisions of the Fourteenth Amendment, which gave "affirmative sanction" to the exclusion of convicted persons from the vote. The case was decided 6–3 with Justices Marshall, Brennan, and Douglas in dissent. In his minority opinion, Justice Marshall pointed out that endorsement for full suffrage rights for former felons came from the National Conference on Uniform State Laws, the American Law Institute, the National Probation and Parole Association, the National Advisory Commission on Criminal Justice Standards and Goals, the President's Commission on Law Enforcement and the Administration of Justice Task Force Report (1967), and the California League of Women Voters.[21] Indeed, the issue had garnered considerable attention in liberal circles—enough so that the Democratic party had in fact made the ex-felon enfranchisement part of their 1972 party platform.

It was, significantly, the federal government—not the state legislatures or, for that matter, public opinion—that slowed the movement to extend the rights of citizenship to ex-prisoners. Following the Supreme Court decision, the California legislature proposed a constitutional amendment that was ratified by popular vote in 1974. Earlier, a court decision in New York upholding disenfranchisement provisions was followed by a legislative act in 1968 to amend the laws. Similar chronologies were followed in (ironically) Florida (1973) and North Carolina (1973) (Tims 1975, 126n14). At the federal level, following on *Ramirez,* Congress scuttled the issue. On December 11, 1974, the House Judiciary Committee voted 21–11 to extend the right to vote in federal elections to all criminal offenders, but the bill died in session.[22]

The push for broad reform had its limits. By 1975 there were twenty-eight states that continued to bar ex-felons from voting (Tims 1975, 126n15). The vast majority of states barred prisoners from voting. Indeed, the Model Penal

Code (1962 draft, Grant et al. 1970) and the Uniform Act on the Status of Convicted Persons (1965) recommended the disqualification of convicted persons for the period of their confinement in prison. Although many liberals had become dedicated advocates of political citizenship—at least for ex-prisoners—less attention was directed to the economic requisites of citizenship. Prisoners participated in vocational and other educational programs (and indeed some prisoners were able to utilize these opportunities to good effect), but there was no concerted campaign to win prisoners market wages, to assure that in-prison work experience or training had postprison relevance. Scholars and policy makers drafted articles on the civil disabilities that prisoners confronted on release—the laws and licensing that often barred ex-felons or even ex-prisoners from public and private employment. A small number of organizations ran programs to prepare newly released prisoners for future employment,[23] but economic issues took a backseat to the electoral questions that liberals addressed with considerably more vigor. Policy makers who subscribed to the 1950s view of rehabilitation endorsed vocational and educational programs and advocated work experience for inmates but in ways that fell short of seeming to offer (as the more radical claims demanded) the likelihood of real wage-earning power either during or following a prisoner's time behind bars. Paid labor that went beyond the upkeep of the prison itself and that produced for the market (as opposed to "state use") had mostly disappeared from the prisons by the 1960s.[24] With the opposition of organized labor likely, liberal reformers had scant reason to argue for the establishment of a vibrant prison industry.

When all was said and done, as much as the reform movement had spurred attention to the conditions of prison life, the broader agenda of the 1960s and early 1970s radical prison movement, which sought to connect the issue of prisons to the racial and class structure of society, and the more limited agenda of liberals, which sought to secure the basic right to vote for those who had done their time, came to very little. Issues of citizenship were on the table, but what was there was hardly more than a passing taste.

1985 to the Present: The Recession of Rights and the Deflation of Standing

The 1980s ushered in a period typically recognized as "harsh on crime." What that meant in terms of both "rights and citizenship" were two developments: (1) the receding receptivity of the state (the courts and the legislature) to prisoner litigation; (2) the criminalization of what in other country contexts has been regarded as social/medical issues such as drug use or mental illness—a criminalization that followed its "convicts" long after completion of the time served.

The shift in the state's response to prisoner rights can be captured in a description of a few key judicial cases—a shift from *Bounds* to *Lewis*. In 1977, in *Bounds v. Smith* (430 U.S. 817, 828) the Supreme Court held that "the fundamental constitutional right of access to the courts requires prison authorities to assist inmates in the preparation and filing of meaningful legal papers by providing prisoners with adequate law libraries or adequate assistance from persons trained in the law." In 1996, *Lewis v. Casey* (518 U.S. 343) narrowed the *Bounds* decision by "limiting it to the right of access to the courts and not to a law library or to legal assistance" (Columbia Human Rights Law Review 2000, 37). In the last several years, prison systems in Arizona and Idaho have closed their law libraries (*Prison Legal News,* January 2, 2001), and the question of what constitutes a denial of access to the courts has become increasingly difficult to demonstrate. In 1995, as mentioned at the outset of this chapter, prisoners' access to the courts was dealt its strongest blow when Congress passed (and the president signed the next year) the Prison Litigation Reform Act (PLRA). The law encumbers prisoners' ease of access through a requirement of court fees, a mandate that other grievance avenues be exhausted first, by imposing a penalty for "frivolous" filings, and other requirements.[25]

Another pair of cases also records the shift in prisoner rights. In 1974 in *Procunier v. Martinez* (416 U.S. 396), the Supreme Court required the application of a strict scrutiny standard of review in addressing the constitutionality of prisoners' complaints. By 1987, the Supreme Court, in *Turner v. Safley,* softened the standard considerably, declaring:

> When a prison regulation impinges on inmates' constitutional rights, the regulation is valid if it is reasonably related to legitimate penological interests. In our view, such a standard is necessary if prison administrators and not courts [are] to make the difficult judgments concerning institutional operations . . . subjecting the day-to-day judgments of prison officials to an inflexible strict scrutiny analysis would seriously hamper their ability to anticipate security problems. (*Turner v. Safley,* 107 S.Ct at 2262)

The Burger Court, which initially handed down decisions that were favorable to prisoners' claims (coinciding with the lower federal courts imposing remedial decrees over entire state systems), began as early as the mid-1970s to restrict due process guarantees to limit the courts as a redress for a prisoner's complaints by requiring that there be a demonstration of "deliberate" indifference on the part of prison authorities, by affirming that the press and public may be denied access to prisons, by finding no constitutional obstacle to double-celling, and, as is well known, by effectively reinstating the death penalty through the *Gregg v. Georgia* 1976 decision. As John Fliter concludes his review of the latter part of the Burger Court, "While the Burger Court rejected the hands-off doctrine as a jurisdictional bar to reviewing inmates' complaints and acknowledged that prisoners have constitutional rights, a policy of deference has the same effect as the original hands-off doctrine" (2001, 137).

The partial retrenchment of prisoner rights in the 1980s was far less severe, however, than the negative construction—that is, the harsh criminalization—of an expanding class of the population. This was a three-fold process.

The process was, first, about numbers—the rapidly growing prison population that rose from about 200,000 in state and federal prisons in 1970 to 2 million in 2001.[26] Simply by sending increasingly huge numbers of people to jails and prisons, the law was, by its very definition, creating an ever-expanding criminal class.

The second process was about the passage of laws that expanded the class of "convicts" through its definitional reach. Mandatory sentences required judges to commit drug users and traffickers to prison; parole reform abolished or reduced parole possibilities and returned parolees to prison for violation of the conditions of parole rather than the commission of serious new crimes (Petersilia 2003); "broken windows" policing caused large numbers of people to be arrested for crimes that were relatively petty, defining disorderly persons as dangerous and threatening (Harcourt 2001, 21); "three strikes and you're out" legislation that made repeat offenders eligible for life sentences, even where the trigger offense was not an act of violence. The severity of these penalties was evident, too, in the postprison burden that they inflicted. Jeremy Travis summarizes the increasingly severe collateral penalties:

> A new analysis of state statutes, conducted in 1996, documented the reversal [of the decline in collateral sanctions]. Compared with 1986, there were increases in the number of states (a) permanently denying convicted felons the right to vote (from eleven to fourteen states); (b) allowing termination of parental rights (from sixteen to nineteen); (c) establishing a felony conviction as grounds for divorce (from twenty-eight to twenty-nine); (d) restricting the right to hold public office (from twenty-three to twenty-five); and (e) restricting rights of firearm ownership (from thirty one to thirty-three). (Travis 2002, 22)

Most dramatically, the "war" on drugs cast a net over a whole new class of people, those who were—many of them—victims of addiction. The Anti-Drug Abuse Acts of 1986 and 1988 resulted in harsh sentences for drug users and dealers, and through the provision that penalized crack at a rate one hundred times more than powder cocaine, brought large numbers of young, black and Hispanic city youths into the criminal justice system. But the war on drugs also imposed continuing sentences on those released from prison; the Temporary Assistance to Needy Families (TANF) Act required states to bar individuals with drug-related felony conviction from receiving federally funded public assistance and food stamps during their lifetime. (States can exempt themselves from the lifetime ban.) Laws in 1996 and 1998 enabled public housing officials to exclude anyone with a drug background (Travis 2002; Allard 2002; Rubinstein and Mukamal 2002).

A third process through which, in this post-1980s period, the construction of criminality has resulted in the diminished standing of a sector of the population has been more discursive.[27] One example involved the terminology used to describe young people charged with or convicted of violent crimes. Some six years before his appointment by President George W. Bush, John Walters—the present drug czar—coauthored a book with Walter Bennett (formerly the secretary of education and also for a period the drug czar himself) and John DiIulio, in which juveniles who committed violent crimes were depicted as a new breed of "superpredators" (Bennett, DiIulio, and Walters 1996). The imagery was powerful. Reflecting its influence in part, state legislators adopted measures to have juveniles tried as adults in the criminal courts. It was only one sign of the harshness of the times. David Garland writes of the ways that stigmatizing offenders ("once thought to be counterproductive insofar as it lessened the offender's self-esteem and prospects of reintegration") have now returned. The "demeaning symbols such as the convict haircut or the broad stripe uniform" have been reinvented (2001, 181).

It is possible, given the history of the last decades, to conceptualize concretely what a fuller restoration of prisoner rights might look like,[28] but is some modicum of citizenship as it might be relevant to prisoners imaginable? If one were to simply take the issue of enfranchisement for prisoners as a basic insignia of citizenship, one need not look far: In Germany, prisoners vote unless at their individual sentencing the proscription against doing so is added as a penalty to the terms of their confinement. There is no ban against prisoners voting in Bosnia, Croatia, Cyprus, Denmark, Iceland, Ireland, Finland, Greece, Latvia, Lithuania, Macedonia, the Netherlands, Poland, Slovenia, Spain, Switzerland, and the Ukraine. In a number of other countries, specific crimes (of treason, for instance) bar particular prisoners from voting, even where many other prisoners are permitted to vote (Austria, Belgium, France, Germany, Italy, Malta, Norway, and San Marino are such cases).[29] In Canada, the Supreme Court recently upheld the right of prisoners to vote. The majority opinion concluded that the "denial of the right to vote on the basis of attributed moral unworthiness is inconsistent with the respect for the dignity of every person that lies at the heart of Canadian democracy."[30]

In the United States, the debate is over ex-prisoners. The issue of citizenship/voting rights for prisoners while confined is not, presently in the United States, even on the table.

Conclusion

Prison reform activism ushered in the modern era of prisoner rights—but on terms that segmented individual rights from political and social citizenship. The radical prisoner movement of the late 1960s and 1970s organized around the protest of oppressive prison conditions. But the movement sought much more. In the conversion to Islam, and in the critique of capitalism and racism, radical prisoner activists found the possibilities of claiming something for themselves that went far beyond better prison conditions: an identity that could be respected and in which the possibility of social standing could be realized. The liberal flank of the movement—prisoner rights advocates, the lawyers and legal service activists, and reformist judges—made their main cause the rights to more humane conditions within prisons. But liberal activists also sought to address broader issues of citizenship, writing critiques and working on litigation that assailed the disenfranchisement and disabilities that ex-prisoners with felony convictions continued to incur long after their prison sentences were over. By the mid-1980s, however, it was clear that the state was far readier to respond to rights claims than to matters of citizenship.

Relative to the next decade, the 1970s were halcyon days. While the institutionalization of prisoner rights activism has not been dislodged—witness the large numbers of prisoner rights cases cited in this chapter's opening—the ease of access to the courts for prisoners and the probabilities that the courts will hand down decisions favorable to the prisoner plaintiff are now vastly reduced. Numerous legislative requirements continue to burden those who have served prison sentences with disabilities (felony disenfranchisement, bars to social policy supports) that carry well beyond the term of incarceration. Policy discourse, moreover, through its use of demonizing categories and nomenclature has deepened the chasm separating those convicted of crimes from everyone else.

In his ambitious comparative analysis of legal rights in four countries, Charles R. Epp argues that the establishment of civil rights in the 1950s and 1960s was not a constitutional endowment nor was it the invention of enlightened judges. It was, he contends, the product of political activism and of the advocacy work of organizations (1998, 2–3).[31] Democratic organization may indeed be necessary to the creation and institutionalization of rights. But the acquisition of civil rights can still leave a vast inequality of citizenship as it has done in the case of prisoner rights. The much needed reform of prison conditions has been important as an end in itself. But unlike some rights that invest the bearer with the capacity to become active well beyond the immediate domain in which the right is exercised, the right to protest unconstitutional prison conditions was curtailed before it could become the basis of such possibility. By the late 1970s, it became clear that these rights were not to become the foundation for either prisoners or their advocates to seek broader political engagement or economic status.[32] The history of prison reform activism in the last few decades needs to be read as a narrative of "rights without citizenship."

Notes

Many thanks to Mitali Nagrecha and Sabina Neem for their research assistance. For his unsparing and very helpful comments on an earlier draft, particular thanks to Sidney Tarrow. These revisions owe much as well to the comments of the volume's editors, Helen Ingram, Val Jenness, and David Meyer, as well as to those of the volume's fellow contributors. My gratitude as well to Marie Gottschalk and Peter Katzenstein. Much of the work on this chapter was completed during a fellowship year at the Russell Sage Foundation.

1. In the film *The Green Mile* (1999), a guard sadistically crushes a mouse that an inmate has been feeding and caring for in his cell.

2. *Jackson v. Austin*, 241 F. Supp. 2d 1313 (D. Kan. 2003).

3. *Hope v. Pelzer*, 240 F.3d 975 reversed. Argued April 17, 2002; decided June 27, 2002.

4. Prisoner suits rarely succeed. One study finds that 4 percent of civil rights lawsuits were settled prior to trial in favor of the inmate. About one percent (half of those that went to trial) resulted in favorable verdicts (Marquart and Belbot 1998). Only on rare occasions do these suits spark a broad investigation.

5. Schlanger (2003) notes that plaintiffs won their suits in less than 15 percent of the cases. See also Sturm 1993b for a broad analysis of corrections litigation.

6. As Margo Schlanger explains, most non-inmate civil cases (against "landlords" "tailors," "neighbors," or "bankers") tend to be filed in state rather than federal court (2003, 1576).

7. For an estimate of 22,000 cases in the federal courts in 1998, see Collins 1998. In Washington, DC, alone, inmates filed 2,328 lawsuits against the Department of Corrections and its officials between 1996 and 1999 (Ripley 1999).

8. Another such extraordinary text is Boston and Manville 1995.

9. These figures are drawn from the U.S. Department of Justice, Bureau of Justice Statistics, "Key Facts at a Glance" and "Additional Corrections Facts at a Glance," at http://www.ojp.usdoj.gov/bjs/tables/corr2tab.htm and http://www.ojp.usdoj.gov/bjs/gcorpop.htm.

10. On Black Muslims, see Jacobs 1976, 1983; Berkman 1979, 51–57; Sullivan 1990, 87–88; Cummins 1994, 63–128.

11. Prisoners and their lawyers received a $12 million settlement in August 2000 (David W. Chen, "Compensation Set on Attica Uprising; Former Inmates Are to Receive from $6,500 to $125,000," *New York Times,* August 28, 2000, 1).

12. Frank R. Kemerer, *William Wayne Justice: A Judicial Biography* (1991), 358, as quoted in Feeley and Rubin 1999, 81.

13. The period of "judicial policy making" in Texas, Georgia, Alabama, Connecticut, and elsewhere has been well documented. See Chilton 1991 on Georgia; Crouch and Marquart 1989 on Texas; Feeley and Rubin 1999 on Arkansas and Texas; Storey 1990 on New York City jails; DiIulio 1990 on Texas; Rhine 1990 on New Jersey.

14. The American Correctional Association drew up a set of minimum standards for adult correctional institutions in 1977; the Joint Committee on the Legal Status of Prisoners of the American Bar Association published, the year before, the "Tentative Draft of Standards Relating to the Legal Status of Prisoners." Launched in New York in the 1970s, a year prior to Attica, a new Department of Correctional Services was created. Signifying the new approach, a change was put into operation in July 1970 in which "the names of all the state's maximum security prisons were changed. There were no more prisons; in their places, instead, stood six maximum security 'correctional facilities.' The prison warden became 'institution superintendent'; the former principal keepers became 'deputy superintendents'; and old-line prison guards awakened that morning to find themselves suddenly 'correction officers.' No one's job or essential duties changed, only his title" (Meunier and Schwartz 1973, 933).

15. All interviews were conducted by Chase Riveland (1999), 171–79.

16. Gerald Benjamin and Stephen P. Rappaport reported in 1974 that 150 prison reform bills were introduced in the Albany legislature during 1972 and eight were adopted. Interestingly, funds for the governor's controversial proposed super-maximum facility were cut from the $12 million package for new prison initiatives at that time. Passed were "a bill authorizing short furloughs for carefully screened inmates within a year of their release date, a measure equalizing parole eligibility for men convicted before and after penal law reform in 1967, an increase in clothing allowances, an authorization for the Dormitory Authority to help finance new prison facilities." Administrative changes included the easing of visiting

restrictions and censorship of mail, new clothing, improved commissary and food services, and a newly opened law library (1974, 211). See also the exhaustive report by Meunier and Schwartz (1973) that looks at the implementation side of these legislatively mandated changes. On the California defeat, see Cummins 1994 (270). Super-max facilities enclose prisoners in a cell twenty-three of twenty-four hours a day, isolated entirely from the general population. See Hallinan 2001, 114–30; and Human Rights Watch 1997.

17. See also the entire special issue of the *Vanderbilt Law Review* (Grant et al. 1970), among others.

18. *Otsuka v. Hite* 64 Cal 2d 596, 414 P.2d 412, 51 Cal. Rptr. 284 (1966).

19. *Green v. Board of Elections,* 380 F. 2d 445 (2d Circ. 1967), cert denied, 389 U.S. 1048; *Beacham v. Braterman,* 300 F. Supp 182 (S. D. Fla. 1969), aff'd mem., 396 U.S. 12 (1969); *Stephens v. Yeomans,* 327 F. Supp. 1182 (D. N.J., 1970); *Dillenburg v. Kramer* 469 F. 2d 1222 (9th Cir. 1972); among others.

20. There were three respondents. One was convicted of a felony (robbery by assault), served three months, and successfully terminated his parole ten years after his conviction. Ten years later the San Luis Obispo County clerk refused to permit him to register. The second person was convicted of heroin possession, served two years in prison, terminated his parole two years later, and was refused permission to register twelve years after that. The third respondent was convicted of second-degree burglary and of forgery and had a similar history of successful parole and refusal when attempting to register to vote.

21. The ACLU supported the effort to bring the case to court and was one of the parties that submitted an amicus curiae brief.

22. In 1971 and again in 1972, hearings were held before the Subcommittee on National Penitentiaries of the Senate Committee on the Judiciary.

23. The Vera Institute was an early advocate of this kind of retraining.

24. The Walsh-Healy Act of 1935 that prohibited the use of convict labor for government contracts over $10,000, the Hawes-Cooper Act of 1929, and the Sumners-Ashurst Act of 1940 limited the interstate sale of prison-made goods. None of this prohibits states from setting up their own prison training or production facilities. The 1994 Oregon state constitution was amended to require all prisoners to work a forty-hour week or be "in training."

25. There is extensive discussion in the law review literature of the PLRA. One useful review is Adlerstein 2001.

26. The Sentencing Project, "Facts about Prisons and Prisoners," at http://www.sentencingproject.org, October 2003.

27. See Jenness and Grattet 2001 for an analysis of how social movements construct understandings of victims and criminals and Schneider and Ingram

1993 for a broad discussion of how the social construction of target groups shapes policy outcomes.

28. The restoration of prisoner rights would certainly need to address both the death penalty and the now rapidly increasing practice of managing prison orderliness by making heavy use of solitary confinement in super-max facilities, particularly solitary confinement of mentally ill prisoners. The means of delivery of the death penalty may be more refined than before (when hanging, use of the electric chair, and so on, were still practiced), but the state's delivery of the final punishment of death is still that—final. It is hard to imagine how to compare confinement for twenty-four hours a day (with one hour in an outdoor "dog pen" for exercise)—in a cell twelve feet ten inches by five feet eleven inches, being unable to hear or talk with any other prisoner through a solid steel or clear plastic (Lexan) door shield, where air temperatures may rise to well over 100 degrees or fall to below 40 degrees—with the "plantation-style" abuses of earlier 1950s and 1960s prisons (Human Rights Watch 1997). It may be "apples and oranges," but it is hard to see it as better.

29. Prison Reform Trust, "Barred from Voting," at http://www.prisonreformtrust .org.uk/file_25_5_2001.html, May 25, 2001.

30. The full decision is at http//www.lexum.umontreal.ca/csc-scc/en/rec/ html/sauve2.en.html.

31. The importance of *both* organizational pressures *and* judge-led initiatives needs to be acknowledged in the case of criminal rights. Liberal judges were certainly crucial to the history of consent decrees and what Feeley and Rubin (1998) call judicial policy making. The role of elite-led reform is also evident in the modern history of the death penalty, where Europe's abandonment of the death penalty happened in the absence of anything like the kind of movement activism that has existed in the United States and in the absence, too, of popular support for ending the death penalty.

32. See Sturm 1993a for a discussion of the difference between law that protects and law that empowers.

References

Adlerstein, David M. 2001. "Note: In Need of Correction: The Iron Triangle of the Prison Litigation Reform Act." *Columbia Law Review* 101 (November): 1681.

Allard, Patricia. 2002. *Life Sentences: Denying Welfare Benefits to Women Convicted of Drug Offenses.* Washington, DC: Sentencing Project. February.

Atkins, Burton M., and Henry R. Glick. 1972. *Prison, Protest, and Politics.* Englewood Cliffs, NJ: Prentice Hall.

Barletta, C. Thomas, and Ronald F. Kennedy. 1998. "State Legislature Recess: Early and Lackluster." *State Bar News* 40, no. 5 (July–August).

Benjamin, Gerald, and Stephen P. Rappaport. 1974. "Attica and Prison Reform."
In *Governing New York State: The Rockefeller Years,* Robert H. Connery and
Gerald Benjamin. *Proceedings of the Academy of Political Science* 31, no. 3 (May).

Bennett, William J., John J. DiIulio, and John Walters. 1996. *Body Count.* New
York: Simon and Schuster.

Berkman, Ronald. 1979. *Opening the Gates: The Rise of the Prisoners' Movement.*
Lexington, MA: Lexington Books.

Boston, John, and Daniel E. Manville. 1995. *Prisoners' Self-Help Litigation Manual.*
3rd ed. New York: Oceana.

Bronstein, Alvin J. 1977. "Reforms without Change: The Future of Prisoners'
Rights." *Civil Liberties Review* 4, no. 3 (September–October): 27–46.

Carleton, Mark T. 1971. *Politics and Punishment: The History of the Louisiana State
Penal System.* Baton Rouge: Louisiana State University Press.

Chilton, Bradley Stewart. 1991. *Prisons under the Gavel: The Federal Court Takeover of Georgia Prisons.* Columbus: Ohio State University Press.

Cohen, Neil P., and Dean Hill Rivkin. 1971. "Civil Disabilities: The Forgotten
Punishment." *Federal Probation* 25 (June).

Collins, William C., and Darlene C. Grant. 1998. "The Prison Litigation Reform
Act." *Corrections Today,* August 1.

Columbia Human Rights Law Review. 2000. *A Jailhouse Lawyer's Manual.* 5th
ed. Available from 435 W. 116th St., New York, NY 10027.

Crouch, Ben M., and James W. Marquart. 1989. *An Appeal to Justice: Litigated
Reform of Texas Prisons.* Austin: University of Texas Press.

Cummins, Eric. 1994. *The Rise and Fall of California's Radical Prison Movement.*
Stanford, CA: Stanford University Press.

DiIulio, John J. 1990. "The Old Regime and the Ruiz Revolution: The Impact of
Judicial Intervention on Texas Prisons." In *Courts, Corrections, and the Constitution,* ed. John J. DiIulio. Oxford: Oxford University Press.

Epp, Charles R. 1998. *The Rights Revolution: Lawyers, Activists, and Supreme
Courts in Comparative Perspective.* Chicago: University of Chicago Press.

Feeley, Malcolm M., and Edward L. Rubin. 1998. *Judicial Policy Making and the
Modern State.* Cambridge: Cambridge University Press.

Felner, Jamie, and Mark Mauer. 1998. *Losing the Vote: The Impact of Felony
Disenfranchisement Laws in the United States.* Washington, DC: Sentencing
Project; New York: Human Rights Watch.

Ferretti, Fred. 1971. "Two Views of Attica Legacy: 'Repression' and 'Terror.'" *New
York Times,* September 26, 1.

Fliter, John A. 2001. *Prisoners' Rights: The Supreme Court and Evolving Standards
of Decency.* Westport, CT: Greenwood Press.

Garland, David. 2001. *The Culture of Control: Crime and Social Order in Contemporary Society.* Chicago: University of Chicago Press.

Grant, Walter Matthews, John LeCornu, John Andrew Pickens, Dean Hill Rivkin, and C. Roger Vinson. 1970. "The Collateral Consequences of a Criminal Conviction." Special issue, *Vanderbilt Law Review* 23, no. 5 (October).

Hallinan, Joseph T. 2001. *Going Up the River: Travels in a Prison Nation.* New York: Random House.

Harcourt, Bernard E. 2001. *Illusion of Order: The False Promise of Broken Windows Policing.* Cambridge, MA: Harvard University Press.

Human Rights Watch. 1997. *Cold Storage: Super-Maximum Security Confinement in Indiana.* New York: Human Rights Watch.

Jacobs, James B. 1976. "Stratification and Conflict among Prison Inmates." *Journal of Criminal Law and Criminology* 66: 476–82.

———. 1983. *New Perspectives on Prisons and Imprisonment.* Ithaca, NY: Cornell University Press.

Jenness, Valerie, and Ryken Grattet. 2001. *Making Hate a Crime: From Social Movement to Law Enforcement.* New York: Russell Sage Foundation.

Manfredi, Christopher P. 1998. "Judicial Review and Criminal Disenfranchisement in the United States and Canada." *Review of Politics* 60, no. 2 (Spring): 277–307.

Marquart, James W., and Barbara A. Belbot. 1998. "The Political Community Model and Prisoner Litigation." *Prison Journal,* September.

Marshall, T. H. 1950. *Citizenship, Social Class, and Other Essays.* Cambridge: Cambridge University Press.

Mauer, Mark. 1999. *Race to Incarcerate.* The Sentencing Project. New York: New Press.

Mauer, Mark, and Meda Chesney-Lind. 2002. *Invisible Punishment: The Collateral Consequences of Mass Imprisonment.* New York: New Press.

Meunier, Paul D., and Howard D. Schwartz. 1973. "Beyond Attica." *Cornell Law Review* 58, no. 5 (June): 929–1034.

Myers, Martha A. 1988. *Race, Labor, and Punishment in the New South.* Columbus: Ohio State University.

Petersilia, Joan. 2003. *When Prisoners Come Home: Parole and Prisoner Reentry.* Oxford: Oxford University Press.

Rebeck, G. L. 1973. "Disenfranchisement of Ex-Felons: A Reassessment." *Stanford Law Review* 25 (June).

Rhine, Edward E. 1990. "The Rule of Law, Disciplinary Practices, and Rahway State Prison: A Case Study in Judicial Intervention and Social Control." In *Courts, Corrections, and the Constitution,* ed. John J. DiIulio. Oxford: Oxford University Press.

Ripley, Amanda. 1999. "Closing Arguments." *Washington Citypaper,* August 20–26.

Riveland, Chase. 1999. "Prison Management Trends, 1975–2025." In *Prisons: Crime and Justice; A Review of Research,* vol. 26, Michael Tonry and Joan Petersilia. Chicago: University of Chicago Press.

Rubinstein, Gwen, and Debbie Mukamal. 2002. "Welfare and Housing—Denial of Benefits to Drug Offenders." In *Invisible Punishment, the Collateral Consequences of Mass Imprisonment,* ed. Marc Mauer and Meda Chesney-Lind. New York: New Press.

Rudenstine, David. 1979. *The Rights of Ex-Offenders.* New York: Avon.

Schlanger, Margo. 2003. "Inmate Litigation." *Harvard Law Review* 116 (April): 1555.

Schneider, Anne, and Helen Ingram. 1993. "Social Constructions and Target Populations: Implications for Politics and Policy." *American Political Science Review* 87: 334–47.

Shklar, Judith N. 1991. *American Citizenship: The Quest for Inclusion.* Tanner Lectures on Human Values. Cambridge, MA: Harvard University Press.

Simson, Elizabeth. 2000. "Justice Denied: How Felony Disenfranchisement Laws Undermine American Democracy." Report for Americans for Democratic Action, March.

Storey, Ted S. 1990. "When Intervention Works: Judge Morris E. Lasker and New York City Jails." In *Courts, Corrections, and the Constitution,* ed. John J. DiIulio. Oxford: Oxford University Press.

Sturm, Susan P. 1993a. "Lawyers at the Prison Gates: Organizational Structure and Corrections Advocacy." *University of Michigan Journal of Law Reform* 27 (Fall): 1.

———. 1993b. "The Legacy and Future of Corrections Litigation." *University of Pennsylvania Law Review* 142 (December): 639.

Sullivan, Larry E. 1990. *The Prison Reform Movement: Forlorn Hope.* Boston: G. K. Hall.

Tims, Douglas R. 1975. "The Disenfranchisement of Ex-Felons: A Cruelly Excessive Punishment." *Southwestern University Law Review* 7: 125–61.

Travis, Jeremy. 2002. "Invisible Punishment: An Instrument of Social Exclusion." In *Invisible Punishment: The Collateral Consequences of Mass Imprisonment,* ed. Marc Mauer and Meda Chesney-Lind. New York: New Press.

Yale Law Journal. 1974. "The Need for Reform of Ex-Felon Disenfranchisement Laws." *Yale Law Journal* 83, no. 3.

9

Policy Threats and Social Movement Coalitions: California's Campaign to Restore Legal Immigrants' Rights to Welfare

Ellen Reese

Democracy and the Politics of Welfare Ex/Inclusion

According to T. H. Marshall's classic model, the development of democracy involves the development of social as well as civil and political rights. Social rights "range from the right to a modicum of economic welfare and security to the right to share to the full in the social heritage and to live the life of a civilized human being according to the standards prevailing in the society" (Marshall 1950, 3). It is precisely these rights that were gutted by the passage of the 1996 Personal Responsibility and Work Opportunity Reconciliation Act (PRWORA). Along with introducing time limits and stronger work requirements for welfare mothers, PRWORA denied federal public assistance—food stamps, Supplemental Security Income (SSI), Medicaid, and Temporary Aid to Needy Families (TANF)—to most legal immigrants for the first time in history.[1]

One might have expected little resistance to PRWORA's anti-immigrant provisions for several reasons. First, the groups most likely to oppose them—poor people, Asians, Latinos, and first-generation immigrants—have particularly low levels of political participation in the United States (Boggs 2000, 30–31; Piven and Cloward 2000; Ramakrishnan and Espenshade 2000). Second, social groups that are negatively constructed by policy makers often fail to mobilize because they view politicians as unsympathetic, and even punitive, toward them (A. Schneider and Ingram 1993). Consistent with this, some legal immigrants contemplated, or actually committed, suicide when they received news that they were no longer eligible for welfare (*Wisconsin State Journal* 1997).

259

Nevertheless, threats to a group's interests and values often stimulate dissent (Tarrow 1998; Meyer 1999; Tilly 1978). PRWORA's passage, along with the passage of the Illegal Immigration Reform and Immigrant Responsibility Act (IIRIRA) shortly afterward, galvanized immigrants and their allies into action. Many began to assert their rights and desire to become citizens, while community-based organizations increased their efforts to help them naturalize. Partly in response to these two punitive laws, the number of naturalizations rose sharply, more than doubling between 1995 and 1996.[2] Immigrants were also becoming more politicized. Between 1994 and 1998, there was a significant rise in the share of naturalized citizens, especially Latino ones, who registered to vote (Ramakrishnan 2001). A broad coalition of immigrants and community organizations mobilized in opposition to PRWORA and IIRIRA. Through protests, letter-writing campaigns, and public testimonies, they contested the negative construction of immigrants and poor people in policy debates and demanded reversal of these two anti-immigrant laws.

In this chapter, I examine the formation and success of the campaign to replace welfare benefits to legal immigrants in California, home of the nation's largest immigrant population. This campaign involved considerable, and effective, coalition work between a wide variety of ethnic groups and immigrant and welfare rights organizations. It provides an excellent case to examine the relationships between public policies, democracy, and social movement coalitions and illustrates how public policies shape the incentives and opportunities for deprived social groups to successfully collaborate in defense of their democratic rights.

My research is based on relevant articles from newspapers and organizational literature and observed testimonies at public hearings. In addition, I interviewed six key activists involved in these campaigns, including staff from five Los Angeles–based groups (two Asian-American organizations, a Filipino community organization, an immigrant advocacy organization focused on Latinos, and a welfare rights organization). I interviewed the lead staff person for the Sacramento-based California Immigrant Welfare Collaborative, who also worked for the Northern California Coalition for Immigrant Rights in San Francisco. These interviews lasted about one hour and focused on their organization's involvement in state-level campaigns to restore legal immigrants' rights to welfare, their collaboration with allied groups, and politicians' responses to their activities.

Before turning to California's campaign to restore welfare to legal immigrants, I first review the theoretical literature on social movement coalitions. Previous research suggests that social movement organizations are most likely to collaborate in response to new opportunities or threats, and/or when resources for organizing expand. Building on these insights, I argue that the scope of policy threats, their timing, and their implementation structures can affect these processes.

Public Policies and Social Movement Coalitions

Coalitions are often vital to activists' success. They improve their access to material resources, social networks, and interorganizational ties (Freeman 1975; McAdam, McCarthy, and Zald 1988, 13; McAdam 1982; Gerhards and Rucht 1992). Forming coalitions with professional associations, experts, celebrities, or business groups often adds legitimacy to activists' demands (Prunty 1984; Epstein 1996; Taylor 1996). Coalitions can also improve activists' access to policy makers, enabling them to broker agreements with the state (Diani 1997; Gamson 1975). For these reasons, coalitions can increase the effectiveness of a single tactic, such as demonstrations, boycotts, or lobbying campaigns (e.g., see Jones et al. 2001; Gerhards and Rucht 1992; Hartman 1984; Jenkins and Perrow 1977; Reese 1996; Shearer 1982; Shaw 1999; Staggenborg 1986). Coalitions also enhance activists' capacity to carry out multipronged strategies or coordinated campaigns involving multiple targets and tactics (Tarrow 1998, 103–4, 152).

While cooperation among SMOs is frequently desirable for these reasons, coalitions do have their pitfalls and challenges. Coalition work can interfere with SMOs' ability to meet their organizational needs. Activists who participate in coalition work divert valuable time, energy, and other resources away from their own organization. By working in coalition with other organizations, SMOs could lose credit for accomplishments and their distinct market niche among supporters and donors. SMOs may also lose their autonomy when they join coalitions. Smaller or less well-funded organizations frequently fear, with good reason, that bigger, better-funded organizations will dominate the coalition and its decision making (Zald and McCarthy 1980; Kleidman and Rochon 1997; Hathaway and Meyer 1997, 61–67; Staggenborg 1986). Elite patronage can channel insurgency into professionalized forms (Jenkins and Eckert 1986) or encourage SMOs' adoption of moderate goals and institutionalized tactics (Piven and Cloward 1977; McAdam 1982), although this depends both on the patrons' politics and the social group's internal capacity and willingness to protest (Cress and Snow 1996).

SMOs may remain divided or in conflict because of deep-seated ideological differences (Arnold 1995). Social cleavages can also prevent groups from working together. For example, ethnic divisions frequently prevent people of color from working together even if they are members of the same class or racial group, while racial prejudices prevent whites from working with nonwhite minorities (Gitlin 1995, 116–25). Likewise, working-class and middle-class activists often have difficulty collaborating because of different values, experiences, organizational practices, and class-based stereotypes (Rose 2000).

Activists' incentives to overcome such differences partly depend on external conditions. According to resource mobilization theory, competition among similar SMOs is fiercer among exclusive organizations than inclusive ones that demand less from their members, and decreases when the availability of organizational resources increases (Zald and McCarthy 1980). The political process model suggests SMOs tend to cooperate in response to new political opportunities or threats, which not only create a sense of urgency among organizers but tend to mobilize constituents and donors, reducing the scarcity of, and competition for, organizational resources (Hathaway and Meyer 1997; Kleidman and Rochon 1997; Staggenborg 1986).

Drawing on these insights, this chapter explores how the content of policy threats and the policy process shape activists' opportunities and incentives to form successful social movement coalitions. As Staggenborg suggests, there are three dimensions of success for social movement coalitions: (1) they last long enough to achieve goals or concessions, (2) they consistently carry out collective action, and (3) they manage to influence their targets in desired ways (1986, 375). Using the "collective goods" criterion, I consider social movements to be influential if they "secure . . . collective benefits for the challenger's beneficiary group," even if the benefits won are concessions rather than the movements' ultimate goals (Amenta, Hoffman, and Young 1999, 6–7; see also Amenta and Young 1999).

Meyer (introduction to this volume) argues that social policies shape the opportunities, constituents, and grievances for social protest. One of the most important consequences of public policy is to carve out target populations, who become subject to particular kinds of treatment (A. Schneider and Ingram 1993). As Mettler (ch. 7, this volume) argues, public policies have both interpretive and resource effects on their targets, both of which influence their political behavior. On the one hand, policies provide more or less generous resources, or take them away, from social groups. They also convey important messages about their targets' worthiness that shape their political behavior. As Mettler's research on World War II veterans shows, policies that provide relatively generous resources and positively construct their target population as deserving and entitled encourage them to participate in politics in conventional ways. On the other hand, as her example of

World War I veterans shows, policies that negatively construct their target populations and provide resources in restrictive or discriminatory ways can, under certain conditions, inspire social protest.

Extending these insights, I argue that the scope of policy threats affect the opportunities for coalition building. If policy threats have inclusive targets, this increases the opportunities for building broad social movement coalitions against them, especially if political opportunities for changing the policy are, or are perceived to be, available. On the other hand, if policy threats have narrow targets, this makes it difficult to build a broad-based social movement.

As political process and resource mobilization theories suggest, whether or not a policy threat stimulates collective resistance to it depends greatly on its organizational strength and perceived opportunities to affect policy. Policy threats are likely to induce resignation if political support for them seems unyielding, the chances of effective repression appear strong, and their target population and its allies have few organizational resources. But policy threats are likely to spark collective resistance if political support for the policy is weak or divided, and the policy's target population and/or its allies have sufficient organizational resources (McAdam 1982; McAdam, McCarthy, and Zald 1988; Meyer 1999; Tilly 1978, Tarrow 1998). Figure 9.1 illustrates my theoretical model under these latter conditions.

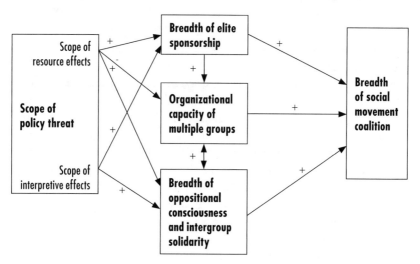

Figure 9.1. Theoretical model of the relationships between the scope of a policy threat and the breadth of a social movement coalition when political conditions for effective protest are, or appear to be, ripe.

As Figure 9.1 suggests, when public policies have "negative resource effects" and reduce or deny a group's access to resources, they limit the group's organizational capacity. For example, if policy changes render a group homeless, they will lack many of the basic resources needed to organize (Cress and Snow 1996). Other factors can compensate for the negative effects of the loss of the target group's resources, however.[3] As Staggenborg (1986) argues, elite sponsors can respond to policy threats by providing more funds to SMOs, which increases their organizational capacity. If a policy's negative resource and interpretive effects are broad, they are likely to stimulate a broad-based response among elite patrons. The greater the variety of patrons responding to the policy threat, the larger the number of social groups that will benefit from their sponsorship. This, in turn, will boost the morale of the affected population and its allies and make it easier for them to form and maintain a broader social movement coalition. At the same time, policy threats are likely to strengthen the oppositional consciousness and build solidarity among the policy's target populations and its allies, which increases their organizational capacity. The broader the policies' targets, the broader opposition and intergroup solidarity will tend to be. This, in turn, makes it easier to build a broader social movement coalition in opposition to a policy threat. Not only are more social groups likely to resist the policy, but vulnerable, resource-poor groups are more likely to find allies with greater power, legitimacy, and/or resources.

Applying this argument to my case study, I argue that PRWORA, and the policy debates surrounding it and IIRIRA, simultaneously threatened the resources of and/or negatively constructed a broad array of social groups, including immigrants, multiple ethnic groups, poor people, and their service providers. This helped to draw these groups, and organizations advocating on their behalf, together. As a result, vulnerable and highly stigmatized groups, such as poor immigrants, could rely on more powerful and less stigmatized coalition partners, such as service providers whose agencies' missions were also threatened by welfare cutbacks. The close timing of PRWORA and IIRIRA, and politicians' justifications of these policies, amplified and broadened the threat to immigrants, which encouraged greater solidarity among immigrants across ethnicity and legal status. PRWORA's anti-immigrant provisions also inspired rich donors and foundation leaders to provide greater funds for organizing around welfare and immigrant rights issues, which facilitated coalition work.

Implementation and policy-making procedures also affect the opportunities for building a successful movement coalition against policy threats as they affect the movement's targets and time frame. In modern democratic states, especially highly decentralized ones such as the United States, the policy process is highly complex. Policies are made by multiple institutions and political actors, located at different levels of government, creating multiple avenues for changing public policy. Groups stymied at the national policy-making stage can minimize, maximize, prevent, or change the impact of public policies by targeting agents responsible for its implementation at the state and/or local levels (Hall 1995, 409). If policy makers at these lower levels of government are more supportive of a movement's demands than those at higher levels, this can improve its ability to influence policy. Implementation deadlines, legislative calendars, and the budget process also influence the pace of movement activities.

Although federal implementation has generally allowed local elites to make state welfare policies more restrictive than federal ones (Noble 1997; Lieberman 1998), it can also increase the political influence of welfare advocates. In the case examined here, federal implementation of public assistance provided California's activists a more favorable political environment to halt welfare cutbacks for legal immigrants. Because the state legislature met and adopted their budget at a certain time each year, activists could focus on short-term policy goals and relatively short concentrated bursts of activity. This minimized the time commitments necessary for collaboration and the need for long-term planning, which reduced the potential for interorganizational conflict. As activists won policy improvements each year, this also helped to maintain the campaign's momentum.

From the Nation to the State: Responses to PRWORA

Welfare cutbacks are risky for politicians, even when they involve a negatively constructed group such as immigrants. They tend to arouse opposition from beneficiaries as well as service providers, frequently organized through public sector unions and professional organizations (Pierson 1994, 30, 127). For these reasons, there would probably have been strong opposition to PRWORA's anti-immigrant provisions even if it had not been followed by other attacks on immigrants' rights. The adoption of IIRIRA shortly after PRWORA's passage added fuel to the fire.

IIRIRA represented a highly punitive response to the recent wave of immigration. Unlike the Immigration Reform and Control Act of 1986, which penalized employers who hired undocumented workers, this act was almost entirely directed toward immigrants. To reduce illegal immigration, IIRIRA strengthened border enforcement, raised penalties for forging or misusing immigration papers, and increased resources for cracking down on visa overstays and other undocumented immigrants. Significantly, the act also targeted legal immigrants. It expanded the number of crimes for which they could be deported and increased the income requirements for, and obligations of, legal immigrants' sponsors. Sponsors now had to prove that they could support immigrants at 125 percent of the poverty line, which made it difficult for poor people to enter the United States. Congress also increased the years that sponsors' income was "deemed" available to immigrants, making it harder for otherwise qualified legal immigrants to receive welfare (Chang 2000, 61; Kilty and de Haymes 2000, 11–12; McBride 1999; Newton 2004; Parenti 1999, 139–60; Ramakrishnan 2001; D. Schneider 2000).

These closely timed policies—IIRIRA and PRWORA—had important resource and interpretive effects on immigrants and the ethnic communities to which they belonged. First, they posed a considerable threat to legal immigrants' access to income and services. Not only did these policies render most legal immigrants ineligible for welfare, they had a "chilling effect" on immigrants' use of welfare. Even legal immigrants who still qualified for welfare stopped accessing it because of confusion or fear that it would interfere with their naturalization process. After the passage of PRWORA, the number of immigrant welfare applications approved dropped sharply—71 percent between January 1996 and January 1998, draining resources away from communities of color (Burnham 2001, 46). Second, PRWORA and IIRIRA posed a more general threat to immigrants' social and political standing within the United States. These policies expressed politicians' devaluation of immigrants and their needs, sending strong policy signals that they were unwelcome and not considered full, or potentially valuable, members of the polity. Politicians justified these policies through all sorts of racist myths about immigrants. In particular, they constructed immigrants, even legal ones, as lazy freeloaders who were purposefully entering the United States to avoid work and/or retire at taxpayers' expense (Chang 2000; Newton 2004; Reese and Ramirez 2002).

PRWORA and IIRIRA threatened all immigrants and so strengthened immigrant solidarity across ethnicity and legal status. Korean and Mexican activists, and undocumented and legal immigrants, who might not otherwise collaborate, worked hand in hand to combat the policies that threw them together. Shortly after PRWORA's passage, and during congressional debates on IIRIRA, activists organized eighty-five thousand people for a march for immigrants' rights in Washington, DC (City News Service 1996). Activists also formed new coalitions, such as the "Fix '96" campaign, which called for the reversal of IIRIRA's and PRWORA's anti-immigrant provisions.

Because the "Fix '96" campaign involved close collaboration among a variety of Asian, Latino, and immigrant organizations, it brought together the most stigmatized and vulnerable immigrants, such as undocumented Mexican immigrants, with less stigmatized and vulnerable immigrants, such as legal Korean immigrants. Not only did this increase activists' organizational resources and reach, it helped to legitimize their demands. To contest politicians' negative construction of immigrants as a fiscal burden, "Fix '96" activists attached mock tax forms from immigrants to letters urging politicians to restore their welfare rights (interviews, staff members from CHIRLA and APALC).

Because PRWORA's anti-immigrant provisions cut across several policy domains, they also encouraged greater collaboration between immigrant and civil rights activists on the one hand, and welfare advocates on the other. As one activist explained,

> If there is a good thing about welfare reform . . . it is that it has brought all these different types of folks together. So immigrant rights groups who never worked with [anti]hunger advocates are now working on food stamps. I guess that is the silver lining of welfare reform. . . . We have been able to establish a good network, a diverse group of folks who have become invested in these issues of hunger, these issues of fairness to immigrants. (Interview, APALC staff)

Ethnic and immigrant advocates viewed immigrants' welfare rights as part of their broad agenda of protecting the rights of immigrants and/or racial and ethnic minorities. Welfare advocacy organizations, on the other hand, supported immigrants' rights to welfare as part of their broad agenda to improve the social safety net. Because PRWORA threatened immigrants' rights to SSI, food stamps, TANF, and Medicaid, it mobilized a wide variety of service providers and other welfare advocates, including senior citizens' groups, antihunger activists, grassroots welfare rights organizations, and disability rights groups.

Together, these groups exerted considerable pressure on Congress to overturn PRWORA's anti-immigrant provisions. Against the perception that immigrant recipients did not truly need help, advocates highlighted the suffering that the impending cutoffs would create. They publicized stories of people who had committed suicide in response to losing their benefits and warned of "mass evictions, increased homelessness, and hunger as aid ceases" (McDonnell 1997b). They also gathered thousands of letters on paper plates from recipients providing personal testimonies about how food stamps kept their families from going hungry (interviews, CHIRLA and

LACEH&H staff). Through public demonstrations, lobbying, and high-profile legal challenges, advocates demanded the full restoration of legal immigrants' welfare rights.

This mobilization and coalition building was facilitated by elite donors' and foundations' decisions to provide new funds for immigrant and/or welfare rights organizing in response to PRWORA and IIRIRA.[4] One of the most notable new funding sources was George Soros's $50 million Emma Lazarus Fund for organizations that helped legal immigrants to naturalize or to campaign for their rights (Moody 1997).

Politicians' mixed support for PRWORA's anti-immigrant provisions also encouraged mobilization on this issue as it gave people hope that policy makers would respond to popular pressure. Indeed, even as he passed PRWORA, President Clinton vowed to restore legal immigrants' rights to welfare (Zimmerman and Tumlin 1999). The National Governor's Association, fearing the fiscal impacts of federal welfare cutbacks, also urged Congress to reinstate benefits (Fresno Bee 1997). Even Republican politicians were mixed and/or lukewarm in their support of cutting immigrants' rights to social services since it might alienate Latino voters (Unz 1994).

Within a year, most congressional politicians supported partial benefit restorations for legal immigrants (Healy 1997). As politicians often do in response to policy debates affecting negatively constructed groups, Congress subdivided the controversial group into those who were deserving and undeserving of aid (Schneider and Ingram 1993, 336). In 1997 and 1998, Congress reclassified certain refugee groups, such as the Hmong, and legal immigrants who were young, disabled, or elderly so that they qualified for federal public assistance. However, new legal immigrants who entered the United States after August 22, 1996 (the day PRWORA was enacted), and able-bodied working-age legal immigrants were still deemed the "undeserving poor" (Zimmerman and Tumlin 1999). While partial benefit restorations narrowed the base of support for subsequent restoration battles, many ethnic, welfare, and immigrant rights groups continued to push Congress to adopt full benefit restorations.

Advocates also pressured state politicians to halt the implementation of federal cutbacks by creating benefit restoration programs. In response, just over half of all states restored legal immigrants' access to at least one public assistance program by 1999. Quantitative research shows that states were significantly more likely to replace benefits if they had larger immigrant populations, spent a greater share of their budget on welfare, and had a larger tax base, measured in terms of per capita income (Ramirez and Reese 2002). But how were coalitions built, maintained, and utilized within these campaigns?

In the rest of this chapter, I provide an in-depth look at the rise and success of California's campaign, focusing on how activists collaborated to produce an effective multipronged strategy and overcame the classic pitfalls of coalitions. California's benefit restoration campaigns were the most successful in the nation. Besides Maine, California was the only state that restored most legal immigrants' rights to all four major public assistance programs: SSI, Medicaid, TANF, and food stamps. In Maine, where noncitizens made up less than 1 percent of the state's population, these restorations, though significant to recipients, benefited a very small portion of the nation's legal immigrants (Zimmerman and Tumlin 1999, 22–23, 58). By contrast, California's replacement programs served tens of thousands of legal immigrants. The state's food stamp replacement program alone benefited 83,596 legal immigrants in July 2000 (California Department of Social Services 2000). How and why did activists manage to achieve such an important victory in California?

Collaborating for Welfare Inclusion: The Rise of California's Campaign

In California, home of the largest immigrant population in the nation, attacks on legal immigrants' welfare rights sent shock waves through both immigrant communities and activist circles. To their relief, legislators quickly approved state replacement funds for TANF (which replaced Aid to Families with Dependent Children) and didn't change state Medicaid requirements to exclude legal immigrants. State politicians were more reluctant to restore food stamps and SSI, especially to new and able-bodied immigrants. Only after five years of pressure by activists did politicians agree to cover food stamps and SSI to these groups and to make these benefit restoration programs a permanent part of the state budget. This decision represented the hard-won victory of a broad-based coalition of ethnic, immigrant, and welfare rights activists.

The campaign to restore legal immigrants' access to welfare confronted a number of serious challenges. First, nativism was strong within the state. In 1994, California's voters passed Proposition 187 to restrict undocumented immigrants' access to public services. Governor Pete Wilson, a strong supporter of Proposition 187, was also a powerful foe to immigrants. Five days after PRWORA's passage, Governor Wilson ordered state agencies to cut off most public services to undocumented immigrants, arguing that they "serve as a magnetic lure drawing illegal aliens across our border" (Capps 1997b). Although Wilson was more supportive of restoring legal immigrants' welfare rights, he opposed restoring them to working-age adults and new immigrants (Fresno Bee 1997; interviews, APALC and LACEH&H staff; McDonnell 1997c).

Because of California's large immigrant population, welfare replacement programs were very expensive. The legislative analyst's office estimated the price of the initial California Food Assistance Program (CFAP) for legal immigrants at $175 million a year, based on the assumption that 345,000 legal immigrants would benefit from it (Morain 1997). Although the Cash Assistance Program for Immigrants (CAPI) provided benefits to a much smaller number of recipients, it provided much more generous benefits and so cost almost as much: an estimated $274 million over two years (Ellis 1997). Given the relative cost of CAPI, its passage was "nothing short of miraculous" (interview, LACEH&H staff).

On the other hand, California provided a far more favorable context for defending legal immigrants' welfare rights than the nation did. Most important, the state had a large and growing population of immigrants. About 26 percent of the state's population was foreign-born by 1996, and on average more than 200,000 legal immigrants were entering the state each year (California Department of Finance 2000; Zimmerman and Tumlin 1999, 57).[5] Moreover, approximately 400,000 of the state's 2.5 million legal immigrants received some form of public assistance (Fagan 1996). The state had large Asian and Latino populations, who respectively made up 12 and 28 percent of the state's total population in 1996 (U.S. Census Bureau 2000). Many of these Asians and Latinos were first- or second-generation immigrants, and so were likely to identify with the plight of new immigrants. The state had numerous community organizations, especially in Southern California and the Bay Area, representing these ethnic and immigrant groups, which not only provided a large pool of potential supporters for benefit restoration programs, but also increased electoral pressure on politicians to make concessions. In addition, unlike Congress, which was dominated by Republicans, Democrats made up the majority of California's legislature. The legislature also included a number of Latino politicians who were especially sympathetic to the plight of legal immigrants.

California's campaign to restore SSI and food stamps to legal immigrants involved considerable coalition work between welfare, ethnic, and immigrant rights coalitions. Support for benefit restorations was both multiethnic and broad-based. There were five main kinds of organizations that supported legal immigrants' welfare rights: (1) welfare advocacy organizations; (2) social service agencies, including faith-based organizations; (3) immigrant rights organizations; (4) ethnic organizations; and (5) legal organizations.[6] Because PRWORA's anti-immigrant provisions simultaneously threatened multiple social groups, it drew them together into a powerful coalition. Social welfare professionals, concerned about losing their funding and having their core missions threatened, and middle-class lawyers, concerned about the violation of state and national laws, helped to legitimate the demands of poor legal immigrants, worried about losing their welfare benefits.

Within ethnic and immigrant organizations there was considerable cross-ethnic coalition work going on. For example, Asian Pacific Islander American (APIA) organizations mobilized a variety of ethnic groups, including Korean, Chinese, Hmong, and Vietnamese Americans, while Latino organizations mobilized both Central Americans and Mexican Americans. Immigrant rights activists also claim that there was considerable support for this campaign among undocumented as well as legal immigrants (interviews, AP3CON, APALC, and CHIRLA staff). As a staff member from the Coalition for Humane Immigrant Rights in Los Angeles (CHIRLA) explained,

> Our ability to turn out [for protests] is also our ability to organize at the local level. We do have [day laborers], we have domestic workers, two pools of the community that are almost completely undocumented. . . . Even smaller protests that we've done, like on state programs, will definitely get the [day laborers] out. . . . It wasn't the link [to them] as much as knowing this is a program for immigrants [that brought them out].

This kind of solidarity among immigrants was encouraged not only by the passage of IIRIRA and PRWORA, but also by a series of state-level attacks on immigrants. In addition to Proposition 187, California's voters passed an anti-bilingual education measure in 1998, and Governor Wilson threatened to cut prenatal care to undocumented immigrants in 1996. This series of political threats politicized immigrants. Naturalized immigrants, especially Latino ones, were registering to vote in record numbers.[7] Activists helped to maintain immigrant solidarity by not favoring legal over undocumented immigrants. To do so would not only alienate undocumented immigrants, but undermine political support for other campaigns they were undertaking. As a staff member of the Asian Pacific American Legal Center explained, "Most politicians these days, I think, will draw the line between legal and 'illegal' immigration. . . . We tried to stay away from that argument, because obviously we were working on other issues, like prenatal care, that impacted undocumented immigrants."

To coordinate their activities, activists involved in this campaign engaged in considerable coalition work. Sometimes they utilized preestablished formal umbrella organizations. For example, the California Hunger Action

Coalition coordinated the lobbying of hunger activists and organizations. In Los Angeles, Asian Pacific Policy Planning Council (A3PCON), played a key role in mobilizing the APIA community around this issue. A3PCON, composed of representatives from more than fifty Asian-American social service agencies, mobilized its member organizations that, in turn, identified and recruited their clients to make testimonies for press conferences and public hearings (interview, A3PCON staff).

Activists formed new formal umbrella organizations to oppose welfare cutbacks and/or attacks on immigrants' rights. In 1997, immigrant rights organizations decided to form the California Immigrant and Welfare Collaborative (CIWC) and jointly hired a full-time lobbyist in Sacramento. As of 2001, the organization coordinates the activities of five immigrant rights organizations. Activists formed the Northern California Coalition for Immigrants' Rights, which included about thirty staff members and represented more than 130 organizations (interview, CIWC staff). Welfare advocates created new welfare rights coalitions. For example, Los Angeles–based welfare rights activists received foundation grants to organize the Human Services Alliance, a coalition of progressive social service providers, and the Welfare Reform Network, an umbrella group of welfare rights organizations. These groups helped to enlist service providers' support for letter-writing campaigns or other activities on behalf of legal immigrants' welfare rights (interview, APALC).

Activists formed informal coalitions between groups that were mobilizing around immigrant and welfare rights issues, especially at the local level. As a Los Angeles hunger activist elaborated:

> There's always been an informal or formal coalition working on this issue that was always keeping in touch—it's almost like we were all working on the same agency. I've worked on a constant basis with . . . California Food Policy Advocates, . . . CHIRLA, . . . the Asian Pacific [American] Legal Center. . . . It was like we were one big group, not just on the immigrant issue, but on other welfare reform issues—constant coalition work. (Interview, LACEH&H staff)

Staff from these organizations shared information and collectively planned their ongoing strategies. Ad hoc coalitions also formed between progressive legal centers, such as the Western Center on Law and Poverty, the American Civil Liberties Union, the Mexican American Legal Defense and Education Fund, and the Asian Pacific American Legal Center. These legal groups coordinated and/or jointly filed legal challenges to welfare policies toward immigrants (interview, APALC; McDonnell 1996).

The formation and maintenance of these coalitions were facilitated by various foundation grants. Many of the organizations received special grants to organize on behalf of legal immigrants' welfare rights from George Soros's Emma Lazarus Fund or other foundations. The California Endowment, the California Wellness Foundation, and Liberty Hill Foundation were other major donors for this campaign.[8] In addition to funding new umbrella organizations, grants from these and other foundations enabled preexisting ethnic, immigrant, and welfare advocacy organizations to hire additional staff to focus on immigrants' rights and/or welfare rights. These funds, and the staff they paid for, minimized the extent to which coalition work for this campaign drained resources away from other organizational activities (interviews, APALC, CIWC, CHIRLA).

Overcoming Differences and Maintaining Cooperation

Even when conditions are ripe for coalition building, as they were in California, building trust and working relationships among diverse groups requires careful consideration of each others' needs, mutual respect, and "honest face-to-face dialogue" (Rose 2000, 143). Such respectful, open communication often breaks down, however, especially when groups organize across racial, ethnic, class, or gender divides and/or when serious disagreements about goals or strategies arise.

In California's campaign to restore legal immigrants' access to welfare, cooperation across racial groups was sometimes difficult to maintain. For example, an Asian-American activist in AP3CON felt extremely frustrated by the cultural insensitivity of "liberal" white advocates. For example, her organization had spent a long time identifying and preparing an APIA recipient to testify at a press conference organized by the Welfare Reform Network, but they were cut off to save time and didn't get a chance to testify. She and other Asian-American activists eventually stopped working with the group because of such incidents (interview, AP3CON).

There was also tension between immigrant rights activists and hunger activists over goals. For example, a hunger activist recalls:

> We wanted to raise the debate around both issues—immigrants and single adults. . . . It was hard to galvanize people around [single adults' welfare rights], which I found disappointing. . . . Even a lot of the [nonprofit organizations] who we had supported on the immigrant issue, which was as much our issue as theirs, they really didn't seem to be forthcoming on some of these issues dealing with single adults. (Interview, LACEH&H)

Similarly, a staff member from an Asian-American advocacy group explained:

> There was some disagreement between us and the hunger advocates [around the issue of finger imaging food stamp applicants]. . . . In the case of mixed [immigrant status] households . . . we're arguing that if they're not applying for the program then they shouldn't have to finger-print. . . . We would say, if we can get that piece, we'd be happy. . . . But the hunger advocates were pushing for the elimination of the [whole finger imaging] program. . . . We would advocate, too, but when it comes to having to choose whether to wait until next year or try to push for this one small piece this year . . . There was some tension [over this]. (Interview, APALC)

He also recalled "more subtle," less explicit tension between professional advocates and grassroots organizations around tactics.

However, activists involved in this campaign were generally able to over-come their differences. Most organizations involved were reform-oriented, which prevented deep ideological splits from developing. Because of the looming implementation of federal cutbacks, activists also felt a tremen-dous sense of urgency. As an antihunger activist explained, "Right after the [federal welfare] bill was passed, we thought, woe is us, disaster, we're doomed. Hunger advocacy is dead and low-income people are going to be dying by the thousands" (interview, LACEH&H). Similarly, immigrants and their allies viewed the struggle for welfare rights as a matter of life and death. As one recipient testified at a public hearing, "Speaking for me and my husband, when you take away SSI, you take away our lives" (McDonnell 1997a). This kind of urgency helped to inspire cooperation among organi-zations, even across ethnic divides and policy domains.

Because the legislature met every year and adopted an annual budget at about the same time each year, activists were able to focus on common, short-term, winnable legislative goals and concentrate most of their joint activity in a few months. This helped to reduce the time commitment needed for coalition work and the potential for interorganizational con-flict. Because activists managed to win small victories each year, this also provided momentum to the campaign. Full restoration of legal immigrants' welfare rights was achieved through a series of campaigns that gradually expanded the pool of immigrants eligible for welfare (interviews, APALC and LACEH&H staff members).

Activists also agreed to disagree about other policy issues, and mainly focused around their "main goal of trying to pass [these] policies" (inter-view, APALC). Facilitating this was the loose, dynamic, and complex struc-

ture of coalitions in this campaign. Rather than one large statewide umbrella organization, California's campaign involved a number of coalitions
differentiated by locality or policy domain, and sometimes overlapping in
their memberships. There were also ad hoc, short-lived coalitions that came
together to organize particular events, such as a public demonstration or a
day of lobbying. The reliance on ad hoc, shifting, and multiple coalitions
helped to maintain the autonomy of SMOs who had different, and more
or less radical, political agendas. It also provided activists with multiple
opportunities for participating in the campaign. For example, a grassroots
Filipino community organization with a broad anti-imperialist, antiracist
agenda participated in antihunger advocates' Hunger Lobby Day, as well
as a welfare reform task force organized by a coalition of Asian-American
community groups (interview, People's CORE).

Friendships, prior relations, and everyday interactions between organizational staff also facilitated collaboration among SMOs. A number of
groups were located in the same building, facilitating the exchange of information and fostering friendships across organizations. A former staff member of LACEH&H became employed by CHIRLA, increasing these groups'
ties (interviews, LACEH&H, CHIRLA, APALC, People's CORE).

Autonomy of coalition partners was maintained in this campaign
through "cooperative differentiation" (Hathaway and Meyer 1997). Groups
cooperated but divided the work in terms of targets, tactics, and tasks.
Legal advocacy groups filed court cases, while community organizers and
service providers mobilized community support for benefit replacement programs among their respective constituents (interviews, APALC, A3PCON,
CHIRLA, People's CORE, and LACEH&H staff). Meanwhile, state-level
umbrella organizations, such as the CIWC and the California Food Policy
Advocates, focused on "meso-mobilization," sending fax and e-mail alerts
to hundreds of organizations, enabling them to quickly organize phone
calls to politicians in support of legislation (interviews, APALC, CIWC,
and LACEH&H staff). By engaging in cooperative differentiation, coalition partners were able to maintain their distinct identities and simultaneously carry out multiple strategies, which reduced the potential for interorganizational competition and conflicts over which strategy was the best.

In short, activists' successful coalition work was partly a response to
the urgency created by looming welfare cutoffs and conditioned by most
groups' reformist tendencies. They avoided interorganizational conflict by
setting easy-to-reach and time-limited goals, agreeing to disagree, maintaining a flexible structure, and using cooperative differentiation. These
findings are consistent with previous research, which identified these same

features as key to cooperation within coalitions affiliated with the peace and antinuclear movements (Hathaway and Meyer 1997; Kleidman and Rochon 1997).

Explaining Activists' Success

Activists' success in California was due to a combination of favorable political conditions and good coalition work. By engaging in "cooperative differentiation," activists were able to carry out an effective multipronged strategy. Legal advocates stalled the implementation of federal cuts through court cases, which provided organizers more time to mobilize political support for benefit restorations (interview, APALC staff; McDonnell 1996). Had the cutbacks been implemented sooner, it may have been more difficult to mobilize recipients because community organizations would have diverted more energy into providing help for legal immigrants who had lost their benefits.

Organizers and service providers employed cooperative differentiation by mobilizing different kinds of constituents. Pooling their networks, they mobilized large collective actions. For example, approximately 2,000 people marched through downtown Los Angeles to protest federal cutbacks in immigrants' right to welfare and urged state politicians to help those affected by the cuts. About fifty civil rights and immigrant advocacy groups, including CHIRLA, sponsored this multiethnic march, which also included social service groups, labor unions, and gay rights groups (Albano 1997). About a week later, activists held their first Immigrant Lobby Day in the state's capital. Latino and Southeast Asian immigrant activists, who usually do not collaborate, jointly lobbied legislators for benefit restorations and then rallied on the capitol's steps (Capps 1997a). A few months later, about 1,200 people participated in a second Immigrant Lobby Day at the state capitol (Bee 1997). Hundreds of activists filled the legislative halls, making a big impression on state politicians (interview, CIWC staff). Similarly, California Food Policy Advocates and California Hunger Action Coalition helped to organized annual Hunger Action Days to lobby state politicians to restore food stamps to legal immigrants (interviews, People's CORE and LACEH&H staff).

There was also effective cooperation between state-level lobbyists and local groups. Because groups in Southern California could not easily travel to the state's capital, they often relied on CIWC staff to keep them informed about state-level developments. There was continual communication between the CIWC and its member organizations throughout this campaign. As one activist explained:

> On a weekly basis, we try to communicate what we are doing here on a
> local level, what needs to be done at the local level to respond to what is
> going on at the state level, and vice versa. . . . If there is a legislator that
> needs to hear from us, we are not sure if he will be helpful to us, we target
> him, we make calls, try to hold rallies at his office. We try to do as many
> things at the local level as possible because this is where the communities
> are. (Interview, APALC staff)

By focusing on lobbying state politicians and officials in Sacramento, the
CIWC often gained privileged inside knowledge from its governmental al-
lies. It kept local activists continually informed about the progress of key bills,
enabling them to make strategic decisions about whom to target and when.
For example, when the CIWC learned through the Division of Finance that
Governor Davis (Wilson's successor) wanted to eliminate the Cash Assistance
Program for Immigrants [CAPI] in 1999, it relayed the message to local ac-
tivists, who held a sit-in protest in his Los Angeles office, demanding that
Davis reauthorize the program, a demand that was met shortly afterward
(interviews, CIWC, APALC, CHIRLA, and LACEH&H staff).

All of this good coalition work could have amounted to little, however,
had political conditions been unfavorable. Advocates benefited from a number of political circumstances. While opposition toward undocumented immigrants' use of social services in California was strong (as indicated by the
passage of Proposition 187), there was greater public support for restoring
legal immigrants' welfare benefits. A Field Institute survey found that about
75 percent of respondents said the state should reinstate welfare benefits to
legal immigrants (Pols 1997).

There was also active support for benefit replacements from county
officials who highlighted the fiscal impacts of the looming cutoffs. The
California State Association of Counties estimated that the restrictions on
legal immigrants' rights to welfare could cost the state's counties $850 mil-
lion as poor immigrants would flood county-funded general relief programs
(Press Enterprise 1996). County officials provided additional media coverage and political weight to activists' demands (interview, CIWC staff).

Activists benefited from the state legislature's Democratic majority
since Democrats were more supportive than Republicans of replacing legal
immigrants' benefits. The state traditionally provided more generous welfare spending compared to most other states (Ramirez and Reese 2002).
It is likely that politicians feared electoral reprisals from, or felt beholden
to, a growing immigrant, Latino, and Asian electorate (interview, CIWC
staff). The growth of the Latino vote was particularly sharp. By 1998,

Latinos made up 12 percent of all voters in California's primary election, more than double their share in 1994 (Pyle, McDonnell, and Tobar 1998; Ramakrishnan 2001).[9]

By far the most active legislative supporters of this campaign were Latino Democrats, especially Marta Escutia, Cruz Bustamante, Gil Cedillo, Richard Polanco, Hilda Solis, and Antonio Villaraigosa (interview, LACEH&H and APALC staff). These politicians acted as "institutional activists" (Santoro and McGuire 1997). They mobilized within the state, tirelessly lobbying their colleagues and the governor to replace immigrants' benefits. Pooling their resources, they produced a television ad urging Wilson to support $124 million worth of new state programs to aid legal immigrants (Jacobs 1997; Mendel 1997b). The Democratic caucus pressured Wilson to compromise on this issue by holding up the passage of the state budget bill for three weeks (interview, CIWC staff). By August, Wilson was willing to make a compromise and hammered out the details of the state food stamp plan in a face-to-face meeting with Bustamante (Mendel 1997b).[10] In 1998, Villaraigosa spearheaded the campaign for bills to expand food stamp coverage to the working-age poor and new immigrants and replace benefits for SSI (Ellis 1998).

In response to activists' mobilization from within and outside the state, both Governor Wilson and his successor, Governor Davis, agreed to restore food stamps and SSI benefits and to make these restoration programs more inclusive. In 1998, legislators also created CAPI, which provided aid to elderly and disabled legal immigrants who lost access to SSI, except for new immigrants who still had active sponsors. That year, state politicians also extended CFAP to cover working-age adults and created exemptions for new immigrants who had no active sponsor (e.g., due to death or an abusive relationship).[11] In 1999, both CFAP and CAPI were extended to cover all new legal immigrants. In 2001, Governor Davis finally agreed to make CFAP and CAPI into permanent programs (interviews, APALC, CHIRLA, and LACEH&H staff). Nevertheless, advocates were not completely successful in their aims. While Governor Davis reauthorized these programs, he also extended the number of years that sponsors were required to support immigrants, preventing many from qualifying for the program (interview, CIWC staff).

Conclusion

The protection and improvement of democratic rights rarely occurs without a struggle in the United States, especially when poor racial and ethnic minorities are concerned. When a growing backlash against Latino, Asian, and

Caribbean immigrants entering the country coincided with a strong welfare backlash, Congress responded by denying most legal immigrants their basic social rights to food, income, and medical care in 1996. PRWORA's anti-immigrant provisions did more than deprive many legal immigrants the resources necessary for survival. They sent a strong policy signal to them that they were unwelcome and reinforced all sorts of racist stereotypes about poor immigrants as lazy, dishonest, and self-serving that prevent them from participating as equals in a democratic polity. This policy threat did not go uncontested. A broad-based coalition of immigrants, ethnic minorities, welfare recipients, service providers, and state and local policy makers came together and demanded the restoration of legal immigrants' rights to public assistance. They managed to win back some of the social rights lost in 1996 at both the state and federal levels, but the struggle for a full federal restoration of legal immigrants' welfare rights has yet to be won. Although President Bush signed legislation to restore food stamps to most legal immigrants in 2002, he and congressional Republicans do not support broader restorations of legal immigrants' welfare benefits.

This case study of California's benefit restoration campaign has explored how the content of public policies and the policy process shape the opportunities to build a successful social movement coalition. Previous research suggests that SMOs tend to collaborate when organizational resources become plentiful and/or when new political opportunities or threats arise. Building on this work, I have argued that, under relatively favorable political conditions, the broader the scope of a policy threat, the more likely that a broad-based social movement coalition will develop in response. More inclusive policy threats draw together multiple groups and stimulate elite patronage, both of which facilitate coalition building. The implementation structures of policy threats also affect the chances to form a successful movement against them. They determine how much time activists have to mobilize, the pace of their activities, and their choice of political targets.

Applying this argument to California's campaign, I argued that the wide scope of the attack on immigrants through PRWORA, IIRIRA, and state-level anti-immigrant initiatives facilitated the development of a broad-based coalition against cutbacks to legal immigrants' welfare rights. These policies, and the policy debates surrounding them, collectively threatened all immigrants, so it strengthened immigrant solidarity across ethnicity and legal status. Because PRWORA's anti-immigrant provisions crossed welfare and immigrant policy domains and simultaneously threatened the rights of poor people, service providers, immigrants, and a variety of ethnic minorities, it increased the incentives for multiple kinds of SMOs to collaborate.

As a result, highly stigmatized and vulnerable groups, such as poor legal immigrants, found ready support from groups with more resources and social status, such as welfare professionals and Asian and Latino advocates. Coalition work among these groups was facilitated by the creation of new foundation grants that became available in response to PRWORA and IIRIRA.

California's advocates benefited from the federal implementation of public assistance, which enabled them to carry out their campaign in a relatively favorable political arena. Immigrants, Asians, and Latinos were numerous and gaining greater electoral power in California while Democrats controlled the legislature. Latino legislators, sympathetic to the plight of immigrants, and county policy makers, fearful of the fiscal effects of welfare cutoffs, supported the benefit restoration campaign. Yet the success of this campaign was also due to good coalition work. By coordinating their activities, community organizations were able to carry out an effective multipronged strategy. While legal activists stalled the implementation of federal cutbacks, community organizations collaborated to mobilize broad-based support for letter-writing campaigns, public testimonies, legislative visits, and public demonstrations.

This chapter has explored the relationship of the breadth of policy threats and their implementation with coalition building through a case study of a successful social movement coalition emerging in response to broad policy threats. Yet as Mettler (ch. 7, this volume) suggests, the negative resource and interpretive effects of public policies often induce quiescence rather than political activism. I have argued that this could occur either because the scope of policy threats is too narrow to build broad-based opposition to it, or because political conditions are, or appear to be, unfavorable. More empirical research on these kinds of negative cases is needed to examine the veracity of such claims. Subsequent research should also explore how the scope of policy gains, various kinds of implementation structures, and the quality of elite patronage shape the opportunities for building successful social movement coalitions.

Notes

I thank all activists who shared their time, insights, and research with me. I also thank participants of the "Social Movements, Public Policy, and Democracy" conference who provided useful feedback on earlier drafts. For research assistance, I thank Elvia Ramirez, Erin Ladd, and students in Sociology 197 and the Minority Summer Research Internship Program (Nichole Aguilar, Christine Black, Rita Bueno, Benjamin Chen, Sarah Cousins, Jennifer Edney, Alex Garcia, Wolderlibanos

Getachew, Bobby Lee Guillen, George Hernandez, Esther Koeshedi, John Lotfi, Sandee Maung, Tram Nguyen, Rosemarie Ostoich, Jessica Quintero, Nichole Robinson, Guadalupe Saldana, Toni Sandoval, Carol Won, and Alex Ygloria). The Ernesto Galarza Applied Research Center and the Department of Sociology at the University of California, Riverside, provided financial assistance for this project.

1. The "qualified" immigrant category includes (1) lawful permanent residents (who hold "green cards"); (2) refugees, asylum seekers, and persons granted withholding of deportation or removal; (3) Cuban and Haitian immigrants; (4) those with INS parole for at least one year; (5) conditional entrants; (6) those identified as victims of domestic violence and their dependents. "Unqualified" legal immigrants include those without green cards but who are nevertheless in the United States legally and immigrants who entered the country legally on or after August 22, 1996 (the day the law was passed). Recent immigrants are ineligible for the first five years they are in the United States. Legal immigrants are ineligible unless they are (1) veterans, (2) refugees, or (3) have worked in the United States for ten years or more (National Immigration Law Center 2002, 3).

2. This sharp rise was part of a longer-term rise in the number of immigrants naturalizing. Other factors that contributed to this rise were (1) the decision of some Latin American governments to allow immigrants to have dual nationality, (2) the Immigration and Naturalization Service's decision to lower the relative cost of naturalization compared to replacing a green card, and (3) many undocumented immigrants granted permanent resident status in 1986 under the Immigration Reform and Control Act became eligible for naturalization in the 1990s (Ramakrishnan 2001).

3. The indigenous resources of the affected group could also be strong, or growing, because of broad socioeconomic changes unrelated to the policy (McAdam 1982).

4. Whether or not this elite patronage moderated the goals and tactics of the welfare and immigrant rights movements is an interesting research question, but beyond the scope of this study.

5. This figure was based on the average number of legal immigrants that entered the state between 1990 and 1998.

6. A full list of organizations involved in this campaign was compiled using relevant newspaper articles and radio broadcasts available through Lexis-Nexis with help from a team of undergraduate researchers enrolled in Sociology 197 (a research seminar) or the Minority Summer Research Internship program. We considered a group to be active supporters if they organized an action (e.g., a march, demonstration, press conference, and so on) and/or made public statements to the press in favor of restoring immigrants' rights to welfare at the state level.

7. The Latino share of California's immigrant electorate rose 11 percent (from

19 to 30 percent) between 1994 and 1998, compared to a 6 percent rise in the nation as a whole (Ramakrishnan 2001, 8).

8. Personal correspondence with LACEH&H staff, July 29, 2002, and APALC staff, August 8, 2002.

9. The growth in the Latino electorate was encouraged by many factors, including the politicization of Latinos by the Chicano rights movement, voter registration drives, population growth, and the rise in citizenship applications that followed in the wake of Proposition 187 and PRWORA.

10. On August 21, Wilson signed bills that would provide state funds for legal immigrants' food stamps, the day before the federal cutoffs would be implemented.

11. Their campaign was facilitated by federal restorations of food stamps to child and elderly immigrants (seen as more sympathetic than able-bodied, working-age adults). Because California had already restored those groups' access to food stamps, advocates simply had to convince legislators to shift their state funds to cover working-age, able-bodied adults rather than allocating more funds to CFAP.

Interviews

Asian Pacific American Legal Center (APALC). Personal interview with staff member, July 17, 2001.
Asian Pacific Policy and Planning Council (A3PCON). Personal interview with staff member, July 17, 2001.
California Immigrant and Welfare Collaborative in Sacramento (CIWC). Personal interview with staff member, September 17, 2001.
Coalition for Humane Immigrants Rights in Los Angeles (CHIRLA). Personal interviews with staff member, August 9 and 13, 2001.
Los Angeles Coalition to End Hunger & Homelessness (LACEH&H). Personal interview with staff member, July 17, 2001.
People's Community Organization for Reform and Empowerment (People's CORE, a Los Angeles–based Filipino-American organization). Personal interview with staff member, August 9, 2001.

References

Albano, L. 1997. "Up in Arms over Welfare Reform; 2000 Attend Rally to Protest Cuts in Aid to Immigrants." *Daily News of Los Angeles,* March 10, N4.
Amenta, Edwin, Drew Hoffman, and Michael P. Young. 1999. "The Strategies and Contexts of Social Protest: Political Mediation and the Impact of the Townsend Movement in California." *Mobilization* 4, no. 1: 1–23.
Amenta, Edwin, and Michael P. Young. 1999. "Making an Impact: Conceptual and Methodological Implications of the Collective Goods Criterion." In *How*

Social Movements Matter, ed. Marco G. Giugni, Doug McAdam, and Charles Tilly, 22–41. Minneapolis: University of Minnesota Press.

Arnold, Gretchen. 1995. "Dilemmas of Feminist Coalitions: Collective Identity and Strategic Effectiveness in the Battered Women's Movement." In *Feminist Organizations: Harvest of the New Women's Movement,* ed. Myra Max Ferree and Patricia Yancey Martin, 276–90. Philadelphia: Temple University Press.

Bee, P. J. 1997. "Immigrants Lobby State to Address Welfare Losses; Protesters Urge Lawmakers to Restore Key Benefits at Capitol Rally." *Fresno Bee,* May 29, B1.

Boggs, Carl. 2000. *The End of Politics: Corporate Power and the Decline of the Public Sphere.* New York: Guilford Press.

Burnham, Linda. 2001. "Welfare Reform, Family Hardship, and Women of Color." *Annals of the American Academy of Political and Social Science* 577: 39–47.

California Department of Finance. 2000. "Legal Immigration to California by County: Federal Fiscal Year 1990–1998." At http://dof.ca.gov/html/Demograp/repndat.htm.

California Department of Social Services. 2000. "Public Assistance Facts and Figures July 2000: Sacramento; Data Systems and Survey Design Bureau." At http://www.dss.cahwet.gov/research/ (accessed September 24, 2001).

Capps, Steven A. 1997a. "Welfare Cuts Unite Those with Benefits; Immigrants Take Their Cause to Wilson's Doorstep." *San Francisco Examiner,* March 19, A14.

———. 1997b. "Wilson Identifies Cuts for Illegal Immigrants; 200 Public Programs Will Now Require Legal Residence Proof." *San Francisco Examiner,* March 26, A5.

Chang, Grace. 2000. *Disposable Domestics: Immigrant Women Workers in the Global Economy.* Cambridge, MA: South End Press.

City News Service. 1996. "Midnight Headlines." *City News Service,* October 11.

Cress, Daniel M., and David A. Snow. 1996. "Mobilization at the Margins: Resources, Benefactors, and the Viability of Homeless Social Movement Organizations." *American Sociological Review* 61: 1089–109.

Diani, Mario. 1997. "Social Movements and Social Capital: A Network Perspective on Movement Outcomes." *Mobilization* 2, no. 2: 129–47.

Ellis, Virginia. 1997. "Democrats Propose Welfare Package: Aid Plan Calls for State to Help Legal Immigrants Whose Benefits Will Be Cut Off under New U.S. Rules." *Los Angeles Times,* May 9, A3.

———. 1998. "Study Says More Immigrants Are Going Hungry." *Los Angeles Times,* July 27, A1.

Epstein, Steven. 1996. *Impure Science: AIDS, Activism, and the Politics of Knowledge.* Berkeley: University of California Press.

Fagan, K. 1996. "Welfare Limbo Reigns As New Reform Kicks In." *San Francisco Chronicle,* October 2, A1.

Freeman, Jo. 1975. *The Politics of Women's Liberation.* New York: David McKay.

Fresno Bee. 1997. "Fixing Congress' Callousness." *Fresno Bee,* February 10, B4.

Gamson, William. 1975. *The Strategy of Social Protest.* Homewood, IL: Dorsey Press.

Gerhards, Jurgen, and Dieter Rucht. 1992. "Mesomobilization: Organizing and Framing in Two Protest Campaigns in West Germany." *American Journal of Sociology* 98, no. 3: 555–95.

Gitlin, Todd. 1995. *The Twilight of Common Dreams: Why America Is Wracked by Culture Wars.* New York: Metropolitan Books.

Hall, Peter M. 1995. "The Consequences of Qualitative Analysis for Sociological Theory: Beyond the Micro-Level." *Sociological Quarterly* 36, no. 2: 397–423.

Hartman, Chester. 1984. "Running a Rent Control Initiative Campaign." In *Community Organizers,* 2nd ed., ed. Joan Ecklein, 161–68. New York: John Wiley & Sons.

Hathaway, Will, and David S. Meyer. 1997. "Competition and Cooperation in Movement Coalitions: Lobbying for Peace in the 1980s." In *Coalitions and Political Movements: The Lessons of the Nuclear Freeze,* ed. Thomas R. Rochon and David S. Meyer, 61–79. Boulder, CO: Lynne Rienner.

Healy, M. 1997. "GOP May Agree to Restore Some Non-citizen Aid." *Los Angeles Times,* May 2, A1.

Jacobs, J. 1997. "Bustamante Champions Legal Aliens Assembly Speaker; He Insists the Budget Agreement Include $124 Million in Food Stamps." *Ventura County Star,* July 29, D9.

Jenkins, J. Craig, and Craig M. Eckert. 1986. "Channeling Black Insurgency: Elite Patronage and Professional Social Movement Organizations in the Development of the Black Movement." *American Sociological Review* 51: 812–29.

Jenkins, J. Craig, and Charles Perrow. 1977. "Insurgency of the Powerless: Farm Worker Movements (1946–1972)." *American Sociological Review* 42: 249–68.

Jones, Andrew W., Richard N. Hutchinson, Nella Van Dyke, Leslie Gates, and Michele Companion. 2001. "Coalition Form and Mobilization Effectiveness in Local Social Movements." *Sociological Spectrum* 21: 207–31.

Kilty, Keith M., and Maria Vidal de Haymes. 2000. "Racism, Nativism, and Exclusion: Public Policy, Immigration, and the Latino Experience in the United States." *Journal of Poverty* 4: 1–25.

Kleidman, Robert, and Thomas R. Rochon. 1997. "Dilemmas of Organization in Peace Campaigns." In *Coalitions and Political Movements: The Lessons of the Nuclear Freeze,* ed. Thomas R. Rochon and David S. Meyer, 47–60. Boulder, CO: Lynne Rienner.

Lieberman, Robert C. 1998. *Shifting the Color Line: Race and the American Welfare State.* Cambridge, MA: Harvard University Press.

Marshall, T. H. 1950. *Citizenship and Social Class and Other Essays.* Cambridge: Cambridge University Press.

McAdam, Doug. 1982. *Political Process and the Development of Black Insurgency, 1930–1970.* Chicago: University of Chicago Press.

McAdam, Doug, John D. McCarthy, and Mayer N. Zald. 1988. "Social Movements." In *Handbook of Sociology,* ed. Neil J. Smelser, 695–737. Newbury Park, CA: Sage.

———. 1988. Introduction to *Comparative Perspectives on Social Movements: Political Opportunities, Mobilizing Structures, and Cultural Framings,* ed. Doug McAdam, John D. McCarthy, and Mayer N. Zald, 1–20. Cambridge: University of Cambridge Press.

McBride, M. J. 1999. "Migrants and Asylum Seekers: Policy Responses in the United States to Immigrants and Refugees from Central America and the Caribbean." *International Migration* 37, no. 1: 289–314.

McDonnell, Patrick. 1996. "Legal Advocacy Groups Sue over Food Stamp Changes." *Los Angeles Times,* October 18, A3.

———. 1997a. "Immigrants Warned of Impending Aid Cuts." *Los Angeles Times,* February 1.

———. 1997b. "INS Backlog Growing As Aid Cutoff Gets Closer." *Los Angeles Times,* February 3.

———. 1997c. "Wilson Assails U.S. Plan to Restore Aid to Legal Immigrants." *Los Angeles Times,* February 13, A3.

Mendel, E. 1997a. "Agreement Reached on State Budget; Food Stamps Included for Legal Immigrants." *San Diego Union-Tribune,* August 8, A3.

———. 1997b. "Wilson Urged to Back Legal Immigrant Aid." *San Diego Union-Tribune,* July 22, A3.

Meyer, David S. 1999. "Tending the Vine: Cultivating Political Process Research." *Sociological Forum* 14, no. 1: 71–77.

Moody, James. 1997. "George Soros: Financial Wizard with a Halo." *Horizon Magazine.* At http://www.horizonmag.com/1/soros.htm (accessed July 31, 2002).

Morain, D. 1997. "Estimated Cost of State Food Stamp Plan for Legal Immigrants Quadruples; Panel to Urge States' Congress Members to Seek Restoration of Federal Aid." *Los Angeles Times,* June 14, A19.

National Immigration Law Center. 2002. *Guide to Immigrant Eligibility for Federal Programs,* 4th ed. Los Angeles: National Immigration Law Center.

Newton, Lina. 2004. "'It Is Not a Question of Being Anti-Immigration': Categories of Deservedness in Immigration Policymaking." In *Deserving and Entitled: Social Constructions and Public Policy,* ed. Anne Schneider and Helen Ingram. Albany: State University of New York.

Noble, Charles. 1997. *Welfare As We Knew It: A Political History of the American Welfare State.* New York: Oxford University Press.

Parenti, Christian. 1999. *Lockdown America: Police and Prisons in the Age of Crisis.* London: Verso.

Pierson, Paul. 1994. *Dismantling the Welfare State? Reagan, Thatcher, and the Politics of Retrenchment.* New York: Cambridge University Press.

Piven, Frances Fox, and Richard A. Cloward. 1977. *Poor People's Movements: Why They Succeed, How They Fail.* New York: Vintage Books.

———. 2000. *Why Americans Still Don't Vote and Why Politicians Want It That Way.* Boston: Beacon Press.

Pols, M. F. 1997. "Poll Finds 84% Favor Public Aid to Poor." *Daily News of Los Angeles,* June 5, N8.

Press Enterprise. 1996. "Welfare Study Says Counties' Costs Not As High As Seen." *Press Enterprise,* October 25, A7.

Prunty, Howard. 1984. "Businessmen as Welfare Advocates." In *Community Organizers,* 2nd ed., ed. Joan Ecklein, 230–32. New York: John Wiley & Sons.

Pyle, A., P. J. McDonnell, and H. Tobar. 1998. "Latino Voter Participation Doubled since '94 Primary." *Los Angeles Times,* June 4.

Ramakrishnan, S. Karthick. 2001. "Unpacking the Backlash: Political Threat, Institutional Mobilization, and Immigrant Electoral Participation in the Mid-1990s." Paper presented at the 2001 annual meeting of the American Political Science Association in San Francisco, California. At http://www.princeton.edu/~karthick.

Ramakrishnan, S. Karthick, and Thomas J. Espenshade. 2000. "Political Participation and Immigrant Incorporation: Generational Status and Voting Behavior in U.S. Elections." Paper presented at the annual meeting of the Midwest Political Science Association. At http://www.princeton.edu/~karthick.

Ramirez, Elvia, and Ellen Reese. 2002. "The Politics of Welfare Inclusion: Explaining State-Level Restorations of Legal Immigrants' Welfare Rights." Paper presented at the Society for the Study of Social Problems conference, Chicago.

Reese, Ellen. 1996. "Maternalism and Political Mobilization: How California's Postwar Child Care Campaign Was Won." *Gender & Society* 10, no. 5: 566–89.

Reese, Ellen, and Elvia Ramirez. 2002. "The New Ethnic Politics of Welfare: Political Struggles over Immigrants' Rights to Welfare in California." *Journal of Poverty* 6, no. 3: 29–62.

Rose, Fred. 2000. *Coalitions across the Class Divide: Lessons from the Labor, Peace, and Environmental Movements.* Ithaca, NY: Cornell University Press.

Santoro, Wayne A., and Gail M. McGuire. 1997. "Social Movement Insiders: The Impact of Institutional Activists on Affirmative Action and Comparable Worth Policies." *Social Problems* 44, no. 4: 503–19.

Schneider, Anne, and Helen Ingram. 1993. "Social Construction of Target Populations—Implications for Politics and Policy." *American Political Science Review* 87, no. 2: 334–47.

Schneider, Dorothee. 2000. "Symbolic Citizenship, Nationalism, and the Distant State: The United States Congress in the 1996 Debates on Immigration Reform." *Citizenship Studies* 4, no. 3: 255–73.

Shaw, Randy. 1999. "From Challenging American Sweatshops to a Movement for a Global Living Wage." In *Reclaiming America: Nike, Clean Air, and the New National Activism.* Berkeley: University of California Press.

Shearer, Derek. 1982. "How the Progressives Won in Santa Monica." *Social Policy* 12, no. 3: 7–14.

Staggenborg, Suzanne. 1986. "Coalition Work in the Pro-Choice Movement: Organizational and Environmental Opportunities and Obstacles." *Social Problems* 33, no. 5: 374–90.

Tarrow, Sidney. 1998. *Power in Movement: Social Movements and Contentious Politics,* 2nd ed. Cambridge: Cambridge University Press.

Taylor, Verta A. 1996. *Rock-a-by Baby: Feminism, Self-Help, and Postpartum Depression.* New York: Routledge.

Tilly, Charles. 1978. *From Mobilization to Revolution.* Reading, MA: Addison-Wesley.

U.S. Census Bureau. 2000. "Population Estimates for States by Race and Hispanic Origin: July 1, 1996." Washington, DC: Population Estimates Program, Population Division, U.S. Census Bureau. Internet release date, August 30, 2000. At http://www.census.gov/population/estimates/state/srh/srh96.txt.

Unz, R. K. 1994. "Immigration or the Welfare State: Which Is Our Real Enemy?" *Policy Review* 79: 33–38.

Wisconsin State Journal. 1997. "Group Asks Legislators to Restore Welfare Cuts to Aid Immigrants." *Wisconsin State Journal,* June 18, 3C.

Zald, Mayer N., and John D. McCarthy. 1980. "Social Movement Industries: Competition and Cooperation among Movement Organizations." *Research in Social Movements, Conflicts, and Change* 3: 1–20.

Zimmerman, Wendy, and Karen C. Tumlin. 1999. *Patchwork Policies: State Assistance for Immigrants under Welfare Reform.* Occasional Paper 24. Washington, DC: Urban Institute.

Conclusion

Social Movements, Public Policy, and Democracy: Rethinking the Nexus

Valerie Jenness, David S. Meyer, and Helen Ingram

Social movements, public policy, and democracy interact and develop around us. As we write, in December 2004, the issue of same-sex marriage occupies a prominent place on the political agenda at multiple levels of government. The executive and legislative branches of government have politicized the definition of marriage in the United States, as have candidates for office. Local elected officials have solemnized marriages, in violation of state laws, while judges at the state level have pronounced judgments, not always favorable, on the constitutionality of those laws. The Supreme Court has declined to hear a case challenging the decision of the Supreme Judicial Court of Massachusetts, which ruled that marriage had to be accessible to same-sex couples. The gay and lesbian movement continues to sponsor grassroots activism, coalition politics, and lobbying efforts to ensure such access to marriage for same-sex couples; at the same time, groups such as the Family Research Council and the Christian Coalition continue to sponsor grassroots activism, coalition politics, and lobbying efforts to ban same-sex marriages, including an effort to amend the U.S. Constitution.

Playing out at the national, state, and local levels, controversy around same-sex marriages erupted with the first civil nuptials, when the mayor of San Francisco, Gavin Newsome, ordered clerks at city hall to issue marriage licenses to same-sex couples. Within days, the city issued more than four thousand marriage licenses to same-sex couples from forty-six states and eight countries. A few elected officials across the country followed Newsome's lead. A countermovement organized to put referenda that offered a restrictive definition of marriage (as between one man and one woman only) on the ballot in eleven states. The placement of these propositions on state ballots, in conjunction with President George W. Bush's championing of a similarly worded federal constitutional amendment, played a role in the 2004 presidential election.

The issue of same-sex marriage, which has only recently come to the fore in the political arena in a discernible way, serves as a shining example of many of the themes contained in this book. That is, this spate of gay marriages, the countermovement they inspired, and the role both played in formal electoral politics follow from the interaction of social movements, existing public policy, and the structure of government. First, public policy provides benefits and burdens, creating supportive and contesting constituencies that seek to defend, repeal, and modify the policy. Policy is its own cause (Lowi 1964; Schneider and Ingram 1997; Wildavsky 1987), and, as such, it structures the opportunities for social movements. Second, policy contains not just the substantive benefits and costs and resource effects with which we have long been familiar, but it also has symbolic effects. That is, policy positively portrays some people—for example, gays and lesbians—who gain status, and removes some of the stigma attached to them by previous policies like the Defense of Marriage Act. Third, the American political context offers potential relevance to a broad range of institutional actors—in this case including elected officials at local, state, and national levels, as well as elected and appointed judges. Those political figures respond to pressures not only from institutional politics, but also from social movements operating on all sides of the political conflict. Fourth, the policy process does not have discrete beginnings and endings; rather, it unfolds in jumps and starts, with no permanent resolution. Prior policies shape the context in which subsequent policies are considered and sometimes contested.

The developing story of the struggle to define marriage points to the importance of the central issues raised here: How does context matter when it comes to understanding the development, content, and implementation of public policy at all levels of government? Under what conditions do public policies incite or inhibit political mobilization? Under what conditions do social movements influence public policy? And what structures and processes characterize the nexus comprised by both public policy and social movements? Enter the chapters presented in this volume, each of which helps develop a fuller understanding of the social movements–public policy connection in American democracy. We conclude this volume by summarizing the key arguments, linking them together in ways that offer an advance and a synthesis over previously disparate research efforts, and suggesting a range of connections between protest and policy that might guide future research.

Context Matters: Moving beyond Identifying Precursors

Over a half century ago Edwin Sutherland published one of the most cited studies of the formation of a type of public policy that is now reemerging as a highly visible and increasingly popular form of crime control policy. What Sutherland (1950a, 1950b) called "sexual psychopath" laws in the 1950s are now commonly described as "sex offender laws" (Winick and La Fond 2003). In his groundbreaking study of the origins and the diffusion of sexual psychopath laws, Sutherland argued that public policy is largely the result of two things: the manipulation of public opinion by the press and the influence of experts on the legislative process. Since the publication of this study, criminologists, sociologists, political scientists, and sociolegal and policy scholars alike have affirmed the crucial role the media and experts play in shaping the development, content, and institutionalization of various forms of public policy. Further, they add a plethora of other geographic, demographic, cultural, organizational, political, structural, and institutional conditions that shape when and how public policy comes into being in modern democracies.

As we move into the twenty-first century, scholars studying diverse types of public policy are adding yet more factors that provide the context and the impetus for public policy formation. These factors include, but are not limited to, the social location of individual moral entrepreneurs and experts (Hagan 2003), triggering events (Galliher and Cross 1983) and moral shocks (Jasper and Poulsen 1995), interest groups and interest group politics (Burstein 1999; Burstein and Linton 2002; Earl and Soule 2001; Klingemann, Hofferbert, and Budge 1994; Meyer and Imig 1993), policy monopolies (Baumgartner and Jones 1993), the shape of political opportunities (Meyer and Staggenborg 1996; Saguy 2000), the social construction of target groups (Schneider and Ingram 1997; Soss 2000), diverse structural conditions (Boyle 2002; Chambliss and Zatz 1993; McGarrell and Castellano 1993; Meyer and Tarrow 1998), and institutional logics (Baumgartner and Jones 2002; Boyle 2002; Clemens 1997; Garland 2001; Rao, Morrill, and Zald 2003). Most important for our purposes here, the interaction of social movements with these contextual factors increasingly has been recognized as significant. Our focus moves beyond identifying the contextual precursors to public policies and their intersection with social movements to tracing the complex patterns that categorize how opposition develops and, in our terms, is *routed* into policy consequences. Changes in structural conditions result in shifts in the political landscape of democratic societies, which in turn provide the impetus for the development and implementation of public policies as well as social movements that challenge them. Changes in structural conditions can be manifested as demographic shifts that result in new social cleavages in society, shifts in the stratification order such that existing inequalities are rendered visible or new inequalities are created, and dislocations and tensions in the economic structure of society that serve to create structural contradictions and incite social change of some sort. Likewise, changes in the political landscape and institutional workings can appear as shifts in public opinion that magnify tensions among social groups, the reconstitution or realignment of political parties and political cultures that serve to alter the opportunity structure for oppositional claims, and social constructions about a set of activities or group of people targeted by public policy (Fisher 2000; Landy 1993; Schneider and Ingram 1997).

Under these conditions, "issue creation" is likely to occur. However, as Meyer argued in the introduction, identifying conditions under which issue creation is likely to occur does not suffice unless one is willing to treat the policy process as a black box. To advance our understanding of the mutually constitutive nature of social movements and public policy, we must devote analytic attention to the multiple and reciprocal feedback mechanisms by which social policies result in social movements and the mechanisms by which social movements affect the policy process and content.

Adopting a broader and more inclusive view requires examining *how* context matters or, more precisely, how changing contexts matter, especially in the Madisonian institutional structure described in the introduction as a system designed to embrace and institutionalize political conflict. Accordingly, the chapters in part II reveal the important role historical, political, and organizational contexts play in setting the stage for collective action that results in issue creation and newfound social policies and vice versa. That is, how existing institutions and policies encroach on, thwart, or marginalize the emergence and effectiveness of social movements can only be understood by examining layers of context.

Edwin Amenta empirically examines the U.S. Depression-era Townsend Plan to reveal how the collective action of challengers is politically mediated within governmental institutions. He moves beyond the identification of casual precursors to provide a model of how two key elements of the context—changing political circumstances and political institutions— influence the effectiveness of different challengers and their efforts over time. Surprisingly, he finds that the Townsend Plan did not enjoy its most noteworthy successes when its supporters were most active or when they implemented the most aggressive mobilization strategies under the most favorable political conditions. Rather, he argues, making policy gains "depends on a coincidence of strategy and political context." To make sense of how this "coincidence" works, Amenta offers a model of how political institutions mediate mobilization efforts under varying conditions such that those most proximate to the policy-making process—elected officials and state bureaucrats—adopt the goals of extra-institutional players, most notably social movement activists. His work emphasizes that social movements cannot directly effect policy change by, for example, introducing a bill in Congress; rather, they depend on the efforts of others located within mainstream political institutions. The outcomes of social protest depend on the political regimes in place, the relevant bureaucrats in charge, and the nature of current programs in place (also see Barker 2004).

Frank Baumgartner and Christine Mahoney pick up where Amenta leaves off by examining the development and composition of the government agenda. Baumgartner and Mahoney address important questions about the context in which social movement and public policy intersect by documenting dramatic changes in governmental activity over the last half of the twentieth century (see also Baumgartner and Jones 2002). Relying on an analysis of congressional hearings, they document a precipitous growth in state attention paid to issues affecting women, the environment, civil rights and minorities, human rights, and the elderly, while there was a sharp decline in attention being paid to public policy on public lands, government operations, and defense. They make sense of these empirical patterns by demonstrating a concomitant growth in several sectors of social movement activity, including women's movement groups, human rights organizations, minority and civil rights groups, environmental groups, and membership in the American Association of Retired Persons (AARP). They argue that much of the impetus for these changes on the public agenda in the last fifty-plus years comes from social movements and the organizations that sustain them. Moreover, they contend, consistent with the diversification of social movements in the latter half of the twentieth century, there has been a proliferation of issues on the public policy agenda. Of course, along with diversification and proliferation comes increased competition for space on the U.S. government's policy agenda. Thus, the number and content of policies already in place in an issue area, as well as the extent to which policy space is crowded, affects the opportunities and strategies of social movements.

Taking increased competition for space in the "social problems market-place" seriously (Hilgartner and Bosk 1988; cf., Baumgartner and Jones

2002), John McCarthy brings us one step closer to understanding how the composition of the social movement–public policy nexus affects the process of translating social movement claims into public policy. McCarthy demonstrates how elite-sponsored coalition politics shape the political and resource terrain over which collective demands for social change develop. Drawing on the case of a substance-abuse community coalition, he argues that community-level coalitions are a historically specific institutionalized type of collective action that has proliferated over the last few decades and, in the process, has enabled elites to mobilize citizen groups to advocate for policies that come to be seen as grassroots policies. As more or less formally constituted agreements among preexisting groups, such coalitions are comprised of multiple sectors of the community, including businesses, the media, law enforcement, school, faith-based organizations, members of the health industry, social service agencies, and, most important, the government. Insofar as the policies derived from coalition politics are elite engineered, they actually reflect the complete interpenetration between the state and so-called outsiders. The result, McCarthy argues, is the "elite social construction of issues and top-down mobilization of citizen preferences" through the related mechanisms of channeling and crowding. These processes ensure some issues get public policy attention and some do not.

At this point it becomes doubtful that a clear line between forces in the context (the outsiders) and actors in political institutions (the insiders) actually exists. Successful issues move from the inside out as or more seamlessly than from the outside in. Recognizing this brings us to the central concern of this volume: understanding the ways in which social movements and government entities interpenetrate such that the boundaries between the two become both hard to discern and highly permeable.

The Social Movement–Public Policy Nexus: Understanding the Contours

Based on her research on the contemporary feminist movement within the Roman Catholic Church and the U.S. military, Mary Fainsod Katzenstein demonstrated how "protest in American society has moved inside institutions" and, in so doing, has changed what constitutes protest (1998, 3). It is a mistake to envision social movements and the state as distinct and easily discernable entities (see, for example, Binder 2002; della Porta and Rucht 1995; Diani 1992; Eisenstein 1996; Mazur 2002; Santoro and McGuire 1997; Werum and Winders 2001). Other scholars delineate the ways in which the work of activists, community and professional groups and networks, social movement organizations, and the state intersect to result in public policy and, on occasion, incite social protest.

For example, in *The Fight against Big Tobacco: The Movement, the State, and the Public's Health,* Mark Wolfson offers a compelling analysis of how "the movement has built upon a preexisting 'infrastructure' of health organizations and professionals and the close, collaborative relationship between movement organizations and state agencies" (2001, 45). The former includes health care organizations and professionals, as well as health voluntaries such as the American Lung Association, the American Heart Association, and the American Cancer Society; the latter includes federal, state, and local agencies, such as the Office of the Surgeon General, the National Cancer Institute, the Centers for Disease Control and Prevention, and a slew of state-sponsored regulatory agencies.

Wolfson argues that this pattern of "state-movement interpenetration" resulted in sweeping policy changes at every level of government and that it generalizes beyond the case of tobacco policy in the latter part of the twentieth century. This formulation moves well beyond envisioning the state as merely a target of social movements, as a provider of constraints and opportunities for social movements, and as a facilitator or sponsor of social movement goals. As he puts it, "it is next to impossible to think about the movement without thinking about the state. The state is not limited to being an external force that acts on, or is acted upon by, the movement, but is in fact an integral part of the movement" (Wolfson 2001, 145). This theme is further developed in Binder's (2002) recent analysis of competing efforts by advocates of Afrocentrism and of creationism to reform public school curricula (see also Goldstone 2003).

These insights are echoed in the efforts to rethink the role of "institutionalist activists" operating within state structures to influence bureaucratic decision making. In their work on affirmative action and comparable worth policies, Santoro and McGuire (1997, 503) defined "institutionalist activists" as "actors located within political institutions but who pursue outsider goals" (but see also Mazur 2002; cf. Banaszak, ch. 5 this volume). This shift in location of at least some activism opens additional possibilities for complicated alliances among activists, the media, experts, and governmental officials. For example, Joel Best's (1999) work on crime control policies explains the formation of current constructions of random violence as a social problem and the development of attendant crime policies as a function of this type of alliance. Specifically, he argues, in the last quarter of the twentieth century numerous major social movements—the civil rights movement, the women's movement, the gay/lesbian movement, the victim's rights movement, and the self-help movement—have joined forces with the media, professional experts, and the state to successfully portray particular groups of citizens as systematically victimized by a society organized around inequality and corresponding discrimination. This and other notions of victimization, especially those promulgated by experts speaking on behalf of the modern self-help movement and various sectors of the therapeutic industry, have been furthered by state-sponsored activities, which laid the foundation for talking about new victims and developing public policies designed to curb random violence and provide relief to those who are victimized by it. This language culminates in producing a contemporary ideology of victimization[1] that has been made possible by the workings of an Iron Quadrangle. For Best, what was once a policy monopoly (Baumgartner and Jones 1993) or an "iron triangle" has now become the "Iron Quadrangle." The Iron Quadrangle is defined by fluid interactions among experts, mass media, activists, and government, which can produce broad social consensus, offering selected facts and interpretive stories that suggest causality and the prospects for solutions.

Mrill Ingram and Helen Ingram illustrate the ways in which various sectors of society are implicated in the iterative process of introducing claims about a new "problem," reaching consensus about its parameters, and defining and implementing public policy in the case of organic foods. They draw on a wealth of historical, interview, and media data to trace the evolution of claims making and policy making surrounding the formulation, passage, and implementation of the Organic Food Production Act of 1990. They show numerous players moving in and out of the state as policy is developed and as challengers, bureaucrats, and elected officials respond to, and affect, market conditions. In this case, marginal groups, including farmers and consumers, mobilized and framed their arguments in ways that helped them to establish themselves as experts *within* the boundaries of legitimate policy-making discourse in federal policy making. Two things in particular proved crucial to the organics movement's ability to advance the cause of "credible edibles": (1) support from the marketplace, which created institutional opportunities; and (2) the ability of activists and farmers to capitalize on market failures and to develop new institutions, most notably certification processes, crucial to deeming products "organic." By detailing how this process occurred, Ingram and Ingram shed insight into how social movements interpenetrate with state structures and vice versa, changing over time, and blurring boundaries between the two. They show how the content of policy shapes the strategies of movements, how the influence of social movements on policy varies substantially across different stages in the policy process, and, most important for the purposes of this volume, how the boundaries between insiders and outsiders are fluid and shifting and thus open to reconstitution.[2]

Formulating the state-movement nexus in decidedly structural terms, Lee Ann Banaszak also challenges the traditionally sharp distinctions between social movements and states. In her chapter, Banaszak investigates how social movements and state structures composed of overlapping memberships affect both social mobilization and policy making. She proposes that three dimensions of the "state-movement intersection" are particularly consequential for how social movements, in this case the modern women's movement, create opportunity for outsiders to mobilize (also see McCammon et al. 2001). For Banaszak, the size, location, and historical context of the state-movement intersection is influenced by public policies, and, in turn, the size, location, and historical context of the state-movement intersection influence the development of the larger social movement's strategies and outcomes. This formulation recognizes the range of actors operating within the state and the potential for shifting, and sometimes competing, alliances. If social movements can operate within as well as outside the state, we need to reconsider our understanding of both phenomena. Such reconsideration can advance our understanding of how public policy is a crucial link to the formation of particular types of state-movement interpenetrations, as well as the conditions under which social movement actors "take to the streets" and/or "work in the air-conditioned halls of government."

Consistent with this connection between structure and process, Ryken Grattet demonstrates the ways in which the development of a "policy nexus" is an important precursor to the formulation and adoption of public policy. He does so by addressing a provocative question—why did the United States adopt workers' compensation laws in the Progressive era—despite the fact that models for how to do so were readily available substantially earlier. As he observes, "despite availability of a discursive foundation, ideological resources, institutional models, and a receptive policy-making audience that was concerned about finding a solution to the issue [of injured workers]—all of which provided an opportunity for reform—reform itself was not forthcoming. What was missing?" Stated in theoretical terms, he asks, what factors needed to be present to translate calls for reform into concrete policy that diffuses across time and space? Based on careful historical work and skillful quantitative confirmatory analyses, he concludes that the formation, structure, and workings of a particular type of social movement–state nexus proved crucial. Defined as "connections among activists and connections among activists, experts, and state officials," the policy nexus is the organizational and interactional space in which challengers and policy makers meet, manage differences among themselves, formulate policy, and institutionalize some forms of public policy and not others. The back and forth among experts, activists, and government leads to institutionalization of some forms of policy and the simultaneous exclusion of other alternatives.

Of course, as this process unfolds, public policy itself becomes part of the institutionalized political field to which all actors must respond. As the chapters in part III show, public policies can become the stimulus to which challengers respond, the authoritative source of state-sanctioned discourse around which the state-movement nexus is structured and operates, and the motor around which the allocation of social, legal, and economic rights (of some sorts and not others) is articulated, justified, and enforced. The consequences of these outcomes for who engages in social movement mobilization, how mobilization is undertaken and sustained, and what types of collective identities and citizens are produced in the process are especially important in a democratic context.

The Nature of the Field: Policy Impacts on Participation, Mobilization, and Identities

Democracy is both a process of making policy and the outcome of public policies. Without engaging thousands of years of debate on the ideal and real forms of democracy, we suggest that democracy is best conceived as the provision of the opportunity for equal and meaningful influence on policy to all citizens within a polity. This necessarily entails the ability to participate in informed debate, which means citizens must have access to usable information and to forums in which to engage in discourse with a larger community. Of course, democracy requires more than a mechanistic adherence to a one-person, one-vote process. After all, majorities can honor formal democratic processes while systematically withholding state benefits from minorities, as seen, for example, in the case of same-sex marriage that introduced this chapter. Democracy must be seen not only as a process, but also as a goal of public policy (e.g., Ingram and Smith 1993), one that can be more closely approached over time through public policies that enhance not only the opportunities for citizens to influence policy, but their capacity to develop wisdom as well as efficacy. In this regard, the recognition that even well-established, self-declared democratic polities (e.g., Curtis, Baer, and Grabb 2001; Klingemann, Hofferbert, and Budge 1994; Mitchell and Wood 1998; O'Donnell 1994) fall short of the democratic ideal is less an indictment than a call for continued action (Young 2003).

Although we are quick to recognize the importance of political equality—access to the ballot, subject to the laws—to democracy, it is doubtful that real political equality can exist without some degree of social and economic equality. In this regard, democracy requires recognition of a community whose members have not only individual values and aspirations but also a shared destiny. To the extent that structural inequalities, operating without formal government endorsement, produce gaps between the ideal of democracy and the operation of politics in the United States, both states and social movements have their work cut out for them. Public policy can enable new actors to make claims on government, and social movements can win recognition and new advantages for the underrepresented and underserved, thus building toward democracy.[3]

Public policy can enable the practice of democracy (Ingram and Smith 1993). Some policies explicitly address democratic processes, such as qualifications for voting or rules and procedures for campaigning for office; nonetheless, we must embrace a larger vision of policy to understand its relation to democracy. As Landy notes, all public policies "instruct the public about the aims of government and the rights and responsibilities of citizens" (1993, 19). In this regard, the making of policy reflects and shapes not only public policy, but also its content. Through the distribution of benefits, burdens, honors, and condemnations, public policy signals what behaviors are valued by the state and which citizens are important. By the agendas pursued by policy, citizens learn whether the problems important to them are also public problems worthy of government action or matters they must solve themselves. Policy rules and tools provide resources and opportunities to be heard in public forums, and they can foster a sense of civic duty that affects beneficiaries their entire lifetime. Alternatively, policies that have no component for outreach to constituents and do nothing to provide information important for instigating citizen mobilization undercut the democratic system.

For example, Suzanne Mettler's chapter examining the effects of veterans' benefits demonstrates how policy design shapes civic engagement, including collective action. By tracing how three generations of policy designs have defined the range of entitlements for U.S. veterans of the Civil War, World War I, and World War II, she demonstrates how features of policy design (i.e., scope of eligibility, value of resources, procedures for determining eligibility, and procedures for benefit delivery) influence not only the resources but also the attitudes veterans have long after their service, and how these material and symbolic resources shape veterans' subsequent civic and political engagement. The larger lesson here is important: by designing and implementing policy, the state shapes the possibilities for collective action among target populations as well as their likely concerns. This can result in constituencies being enabled into democratic membership in the polity or in the exclusion, marginalization, or demonization of others.

Whereas Mettler notes the empowering and enabling effects of at least one version of the GI Bill targeted toward a constituency constructed as worthy and deserving of benefits, Mary Fainsod Katzenstein's chapter concerns a constituency constructed as problematic. She provides a clear view of how decades of public policy can incrementally bestow a band of rights on a target population while, at the same time, denying categorical and robust citizenship for that same population. Investigating more than a quarter century of the politics of incarceration in general, and the prisoner rights movement in particular, she details how the prisoner rights movement has made modest advances through the courts, especially in the arena closest to home: improving prison conditions. At the same time, however, the prisoner rights movement has failed to secure the most basic entitlements of citizenship for prisoners. For example, prisoners continue to experience civil disabilities, such as the inability to earn a living wage and disenfranchisement.[4] Taking the historical record into account, she concludes that the successes of the movement were more than counterbalanced by the larger failure on citizenship. The movement was blocked, in large part because it was unable to construct a sustainable sympathetic identity for incarcerated felons.

Ellen Reese's chapter tells a more encouraging story of a disadvantaged constituency constructing a sympathetic collective identity and resisting unfavorable policies by political mobilization and coalition building. In looking at the legal rights of immigrants, Reese traces substantial reactive political mobilization to the adoption of two federal policies in 1996, the Personal Responsibility and Work Opportunity Act and the Illegal Immigration Reform and Immigration Responsibility Act. Constituencies targeted by this legislation organized and forged coalitions with supporters within government. The provocation of threatening legislation generated substantial proactive claims about democratic rights from a broad coalition of previously marginalized groups. She contends that the coalition ties forged in this campaign can serve as the basis for effective political action in the future.

The chapters in part III reveal the ways in which diverse elements of policy design are influenced by, and then in turn influence, citizen preferences, collective action, and collective identities. Clearly, the links between social movements, governmental action, and policy are multifaceted. For example, social movements can be at the core of attracting attention to an issue and getting it put on the public agenda; however, once there, existing policies and the ways in which they are implemented have strong influences on the opportunities and constraints facing challenger movements. The obstacle course of American federalism and fragmentation, identified by Reese and others here, makes the linkages more complicated because of the multiple channels through which interested actors can mobilize and promote—or prevent—policy reform (e.g., Werum and Winders 2001).

In addition, because of the multiplicity of access points, each operating under different institutional and cultural constraints, the routes through which movements can influence policy vary in character as well as location. Further, all of these levers are constrained by the broader cultural constructions of government and target populations, meaning that only a small portion of possible policy responses could actually take place (Fisher 2000; Ingram and Ingram, ch. 4 this volume; Jenness and Grattet 2001; Schneider and Ingram 1997). We can think about the relevant actors involved in a policy area as a "domain" (Burstein 1991). Recognizing that policy domains are rooted in social constructions acknowledges that how problems are defined and responded to is contingent on available frameworks of meaning that actors appropriate and deploy in key institutional settings (e.g., Armstrong 2002). Analytically, the term "policy domain" refers to (1) the range of collective actors—for example, politicians, experts, agency officials, and interest groups—who have gained sufficient legitimacy to speak about or act on a particular issue; and (2) the cultural logics, frameworks, and ideologies those actors bring to bear in constructing and narrating the "problem" and the appropriate policy responses.

Finally, the culture and structure of a policy domain is organized around at least four points in time: (1) issue creation, where a problem is recognized, named, and deemed in need of a solution; (2) the adoption of a particular policy solution from a range of alternatives; (3) the rule-making phase where government officials and the courts determine the precise meaning of the policy; and finally, (4) the classification and application of the rules by enforcement agents to specific "real world" circumstances[5]— although these stages frequently appear simultaneously or out of sequence. Policy making occurs not just at the moment of legislative enactment, but is renegotiated and redefined repeatedly. The many layers of government and multiple access points associated with this larger policy-making process have the capacity to stimulate or curtail civil engagement in general and social movements in particular. As such, they are crucial to processes of democratization and the functioning of a democracy.

Discussion and Conclusion

The shifts in intellectual terrain shown in this volume, and also evidenced in other recent social movements and public policy literature, are significant on both empirical and theoretical grounds. Empirically, scholars are exploring an increasing number of substantive domains of social life and explicating the mutually constitutive nature of social movements and public policy. In the process, new features of social life are recognized as part and parcel of social movements and acknowledged as intimately connected to public policy. Theoretically, the literature has moved beyond a preoccupation with one-way theories of the influence of social movements on public policy and the impact of public policy on social movements. Indeed, the chapters in this book point to the limitations of thinking about states and social movements as separate entities in the policy-making process and to the value of conceptualizing them as a nexus of political activity in democratic societies.

There are also a number of specific conceptual and theoretical advances. First, it is extremely helpful to understand the social movement–public policy making relationship as both (1) a set of structures that compose the historical, political, and organizational context in which mobilization emerges, develops, and effects influence (or not); and (2) a set of processes, such as issue creation, agenda setting, coalition building, and policy framing and implementation. By attending to both structure and process along these lines, the nature of the social movement–state nexus becomes a more potent predictor of the timing, content, and consequences of both public policy making and social movement mobilization.

Second, the work presented here demonstrates the complicated ways in which parties to this relationship come into being, engage in an array of political processes, and produce social change in America. In particular, the social movement–state intersection, as Mettler calls it, is where protest and accompanying grievances get most immediately translated into influence on policy. This process of translation is, as chapters in this volume reveal, both constrained and enabled by a variety of factors, including the institutional field and its workings (and failures) and attendant logics, the political structures dictating the rules of engagement, the organizational contexts proscribing the range of possibilities for both actors and policies, and the parameters of existing policy. All of these factors shape the design, content, and implementation of policy, which in turn shapes the field of opportunities for subsequent collective action. As these chapters show, policies create constituencies, the range of possibilities for constituencies to mobilize, and types of grievances that accompany mobilization. In short, social movements mold opportunities for policy and policy molds opportunities for social movement mobilization. However, the recursive effects are sometimes obscure and must be teased out in analysis.

Third, these chapters demonstrate that the causality that underlies the relationship between social movements and public policy is composed of multiple feedbacks that transform both movements and policies over time.[6]

A central message of this book is that the permeable boundaries between social movements and various domains of the state (i.e., the courts, legislatures, bureaucracies) ensure that the relationship between policy and social movements is best characterized as an ongoing dialogue, with changes occurring in both policy and social movements. In this dialogue, the influence of public policy on social movement and vice versa may vary substantially across different stages in the policy-making and implementation processes.

Finally, the relationship between the dialogue of social movements and public policy and the fortunes of democracy is critical. Social movements are important vehicles through which American democracy becomes more inclusive by enlisting losers in a policy debate, including the poor, people of color, gays and lesbians, veterans, injured workers, the elderly, prisoners, and many other groups in active political engagement. Public policies institutionalize gains sought by such groups and provide resources that sustain and reinforce these social movements. Unfortunately, what can positively reinforce can also undercut and weaken. Recent and not-so-recent history is filled with examples of the stifling of protest through policies with putatively lofty goals like public safety and security. More subtly, institutions and processes put in place by policy can thwart even the recognition of shared aspirations for change. Past research has demonstrated the plethora of ways in which participation in democratic decision making and government structures are derailed. We hope that this book will continue that research tradition but also encourage research on ways in which policies can promote a more substantial democracy in America. It is likely that social movements will be an important part of both the analytical and political stories.

Notes

1. This ideology is anchored in the notion that victimization is widespread, victimization is consequential, victimization is relatively straightforward and unambiguous, victimization often goes unrecognized, individuals must be taught to recognize others' and their own victimization, claims of victimization must be respected, and the term "victim" signals undesirable consequences. Best convincingly demonstrates how "this set of beliefs makes it easy to label victims, and very difficult to dispute those labels" (1999, 117). Moreover, "the contemporary ideology of victimization offers a formula—a familiar set of claims—that can be adapted by would-be advocates of new forms of victimization" (117–18), including those in the therapeutic community and helping professions and those employed by the state.

2. A central lesson here, also found in other issue domains (see, for example, Jenness and Grattet's [2001] work on the development and implementation of hate crime policy in the United States and Kelmes's [2004] work on the development

and implementation of drug policy in the United States), is that while challengers' ideas come to the fore during the issue-creation phase of policy making, established interests enjoy tremendous influence in shaping outcomes during the implementation phase of policy making.

3. Social movements can also produce democratic cultures and processes within their sponsoring organizations and constituencies (Polletta 2002).

4. Uggen and Manza (2002) demonstrate that denying convicted felons, who are disproportionately drawn from the ranks of racial minorities and the poor, the right to vote has played a decisive role in at least 7 percent of U.S. Senate elections; moreover, at least one Republican victory would have been reversed if former felons recovered the right to vote. As the prison population grows, they argue, the United States steps backward on the road to democracy.

5. For a contrasting view, see models proposed by Sabatier (1994, 1999), Sabatier and Jenkins-Smith (1993), and, more recently, Baumgartner and Jones's (2002) work on "punctuated equilibrium."

6. Baumgartner and Jones argue that both positive and negative feedback loops shape public policy as well as the institutions in which they are created, modified, and institutionalized. Negative feedback processes enhance stability and incrementalism and "are fundamental to most models of bureaucratic behavior, the functioning of policy subsystems, concepts of interest group–pluralism, models of democratic gridlock, and to other prominent views of the policy process" (2002, 6). In contrast, positive feedback models of politics and policy making are "models in which ideas of momentum, bandwagon effects, thresholds, and cascade play critical roles" (7).

References

Armstrong, Elizabeth A. 2002. *Forging Gay Identities: Organizing Sexuality in San Francisco, 1950–1994.* Chicago: University of Chicago Press.

Barker, Vanessa. 2004. "Politics of Pain: State Governance, Moral Protest, and the Varied Impacts of Social Movements." Unpublished paper.

Baumgartner, Frank R., and Bryan D. Jones. 1993. *Agendas and Instability in American Politics.* Chicago: University of Chicago Press.

———, eds. 2002. *Policy Dynamics.* Chicago: University of Chicago Press.

Best, Joel. 1999. *Random Violence: How We Talk about New Crimes and New Crime Victims.* Berkeley: University of California Press.

Binder, Amy. 2002. *Contentious Curricula: Afrocentrism and Creationism in American Public Schools.* Princeton, NJ: Princeton University Press.

Boyle, Elizabeth Heger. 2002. *Female Genital Cutting: Cultural Conflict in the Global Community.* Baltimore, MD: Johns Hopkins University Press.

Burstein, Paul. 1991. "Policy Domains: Organization, Culture, and Policy Outcomes." *Annual Review of Sociology* 17: 327–50.

———. 1999. "Social Movements and Public Policy." In *How Social Movements Matter,* ed. Marco Giugni, Doug McAdam, and Charles Tilly, 3–21. Minneapolis: University of Minnesota Press.

Burstein, Paul, and A. Linton. 2002. "The Impact of Political Parties, Interest Groups, and Social Movement Organizations on Public Policy: Some Recent Evidence and Theoretical Concerns." *Social Forces* 81: 380–408.

Chambliss, William J., and Marjorie S. Zatz. 1993. *Making Law: The State, the Law, and Structural Contradictions.* Bloomington: Indiana University Press.

Clemens, Elisabeth S. 1997. *The People's Lobby: Organizational Innovation and the Rise of Interest Group Politics in the United States, 1890–1925.* Chicago: University of Chicago Press.

Curtis, James. E., Douglas E. Baer, and Edward G. Grabb. 2001. "Nations of Joiners: Explaining Voluntary Association Membership in Democratic Societies." *American Sociological Review* 66: 783–805.

della Porta, Donatella, and Dieter Rucht. 1995. "Left-Libertarian Movements in Context." In *The Politics of Social Protest: Comparative Perspectives on States and Social Movements,* ed. J. Craig Jenkins and Bert Klandermans, 229–72. Minneapolis: University of Minnesota Press.

Diani, Mario. 1992. "The Concept of Social Movement." *Sociological Review* 40: 1–25.

Earl, Jennifer, and Sarah Soule. 2001. "The Differential Protection of Minority Groups: The Inclusion of Sexual Orientation, Gender, and Disability in State Hate Crime Laws, 1976–1995." *Research in Political Sociology* 9: 1–31.

Eisenstein, Hester. 1996. *Inside Agitators: Australian Femocrats and the State.* Philadelphia: Temple University Press.

Fisher, Frank. 2000. *Citizens and Experts in the Environment: The Politics of Local Knowledge.* Durham, NC: Duke University Press.

Galliher, John F., and John R. Cross. 1983. *Morals Legislation without Morality.* New Brunswick, NJ: Rutgers University Press.

Garland, David. 2001. *The Culture of Control: Crime and Social Order in Contemporary Society.* New York: Oxford University Press.

Goldstone, Jack. A., ed. 2003. *States, Parties, and Social Movements.* New York: Cambridge University Press.

Hagan, John. 2003. *Justice in the Balkans: Prosecuting War Crimes in the Hague Tribunal.* Chicago: University of Chicago Press.

Hilgartner, Stephen, and Charles L. Bosk. 1988. "The Rise and Fall of Social Problems: A Public Arenas Model." *American Journal of Sociology* 94: 53–78.

Ingram, Helen, and Steve Rathgeb Smith, eds. 1993. *Public Policy for Democracy.* Washington, DC: Brookings Institution.

Jasper, James M., and Jane D. Poulsen. 1995. "Recruiting Strangers and Friends: Moral Shocks and Social Networks in Animal Rights and Anti-Nuclear Protest." *Social Problems* 42: 493–512.

Jenness, Valerie, and Ryken Grattet. 2001. *Making Hate a Crime: From Social Movement to Law Enforcement.* New York: Russell Sage Foundation.

Katzenstein, Mary Fainsod. 1998. *Faithful and Fearless: Moving Feminist Protest inside the Church and the Military.* Princeton, NJ: Princeton University Press.

Kelmes, Glenda. 2004. "Taking the High Road: A Qualitative Analysis of the Passage and Implementation of California's Substance Abuse and Crime Prevention Act of 2000." Unpublished paper.

Klingemann, Hans Dieter, Richard I. Hofferbert, and Ian Budge. 1994. *Parties, Policies, and Democracies.* Boulder, CO: Westview Press.

Landy, Marc. 1993. "Public Policy and Citizenship." In *Public Policy for Democracy,* ed. Helen Ingram and Steven Smith. Washington, DC: Brookings Institute Press.

Lowi, Theodore. 1964. "American Business, Public Policy, Case Studies, and Political Theory"; review of R. A. Bauer et al., *American Business and Public Policy* (New York: Atherton, 1963). *World Politics* 16, no. 4: 677–715.

———. 1965. *Legislative Politics USA.* Boston: Little, Brown.

———. 1969. *The End of Liberalism: Ideology, Policy, and the Crisis of Public Authority.* New York: Norton.

Mazur, Amy. 2002. *Theorizing Feminist Policy.* Oxford: Oxford University Press.

McCammon, Holly J., Karen E. Campbell, Ellen M. Granberg, and Christine Mowery. 2001. "How Movements Win: Gendered Opportunity Structures and the State Women's Suffrage Movements, 1866–1919." *American Sociological Review* 66: 49–70.

McGarrell, Edmund, and Thomas Castellano. 1993. "Social Structure, Crime, and Politics: Conflict Model of Law Formation." In *Making Law: The State, the Law, and Structural Contradictions,* ed. William J. Chambliss and Marjorie S. Zatz, 347–78. Bloomington: Indiana University Press.

Meyer, David S., and Douglas R. Imig. 1993. "Political Opportunity and the Rise and Decline of Interest Group Sectors." *Social Science Journal* 30: 253–70.

Meyer, David S., and Suzanne Staggenborg. 1996. "Movements, Countermovements, and the Structure of Political Opportunity." *American Journal of Sociology* 101: 1628–60.

Meyer, David S., and Sidney Tarrow, eds. 1998. *The Social Movement Society: Contentious Politics for a New Century.* Lanham, MD: Rowman & Littlefield.

Mitchell, Michael J., and Charles H. Wood. 1998. "Ironies of Citizenship: Skin Color, Police Brutality, and the Challenge of Democracy in Brazil." *Social Forces* 77: 1001–20.

O'Donnell, Guillermo. 1994. "Delagative Democracy." *Journal of Democracy* 5: 55–69.

Polletta, Francesca. 2002. *Freedom Is an Endless Meeting: Democracy in American Social Movements.* Chicago: University of Chicago Press.

Rao, Hayagreeva, Calvin Morrill, and Mayer Zald. 2003. "Power Plays: How Social Movements and Collective Action Create New Organizational Forms." *Research in Organizational Behaviour* 22: 237–81.

Sabatier, Paul A. 1994. Introduction to *Parties, Policies, and Democracies,* ed. Hans Dieter Klingemann, Richard I. Hofferbert, and Ian Budge, xix–xxii. Boulder, CO: Westview Press.

———, ed. 1999. *Theories of the Policy Process.* Boulder, CO: Westview Press.

Sabatier, Paul A., and Hank C. Jenkins-Smith. 1993. *Policy Change and Learning: An Advocacy Learning Approach.* Boulder, CO: Westview Press.

Saguy, Abigail C. 2000. "Employment Discrimination or Sexual Violence? Defining Sexual Harassment in American and French Law." *Law and Society Review* 34: 1091–128.

Santoro, Wayne A., and Gail M. McGuire. 1997. "Social Movement Insiders: The Impact of Institutional Activists on Affirmative Action and Comparable Worth Policies." *Social Problems* 44: 503–19.

Schneider, Anne L., and Helen Ingram. 1997. *Policy Design for Democracy.* Lawrence: University of Kansas.

———. 2004. *Deserving and Entitled.* Albany: State University of New York Press.

Soss, Joe. 2000. *Unwanted Claims: The Politics of Participation in the U.S. Welfare System.* Ann Arbor: University of Michigan Press.

Sutherland, Edwin H. 1950a. "The Diffusion of Sexual Psychopath Laws." *American Journal of Sociology* 56: 142–48.

———. 1950b. "The Sexual Psychopath Laws." *Journal of Criminal Law and Criminology* 40: 543–54.

Uggen, Christopher, and Jeff Manza. 2002. "Democratic Contraction? Political Consequences of Felon Disenfranchisement in the United States." *American Sociological Review* 67: 777–803.

Werum, Regina, and Bill Winders. 2001. "Who's 'In' and Who's 'Out': State Fragmentation and the Struggle over Gay Rights, 1974–1999." *Social Problems* 48: 386–410.

Wildavsky, Aaron. 1987. *Speaking Truth to Power: The Art and Craft of Policy Analysis.* New Brunswick, NJ: Transaction Books.

Winick, Bruce J., and John Q. La Fond, eds. 2003. *Protecting Society from Sexually Dangerous Offenders: Law, Justice, and Therapy.* Washington, DC: American Psychological Association.

Wolfson, Mark. 2001. *The Fight against Big Tobacco: The Movement, the State, and the Public's Health.* New York: Aldine de Gruyter.

Young, Iris. 2003. *Inclusion and Democracy.* New York: Oxford University Press.

Contributors

EDWIN AMENTA is professor of sociology at New York University. His interests include political sociology, social movements, comparative and historical sociology, and social policy. He is the author of *Bold Relief: Institutional Politics and the Origins of Modern American Social Policy.*

LEE ANN BANASZAK is associate professor of political science and women's studies at Pennsylvania State University. Her research focuses on women's movements in the United States and Western Europe and the comparative study of public opinion on abortion, gender roles, and feminism. She is the author of *Why Movements Succeed or Fail: Opportunity, Culture, and the Struggle for Woman Suffrage* and coeditor of *Women's Movements Facing a Reconfigured State.* She has also published in *American Political Science Review, Public Opinion Quarterly,* and *Political Research Quarterly.*

FRANK R. BAUMGARTNER is professor of political science at Pennsylvania State University. His work focuses on public policy, agenda setting, and interest groups in American politics. His books include *Agendas and Instability in American Politics* (with Bryan D. Jones) and *Basic Interests: The Importance of Groups in Politics and in Political Science* (with Beth L. Leech). He is codirector, with Bryan Jones, of the Policy Agendas Project (www.policyagendas.org).

RYKEN GRATTET is associate professor of sociology at the University of California, Davis. His work examines the social and cultural dimensions of lawmaking. He is the coauthor of *Making Hate a Crime* (with Valerie

Jenness), and his articles have appeared in *American Behavioral Scientist, American Sociological Review, Social Science History, Journal of Criminal Law and Criminology, Law and Society Review,* and *Sociological Perspectives.* His current work focuses on the ways local police and sheriff's agencies in California are responding to hate crime laws.

HELEN INGRAM is Warmington Endowed Chair in Social Ecology at the University of California, Irvine, where she holds joint appointments in the Departments of Planning, Policy, and Design; Political Science; and Criminology, Law, and Society. She has written widely on natural resources and environmental policy and public policy theory and design, and is the coauthor (with Anne Schneider) of *Policy Design for Democracy.*

MRILL INGRAM holds a research and outreach position at the Environmental Resources Center at the University of Wisconsin–Madison. Her work focuses on the arena of agriculture, and in this context she has explored science in policy making, community-based research, and public understanding of science. She has written many articles about science for lay audiences and is working on a book exploring the definitions of nature and the use of science by agricultural social movements.

VALERIE JENNESS is professor and chair in the Department of Criminology, Law, and Society and professor of sociology at the University of California, Irvine. Her research focuses on the links between deviance and social control (especially law), and social change (especially social movements), and the formation and implementation of public policy. She is the author of *Making Hate a Crime* (with Ryken Grattet), *Hate Crimes: New Social Movements and the Politics of Violence* (with Kendal Broad), and *Making It Work: The Prostitutes' Rights Movement in Perspective,* as well as numerous articles on the politics of prostitution, AIDS and civil liberties, hate crimes and hate crime law, and the gay/lesbian movement and the women's movement in the United States. She is working on a study of hate crime law enforcement policy and a study of the development and implementation of policies and programs designed to reduce prison rape.

MARY FAINSOD KATZENSTEIN is professor of government at Cornell University. She is the author or editor of several books on ethnic politics in India and women's movement politics in Europe and the United States, including *Faithful and Fearless: Moving Feminist Protest inside the Church and Military.* She coedited a book with Judith Reppy on race and gender issues in the U.S. armed forces and is now coediting a book on social movements and poverty in India with Raka Ray. Her recent work has focused on prison reform activism in the United States.

CHRISTINE MAHONEY is a PhD candidate in political science at Pennsylvania State University. She has published in *European Union Politics* and the *Encyclopedia of Social Science Research Methods*. Her research focuses on interest groups and lobbying in the United States and the European Union. She has conducted over one hundred interviews with advocates in Washington, DC, and Brussels, Belgium. Her research has been supported by a Fulbright Fellowship to the European Union and a position as visiting junior scholar at Nuffield College, Oxford University.

JOHN D. MCCARTHY is professor of sociology and director of the graduate program at Pennsylvania State University. His research interests include social movements and collective behavior, the sociology of protest, the policing of protest, and the sociology of organizations. He is collaborating with Andrew Martin and Clark McPhail on a study of campus community public order disturbances and with Frank Baumgartner on a study of the expansion of U.S. interest organizations during the past four decades.

SUZANNE METTLER is alumni associate professor of political science in the Maxwell School at Syracuse University. Her research interests include American political development, public policy, and citizenship. She is author of *Dividing Citizens: Gender and Federalism in New Deal Public Policy* and *Soldiers to Citizens: The G.I. Bill and the Making of the Greatest Generation*. Her new work examines how changes in the welfare state over recent decades have affected citizens' attitudes about government and participation in politics.

DAVID S. MEYER is professor of sociology and political science at the University of California, Irvine. He is author or coeditor of four other books on social movements, as well as numerous articles. He is most interested in the relationships among social movements, institutional politics, and public policy.

ELLEN REESE is assistant professor of sociology at the University of California, Riverside. Her research focuses on the politics of welfare in the United States. She is author of *Backlash against Welfare Mothers: Past and Present*. Her latest work investigates political struggles over the implementation of welfare reform.

Index

Office of Minority Health (U.S.), 102
Office of National Drug Control Policy (ONDCP), 92
OFPA. *See* Organic Food Production Act
Old Age Revolving Pensions, Ltd. *See* Townsend Plan
ONDCP. *See* Office of National Drug Control Policy
Organic, defined, 122, 129, 132
Organic agriculture movement, 121–48, 295; background, 128–30; certification, 129–30, 140; critique of, 127, 135, 142n.3; economics, 123–24, 130–31; field conditions for, 122–23, 125–28; regulations, 124–25, 136–40; rule-making, 135
Organic Food Production Act (OFPA), 118, 122, 123–24, 131–33, 295
Organic Trade Association (OTA), 132
OTA. *See* Organic Trade Association
Outshoorn, Joyce, 154
Outsider claimsmaking, 117

Pacifism. *See* Antiwar movements
Partnership for a Drug-Free America (PDFA), 98–99
PATCH program, 102
PDAC. *See* President's Drug Advisory Council
PDFA. *See* Partnership for a Drug-Free America
Personal Responsibility and Work Opportunity Reconciliation Act (PRWORA), 259, 260, 264, 265–69, 279–80, 299
Pesticides, 127, 130
Peterson, Esther, 150, 151
Pierson, Paul, 213
Piven, Frances Fox, 5, 16, 157, 159, 212

Policy. *See* Public policy
Policy Agendas Project, 65–66, 74–75
Policy makers: collective mobilization influence on, 18–19, 31–33, 35–36, 55–56, 77–82, 87; and social movements, 21–22, 27–28, 77–82, 117–19, 151–63; and women's movement, 153–54, 162–70. *See also* Congressional hearings
Political context: and mobilization, 29–30, 34–40, 290–93; and strategy, 30, 34–40; of Townsend Plan, 45–55
Political freedom: limiting, 13
Political institutions. *See* Policy makers
Political opportunity, 14
Political system, U.S., 32–33, 67, 73–77
Pollution, water. *See* Water pollution
Poor people: and social movements, 5–6
Powell, Walter, 67, 80
President's Commission on the Status of Women, 149–50, 165
President's Drug Advisory Council (PDAC), 92
Prisoners' rights, 236–55; and citizenship, 239–40, 246–51; institutionalized claims, 244; and radical politics, 240; and self esteem, 241; voting, 246, 250–51; wage earning, 242
Prison Litigation Reform Act, 237
Prison reform, 208–9, 236–55; 1960s, 240; 1970–1985, 240–47; 1985 to present, 247–51; overview, 239–40; state legislation, 245; statistics, 239
Procunier v. Martinez, 248
Protest movements: causes for, 15–16; cycles of, 78, 212; institutionalization of, 19–21, 212, 293; and public

Veterans' organizations, 230n.1
Vietnam Conflict *(1961–1975)*, 1–2, 4
Volunteerism, 96, 214

Walker, Jack, 80, 103
Walsh-Healy Act, 254n.24
Walters, John, 250
War of 1812, 216
War on Drugs, 90–91
Wars. *See specific wars and conflicts*
Water pollution, 130
Watrous, Paul, 192
Weakley, Craig, 134
WEAL. *See* Women's Equity Action
    League
Welfare, 6
Werner, Richard, 227
White House Conference on Aging, 72
Wieringa, Saskia, 154

Willoughby, William F., 181
Wolfson, Mark, 14, 97, 294
Women and employment, 163–65,
    167–68
Women's Equity Action League
    (WEAL), 164
Women's movement, 68–70, 149–50,
    213; insiders vs. outsiders, 154,
    162–63, 165–68; and state, 153–54,
    162–70
Wood, Frank, 245
Workers' compensation, 181–200, 296
World War I *(1914–1918)*, 217–18
World War II *(1939–1945)*, 28, 219,
    221–22

Youngberg, Garth, 143n.5

Zald, Mayer, 122, 124, 130